To Andy Davies
Beloved br[illegible]
and coworker in the Lord -
Bob & Janelle Owen

The Churches of Christ in the Twentieth Century

RELIGION AND AMERICAN CULTURE

Series Editors

David Edwin Harrell, Jr.

Wayne Flynt

Edith L. Blumhofer

THE Churches OF Christ

IN THE TWENTIETH CENTURY

Homer Hailey's Personal Journey of Faith

David Edwin Harrell, Jr.

THE UNIVERSITY OF ALABAMA PRESS
TUSCALOOSA AND LONDON

1 2 3 4 5 6 7 8 9 · 08 07 06 05 04 03 02 01 00

Text design by Shari DeGraw
Jacket design by Mary Frances Burt

∞
The paper on which this book is printed meets
the minimum requirements of American National Standard for
Information Science–Permanence of Paper for Printed Library Materials,
ANSI Z39.48-1984.

Library of Congress Cataloging-in-Publication Data

Harrell, David Edwin.
The Churches of Christ in the twentieth century : Homer Hailey's
personal journey of faith / David Edwin Harrell, Jr.
p. cm. — (Religion and American culture)
Includes bibliographical references and index.
ISBN 0-8173-1008-8 (cloth : alk. paper)
1. Hailey, Homer, 1904– 2. Churches of Christ—Clergy Biography.
3. Churches of Christ—History—20th century. I. Title. II. Series:
Religion and American culture (Tuscaloosa, Ala.)
BX7077.Z8 H354 2000
286.6′092—dc21
[B]
99-6566
CIP

British Library Cataloguing-in-Publication Data available

To the memory of
Dr. David Edwin Harrell, Sr., and Mildred Lee Harrell,
who would have taken great pride in this book.

Contents

Preface

THE HISTORY of churches of Christ in America was largely an untold story until near the end of the twentieth century. In the past two decades, however, a flurry of books have been written about the group's separation from the Disciples of Christ/Christian Church, a schism that was recognized in the Religious Census of 1906, and its stormy history since that time. Reasons for this heightened interest are readily apparent. For many years the larger and more reputable Disciples of Christ claimed historical precedence as heir of the American restoration tradition; most of the histories written about the movement in the first two-thirds of the twentieth century deemed churches of Christ to be an ecclesiastical ephemeron, the more or less irrelevant sectarian refuse of the nineteenth-century restoration movement. By the last third of the twentieth century, that judgment had proven to be premature. Like most mainstream Protestant groups in the United States in the last third of the twentieth century, the Disciples of Christ/Christian Church suffered serious membership losses, but churches of Christ boomed. By the end of the century, several million Americans' spiritual world view had been formed in churches of Christ. So, it is both understandable and fitting that a group of historians born into this tradition should arise at the end of the century to probe the meaning of their own religious heritage.

This book is about both a church and a man—Homer Hailey. I began with the intention of simply writing a biography of Hailey, but I discovered that it would be impossible to write perceptively about Hailey without exploring the churches of Christ. On the other hand, while it might be possible to write a history of churches of Christ in the twentieth century without mentioning him, Hailey's life provides an extraordinary window on the movement. Like most members of churches of Christ, Hailey defies most of the generalizations that seem so clear when one surveys the broad landscape of restoration history.

Combining the vagaries of individual biography with the regularities of institutional history throws a bright light on the dangers of easy generalization. One portion of this book outlines the patterns of intellectual dissonance, sociological change, and schism that are an integral part of the history of churches of Christ, and, indeed, of other churches. However, such histories cannot describe the dissimilar lives of the individuals who worked and worshiped in thousands of local churches. While groups and institutions often seem to follow predictable patterns and fit neat models that repeat themselves in history, individual behavior is never so tidy. Ironies abound in the entangled tales of lives as long as that of Homer Hailey.

"Homer Hailey," mused his old friend Harry W. Pickup, Sr., in 1988, "became great in his own time." This was a judgment entirely true from Pickup's perspective. In a lifetime spanning nearly the entire twentieth century, Homer Hailey became a household name to hundreds of thousands of members of churches of Christ. He taught the Bible to hundreds of college students, many of them preachers, and he preached in hundreds of churches to hundreds of thousands of people. He also wrote books that were widely read, both inside and outside his own religious communion; his commentary on the minor prophets was selected by *Christianity Today* as one of the twenty-five most influential books written during the year it was published.

Fame is relative, and Hailey's accomplishments hardly mark him as a critical figure in the development of twentieth-century American religion or thought. He would have never imagined that they did. Hailey's achievements are significant largely to members of churches of Christ. Even in that context, Hailey was not a pivotal figure. He never sought power or influence; he never led campaigns (as editors within the churches of Christ are apt to do); nor was he often a critical figure in the movement's endless controversies. Hailey contributed almost nothing in the way of crucial concepts or arguments to the twentieth-century development of the movement's perpetually open-ended thought.

Why, then, tell the story of Homer Hailey? Partly, I confess, because it is a personal tale that seems so transparently admirable to me that it deserves being told. It is also a piece of Americana, a parable about the ending of the frontier, about the end of American innocence. My father loved Homer Hailey; my readers will like him, I think, as I have liked him for many years.

But there are other reasons for combining the telling of these stories. Homer Hailey's life weaves its way through the twentieth-century history of churches of Christ in a way that illuminates the entire history of the movement. While not often in the forefront of the many controversies that defined churches of Christ, Hailey, like other preachers and church members, was forced repeatedly to make life-changing choices. Over and over, members of churches of Christ made faith decisions that changed the shapes of their futures. Hailey's life story puts in perspective the complexity of serving God in the loose and unfettered environment of the restoration movement.

The American restoration movement that began in the early nineteenth century in diverse reforms led by Thomas and Alexander Campbell, Barton Stone, and others was an amorphous, dynamic movement when Homer Hailey was born in 1903. In Hailey's lifetime, the movement went through two major divisions and numerous smaller ones, offering its adherents choices that reached from one end of the theological and sociological spectrums to the other. At the beginning of the twentieth century the movement was ostensibly still united in its quest for the ancient order of things, though in fact a division between the Christian Churches and churches of Christ was pretty well defined. By the end of the twentieth century, the movement had divided and redivided into several distinct religious groupings.

The divisions in the American restoration movement sparked fractious debates and manufactured a body of arguments that is an almost impenetrable maze to outsiders. The arguments over missionary societies, instrumental music in worship, methods of congregational cooperation, and the role of church-supported institutions were nuanced by history and embodied language and logical differentiations foreign to traditional evangelical theology. Nonetheless, these arguments and divisions are the essence of the twentieth-century history of churches of Christ.

Homer Hailey's spiritual odyssey spans the complex and factious history of the American restoration movement. He began his spiritual life as a member of the Christian Church in Willcox, Arizona, became a member of a church of Christ in the 1920s, and, in the 1950s, left the mainstream churches of Christ to work among a minority who opposed certain institutional practices. Finally, in the 1980s Homer Hailey's name became enmeshed in another type of controversy that is endemic in the churches of Christ. He became a target of attacks because of his beliefs about divorce and remarriage. Such internecine quarrels were another persistent part of the history of the American restoration movement.

Hailey's religious pilgrimage is instructive partly because, while always a respected leader and a widely used preacher, he was rarely a combatant. He made his spiritual choices on much the same basis as hundreds of thousands of people in the pews who were trapped in the midst of battle lines that they did little to form or control. To follow his life is to examine one line of thinking that has been a historic part of the American restoration movement and to view passingly the scores of other options embraced by members of churches of Christ. Hailey's life is not a history of the churches of Christ, but he peered down most of the theological byways that appeared during the turbulent twentieth century, and, given his character, he made predictable choices.

After a division was more or less completed in churches of Christ over certain institutional issues in the mid-1960s, Hailey's influence and his circle of friends grew narrower, as did those of every other person who embraced noninstitutional views. Yet, both at a personal and at a general level, Hailey's influence continued to reach across the escalating walls that compartmentalized churches of Christ. He maintained a cordial, and sometimes close, relationship with former students who by the 1990s were scattered across the theological spectrum. In 1988, Hailey returned to Abilene Christian University to attend the fiftieth reunion of the class of 1938, having served for four years as the class's faculty sponsor. During a chapel service, Paul Faulkner, a Hailey student and ACU faculty member, fought back tears as he struggled to explain to a new generation the meaning of Homer Hailey.

In a more general way, Homer Hailey's biography is a story that belongs to the broader history of the churches of Christ. To those of his generation, at the end of the twentieth century, the churches of Christ remained one people. Hailey's generation feuded, debated, and divided, but they began and ended their lifetimes as brethren. Ties of friendship, kinship, and comradeship are finally severed only with the passing of a generation. Alexander Campbell and Barton Stone lived and died regarding the evangelical Christians they left behind as brethren who needed reforming. David Lipscomb regarded the leaders of the Disciples of Christ/Christian Church as erring brethren. Clear-cut schism is the finished work of strangers. In the 1990s, most people on the extremes of the restoration movement no longer know one another.

Whatever the justifications for writing these two stories together, I recognize that this is an unusual literary venture. I have therefore divided the book into three parts. Part I introduces both Homer Hailey and the churches of Christ up to the time that he entered Abilene Christian College in 1926. Part II, composed of Chapters 2, 3, and 4, is a history of the mainstream churches of Christ from 1920 to the end of the century. Those interested primarily in Homer Hailey may find these chapters somewhat disruptive. Hailey appears in them, but only here and there and in relatively unimportant roles. However, Homer Hailey will become a much more plausible figure for readers after they read these chapters. On the other hand, those interested only in the history of the churches of Christ in the twentieth century will find it mostly in these chapters. If they read on, however, following the journey of Homer Hailey will greatly enrich their understanding of the nuances in the movement's history. Part III, which includes Chapters 5, 6, 7, and 8, provides both a biography of Homer Hailey and a history of noninstitutional churches of Christ, the minority collection of churches with which Hailey cast his lot when he left Abilene Christian College to go to Florida Christian College in 1951.

For those unversed in the beliefs held by members of churches of Christ, the terminology in this book will, no doubt, often seem obscure and confusing. While it would be impossible to clarify all of the theological distinctions that have contributed to what could well be viewed as a "restoration language," I do feel compelled to make a few comments about the terminology I have used. Theoretically, churches of Christ are an undenominational movement of autonomous local churches. In deference to that notion, I have avoided using the formal title—Churches of Christ—and use instead a lowercase *c* when referring to the thousands of independent congregations that make up the churches of Christ. Actually, the churches of Christ sometimes act like a denomination and church members (called "Christians") often think denominationally. The most common euphemism for "denomination" is "brotherhood." That term may be used in an undenominational context, but frequently it is no more than a circuitous way to describe the goings-on in a self-consciously denominational Church of Christ. Nonetheless, congregational independence and resistance to outside coercion are still stronger in churches of Christ than in almost any other corner of the religious world. Even in the most structured wings of the movement, churches of Christ emerge as an unruly and petulant denomination, and in other locales undenominational Christianity in its most individualistic form still prevails. I prefer calling the churches of Christ a "movement," rather than a "brotherhood"—thus recognizing the group's vagueness and fluidity. I lapse into use of the term *brotherhood* from time to time, however, to describe the collective chaos of the thousands of scattered churches of Christ.

It would be nonsense to pretend that I could tell this story in an entirely disinterested manner. Beyond the hidden passions and agendas that lurk behind all of our representations of the past, this narrative is *my story*. I have tried to deal fairly and honestly with the rascals and charlatans, with the arrogant and the deluded, but I suspect that my language may sometimes give me away. Fortunately, few of the heated debates in the history of churches of Christ have pitted morality versus immorality, righteousness versus venality; they have more often reflected different visions of God and the meaning of righteousness. The percentage of rogues and rascals is spread pretty evenly across the landscape from right to left.

One additional personal dilemma inherent in writing about my own religious heritage is that, from time to time, I have been a spokesman in the debates that have taken place. As a literary strategy, I have chosen to write about myself in the third person. After fifty years of writing history, I am simply more comfortable in telling stories in the third person, although it is passing strange to report that "Ed Harrell said . . . " I am not always comfortable with what I wrote in the 1960s, or even what I wrote in the 1990s, but I have tried to treat my own ideas with a degree of historical objectivity, as I do those of other people.

Readers of this manuscript, which is buttressed with copious notes, will discover the depth of my debt to a number of sources. One such debt is so large that it demands special recognition. In the late 1980s, when I first began to ponder writing a book about Homer Hailey, I discovered that one of his devoted students, John Kilgore, of Houston, Texas, was also thinking of writing a biography of his friend and teacher and had taped more than eighteen hours of conversation with him. When John learned that I had proposed a book project to Hailey, he generously turned over to me the hours of interviews that he had taped and, ever since, has patiently waited for something to come of it.

I also thank Homer Hailey, the Center for Restoration Studies at Abilene Christian University, and the Disciples of Christ Historical Society for allowing me to publish the photos that appear in this book. In addition, I am grateful to the William B. Eerdmans Publishing Company for granting permission to quote generous portions of Richard T. Hughes's extremely important history titled *Reviving the Ancient Faith: The Story of the Churches of Christ in America* (copyright 1996). Every study of the churches of Christ will be compelled to build on this pivotal book. I am very grateful to Scott Billingsley, my Ph.D. student at Auburn University, for compiling a splendid index. Finally, I thank Kathy Cummins for her extremely careful and helpful editorial labors that covered a multitude of sins.

Whatever my readers may think of Homer Hailey, I will be surprised if they do not find his life story engaging. I visited Homer shortly after his ninety-fourth birthday in 1997, just before he moved out of the house that he and Widna had built in

Tucson. He was fragile but robust in spirit. "How are you do ing, Homer?" I asked. "Well, brother Eddie," he replied with an intellect and wit as sharp as ever, "I can't get around real well anymore, but I sit real good." Few people have lived life so fully or have given themselves to it more robustly. The hundreds of thousands of Christians who are now living their lives in churches of Christ will profit from knowing about him and his century.

The Churches of Christ in the Twentieth Century

PART I

Homer Hailey and the Churches of Christ

Origins

1

Homer Hailey and the Churches of Christ

An Institutional History and a Personal Saga

HOMER HAILEY WAS BORN IN 1903, three years before the United States Census Bureau formally recognized the Churches of Christ as a religious body distinct from the Disciples of Christ. Still alive near the end of the century, Hailey experienced in his life the entirety of the turbulent twentieth-century history of the churches of Christ. During those years, the loose movement effectively divided into three estranged groups, all using the name churches of Christ, and into many smaller factions. Like most members of the churches of Christ, Hailey was usually a spectator in the controversies that framed the church's history rather than a major player, but he remained widely known and respected throughout the churches of Christ at the end of the century. Occasionally he was a key participant in the conflicts that shaped the movement, but even when he was not, Hailey, like every other member of the churches of Christ in the twentieth century, was repeatedly compelled to make life-changing choices about where his allegiances lay in the crazy-quilt pattern of churches of Christ in America.

The Churches of Christ at the Beginning of the Twentieth Century

The theological primitivism embraced by members of the

churches of Christ nullified in their minds all questions of origin because they believed that any church in any age that replicated the organization, worship, and work of New Testament churches was a church of Christ. Such primitivist notions, in one form or another, have long existed in Christian history, and the earliest conceptualizers of the American restoration movement of which the churches of Christ were a part were well aware that others before them had shared their vision of restoring New Testament Christianity.[1] The more proximate origins of the twentieth-century churches of Christ, however, lay in the dynamic and democratic religious ethos of early nineteenth-century America.[2] In those heady early years of the republic, Americans were confident that, unleashed from the repressions of tyranny and bigotry, they were on the verge of unlocking primal and undefiled truths that would establish political, social, and intellectual rectitude. Such aspirations blended easily with longings for a return to the simple and pure truths of New Testament Christianity.

The American restoration movement that took organized form in the early nineteenth century drew on several different primitivist reforms.[3] The two largest of these reforming streams were a group of churches led by Thomas and Alexander Campbell of western Virginia and another led by Barton Stone of Kentucky. These two movements informally united in 1832. Most of the early leaders of the restoration movement rejected all denominational structure; thus, the union meant simply that in some communities congregations merged and in others local churches agreed not to compete with one another. The movement's central plea was "to speak where the Bible speaks and be silent where the Bible is silent." Its early leaders insisted on using "Bible names," calling themselves Christians or Disciples of Christ (denominational opponents frequently used the pejorative term *Campbellites*), and congregations were usually called either Christian Churches or churches of Christ.

The Disciples of Christ, as the movement was generally

called in the mid-nineteenth century, developed several doctrinal distinctives. Perhaps most significant, Disciples differed from traditional evangelical Protestants concerning the significance of baptism, arguing that baptism was an element in the "restored gospel" and that it was essential to salvation, the forgiveness of sins, and the new birth. The Disciples' understanding of baptism was fully developed in a number of debates between Alexander Campbell and Presbyterian ministers and formulated by evangelist Walter Scott in a five-point "gospel restored": faith, repentance, and baptism on the part of human beings and the remission of sins and the gift of the Holy Spirit on God's part. This "five-finger" formula provided a stock sermon for two generations of frontier preachers. Disciples also explored the New Testament to find models for the church; Alexander Campbell contributed a long series of articles entitled "The Restoration of the Ancient Order of Things" that for the most part outlined their beliefs about the proper organization and work of local churches. Among other things, Disciples insisted that each local church should be independent under the rule of its own elders. The most visible difference in Disciples' worship grew out of Campbell's insistence on a weekly observance of the Lord's Supper, a view he inherited from his early contacts with the Haldane and Sandemanian religious reforms in Scotland and northern Ireland.

In 1866 Alexander Campbell died, symbolically ending the first-generation leadership in the Disciples of Christ movement. By that time, more than two hundred thousand people had joined the reform, and the Disciples of Christ had become the sixth-largest religious body in the United States. By 1880 Disciples numbered more than five hundred thousand and a religious census in 1906 listed more than one million members in Christian Churches and churches of Christ.

Growth of the Disciples in the nineteenth century was accomplished amidst an environment of incessant bickering and internal tension. From its beginnings, the restoration movement included ill-defined doctrinal areas in which issues were unresolved, some of them matters of considerable theological and moral import. For half a century before the Census Bureau formally recognized in 1906 the division between the Disciples of Christ and churches of Christ, factions within the movement debated the use of instrumental music in worship services, missionary societies, and the proper role of the "pastor" in local church organization. No formal mechanism existed to pronounce a division within the movement, but by the beginning of the twentieth century, most church-related institutions, religious periodicals, and local churches had aligned themselves with one faction or the other. The parties were defined generally by institutional loyalties. The "progressives," as the more liberal group was called, were known as "society men" or "*Standard* men," identifying them as backers of the United Christian Missionary Society and the leading moderate journal of the late nineteenth century, the *Christian Standard,* published in Cincinnati. On the other hand, conservatives were called "antis" or "*Advocate* men," marking them as opponents of the society and supporters of the most widely circulated conservative periodical, the Nashville-published *Gospel Advocate*. More and more, the name churches of Christ came to be quasi-official among conservatives and the name Christian Church to be used among progressive churches. Well into the twentieth century the name Disciples of Christ continued to be used in both wings of the movement, but it slowly came to be identified mostly with the progressives.

Formal divisions within the restoration movement have always involved differences far more profound than the specific doctrinal issues that were the focus of theological debating; indeed the movement typically existed for long periods when considerable differences in practice and belief were tolerated. Schisms became formal only when leaders on the conflicting sides implicitly or explicitly decided that they no longer had the same understanding of the restoration plea, that they were no longer of the same mind. By the late nineteenth century the movement clearly included people with different theological understandings and different religious agendas.

By 1900 the movement's more astute leaders on both sides of the controversy recognized that they had reached a hermeneutical impasse. In 1884, David Lipscomb, the editor of the *Gospel Advocate,* wrote: "Nothing indicates the wide departure from the landmarks of truth more clearly, that is taking place among those who started out to restore the ancient order, than the loose views put forth by some of the accredited teachers among them in reference to the authority of God. These show that the old standards have been set aside and new ones adopted."[4] While some of those defending instrumental music and missionary societies argued that such "innovations" were consistent with a plea to restore the New Testament church, others confessed that it was a mistake to require specific precedents for church worship and organization. In the Missouri Christian Lectures in 1886, M. M. Goode surmised: "In regard to the methods employed for preaching the gospel to the world, and all benevolent ministrations of the church, and all aids to its service and worship, Christians have no positive specifications and they must be governed by general laws and principles applied according to their best judgment."[5] By the end of the nineteenth century, the movement was awash with more fundamental questionings of the basic hermeneutical premises of the earlier restoration. "A principle may set aside an apostolic precept," wrote George Smith in 1893: "It may brush aside an apostolic decree. We do that constantly. We follow the apostolic example whenever we like it; when we do not, we depart from it."[6]

In short, by the end of the nineteenth century perceptive Christians recognized that their differences reached far deeper than disagreements about instrumental music and missionary societies. Conservatives were united by a commonsense hermeneutic that believed that the New Testament provided a recoverable model of Christianity, though they were far from united about the details of the model. Progressives had begun to apply the restoration hermeneutic much less rigidly. Some generalized the plea for New Testament authority, thus exempting instrumental music and missionary societies from demands for specific authority; others discarded the restoration hermeneutic altogether, regarding it as both impractical and unnecessary.

The growth of schismatic pressures in the larger movement was chronicled by the religious censuses in the first half of the century. In 1906, when the Census Bureau first separated the two groups, it reported that the membership of the churches of Christ was 159,658 people in 2,649 congregations; by 1926 those figures had risen to 433,714 members in 6,226 congregations. During the same period the membership of the Disciples of Christ rose from 982,701 to 1,337,595 but the number of local congregations declined from 8,260 to 7,648.[7] The Religious Census Report in 1926 described the amorphous nature of the division in the movement: "In the census report for 1890 both parties were reported together under the title Disciples of Christ. In the report for 1906 the Conservatives were reported separately as Churches of Christ, but the results were not altogether satisfactory, as it was difficult to draw the line between them and the Disciples of Christ. There is now a clear distinction between the two groups, and the statistics for 1926 are far more complete."[8]

In 1948, Disciples historians Winfred Garrison and Alfred T. DeGroot, conceding that division was far from neat in the restoration movement, pointed out that "the separation in 1906 was . . . only a statistical event."[9] Interestingly, however, in that year, McQuiddy Printing Company, the publisher of the *Gospel Advocate,* printed a pamphlet entitled *List of the Preachers of the Churches of Christ.*[10] Nearly six hundred preachers were listed in the pamphlet, along with a statement of a prospectus of the *Gospel Advocate* that defined the distinctives of the churches of Christ: "It stoutly advocates the doctrine of missions, and argues unceasingly that every Christian is a divinely commissioned *missionary* and every church a scripturally organized *missionary society* . . . It believes in, and stoutly advocates, congregational singing, as opposed to select choirs and instrumental performances, as the best and most soul-stirring church music."[11] Even so, the division began decades earlier and the line between the churches of Christ and the Christian Church did not become clearly fixed until the 1920s. The schismatic pressures in the Disciples movement was not unlike the divisions that separated the most conservative northern Presbyterians and Baptists from their denominations in the modernist/fundamentalist conflict of the 1920s.

Most Disciples historians in the first half of the twentieth century regarded the churches of Christ as a cantankerous and schismatic, though not insignificant, faction, whose views were an aberration that did not represent the mainstream of the Stone-Campbell restoration tradition.[12] In his 1996 history of the churches of Christ, *Reviving the Ancient Faith,* Richard T. Hughes argued that the opposite was true, that it was the churches of Christ who remained faithful to the primitivist vision of the early leaders of the restoration movement.[13] In truth, the churches of Christ seemed to view themselves both as continuous with the American past and as a newly formed incarnation of the ancient church. When Homer Hailey drove from Arizona to Abilene, Texas, in 1926 to become a student at Abilene Christian College, he was entering an old religious tradition with intellectual roots reaching into the nineteenth century and far beyond, but at the same time entering a new religious movement, the churches of Christ, that was just beginning to define its own identity.

Hailey Family Roots

A Confederate soldier at age fourteen, Thomas L. Hailey, Homer's grandfather, was taken prisoner in Richmond in 1865, when he was still only seventeen years old, and paroled a few weeks later when the Civil War ended. After visiting their home in North Carolina, Thomas and his older brother,

Robert, who had also fought for the Confederacy, joined the stream of defeated veterans trekking across the South to Texas, hoping to find a new life in the aftermath of the war. Thomas Hailey homesteaded a farm in Harrison County, where he stayed the rest of his life. Located twelve miles northeast of Marshall, the county seat, the Hailey farm was on rich cotton land, lying in the heavily wooded and well-watered drainage basin of the Red River.

When Harrison County was formed in 1850, it was the most populous and one of the most prosperous counties in the new state of Texas. In 1860, the population of the county was more than fifteen thousand, nearly sixty percent of that total being slaves.[14] The Civil War and Reconstruction turned Harrison County into a social cauldron, as it did all of the postwar South. Many of those who settled there after the war stayed only a few years before pulling up stakes and heading west again. In the late nineteenth century, only about a third of Harrison County's residents remained in place for more than a decade.[15]

Thomas Hailey was one of those who stayed. On October 25, 1876, he married Mollie C. Williams in the Marshall home of Mr. and Mrs. T. Y. Adkins.[16] Hailey was a successful farmer, and in his later years he moved into Marshall where he lived in a modest but comfortable home. His grandchildren remembered the Hailey house as a luxurious place featuring gas lights and regular visits from the "light bread" salesman.

Thomas and Mollie Hailey reared six children on their East Texas farm. Their second child, Robert T. Hailey, born on September 2, 1879, was named for his "Uncle Rob" who had accompanied Thomas to Texas. Robert Hailey never married; in the census of 1880 he was listed as a part of the Thomas Hailey household. He was a successful surveyor who accumulated a modest personal fortune; he traveled widely and earned high wages surveying in Old Mexico. Subsequent generations of Haileys regarded Uncle Rob as the savant of the family; he read widely and was an early advocate of Darwinism in the

Thomas L. Hailey, grandfather of Homer Hailey, at about eighty years of age in a photograph from around 1920.

midst of the Bible Belt. He also gave financial assistance to any of his brother's children and grandchildren who sought a higher education. A man of "high principles," Robert Hailey was highly esteemed by later generations of Haileys, in spite of his heretical religious views.

Robert T. Hailey, the eldest son of Thomas and Mollie, was reared on his father's farm, learning the skills of raising and ginning cotton. A friendly and likeable young man, he was apt and able at whatever job came to hand. Hailey matured into a man's man, two inches over six feet tall, and given to drinking and gambling, as were many of the marginal men who struggled to find self-worth in the degrading poverty of the post–Civil War South.

Hailey's character faults were not so obvious when he met and married Mary Eunice (Mamie) Collins in 1900. A young schoolmarm who had begun teaching at a one-room school between Marshall and Karnack, near the Hailey farm, Mamie Collins heard rumors about Rob Hailey's wild streak before they married. She knew he was a drinker. But, like most young women, she probably was confident that her husband would settle down after marriage.

Mamie Collins was also a native of Harrison County. Born in 1878, she was the second of six children in the family of John Whitehorn Collins and Mary Ida Nesbitt. Shortly after Mamie's marriage, the Collins family joined the stream of population moving west. John Collins spent several years in Lockney, in West Texas, before moving to Arizona in 1909 where he homesteaded a ranch twenty-one miles north of Willcox. The Collins family was among several hundred other families who migrated to the Sulphur Springs Valley of Arizona in the five years after 1905, drawn partly by a recently enacted amendment to the Homestead Act that allowed settlers to claim 320 acres of public land (double the amount allowed by the original 1862 Homestead Act), belatedly recognizing that dry farming in the West required large amounts of land. In addition, between 1905 and 1907 the Sulphur Springs Valley blossomed during a sequence of unusually wet years—the 23.5 inches of rainfall in the area in 1905 was more than twice the long-term average for the valley. Hundreds of homesteaders settled in the valley surrounding the town of Willcox, forming new communities with schools and post offices such as Lompoc and McAlister. The homesteaders staked claims in the midst of existing ranches that had been established twenty-five years earlier. Within a decade many of the farming claims had been abandoned after a series of years with below-average rainfall virtually wiped out dry farming in the valley.[17]

The Collins's move to Arizona was not motivated by economics. They came to Willcox looking for their son, Roy, who had migrated west several years earlier and disappeared. They searched in vain; the family finally concluded that Roy had died in the rambunctious mining town of Bisbee where life was cheap and the law virtually nonexistent, mingling his blood with that of countless other anonymous adventurers who perished on the American frontier. Whatever his fate, Roy's migration was the magnet that drew the Collins family, and later the Hailey family, to frontier Arizona. Grandfather Collins died on his claim in 1919; during his years in Arizona he farmed, raised a few cows, and, like many other homesteaders, worked as a hand on neighboring ranches.

Religious Roots

Granny Collins provided her descendants with their first vague sense of religious identification. Born Mary Ida Nesbitt, she was the fourth of eleven children in the family of Robert Jamerson Nesbitt and Susan Adeline Johnson.[18] Her grandfather and grandmother were staunch Scottish Presbyterian immigrants who respected God, learning, and hard work. Robert J. Nesbitt, a veteran of the Mexican War, was one of the earliest settlers of Harrison County; his family founded the village of Nesbitt just northwest of Marshall.

Some time late in the nineteenth century, Mary Ida Nesbitt attended a religious debate between preachers from the Christian and Presbyterian churches, one of the scores of forgotten skirmishes that marked the front lines of the battle for the religious loyalty of the common people in Texas. A generation of Texas Disciples preachers, including T. W. Caskey, T. R. Burnett, and J. D. Tant, waged incessant war on "the sects." Between 1886 and 1890 Tant conducted fourteen debates. In the absence of other forms of intellectual stimulation and entertainment, religious debates drew large and serious audiences in the late nineteenth and early twentieth centuries; few combatants were more skilled than the coolly logical pioneer preachers who had embraced the American restoration movement. Convinced by the debate that Presbyterianism was doctrinally wrong, Ida Nesbitt joined thousands of others who in the nineteenth century left Presbyterian and Baptist churches to become members of the churches of Christ.

Granny Collins had cast her lot with the most conservative and militant wing of the restoration movement. Since 1845 Texas Disciples churches had formed "co-operations" to support evangelists and to provide occasions for meetings, but in 1886 progressives established a state missionary society, pushing Texas preachers headlong into the brewing national debate on the subject.[19] The debate over the propriety of societies was an old one, but it became increasingly threatening. In 1889, a group of hyperconservatives in Illinois, led by an extremist editor named Daniel Sommer, drafted the Sand Creek Declaration, stating "that those who did not cease using societies and instrumental music in the worship would no longer be regarded as brethren."[20] The declaration had the ring of a sectarian proclamation that offended many, but it was an expression of exasperation from conservatives whose protests were ignored by progressives. The Sand Creek Declaration has been taken by some as the date marking the separate existence of the Christian Church and the churches of Christ. The process was not so neat, however. In reality, in Texas the two groups had issued strong separatist statements three years earlier; in Tennessee a division in the Woodland Street Church in Nashville over the organization of a state missionary society in 1891 may be regarded as the first division in that state.[21]

Granny Collins was a charter subscriber to the *Firm Foundation,* a paper launched in 1884 by Austin McGary that was "respectfully, fraternally, and affectionately dedicated to all that class of brethren, who . . . are willing to turn their steps away from *all* human *systems, plans* and *directions* into this *one* mapped out by the apostles of our Lord."[22] McGary, a Confederate veteran who before his conversion in the 1870s was twice elected sheriff of Madison County, Texas, was a fractious and bellicose editor who led the fight against progressivism in Texas. McGary's pugnacity did not end there; he waged a fifteen-year war on David Lipscomb's conservative paper, the *Gospel Advocate.* McGary charged that the *Advocate* was not sound on the "rebaptism issue." Most churches of Christ in the

Mary Ida Nesbitt on the Collins ranch in Arizona, around 1917. Granny Collins was the first of her family to enter the church of Christ, and she was an ardent reader of the *Firm Foundation*.

nineteenth century accepted Baptists into their fellowship without question, but McGary insisted that they should be rebaptized "for the remission of sins."[23] The rebaptism fight simmered for years, and in the end the *Firm Foundation* view prevailed. In the meantime, some Texas conservatives regarded the *Gospel Advocate* as unreliable, but both parties were so thoroughly conservative that no real division between the two was possible.

Initially a monthly, the *Firm Foundation* became a weekly after its first year of publication. Granny Collins devoured the "Firmey," reading it while doing her churning and other chores. She attended church services regularly; the First Christian Church of Marshall was founded in 1889, and a Church of Christ began meeting in the city hall in 1915. Mamie Collins was instructed by her mother and baptized while a teenager. In later years, during the Collins and Hailey family migrations westward, religious fervor ebbed and flowed, but Mamie and her children inherited from Granny Collins an identity with the strictest wing of the restoration movement, the Texas churches of Christ.

Texas Childhood

Homer Hailey was born August 12, 1903, on the Hailey farm northeast of Marshall, the first of Robert and Mamie Hailey's six children. Fifteen months later a second son, Rob, was born on the farm. Rob and Homer were inseparable companions in the years of their youth. Shortly after Rob's birth, the family moved west to Turkey in the Texas panhandle.

Robert Hailey's skills as a cotton ginner were readily marketable in Texas at the turn of the century, and he moved to Turkey to build a cotton gin. Because the ginning season lasted only about four months, Hailey also operated a small store in the town. During the three years that the family lived in Turkey, two more children were born, a girl, Ruth, in 1907, and a boy, Jack, in 1908. Homer and Rob were fond of hanging around their father's country store; the little boys listened to men talk and were treated to an occasional "sody pop."

Apparently things did not work out well for Robert in Turkey, or perhaps he was just struck by the unquenchable wanderlust that reappeared throughout his life, and in 1909 he packed his family into a covered wagon and journeyed five hundred miles across the New Mexico Territory. In 1909 New Mexico was a wild and sparsely inhabited expanse, still three years removed from statehood; the covered wagon journey was an adventure into America's pioneer heritage that the little Hailey boys never forgot. The trip was filled with high adventure and misadventure. One day while Mamie was cooking on a portable stove a whirlwind swept through their camp, setting off a prairie fire that could be seen for miles and attracting cowboys from all around the horizon to fight it. The unbroken, fenceless plains teemed with wild game and gargantuan rattlesnakes. The boys savored the adventure; for Mamie it was a nightmare, "the worst trip she ever took," and in later years she steadfastly refused to discuss the ordeal when her sons sought to refresh their memories.[24]

Whatever Robert was seeking in his covered wagon journey west, he did not find it, and in the fall the family was back in West Texas, at Lamesa, where Robert rented a farm from his brother-in-law. Lamesa proved to be yet another pause in the Hailey family wanderings, one that left only a few memories. Homer later did recall pulling bolls of cotton in the West Texas fields for a penny a pound, earning five dollars during the summer. He and Rob made hunting trips with their father into the breaks, the wild terrain west of Lamesa where thickets of shrubs and mesquite trees broke the plains and where birds and wild game had lived for centuries largely undisturbed by human beings. Such excursions were manly experiences; they were among the best times the youngsters ever spent with their father.

After two years in Lamesa, Robert Hailey returned to the Hailey farm in Harrison County, a final stutter in the inexorable westward odyssey of the pioneer family. In December 1910, while the move back to East Texas was under way, Mamie boarded the children on the train in Big Spring, Texas, for a journey to visit her parents in Arizona. The trip was another excursion into the Old West that left deep impressions on the young Hailey boys. All along the tracks they saw the makeshift shacks of "nesters," farmers who had homesteaded claims on the prairie lands. In Willcox, Grandfather Collins met the family, loaded them into his wagon, and began the day-long trip to his homestead. There they visited in his two-room house constructed of one-by-twelve boards and a tent. During the two-month stay, Grandfather Collins treated the boys to a twelve-

Robert T. Hailey, father of Homer Hailey, working in a cotton gin around 1916.

mile wagon trip to Fort Grant, an outpost on the Indian frontier only recently vacated by the army.

In February 1911, the family rejoined Robert Hailey on the Hailey farm where they lived for four years. Homer was seven, Rob was six, and neither had ever been to school. For two years after their return, Mamie taught the boys at home; then, for two years they attended Fern School, a one-room schoolhouse about two miles through the woods from the Hailey farm. The school had ten other students, about half of them Baldwin children. Homer and Rob became close friends with the Taylor boys, Tommy and Tony, who also lived only a short distance from the Fern School. Together they played boy's games with makeshift balls and bats, swords and shields. The Taylor boys owned a bicycle that was treated as community property.

The Hailey and Taylor boys often camped and played together. On the evening of December 22, 1912, when Mrs. Taylor gave birth to a daughter, Tommy and Tony Taylor spent the night with the Haileys. The next morning Homer and Rob went home with them and took a look at the newborn baby girl whose name was given to her by a servant who declared the baby as beautiful as a "lady bird." Meeting Lady Bird Taylor Johnson was one of those passing encounters in life that took on poignancy years later.

In February 1915, when Homer was eleven, Mamie once again packed the children on a train for Willcox; this time they went to stay. The children knew instinctively that this was an auspicious moment in their family history. The little village of Hallsville seemed to come alive as they boarded the train: children gathered near the tracks gaping at the great iron horse, black vendors sold chickens and bread, families clung lovingly to relatives who might never be seen again. It was a scene etched in the memory of the Hailey children.

Up to this time, as their train headed away from Texas, the family's vagabond existence had been much like that of thousands of other marginal southern farm families. In the best of times, southern farmers sold their cotton at prices so depressed that they could only scrape a subsistence living from the fertile southern soil. In the worst of times, they could not make ends meet; they moved from place to place, lived with relatives, rented a stake, hoped for a better year. The last best hope for those who dreamed big enough, and the last great American adventure, was a homestead on the frontier.

Growing Up in the Old West

On February 14, 1915, Grandfather Collins again collected Mamie and the children into his wagon for a twenty-one mile ride from Willcox up the Sulphur Springs Valley, into the Gillman Hills, where he was working on the JH Ranch. Eleven-year-old Homer Hailey was stepping into the open range cattle kingdom, the grandest of America's frontier romances. The trail north led through an awesomely wild and majestic countryside; along the way Homer killed a pair of quail with his new double-barrel shotgun. For the next twelve years Willcox and its environs was Hailey's home; it was the time and setting in which Homer Hailey would acquire a sense of place and identity.

The strikingly beautiful Sulphur Springs Valley where Willcox is located sits on a tableland about four thousand feet above sea level. The valley stretches for nearly a hundred miles between rugged mountain chains. It is bounded by the Chiricahua and Dos Cabezas mountains in the east and south and the Pinalenos in the north, where Mount Graham, the dominant peak in southern Arizona, rises to 10,720 feet. Framing the valley on the west are the Dragoon Mountains in the south and the Winchester and Galiuros in the north.[25] Although the region's climate is semiarid, the area was covered with a nutritious grass that turned it into a prosperous ranching area in the 1880s.

The Sulphur Springs Valley was a part of the Gadsden Purchase of 1854. The area was virtually unexplored at the time it was acquired from Mexico; it was assumed to have value only because it lay athwart the only feasible transportation route across the south to California. The first intrusion into the area came with the opening of the Butterfield Overland Mail route in 1858. The first regular transcontinental system of transportation in the United States, the Butterfield Overland Stage, traveled from St. Louis to San Francisco via Fort Smith, Arkansas, El Paso, and the desert Southwest. The company built stations about every twenty miles along the route to supply fresh teams of horses. Just east of the future site of Willcox the stage passed through Apache Pass, a narrow opening between the Dos Cabezas and Chiricahua mountains.

Until about 1875, the Sulphur Springs Valley was disturbed only by the passage of the stage and some minor skirmishes between Confederate and Federal troops during the Civil War. For centuries the land had belonged to the Chiricahua Apache

Indians, a seminomadic people who sometimes welcomed intruders bearing gifts and sometimes wreaked havoc and death on parties passing through their territory. In order to provide a measure of protection to the southern transportation route, the government built Fort Bowie at Apache Pass in 1862 and ten years later constructed Fort Grant in the northern part of the Sulphur Springs Valley, opening an era of running skirmishes and full-scale wars between the Apache and the army. The Apaches were led by Cochise until his death in 1874 and by Geronimo until his capture in 1886. By the end of the century, all Apaches had been settled on reservations, but their presence still hovered like a mist in the desert valley.

Two developments spelled an end to Apache domination of the Sulphur Springs Valley area. First, the Southern Pacific Railroad began constructing the first southern transcontinental railroad through the Gadsden Purchase in the late 1870s. The Southern Pacific pushed into Arizona in 1878, reached the new town of Willcox in August 1880, and linked with the Atcheson, Topeka and Sante Fe Railroad in Deming, New Mexico, before the end of the year. The completion of the railroad opened the area to settlers, particularly encouraging the expansion of the open range cattle business.

The era of open range cattle ranching began shortly after the Civil War, triggered by demands for beef in the East, improvements in refrigeration that made it possible to ship meat long distances, and the availability of millions of longhorn cows in Texas that could be purchased very cheaply. Ranchers began rounding up the cows and driving them to railheads in Missouri and Kansas where they were shipped to stockyards in Kansas City and Chicago. Between 1868 and 1888 millions of cows were shipped from the western range; enterprising cattle barons carved out huge ranches where they could run thousands of cows. These ranches appeared first in Texas but the business quickly expanded westward from New Mexico and Arizona in the south to Montana and Idaho in the north.

Because the grazing land on the western plains was semiarid, the ranches were extremely large. While most ranchers established ownership of small plots of land around crucial watering spots by homesteading or purchase, open range ranches were extralegal arrangements that survived by the consent of the community and by six-shooter law. Cattle barons simply claimed the right to graze certain portions of public lands. They formed cattlemen's associations, registered their claims and brands, and in most places became respected citizens. In later years many of the ranchers established legal ownership to spreads that included hundreds of thousands of acres and in addition leased millions of acres from the federal government.

Much American folklore harks back to the fifty-year period of the open range cattle kingdoms. Easterners were fascinated by the real and fictional exploits of cattle barons and gunfighters, gamblers and marshals, rustlers and stagecoach robbers. Cowboys were the journeyman workers on the open range ranches, driving the cattle to market and exhibiting their riding and roping skills in semiannual roundups in which the cattle that had mingled together on the open range were separated and calves were branded by each ranch. The open range cattle kingdoms began to collapse in the late 1880s for a number of reasons. Increasingly, ranchers were forced to acquire legal ownership of the land because of the encroachments of homesteading farmers; the development of barbed wire made it possible for ranchers to fence in the best grazing land and improve the quality of their livestock; demands for a better-quality beef caused the tough and wiry longhorns to be replaced by Herefords and other cattle that required more care. Nonetheless, these changes came slowly, and vestiges of open range ranching remained for decades in some areas of the west, including the Sulphur Springs Valley.

Open range ranching began in the Sulphur Springs Valley with the establishment of the Sierra Bonita Ranch by Colonel Henry Clay Hooker in 1873. Located about twenty-two miles north of the site of Willcox and just ten miles south of Fort

Grant, for years the Hooker Ranch supplied most of the beef for the army in the Southwest. At its peak the ranch supported a herd of about twenty-five thousand longhorns. By the end of the century, the valley was largely divided into a few open range ranches. The Riggs Home Ranch occupied a huge expanse west of the Chiricahuas; east of Willcox was the Munk Ranch, established by two brothers in 1882; stretching for fourteen miles north of Willcox was the JH Ranch, where cattleman W. H. McKittrick ran a herd of about twenty-eight thousand head. Cattle production in the Sulphur Springs Valley reached its peak in the 1890s, but it remained a big industry well into the twentieth century. Willcox became the most important railhead for the shipment of cattle from the Southwest.

From February until September, Mamie Hailey and her children lived on the JH ranch with the Collins family. Granny Collins was a celebrated cook and cowboys from nearby ranches frequently stopped by to eat a meal and spend the night. Grandfather Collins was a skilled raconteur; in the evenings Homer and Rob sat late into the night listening as he and visiting cowboys swapped tales of Indians and outlaws, of rustlers and train robbers, of gunfights and killings in Willcox. Some evenings, no doubt, the dialogue turned to Wyatt, Virgil, and Morgan Earp whose Battle at OK Corral with the Clanton boys in nearby Tombstone became the most famous gunfight in the West. Or, perhaps they conversed on happenings closer home, such as the shooting of the less-famous Earp brother, Warren, a cowboy on the Hooker Ranch who was killed on a dare by one of his fellow ranch hands. Homer and Rob spent their days doing chores and aimlessly exploring the countryside—visiting the nearby Hooker Ranch, climbing the stark and imposing cliffs of the Gillman Hills, listening for echoes of Apache war whoops, looking for the tracks of Cochise and Geronimo.

The Hailey family expanded again in May 1915 with the birth of Roy. In September Robert rejoined his family, and they moved to the old Collins homestead so that the children could attend the Lompoc public school about a mile and a half away. Homer returned to the ranch the next summer, working his first real job as a helper for Mrs. Brookerson, wife of the JH Ranch foreman. In the evenings he loitered around the cowboys' "poker room," enthralled by the sights and sounds. Many years later the names and personae of the JH cowhands were etched in his memory: Six-shooter Bill, who carried a gun in the pocket of his chaps; Blackey, who wore "dress shirts"; Cal Musgraves, who in later years was a prison guard; and eighteen-year-old "little Tommy." Homer and Rob volunteered to help the cowboys in two roundups, experiencing one of the final scenes in the closing of the open range West, savoring the beefsteak, beans, dried fruit, and coffee served around the campfire by cook Jeff Bacchus.

During the summer of 1917, thirteen-year-old Homer Hailey experienced another novel adventure into the Old West. He was dispatched to fetch a wagon from his Uncle Roger Collins, who had settled seventy-five miles to the east near San Simon. Homer spent the first evening in the bunkhouse of the Shields Ranch; he offered his hosts fifty cents but discovered that hospitality to strangers was a part of the code of the West. After collecting the wagon, Homer spent a second evening sleeping on the ground near San Simon. When he awakened he discovered that his mules had strayed. After a day spent rounding up the team, he was put up for the evening by an elderly settler and his wife. The youngster was given a hearty meal, but first the couple read the Bible and prayed. The ambience of the evening lingered long in the young man's memory. On the way home the wagon broke down between San Simon and Bowie. Homer left it at a ranch, intending to return for it later, but he never did. Leading the two balky mules he headed for home, spending the last evening of his adventure in a line house on the Munk Ranch, an unoccupied shack where provisions were left for cowboys who might be stranded on the range.

In 1917 Homer finished Lompoc school, and the family moved into a small house in Willcox so that he and Rob could attend high school. Homer was a good student, something of a math "whiz." His greatest deficiency, and one that plagued him all his life, was a poor grasp of grammar, a weakness he attributed to the fact that he skipped a year of elementary school.

Willcox was a thriving cow town, shipping thousands of cattle each year to packing houses via the Southern Pacific Railroad. In the evenings, the bellowing of cattle awaiting shipment broke the stillness of the desert. Homer and Rob continued to hunt and camp in the surrounding area, attended an occasional cowboy movie when they could afford it, and got odd jobs loading cattle into the rail cars. In addition, Homer learned to love the novels of Zane Grey and local colorists Harold Bell Wright of Tucson and Jean Stratton Porter. His first summer in Willcox Homer worked as a waiter in a local restaurant where he had a scrap with a bully. He borrowed a Smith and Wesson six-shooter and fully intended to shoot the other youngster. Fortunately, the boy left town and Homer never saw him again. In later years Homer mused about the tragic turn his life might have taken had he, filled with images of gunfights and the code of the West, become a killer himself.

Though no one knows for sure, the family's move to Arizona was apparently motivated by Mamie's desire to join her parents, driven by the increasing irresponsibility of her drinking husband. Robert and Mamie Hailey did not discuss their problems with their children, but it was clear that the marriage had failed. The children heard arguments, and they saw their father drunk, but, like most children, they tried to stay clear of the family's troubles.

Robert worked a variety of laboring jobs in Arizona before becoming a wagon driver in 1917 for Norton-Morgan Commercial Company, one of the pioneer merchant firms in the Southwest. John M. Norton built the first store in Willcox; it became a supply depot for a huge area in the West. The

Norton-Morgan Company operated a major freighting business that supplied most of the army outposts in the area, as well as the region's mining camps and ranches. The freight caravans that supplied the remote outposts of the West provided yet another adventurous chapter in the nation's frontier history. From the 1840s until the second decade of the twentieth century huge wagons supplied remote settlements that could not be reached by rail. The huge wagons, some of them carrying tons of freight, were guided across the rough terrain by skilled drivers called mule skinners and bull whackers.

Robert drove a double-wagon pulled by a team of six mules carrying supplies on a route that ran from Willcox seventy-five miles north to the community of Klondyke. Along the way he made deliveries to the scattered ranches and mining camps and took orders for his return trip. Rob Hailey remembered riding out on Monday morning with his father and returning on Friday, having traversed the incredibly beautiful Sulphur Springs Valley up to Aravaipa Canyon. At one time, Norton-Morgan operated dozens of freight wagons, but Robert's weekly run up the valley was the single surviving route in 1917. After Robert died in 1918, Norton-Morgan discontinued wagon freighting. A piece of the Old West died with Robert Hailey.

On the weekends, Robert returned home; he mostly spent his time gambling and drinking, carousing in the saloon of Ben Pride. He was a "likable" man, easygoing and friendly. In later years his sons probably reflected much of his personality. But by the time he moved to Willcox his financial irresponsibility and drinking had alienated him from his wife and children. In October 1918, in an epidemic that killed hundreds of thousands throughout the nation, Robert fell ill with the flu. He seemed to recover and began preparations for his trip north, but suffered a relapse and died at his home in Willcox. Homer was by his bedside when his father died. None of his family attended his funeral, as all of them were in bed with the flu except for Mamie, who stayed home to care for them.

It was a bitter moment in the family's history. Mamie had long since preserved the marriage only because of her loyalty to her children. She had come to detest her husband. She spoke reluctantly and with few words about her marriage in later years. When she did, she revealed that as she heard the sound of the wheels of the wagon-hearse passing their home bearing the body of Robert Hailey, the wagon wheels seemed to be saying, "I am free. I am free."[26]

Robert's legacy to his family was tragically slight. He left behind an embittered wife who steadfastly refused to discuss her marriage in later years. Homer's and Rob's memories of their father were less harsh, although they were influenced by their mother's bitterness. Rob fondly recalled accompanying his father on trips up the valley. Homer could remember pleasant family evenings playing dominos and cards, but he also had vivid memories of unpleasant scenes when his father came home drunk. Most of all, in later years Homer dreamed of what might have been, of the relationship that he could have had with his father. The tragedy of Robert Hailey was that drinking alienated him from the family and "destroyed love."[27]

Mamie Collins Hailey no doubt held her own in the tense battles with her husband. She was not a spineless or weak woman. From the beginning she was the center of the family; she was the source of the children's education, discipline, and principles. Mamie was a remarkable woman, as tough as any of the calloused cowboys in Arizona—iron willed, courageous, impressively well-read, and deeply prejudiced. The family had no visible means of support. Mamie became the family's foundation rock, although she was a little widow with five children and was five months pregnant with a daughter, Mary Ida, who was born in February 1919. Women played by far the most influential roles in the formation of Homer Hailey's character, and Mamie was the most significant.

The family closed ranks around Mamie. The death of Robert was only one of a series of tragedies that befell the family in

1918. Within the period of a year, Mamie's brother, John Collins, was killed in the Battle of Argonne in France; Grandfather Collins died on his ranch and was buried in Willcox; the rented house where Mamie and the children were living burned to the ground destroying all of their personal possessions; and, most tragically, Homer's thirteen-year-old brother, Jack, was killed when his gun accidentally discharged during a hunting trip. The family was shaken, particularly by the accidental death of Jack, but they "didn't cry about any of it. . . . We just went on." Frontier life was filled with violence and tragedy. The Haileys did not dwell on their misfortunes. "You've got to live in the present," Homer recalled many years later. "I've always done it. Those things are a part of life."[28] With each tragedy the family drew closer together and to Mamie.

When his father died, Homer was fifteen and had just begun his second year of high school. He quit school, accepted a job offered to him by Norton-Morgan to work as a clerk in the Willcox store, and became the chief source of income for the family. For several years, Homer and Rob supported the Hailey family, Homer clerking in stores and Rob working in the bank. The boys opened a common bank account, working as one man to support the family. The Haileys received a small welfare stipend from the state, but they survived mostly because the citizens of Willcox assumed that it was their responsibility to employ Homer and Rob. They endured, "poor as Job's turkey," eating biscuits and molasses for breakfast and cornbread and beans for supper. Mamie bought a little house in Willcox, but no one in the family owned an automobile. They were never hungry, but Homer later recalled a lifelong desire, born of poverty, to have a nice home and to be able to wear good clothes.

Homer's job selling groceries and hardware at Norton-Morgan was a lifesaver for the Hailey family, but he did not like it much. He yearned to roam the wild countryside and dreamed of being a forest ranger, but it was not to be. In later years he came to believe that he had learned valuable lessons working as a clerk, discovering how to relate to people and how to sell, talents that served him well in his years as an evangelist. After a year, Homer changed jobs, becoming a clerk in Huffman's Toggery. He was happier there because he liked selling men's clothing and dressing the windows. More important, he established a lifelong friendship with the Thomas Huffman family.

Though still just a youngster, Homer matured into a respected citizen of Willcox, likable and sociable. Away from work, Homer explored the countryside with Rob and his friends, once climbing Mount Graham. There was little mischief in him, but he drifted into the common life-style of a Willcox bachelor, smoking heavily, occasionally drinking White Mule bootleg liquor, playing penny ante with his friends, and frequenting the local dances. He was "plumb good looking," a little cocky, and a passing good dancer. For several years Homer and Mattie Hamilton were steady companions at the dances, but the courtship held little promise. Mattie was looking for something permanent, and Homer had a mother and family to support.

While working at Huffman's Toggery, Homer returned to high school, finishing three years of class work in two years. These were frantically busy years with little time for frivolity. Homer worked in the store after school and then studied late into the evenings. Still, he was amazingly active in high school. Homer was one of two members of the debate team, played Shylock in the Union High School version of "The Merchant of Venice up to Date," and occasionally dated. He tried to play basketball and football in high school, but there was no room in his schedule. He did play in one football game, after having seen only one; Willcox lost to Douglas 81–0. In 1925, at age twenty-two, Homer Hailey graduated as valedictorian in a class of twenty-five and quivered through a graduation address.

Two circumstances—one a brief incident and the other a lasting friendship—slowly pushed Hailey in new directions.

The one, brief, portentous incident in his life was a somewhat painful and embarrassing whipping he received in a fight. While attending a dance, and while slightly under the influence of White Mule, Hailey accused another young man of stealing his whisky and awoke the next morning with a puffed lip and a damaged ego. The episode started him on the road to reform. He quit smoking, purchased barbells and began lifting, and began to box, determined to "whip that fellow if I never saw the back of my neck." He never saw his mugger again, but in later years he became "very grateful to him for what he did for me that night, because it turned me around." One of his friends in Willcox showed Hailey a copy of Benarr McFadden's *Strength Magazine,* and he began in earnest what would become a lifetime commitment to body building and nutrition. A second, and more important, life-changing influence entered Hailey's life when he was befriended by Mrs. Huffman, the wife of his employer.

A Spiritual Journey to the Churches of Christ

A few months after his unfortunate fisticuffs experience, Hailey began a spiritual journey that put an end to his carousing days and set him on the course he would follow for the next seventy years. When Hailey went to work for Thomas Huffman in 1919, a strapping and likeable sixteen-year-old youngster, Mrs. Huffman treated him like a son. A "very devout woman" who taught a class at the Christian church in Willcox, Mrs. Huffman finally persuaded Hailey to begin attending classes on Sundays. She encouraged and corrected him; Mrs. Huffman always seemed to know when he had been into some mischief, and she particularly "got after him" when he drank. Hailey was vaguely aware that his family had a religious identity inherited from Granny Collins, but he had been without formal religious influence most of his life. Mamie taught the children the principles of right and wrong, but they rarely attended church. The family had never had private devotions or prayers; Mamie had had little opportunity to learn much about religion herself.

The Christian Church was established in Willcox in 1911 by an evangelist supported by the Arizona Christian Missionary Society. W. H. Salyer, the state secretary, vigorously promoted the Christian Church in Arizona, regularly evangelizing in the scattered settlements and erecting "a uniform type of modest church shelter which required usually $600 in materials and was constructed by donated labor."[29] The congregation was visited from time to time by evangelists supported by the missionary society, but on most Sundays a small group of devout women taught a class and presided over the Lord's Supper. In later years Hailey remembered that Mrs. Huffman was a "good teacher" who "knew the Bible quite well." The church had only two male members; neither of them attended unless a visiting preacher was present.

In 1922 the missionary society dispatched an evangelist to Willcox to conduct a protracted meeting, an older man named Talbot, who was, as Hailey later remembered, a "good sound preacher." Talbot harvested a group of young people who had been prepared by Mrs. Huffman's persistence and teaching; Homer, Rob, their sister Ruth, Homer's girlfriend Sybil Bonham, and Rob's future wife Helen Cook were all baptized. Mamie was pleased by the religious transformation of her family. She made it clear that she did not believe in instrumental music, but she deemed the Christian Church to be the best religious option available in Willcox.

When Homer Hailey was baptized at the Willcox Christian Church, the American restoration movement was entering its third generation. The division between the Christian Church and the churches of Christ was fairly well defined; in 1926 in Arizona, there were twenty-one churches of Christ and nineteen Christian churches. In keeping with the national pattern, the Christian churches in Arizona were larger (averaging 130 members to 39 in churches of Christ) and wealthier (Christian churches owned seventeen buildings with an average value of

$13,618 compared with six buildings with an average value of $2,800 for the churches of Christ).[30] The economic disparity between the two groups was less apparent in Arizona than in most other states, however, because of the general poverty of the churches in the West.

The practical differences between the churches of Christ and the Christian Church in an area as remote as Arizona were relatively slight, not reaching much deeper than disagreements over instrumental music and support for missionary societies. Most of the missionary society evangelists who preached in the small Christian churches of the state were "pretty sound old men," Hailey recalled in later years. They were much more likely to preach the five-finger plan of salvation or offer discourses on premillennialism or pacifism than to expound upon liberal theology or the social gospel.

Most of the young people converted in the Willcox meeting in 1922 remained Christians, but Hailey was most deeply changed. He was the "happiest guy in the world." He quit drinking and set out to study the Bible, reading on Sundays and evenings, often sitting under a yucca. "I didn't know what I was reading," he later mused, "but I read it through. That's the only time in my life that I just read the Bible through."[31] Two of the church's leading women, Mrs. Huffman and Mrs. Browning, made Hailey their special project, encouraging him and nurturing the notion that he should be a preacher. Because none of the male members of the church attended regularly, Hailey was usually the oldest man in the services; he began presiding at the serving of the Lord's Supper on Sundays and made a few halting talks. The preachers who visited irregularly encouraged his efforts, supplying him with sermon outlines and pointers.

After graduating from high school, Hailey knew that he wanted to continue his education and become a preacher, but the family still needed his support. He and Rob borrowed five thousand dollars and became partners in a general merchandise store in Willcox with two older merchants. The Valley

Store became a millstone around Homer's neck. The business grew slowly, competing against Norton-Morgan and Huffman Toggery, and young Hailey felt that his two older partners saddled him with most of the responsibility and work. Furthermore, he felt himself slipping spiritually. He began dating a "Methodist girl" and started dancing and drinking again. On Christmas night 1925, he went through something of a personal spiritual crisis. He spent the evening with a bottle of wine, pondering his future. It was the last time he would ever drink. On that evening he resolved to reform and become a preacher. He asked his business partners to buy him out. At first they refused, but in August 1926, he told them he was leaving with or without their consent. Reluctantly, his partners purchased his share of the business, giving him a profit of $550 for the increased value of the store's stock. He split that amount with Rob and entered the next phase of his life with $275.

Homer's decision to go to college and become a preacher uprooted the Hailey family. On August 2, 1926, Homer loaded Mamie, his younger sisters, and all of their belongings into a second-hand 1923 Ford Model T touring car that he had secured in a swap for some bank stock he had purchased. They set out for Hallsville, Texas, where Granny Collins was living; they had planned two stops along the way. Granny Collins had always wanted one of her children to attend Abilene Christian College and Hailey decided to stop in Abilene and look at the campus. One of the members of the Willcox Christian Church had encouraged him to consider attending Texas Christian University in Fort Worth.

The two schools Homer Hailey set out to visit represented the two roads taken by the restoration movement in Texas. Texas Christian University was founded in 1869 when two Disciples preachers, Addison and Randolph Clark, began holding classes in Fort Worth. In 1873 they moved the school to Thorp Spring, forty miles to the southwest, to escape the "sin and corruption" in the booming cow town of Fort Worth. In 1889, the school formally affiliated with the Christian Churches of Texas and three years later moved to Waco, where it operated as AddRan Christian College until its name was changed to Texas Christian University in 1902. The university returned to Fort Worth in 1911; in 1923 Mrs. Mary Couts Burnett gave TCU a large bequest that remains the largest portion of its endowment. By 1926, when Hailey visited TCU, the university was financially secure, academically respectable, and on the verge of becoming a national football power. TCU was one of twenty-seven "colleges and schools of higher grade" identified with the Disciples of Christ movement in 1926.[32]

Abilene Christian College, on the other hand, was only twenty years old when Hailey visited in 1926. Clearly identified with the conservative churches that opposed instrumental music and the state missionary society, ACC was a struggling institution trying to survive in the midst of a religious movement that was strongly anti-institutional and anti-intellectual. In 1926, ACC was unaccredited and looked much like a Bible school, although a full college curriculum was offered. No member of the school's faculty held a doctoral degree.

Texas Christian University and Abilene Christian College symbolized the social context of the division in the Texas restoration movement. The sociological dimensions of the churches of Christ–Christian Church division were much clearer in Texas than in Arizona. The crusty conservative preachers who led the churches of Christ in Texas in the late nineteenth century understood well that the two groups were divided by economic as well as theological differences. Texas preacher Thomas R. Burnett captured the common people's prejudices in an 1895 article that criticized the meeting of the Texas Missionary Society: "Last week about a hundred preachers and fashionable women assembled at Gainesville, Texas, in a state convention, and wasted enough of the Lord's money and time to have held a hundred protracted meetings. . . . They also spent enough money for extra fine toggery, to appear in style, to pay the expenses of a half dozen evangelists to preach the gospel in destitute places all summer. What was their business in Gainesville? Principally a fashionable blow-out, and in addition to this, an effort to push forward the furor for societies and fads in religion, and to supplant the Lord's plan of work and worship in the churches."[33] In the census of 1926 the Disciples of Christ reported 77,150 members in Texas in 489 churches, an average of 158 per congregation. The churches of Christ reported 98,909 members in 1,286 churches, averaging 77 per local church. The average value of the 462 Christian Church edifices in the state was $17,781; the average value of 1,055 churches of Christ was $3,878. While the churches of Christ had more members in Texas than the Christian Church, the progressives had more than twice as many members in such urban counties as Collin, Dallas, Harris, Hunt, and Tarrant.

The Haileys journeyed to Texas with little understanding of such matters. It was an exciting time for them; they stopped for a few days in El Paso to visit Uncle Tom Hailey before driving on to Abilene. There they stayed in a tourist court and Hailey toured the barren campus of the small West Texas school. He talked briefly with the school's diminutive and dour president, Batsell Baxter, and went away unimpressed. They journeyed on to Fort Worth where Hailey strolled around the impressive campus of TCU. In Fort Worth he was intimidated. "This is too big for me," thought the youngster from Willcox. "I'd be lost in this school."[34] The two schools offered starkly different roads to travel, as did the Christian Church and the churches of Christ.

Undecided about his future, and not totally satisfied with either ACC or TCU, Hailey and his entourage headed for Hallsville to visit Granny Collins and Aunt Sudie Bass, Mamie's older sister. It was the "most providential" trip Homer Hailey would ever make. Granny Collins encouraged him to attend ACC. More important, Aunt Sudie's daughter, Sybil, told Homer that she was thinking of returning to school for her final two years and that she would go to ACC with him if he made that choice. They struck a deal. Sybil and Homer would go to school, and Mamie and Ruth would live with them and keep their apartment. Hailey returned to Abilene, rented an apartment, and went back to Hallsville to wait for school to begin in the fall of 1926.

PART II

The Mainstream Churches of Christ

1920–1999

2

The Churches of Christ, 1920–1950

A Heritage of Controversy

LATE IN HIS LIFE, Homer Hailey judged that the years from 1920 to 1950 were a transition period in the history of the churches of Christ, a time when the pioneer preachers who had fought the battles that saved the church from digression faded from the scene and were replaced by better-educated, full-time preachers. He believed that his first two decades of preaching had been part of a golden age in the church's history, an era peopled by selfless evangelists, men of deep convictions and fervent spirits. His own meetings in the 1930s and early 1940s were a part of a fading epoch when an evangelist could pitch a tent, preach for three weeks, and baptize dozens of earnest seekers.[1] There were "giants in those days," wrote Foy E. Wallace, Jr., in 1935, preachers and debaters who harvested a generation of converts who had been "thoroughly indoctrinated."[2] By the end of World War II, times had changed, the nation had changed, and the churches of Christ had changed.

In a series of articles on the "history of the church during the last fifty years," written in 1941, *Firm Foundation* editor G. H. P. Showalter noted an important divide in the early history of the churches of Christ in the twentieth century. "For the first two decades [1895–1915] . . . brethren who had freed themselves from the Christian Church . . . found themselves accomplishing little," Showalter wrote. Most members of the churches of Christ expressed "gratitude that they were delivered from innovation," but the churches exhibited little vision or evangelistic fervor. In fact, many were so intimidated by the debate over missionary societies that they were "rather afraid to do anything for fear they would do something that was wrong." After World War I, however, there had been a "very remarkable activity on the part of loyal churches of Christ in the realm of missionary work. They have been preaching the gospel in destitute places and as a result have built many congregations where a few years ago there were none."[3]

Statistical evidence confirms that the churches of Christ did grow during the first four decades of the twentieth century. In 1936, the Bureau of the Census made an effort to be more discriminating between Disciples of Christ churches and churches of Christ and, as a result, reduced from its 1926 figures the estimated membership of the churches of Christ to 309,551 people in 3,815 congregations. While some knowledgeable preachers believed that the churches of Christ were seriously undercounted in 1936, the Census Bureau insisted that its figures were "far more complete."[4] This census notwithstanding, the period from 1920 to the end of World War II was clearly one of vitality and growth in the churches of Christ. At the end of World War II, M. Norvel Young began collecting information for a 1946 religious census, which was never completed. On the basis of his sampling, however, Young estimated that the churches of Christ had 682,172 members in more than 10,000 congregations.[5]

Wild Democracy

Editor G. H. P. Showalter believed that the remarkable growth in churches of Christ after World War I had been achieved without the appearance of major internal tensions. He noted minor problems, such as a lack of "real genuine piety and spirituality among those who are the professed followers of Christ according to the New Testament order," manifesting itself in the "lack of prayer" and the growth of "levity, frivolity, joking, jesting, etc." at church services. Nonetheless, Showalter thought that the churches of Christ were a homogeneous group at the outbreak of World War II: "It is gratifying to note how little disposition there seems to be at the present time to turn back to a more liberal, human and worldly policy with reference to things required of us in the New Testament."[6] In view of the bickering and strife that filled the papers read by church members, Showalter's assessment seemed visionary, but, at least on the surface, most controversies were local and limited. When World War II erupted, the central intellectual motifs in the movement remained unchallenged and its most cherished shibboleths were mouthed everywhere. A decade later, this apparent uniformity of intent and purpose had vanished. By 1950, the churches of Christ were awash in a sea of strife and the riptides beneath the surface were treacherous indeed.

Even at the time Showalter penned his optimistic assessment, the churches of Christ were riddled by dissension; indeed, the American restoration movement had always been a case study in controversy. Even during the "golden age" of the 1920s and 1930s, the periodicals read by the members of the churches of Christ teemed with impassioned debates about a bewildering array of issues. These disputes often turned uncivil, and they frequently ebbed and flowed for decades. While one issue was being heatedly debated, causing clusters of churches and preachers to coalesce around contrasting positions, the heat of that skirmish would momentarily overshadow equally serious disagreements that cut along different lines. When the *Gospel Advocate* was under attack in the rebaptism controversy in the 1930s, Cled E. Wallace, then a staff writer for the *Advocate,* commented on the tendency of fighting preachers to highlight one issue at a time, wryly charging that the only doctrinal point of agreement among those who insisted on the rebaptism of all denominational converts was that they "had it in for the Gospel Advocate."[7]

Many preachers thrived on the spirit of controversy, while others found the incessant bickering worrisome. The internal battles clearly dissipated a good deal of energy. Yet, most of the rancorous debates of the 1930s and 1940s never threatened to divide the loose unity of the movement. So long as all parties retained an apparent commitment to restoring New Testament Christianity through a common-sense reading of the Bible and saw themselves as a separated remnant of the faithful, the tenuous and informal unity of the churches of Christ remained intact. With the passing of a few years, the bitterest of enemies often declared truces and could be found fighting shoulder-to-shoulder as new battle lines formed in new controversies.

In at least one way, controversy served a useful purpose within the restoration movement. Disdainful of creeds, preachers used altercation to chart the course of the future; argumentation was a stratagem for reaching consensus in an intellectually unrestricted church. While central beliefs were broadly held in all of the churches, on the fringes doctrinal issues were constantly being rethought. Recently settled questions (such as baptism for the remission of sins and the rejection of instrumental music in worship) were universal tests of orthodoxy, but, in fact, the churches of Christ were united only by a hermeneutic that demanded a constant reevaluation of every belief in the light of a common-sense reading of the New Testament and by a primitivist commitment to restoring New Testament Christianity.

G. H. P. Showalter offered a summary of the church's intellectual life in the first half of the twentieth century that could be applied to any period in the history of the churches of Christ: "There has been no small amount of attention given to accurate and careful definitions of terms, and also of what is involved in our aims and purposes."[8] The "peculiar religious teaching of various religious groups may be defined as distinctive dogmata," Showalter continued, because "the denominational churches with their creeds, confessions of faith, and articles of discipline, throw out boundaries and plant limitations on the faith and practice of their members." No such "doctrinal range" existed in the churches of Christ; any belief or practice was open to reexamination. The churches of Christ were no place for "dogmatists," Showalter concluded. The ideas of all "uninspired men" were forced to compete for acceptance in an open market.[9]

This commitment to freedom of thought and expression, often violated in practice in the churches of Christ, was repeatedly set forth as the only allegiance demanded of church members. It was the key to the movement's plea for Christian unity—a unity that necessarily survived within an unruly and petulant arena of disagreement. In a 1906 statement of editorial policy, the *Gospel Advocate* highlighted the movement's commitment to freedom of thought and opposition to intervening clerical elites: "It opposes all human creeds and ecclesiastic councils, and pleads for the right of each individual to study the Scriptures for himself, and formulate his own faith, without dictation or hindrance from churchly dignitaries. It opposes all clerical assumption of official authority in the church."[10] In 1908, the aging David Lipscomb described the invigorating outcome of free discussion: "He who deprecates all discussion must be content with a very imperfect knowledge of the truth of God. Water that is never stirred becomes stagnate and fetid. The mind that is never stirred with new and adverse thoughts . . . becomes stale, commonplace, and effete. The faith of such persons lacks vigor and enterprise."[11] Lipscomb was disdainful of Daniel Sommer, who refused to allow free discussion in his paper, and wrote: "A true lover of truth seeks out and appropriates as his own every truth he finds, no matter who holds or teaches it."[12] Foy E. Wallace, Jr., by many measures the rankest "dogmatist" in the movement, agreed with Lipscomb that "the whole ground of the restoration plea needs repeatedly to be reviewed and restated."[13] Frank B. Shepherd, Homer Hailey's mentor and a respected preacher in the 1930s, believed that "the twenty-seven books [of the New Testament] were written by the Holy Spirit for the express purpose of keeping us rethinking our religion." A constant reassessment of practice and teaching was the only protection against "digression."[14]

This commitment to free thought and discussion made the churches of Christ a "wild democracy" in which the "common sense" of every person was the governing religious authority.[15] A populist confidence in the ability of the common person to understand truth, often accompanied by overt anti-intellectual prejudices, made members of the churches of Christ wary of education and pretentious scholarship. In 1939, L. L. Brigance of Freed-Hardeman College summed up these widely held prejudices: "It is generally believed, and not without reason, that college professors have, upon an average, less common sense than any other class unless it be preachers. There are many Ph. D.'s and D. D.'s whose heads are filled with fanciful, intellectual theories that have so little common practical sense that they need a guardian. Good, sound gospel preachers have been ruined by attending some big university and getting a master's or doctor's degree."[16] Few members of the churches of Christ in the 1930s and 1940s would allow preachers or professors to codify their religious faith.

Schism was inevitable in such an atmosphere of debate and conflict; typically, in the first half of the twentieth century, divisions within the churches of Christ were congregational. By the 1930s, local churches splintered with astounding regularity. In the absence of a denominational organization to declare a congregation either in or out of fellowship with others, splinter congregations continued to relate loosely with some churches of Christ and remain aloof from others. After a decade or two, feuding churches often reconciled, although sometimes peace was restored only with the passing of a generation, giving rise to the adage that most church squabbles were solved by funerals.

Local congregations divided over scores of doctrinal issues

during the first half of the twentieth century. Some of the disputed questions were trivial, even in the minds of the most principled preachers. In 1936, Foy E. Wallace, Jr., composed a list of "hateful problems," practical and doctrinal, that had disrupted local churches: "Preacher's problems and the problem of preachers; the striving for place and the swapping of jobs; exchange meetings, Young People's Meetings, all kinds of meetings; the night service, the song service; missionary work, women's work, and no work."[17] Another preacher, Will J. Cullum, protesting a spread of "hobby riding" that was "very hurtful to the cause of Christ," listed some issues that had caused schisms: "objections to a baptistery, [some] insisting that we should have running water, because Christ was baptized in the River Jordan"; objections to the use of "individual cups in observing the Lord's Supper," to "having a plate for the bread," and to the "preacher extending a gospel invitation [instead of waiting] for sinners to ask what they should do as on Pentecost"; members who claimed "that it is unscriptural to have elders in the church, taking the position that all elders were in the days of inspiration"; objections to "singing any song that is not addressed 'in words' to The Lord"; and, "most ridiculous," Cullum concluded, brethren objecting to "a word formula in baptizing, or in a marriage. And to having a funeral service."[18]

Of course, defining triviality was the essence of an inherent fellowship dilemma in the churches of Christ. One person's triviality was another's test of loyalty to New Testament authority. No clear New Testament teaching was trivial to a serious restorer. Thus, the only test was whether a matter was clearly established by the Scriptures or merely a misguided opinion. Cullum judged that the "most hurtful" hobby of his day was opposition to "systematic study of the word of the Lord" in Bible classes. His article illustrated that the line between hobby riding and loyalty to the truth was thin and subject to individual judgment. He explained that Bible classes under the direction of elders were all right, but "to organize a Sunday School, with Supt., Sec., and Treas. with all of this done as an organization, it is as unscriptural as a Missionary society."[19]

Objections to Bible classes, sometimes called "Sunday Schools" and operated as suborganizations within a local church in the manner that Cullum found objectionable, became the basis for a collective schism in which perhaps five percent of the churches formed a self-conscious minority faction in the 1920s. In 1925 this group assembled a directory of the churches opposed to Bible classes, using one of the informal strategies that provide a mechanism for division in the restoration movement. About half of the non-class churches also objected to the use of more than one container in the observance of the Lord's Supper; several hundred other churches that were not a part of the non-class movement became identified with the "one-cup" position.[20] These dissenting churches often disagreed with one another on a variety of other issues, including whether fermented or unfermented grape juice should be used in communion, whether the loaf must be broken before distribution, the scriptural authority for located preachers, and the propriety of women speaking or teaching in the churches—all issues that were also debated in other churches of Christ. These non-class and one-cup congregations, numbering more than one thousand in the 1990s, were often alienated from one another, but they did develop limited networks in the 1920s and 1930s that survived into the 1990s.[21]

Sometimes crusading preachers launched major attacks to save the churches from minor errors and, unlike the dissent raised by the one-cup and non-class protests, the furor dimmed in time. In 1936, young Guy N. Woods attacked the "menace" of Young People's Meeting Societies: "Not since the shameful defection produced by the innovation of instrumental music and missionary societies, has a more insidious evil encroached on the purity of New Testament churches. For a time covertly, but now brazen and bold, the Y. P. M. Society, rears its ugly head, as religious journals weekly tell of further departures from the ancient order of things and the simplicity of the Lord's arrangement."[22] Others thought that Woods's rhetoric was overwrought. Otis Gatewood chided Woods's intemperance, although he admitted that some local churches structured their teaching programs unwisely. He urged "all churches not to discontinue their young people's meetings, but correct the mistakes."[23] The issue resurfaced from time to time, but more as a general difference in emphasis than as a major "departure from the ancient order of things."

Some questions of considerable moral import, such as a cluster of issues surrounding biblical teachings on marriage, divorce, and remarriage, often caused divisions in local churches but did not become the focus of a broader schism. There was a general consensus among preachers that it would be preferable for a Christian to marry another Christian, but few congregations regarded violations of that rule as being of sufficient gravity to refuse fellowship to a member. The question of divorce was more troublesome. From the beginnings of the American restoration movement, wide disparities of belief existed about divorce and remarriage. A majority believed that such passages as Matthew 19:9 set clear boundaries that allowed remarriage after divorce only if a husband or wife was an innocent party whose partner had committed adultery. That view was not universally held, however. For instance, distressed by the growing "divorce evil" in 1930, G. H. P. Showalter included a second reason for divorce: "there is but one cause (fornication) possible, or at best two (desertion) that may be scripturally urged as a reason or an excuse for divorce."[24] Some preachers were stricter, insisting that there was no scriptural cause for divorce and remarriage, and others held looser views that permitted divorced people to be members of local churches. Many local churches divided over specific cases of enforcement; each local church dealt with its own problems and there was considerable variation from place to place. In some congregations divorced persons were unofficially treated as "associate members," allowed to attend and participate in the communion but not to be leaders in the congregation.

No editor during the 1930s and 1940s demanded that all churches of Christ adopt a single position on the divorce question; no school or paper treated divorce as an issue demanding "brotherhood action." Asked in 1931 why "preachers in the churches of Christ are divided on the divorce question," W. T. Kidwell replied in the *Firm Foundation:* "The only answer I can give to the above question . . . is that some preachers have failed to 'rightly divide the word of truth' on the divorce question." But Kidwell did not resolve the issue; he merely hinted that his own view was not orthodox: "I never interpret anything Jesus said before he was crucified, only in the light of what was taught by the Holy Spirit through the apostles under the last commission."[25] At the end of the thirties the divorce issue was as muddled as ever. In 1939, G. H. P. Showalter noted that he had "received many articles" on the subject, and that they varied widely, convincing him that "all have not studied the subject sufficiently well." Showalter's advice was typically loose and noncommittal: "We kindly suggest that all interested . . . read the Bible for themselves, carefully, conscientiously, thoughtfully, and particularly what Christ, Paul and others have taught in the New Testament."[26]

For all of the sound and fury, the fussing and dividing in churches of Christ in the pre–World War II years took place within an atmosphere of debate, proof-texting, and assumed primitivist commitment that was a familiar arena for all of the combatants. In short, it represented a type of untidy negotiation that characterized churches of Christ in periods of relative homogeneity. The disputes were skirmishes between like-minded people and, with the exception of the one-cup and non-class divisions, they did not segregate the movement into distinctive communities. Consciously or unconsciously, most people within the movement realized that it was an attitude that united them rather than a catalog of beliefs and practices. In 1875, David Lipscomb summarized this often unstated premise: "So long as a man really desires to do right, to serve the Lord, to obey his commands, we cannot withdraw from him. We are willing to accept him as a brother, no matter how ignorant he may be, or how far short of the perfect standard his life may fall from this ignorance. . . . What is needed is patient instruction and discipline in the church, instead of withdrawal from the weak."[27] While the separation of the dissident non-class and one-cup churches in the twenties and thirties established self-conscious networks of churches of Christ that subsequently had their own histories, those schisms simply shattered away the brittle extremes of the movement, those people who proved unable to tolerate the level of dissonance and debate that existed in the wild democracy of the churches of Christ. People on both sides of those issues still intended to "obey" the teachings of the New Testament in the most literal sense; these were separations between like-minded people whose consciences tolerated only so much disparity.

Broader divisions within the restoration movement—such as the Christian Church–churches of Christ schism at the end of the nineteenth century—were much more complex, as the subsequent telling of this story will reveal. Rarely have churches of Christ divided into separated communions simply over differences in belief. Historian Leroy Garrett regarded it as something of an "oddity" that "internal fission" in the movement almost always resulted from *"disputation over methodology more than theology."*[28] Visible differences in practice and worship, rather than propositional affirmations about particular beliefs, have always provided the mechanism for schism in the restoration movement because they caused opposing groups to doubt the other's commitment, in Lipscomb's words, "to do right, to serve the Lord, to obey his commands." In times of crisis, when feuding factions came to suspect the worst of one another, alternate institutional networks arose to define separated groups of churches.

In short, broad and permanent divisions in the churches of Christ became likely when local churches and preachers aligned themselves around visible differences in practice, which they believed signified even more fundamental differences in purpose, and around clusters of church-related institutions. Papers and schools were the most authoritative extra-congregational institutions supported by members of churches of Christ in the 1930s and 1940s; at the local level, people had imprecise and shifting loyalties to these institutions.

Occasionally in the history of the churches of Christ, a leader came close to acknowledging that institutions created a surrogate denominational structure. While editor of the *Gospel Advocate* in the mid-1930s, Foy E. Wallace, Jr., in a series of articles, lambasted the "factious spirit in churches" that had caused "factions and rumors of factions." To thwart the chaos, Wallace published guidelines for churches wishing to receive "the recognition and endorsement of the *Gospel Advocate*." Granting that "the Gospel Advocate has no authority over the churches . . . and any church or individuals who make investigations satisfactory to themselves have the personal right to act accordingly," Wallace nonetheless announced that "the Gospel Advocate will not . . . feel obligated to endorse their decisions."[29] Wallace's series obviously riled some readers. A few months after Wallace's first articles appeared, the editorial page of the *Gospel Advocate* featured an article by B. C. Goodpasture, one of Wallace's staff writers, that attempted to clarify and soften the editorial. Goodpasture explained that "when possible, churches should settle their own troubles among themselves" and that "outside interference" was not usually needed. In the end, however, he supported Wallace's guidelines, arguing that "it is the duty of a religious paper to 'mark' and 'avoid' them that cause divisions" and "in doing this, the paper does not pose as a regulator of the churches, but as a teacher of the truth."[30] These *Gospel Advocate* editorials came about as close as anything ever written to describing an organization within the churches of Christ that was larger than a local church; in the process, Wallace and Goodpasture described the de facto pattern of schism within the restoration movement.

Pacifists Fight a Losing War

The moral issue that generated the bitterest discussions in the first half of the twentieth century was pacifism. The twentieth-century churches of Christ did not inherit a clear-cut pacifist legacy from the nineteenth-century restoration movement. During the Civil War there were pacifist blocks of preachers in both North and South, but most Disciples joined the swelling ranks of the military. Opposition to the Civil War was strongest in the border states of Kentucky, Tennessee, and Missouri; young David Lipscomb, who became the patriarch of the churches of Christ in Tennessee in the late nineteenth century, was a pacifist. He, along with many of the preachers in the border states, refused to serve on either side during the Civil War.[31]

In the late nineteenth century, the churches of Christ in the South drifted toward pacifism, while the more liberal Christian Churches in the North became increasingly nationalistic and patriotic. Protesting the growing support for the Spanish-American War among northern churches, Texas preacher J. D. Tant wrote in 1898, "The digressive preachers who have introduced the organ and society in Texas and have divided the Church of Christ, will go to fight Spain; for many of them are political men who vote and hold office."[32]

Tant's pacifism, like that of many leaders among the churches of Christ, was rooted in a broader sense of alienation from the world. David Lipscomb was the chief architect of a theology of world separation that had a lasting influence on the churches of Christ. Lipscomb wrote extensively in the *Gospel Advocate* on the separation of Christians from the world, opposing military service, voting, and holding office, and in 1889 his views were collected in a small book, *Civil Government:*

Its Origin, Mission and Destiny, and the Christian's Relation to It.[33] Arguing that a Christian's "citizenship is in heaven" and that he or she has no legal relationship with the "kingdoms of the world," Lipscomb believed that it was thoroughly misguided, indeed sinful, for Christians to become embroiled in politics. Lipscomb's book was reprinted repeatedly in the half century after its publication.[34]

It is difficult to estimate how widely Lipscomb's views penetrated into the pews of the churches of Christ. He never believed that his ideas should become a test of fellowship within the churches, and he frequently complained that he was deserted by his friends during times of patriotic fervor. In 1880, Lipscomb reacted with disgust when northern Disciples rallied behind the presidential candidacy of James A. Garfield, who was a former Disciples preacher and college president. Lipscomb used the occasion to taunt the staunchly Democratic church members in the South. "Now, dear brethren of the South who wish to argue for good, pious, religious rulers," he sarcastically asked, "what are you going to do about Bro. Garfield?"[35] While it is difficult to judge what percentage of the people in the churches of Christ agreed with Lipscomb's full-blown argument on civil government, a very large portion probably shared his general disdain for the affairs of the world.

During World War I, pacifists within the churches of Christ faced enormous pressure from the rising tide of patriotism that affected all Americans, but they tried to resist.[36] Six days after the United States entered the war, the *Gospel Advocate* published a statement entitled "How to Prepare Petitions against Carnal Warfare," and the editors urged readers to purchase and read Lipscomb's book. Lipscomb himself was eighty-six years old and died before the year was out, but on the campus of his Nashville Bible School petitions were provided for students who wished to apply for exemption from the draft.[37]

In August 1917 the *Gospel Advocate* reversed itself, announcing that the paper would "be helpful in every possible way to the government."[38] Partly, the editorial change was caused by government intimidation. In June 1917 the government passed the most repressive (and unconstitutional) legislation restricting individual freedom since the early days of the Republic. The Espionage Act of 1917 gave the government broad powers to shut down pacifist publications, and the publisher of the *Gospel Advocate,* J. C. McQuiddy, was summoned to a meeting with Attorney General Lee Douglas to defend the paper's policies. Douglas was satisfied after the meeting that McQuiddy was a "patriot citizen," and the *Gospel Advocate* soon proved him to be correct.[39]

The *Advocate's* change was only partly caused by government intimidation. Many preachers were pacifists all through the war, and some were jailed because of their beliefs, but overwhelmingly the young men in the churches of Christ responded patriotically to the call for volunteers. Furthermore, many preachers were strong supporters of the war from the beginning, including G. H. P. Showalter, editor of the *Firm Foundation,* who labeled the pacifists in the churches "sanctimonious fanatics."[40] By the end of World War I, pacifism had not vanished from the churches of Christ, but it had been badly wounded by the Great War.

Nonetheless, pacifist articles began to appear once again in the years between World War I and World War II. Some local churches took action. In 1933, the church in Valdosta, Georgia, where seasoned pacifist A. B. Lipscomb preached, drafted "Anti-War Resolutions" and requested "the War Department to grant immunity to its young men who were consistent church members and conscientious objectors to war." Scores of other churches followed suit. During the early 1930s, Foy E. Wallace, Jr., urged "preachers to be exhorting Christians to follow Christ and the apostles even to prison and martyrdom [rather than] instilling within them the spirit of militarism, war and hell." He boldly boasted, "I am not a patriot—I am a Christian."[41]

The renewed emphasis on pacifism was not universally welcomed. W. W. Otey warned that "the vast majority would not agree" with such teaching and that pacifist agitation could "result in open division." If elders had a right to commit an entire local church to pacifism, Otey asked, "why not commit them also on the question that Christians should not vote or participate in civil government? . . . The two questions are inseparably linked."[42]

As war clouds gathered in the years leading to World War II, the pacifist tradition in restoration thought was again severely challenged. The most committed pacifists in the church, including H. Leo Boles, James D. Bales, M. Norvel Young, Fanning Yater Tant, Ira Y. Rice, Jr., N. B. Hardeman, J. P. Sanders, and Norman Parks, offered instructions in the various papers telling young Christian men how to file for conscientious objector status.[43] However, after the United States entered the war, a majority of the members of the churches of Christ once again joined the patriotic stampede as their sons volunteered or were drafted into the service.

To a remarkable degree, however, the papers circulated in the churches of Christ remained silent during the war, illustrating that pacifism still had wide support among editors and writers. Reading the *Firm Foundation* and the *Gospel Advocate* from 1940 through 1945, one is struck by the lack of attention given to the progress of the war. In the *Firm Foundation*, G. H. P. Showalter gave reluctant support to the war, but he refused to publish most of the articles that he received on the subject.[44] B. C. Goodpasture, the editor of the *Gospel Advocate*, said little on the issue either before or after the war, but he helped raise financial support for young Christians detained in conscientious objector camps, and he criticized those who were pacifists during peace time but "in time of war . . . goose-step like a German corporal."[45] Historian Earl Irvin West surmised that Goodpasture "did what he could to promote the non-combatant positions."[46] The clearest pacifist voices "crying in the wilderness" in the midst of World War II were found in north Alabama, where a number of church leaders, including John T. Lewis, penned anti-war tracts.[47]

On the other hand, pro-war preachers in the churches of Christ appealed to wartime patriotism to bludgeon the pacifists. In March 1942, after the United States entered World War II, Foy E. Wallace, Jr., reversed himself and became a virulent patriot and militarist; he lambasted those who refused to change with him.[48] N. B. Hardeman, who in the 1930s had been Wallace's warm friend, later charged that "both Foy and Cled [Wallace] tried more than once to line me up with them in favor of carnal warfare. I refused to join them."[49] In an article printed anonymously in the March 1942 issue of the *Bible Banner,* Foy E. Wallace, Jr., branded conscientious objectors "freak specimens of humanity."[50] Cled Wallace, Foy's acerbic brother, labeled pacifists "long-faced crackpots." He believed that pacifist preachers were guilty of undermining young people's will to fight with their "idiotic drivel," and he scored the Abilene Christian College bookstore for selling pacifist tracts. ACC President Don H. Morris defensively responded that the college fully supported the nation's "gigantic effort to subdue lawless men and nations."[51] Wallace bitterly disliked Goodpasture and was elated to find him in a vulnerable position during World War II. He appealed to patriotic prejudice in a reply to Goodpasture's "goose-stepping" article: "Brethren who support the government in its titanic struggle against goose-stepping aggression with their lives, their sons, their toil and their money will think Brother Goodpasture has insulted both them and their government in comparing them to a goose-stepping German corporal."[52] Historian Michael W. Casey judges that Wallace's "mendacity took its worst form" when he wrote an article implying that all conscientious objectors were premillennialists because they "generally hold that human governments belong to Satan."[53]

During World War II, the number of members of the churches of Christ who applied for conscientious objector status was relatively small. It is impossible to know exactly how many church members served in noncombatant duties in the armed services, but about two hundred young men entered conscientious objector camps where they were required to perform public service and to support themselves financially.[54] In 1943, James P. Miller reported the names of more than seventy young "Church of Christ men" who were detained in "the Civilian Service camps of the Quakers, Brethren and Mennonites, with no provision made by any church of Christ for their support." G. H. P. Showalter urged that "it is nothing but common fairness and honesty for those schools and churches of Christ that have taught these young men this faith to provide for their support."[55] The conscientious objectors suffered heroically, being forced to perform "slave labor" according to some sympathizers. Some preachers commended the young men for standing up "for Christ, facing the criticism of the world and the criticism of many in the church." Even under threat of prosecution, many preachers continued to support pacifism and condemned the " 'big' worldly, political, office-loving and office-holding members [who] have frowned upon . . . these young men."[56] Scores of churches responded to the appeals for financial support for the conscientious objectors.[57] In California, a committee of preachers headed by Jimmie Lovell formed a Service Committee for Conscientious Objectors to gather funds for the support of young men in Quaker camps, hoping to wipe away any "stigma . . . and hereafter care for those we call our own."[58]

On the other hand, pro-war militants had little sympathy for the fate of the young conscientious objectors. "Slave labor indeed," sneered W. W. Otey. "They raised not a finger to aid the defense but did all in their power to weaken the government, and so indirectly aided the enemy. . . . When weeping over the 'slave labor' rendered by the objectors, just ask what would be their condition, and all of us, had enough been found to take protection from the service."[59] Otey attacked the efforts to aid the conscientious objectors: "The whole matter is disgusting, humiliating, shameful and at variance with every principle of justice, righteousness, and the dignity of true manhood."[60] Otey insisted that "a very small percentage of our brethren hold the view that Christians dare not take up arms." Others insisted, however, that "thousands of Christians" were pacifists and that "thousands of boys were in uniform who had like beliefs—but because of immaturity, outside influences and other causes, went into uniform against their real convictions."[61]

In the common mind of the churches of Christ, pacifism was most important because it was linked with the broader sense of alienation that was intuitively accepted by many of the poor Christians of the early twentieth century.[62] One may argue, as Michael Casey has, that nothing did more to destroy the outsider identity in the churches of Christ than Wallace's assaults on pacifism during World War II. "In the march of the Churches of Christ to denominational respectability," Casey wrote, "the primitivist pacifists have been mistakenly written off as irrelevant."[63] They were, in fact, central actors in the early twentieth-century image of a peculiar people called to be separate from the world. A minor pacifist tradition survived World War II, and many local churches continued to harbor pacifist members, but World War II and the Wallace-led patriotic crusade greatly diminished the influence of this historic theological belief in the churches of Christ.

The Premillennial Purge

Ultimately more divisive among churches of Christ than pacifism was the theory of dispensational premillennialism, a concept that raised issues about the relationship of the Christian to the surrounding society. According to historian Earl West, between the two world wars "the brotherhood had a boundless preoccupation" with the subject.[64] While premillennial theories have flourished throughout the history of Christianity, a new dispensational version that owed much to the writings of Englishman John Nelson Darby came to have great influence among American evangelicals in the last quarter of the nineteenth century. By 1900, dispensationalism was widely supported by the conservative American Protestants subsequently called fundamentalists, and the idea was spread through a series of national prophetic conferences. The theory was further popularized through the Scofield Reference Bible, first published in 1909, which was an annotated version with copious notes explaining the doctrine.

Premillennial theories have come and gone in the history of Christianity, but dispensationalism drew great credibility beginning in the late nineteenth century because of the emergence of the Zionist movement and the subsequent establishment of the nation of Israel. Generally pessimistic about the future, dispensationalists believed that humanity was hurdling toward an imminent and catastrophic finale that would be followed by the establishment of a millennial kingdom in which Christ would reign for a thousand years on earth. Dividing history into seven dispensations (innocence, conscience, human government, promise, law, grace, and kingdom) dispensationalists believed that the "Church Age" was a "great parenthesis" imposed after Jesus failed to establish God's kingdom on earth because of Jewish resistance. The ending of the Church Age would be preceded by a period of great tribulation, the rise of the Antichrist and the false prophet, the battle of Armageddon, and the second coming of Christ to bind Satan and institute the millennium. In a quirky interpretation of I Thessalonians 4:17, Darby argued that Christians would be caught up in a pretribulation "rapture."[65]

While some early Disciples leaders had accepted William Miller's millennial speculations in the 1830s and others had embraced postmillennial ideas, no single millennial theory won universal acceptance in the restoration movement until the 1920s. The early leaders of the movement held divergent views on prophetic passages and most were too engrossed with restoring the patterns of New Testament Christianity to devote much attention to prophecy. The American restoration movement was primarily an Acts-Epistles movement, intent on common-sense readings of those sections of the New Testament, and its leaders were much less comfortable with the prophetic portions of the Bible.

Historian Richard T. Hughes has argued rather persuasively in recent years, however, that premillennial beliefs formed an important part of the thought of the earliest leaders of the Disciples of Christ movement.[66] Some early Disciples leaders, including Barton W. Stone and Walter Scott, embraced the premillennial calculations of William Miller in the 1840s. Hughes shows that Stone was deeply influenced by millennial ideas. Premillennial speculation waned among the Disciples of Christ, however, as it did in American Protestantism in general, after Jesus did not return in 1844 as Miller predicted.

While Barton W. Stone's premillennial mind set has been overlooked by students of restoration history, Alexander Campbell's interest in the biblical millennium is well documented. In 1830 Campbell chose the name *Millennial Harbinger* for his long-running periodical. However, Campbell, like most Protestants in the antebellum period, was a postmillennialist, believing that prophecy pointed toward a period of prosperity and peace on earth that would be introduced by human endeavor. Campbell believed that the restoration movement and the American nation were providential catalysts chosen to initiate the religious and political reform that would introduce a millennium of peace and righteousness. In his last years, as sectional animosities increased and the Civil War erupted, Campbell became less sanguine about the future of the nation and the world and his postmillennialism became muted.[67]

In the years between the Civil War and World War I, as measured by the bulk of articles produced on the subject, the leaders of the restoration movement showed little interest in premillennialism. When the prophetic movement began to gain momentum among the evangelical churches in the late nineteenth century, liberal Disciples of Christ were the first to take an interest in dispensationalism. That interest quickly collapsed in the early twentieth century, however, as dispensationalism increasingly became a fundamentalist fetish. By 1915, liberal Disciples had become harsh critics of dispensationalism, wholeheartedly backing the optimistic social reforms of the progressive era.

Richard Hughes argues, however, that millennialism remained an important theme in the churches of Christ in the years between the Civil War and World War I. Hughes finds direct links between the millennial thought of Barton W. Stone and the ideas of such patriarchs of the churches of Christ as Tolbert Fanning, James A. Harding, and, most of all, David Lipscomb. While Hughes acknowledges that neither Fanning nor Lipscomb was a traditional premillennialist (Harding clearly was), he insists that their opposition to military service and voting was rooted in an apocalyptic vision of an earthly kingdom of God that, at least in the minds of some, was linked to millennialism.[68]

During the first years of the twentieth century, periodicals in the churches of Christ rarely discussed dispensationalism, although occasional articles did appear espousing diverse views of the millennium. Partly, the religious separatism within the movement sheltered most preachers from the voluminous body of writing on the subject that appeared in fundamentalist publications. The theory was sufficiently well known by 1906, however, to trigger a public debate in which C. R. Nichol opposed premillennialism and A. S. Bradley defended the theory. The debate was published and circulated widely, beginning a significant erosion of support for the idea in the churches of Christ.[69]

Premillennial speculation was greatly stimulated by World War I, a catastrophe that many dispensationalists viewed as a sign of the beginning of the end times, and by 1914 serious debate had erupted in churches of Christ about the theory. The chief defender of dispensationalism was Robert H. Boll, a German immigrant who had been educated at Nashville Bible

School under the tutelage of James A. Harding. Boll was a pacifist during World War I and fully subscribed to Lipscomb's theories about civil government; in the first decade of the twentieth century he added to those ideas a full-blown theory of dispensational premillennialism based on the writings of the leading evangelical theorizers.

Boll was a respected preacher, and in 1910 he became the front-page editor of the *Gospel Advocate*. His premillennial leanings soon appeared in his columns, and in 1914 he began a series of articles elaborating his beliefs. A number of the older *Advocate* staff writers, including F. B. Srygley, J. C. McQuiddy, A. B. Lipscomb, and M. C. Kurfees, objected, both in private and in print, to the Boll articles. The parties negotiated an "agreement" that allowed Boll to retain his position on the *Advocate* staff, but they soon disagreed about the meaning of the settlement, and in 1915 Boll resigned.[70] The aging David Lipscomb made no direct comment on Boll's teaching, but he did reassert his long-held sentiment that prophetic speculation was of little value. Recalling the miscalculations of William Miller, and questioning the contemporary prophetic infatuation surrounding World War I, Lipscomb reaffirmed that he was "not sure of the time of His coming."[71] He concurred in the decision to drop the popular Boll from the magazine. Boll continued to promote premillennialism in *Word and Work*, a small magazine established early in the century, and moved to Louisville in 1915.

By the 1920s premillennialism had become a major topic of discussion. In 1927, R. H. Boll and H. Leo Boles, president of Nashville Bible School, conducted a written debate in the *Gospel Advocate* that lasted from May until November. The articles were written in a "brotherly tone"; at the end of the discussion, Boles urged churches not to divide over the belief. When Boll visited Nashville a few months after the discussion, Boles invited him to speak to the students at chapel services at Nashville Bible School.[72] Boles wrote of Boll: "I believe him to be sincere, pious, and a cultured, Christian gentleman. . . . We differ . . . but our differences and a discussion of them do not keep me from esteeming him very highly as a brother in Christ Jesus."[73] Most people accepted that moderate judgment in 1927.

In the 1930s, the controversy turned uglier. In 1932 F. B. Srygley and R. L Whiteside, two staff writers at the *Gospel Advocate,* began to severely criticize premillennialism in the paper and in July they were joined by editor Foy E. Wallace, Jr., in his first article on the subject. In January 1933, a public debate between Wallace and Charles M. Neal in Winchester, Kentucky, changed the character of the premillennial controversy and made Wallace "the clear leader among refuters of the Boll doctrines."[74] Wallace possessed none of H. Leo Boles's gentle disposition, and the discussion became so acrimonious that the First Christian Church, where the debate was being conducted, insisted that the final two nights not be held in the church auditorium. Wallace laid down new guidelines for maintaining unity in the churches of Christ: "Here is my hand, Brother Neal. . . . Here is my hand, Brother Boll. We will not tell you to quit *believing* them [premillennial ideas]. We only ask you to quit pushing them on us. . . . Hold these opinions if you want to. But *hold* them. Believe these theories if you want to, but keep them for your own comfort and consolation, since the rest of us get none out of them."[75] A second debate with Neal in Chattanooga six months later was equally acrid.

In 1935, William L. Oliphant and J. R. Rice conducted an equally factious debate in Dallas. As it became increasingly clear that premillennialists intended to continue to "push" their ideas, Wallace became obsessed with crushing the movement. Those who persisted in teaching the theory, Wallace warned, were "theorizing themselves out of the fellowship of the churches."[76] Wallace pursued Boll and his "sympathizers" with single-minded purpose for more than a decade. His voluminous corpus of writing refuting dispensationalism was collected in a volume published in 1946, *Modern Millennial*

Theories Exposed, and a book composed of a series of lectures he delivered in Houston in 1945, *God's Prophetic Word*.[77]

On the basis of the historical record, one might have predicted that the premillennial debate would divide some local churches but would have no broader impact. Conservative southern denominations, such as the Southern Baptist Church, tolerated vastly different millennial theories without serious disruption, as the restoration movement had done for a century. However, in the 1930s, schools and papers came under intense pressure to line up on the issue. In short, the controversy advanced to a level of intensity that required institutions to identify themselves clearly on the issue. Foy E. Wallace, Jr., was the chief actor in the premillennial controversy; in later years, after the flight away from any taint of premillennial sympathy became a virtual stampede, Wallace bridled when others claimed partial credit for slaying the prophetic dragon. For twenty years Wallace pushed the debate, brilliantly defining the issues and relentlessly pursuing moderates who hoped that peace could be restored in the churches. Wallace relished the role of heresy hunter, and he used every conceivable tactic to purge premillennialists and their sympathizers from positions of influence. "So intense was the brotherhood's negative response to the premillennial theory," wrote Earl West, "that by 1934 schools were making it clear that they had no sympathy for the Boll viewpoint."[78] By 1940 the battle was over. By that time, every college and every paper except for Boll's organ had renounced premillennialism and premillennialists; Boll had been effectively expelled from the movement along with a small number of supporting churches concentrated in the Louisville area. A by-product of the premillennial purge was the high visibility given to the hard-nosed, militant tactics of Foy E. Wallace, Jr., a legacy he bequeathed to a generation of admiring preachers. Wallace's son, William E. Wallace, summarized his father's impact: "The pre-millennial battle created attitudes, tactics, policies, procedures, precedents, and excesses which were to be employed in the forties, and in the fifties, with reference to the issues of the times."[79]

Wallace's victory in the premillennial controversy was neither as easy nor as complete as it appeared. Some leaders in the churches of Christ never believed that premillennial convictions should be a test of fellowship, and many influential older preachers refused to renounce R. H. Boll, whom they regarded as a pious man. J. N. Armstrong, president of Harding College, argued that premillennialism involved nothing more than personal conviction and that those who held the view should be treated generously, as were brethren who held minority views on other subjects. In fact, Armstrong insisted that dispensationalism should be less divisive than many other doctrinal differences that were overlooked by anti-premillennial zealots: "I am very frank in saying that there is a real difference between certain other questions and the millennium and that difference is that the government question, the eldership question, the war question, the 'College question,' and the re-baptism question involve the practice of the church and of the brethren. This makes these last named questions more serious, indeed. But the difference on the millennium questions has been raging for twenty years and more and has not in its life time changed the practice of the brethren or of a single church."[80] Armstrong's distinction between questions that "involve the practice of the church" and theological issues that involved only matters of individual faith correctly located a general fault line of division in the restoration movement and gave support to his belief that the churches of Christ should not and would not divide on the issue. He was convinced that the controversy had descended to the level of a personal vendetta and that Wallace and Boll were "equally responsible for the breach." He saved his harshest criticism for Wallace and his friends, labeling them "popes," "dictators," "partymakers," and "creedwriters." Their aim, Armstrong contended, was to establish a "creed-bound human sect,"[81] a theme that was echoed by R. H. Boll in *Word and Work*.[82]

In return, Wallace railed against the middle-of-the-roaders who could not differentiate "piety" from "putty." Wallace acknowledged that the "neutralist" stance was still a "popular position" in the mid-1930s. Many preachers acquiesced to his demands that they take a public stand against premillennialism only after years of dragging their feet. In 1939, John T. Lewis surmised that it was only the gallant efforts of Foy E. Wallace, Jr., and Nicholas Brodie Hardeman that had stemmed the tide of " 'Bollism;' sissyism, premillennialism, and other isms" in Nashville, while "some members of the faculty, and board of directors, of David Lipscomb College . . . thought that 'Bollism' or premillennialism was not an issue . . . were admirers, and avowed defenders of Brother R. H. Boll, and did not think there should be any agitation against the theories."[83] Many preachers, Wallace charged, had "assumed the 'watchful waiting' attitude to see how the fight would go." Such equivocation infuriated Wallace: "Surely the gospel preacher who waits to feel the pulse of public sentiment before he will take a stand is not a safe leader in the thought and action of the church. And the preacher who does not know where he stands on vital questions, should stand aside."[84]

While J. N. Armstrong clearly did have both personal and intellectual ties to a premillennial past, many other respected leaders in the churches of Christ were repelled by Wallace's tactics, including many who had no taint of premillennial sympathy. In 1934, in an episode that infuriated Wallace, G. C. Brewer appeared at the Abilene Christian College Lectures as a substitute for Wallace and lambasted the anti-premillennial campaign, without naming Wallace. Long convinced that a division could have been avoided had not "some preachers" used the "unfortunate affair for their own advantage," Brewer was typical of those preachers who were "more critical of men who opposed Boll and his friends than of Boll's promotion of the doctrine."[85] In 1939, when one of Wallace's friends urged the *Firm Foundation* and the *Gospel Advocate* to "rally to the defense of the cause of Christ against this digressive aggression,"

G. H. P. Showalter bruskly retorted that it was "ridiculous how a man can become the victim of 'one-ideaism.'" He warned, "A hobbyist works on one error to the neglect of others; a level headed Christian does not."[86] B. C. Goodpasture replied in the *Gospel Advocate* with similar annoyance, charging that some saw "evil, and only evil continually."[87] By 1940, Wallace had prevailed and premillennialism had been purged, but Wallace had few friends among the most influential leaders in the churches of Christ.[88]

No one resented Wallace's tactics more than the administrators of the colleges operated by members of the churches of Christ. With the exception of Freed-Hardeman College, where President N. B. Hardeman was a staunch Wallace ally, one college after the other was forced to defend itself against charges of harboring Boll sympathizers; there was usually a modicum of truth in the charges. In some cases, the premillennial debate toppled administrations. In 1946, young Athens Clay Pullias rose to the presidency of David Lipscomb College promising to purge the faculty of premillennialists. Pullias fired a few faculty members, but could not force out Boll's best friend on campus, the aged S. P. Pittman.[89]

The battle was most fiercely contested at Harding College, where administrators struggled to remedy its image of being a premillennial institution throughout the 1930s. In 1935, President J. N. Armstrong issued a clear rejection of dispensational premillennial belief, as he had in the past, but his statement fell far short of satisfying Wallace and his lieutenants.[90] Wallace's crusade against Harding College, led by Little Rock preacher E. R. Harper, lasted for years.[91] As early as 1938, according to Richard Hughes, "Harper had egged Wallace on to declare Boll and his premillennial following no longer bona fide members of Churches of Christ."[92] During a meeting with Harper and other critics in 1939, Harding College administrators agreed to add W. B. West, a strong anti-premillennialist, to the college's Bible Department, and Harper agreed "to call off his fight against the college."[93] However, Wallace and

Harper soon returned to the attack, and well into the 1940s Harding College was regarded as unsound by many members of churches of Christ.

Why did the issue of dispensational premillennialism reach the level of brotherhood division? Partly, the reason was theological. Dispensational premillennialism was more than just a prophetic theory, it was a broad scheme of biblical interpretation that had implications in many areas. Over a period of years, many preachers came to view dispensationalism as a serious threat to the basic assumptions of the restoration movement. Most troublesome was the dispensationalists' contention that the "Church Age" was a "parenthesis" in divine history and that Christ was not seated on David's throne as the head of the church. For restorers, the church was the culmination of God's prophetic plan, the glorious institution that they were striving to restore. Therefore, by the 1930s, most leaders in the churches of Christ judged that premillennialism was not only a mistaken interpretation of prophecy but also embodied a nexus of ideas that were clearly and dangerously wrong.

In addition, the powerful personality of Foy E. Wallace, Jr., influenced the outcome of the premillennial controversy. Wallace's prominence in the churches in the 1930s was unprecedented; he was the idol of a generation of preachers, including Homer Hailey. Even those repulsed by his tactics were well aware of his personal charisma and his fighting skills. By the end of the 1930s, some people idolized Wallace as the savior of the churches of Christ and others blamed him for dividing the brotherhood, but no one disputed that he had been the chief architect of the premillennial schism. At best, Wallace stood in the breech against a heretical theory that would have seriously changed the direction of the movement; at worst, he illustrated, in the words of Richard Hughes, "the lust for power and control that often drives contestants in struggles such as this."[94]

In his book *Reviving the Ancient Faith,* Hughes portrayed the

Foy E. Wallace, Jr. (1896–1979). Well into the 1940s Wallace was the most honored and feared preacher in the churches of Christ. He deserved a major share of the credit for expelling premillennialists from the movement, and he encouraged the early opposition to institutionalism, though he later repudiated noninstitutional leaders. Scarred by numerous battles with foes and friends, Wallace saw his influence dwindle after 1950. (Courtesy of the Center for Restoration Studies, Abilene Christian University.)

premillennial division as a defining moment in the twentieth-century history of the churches of Christ. While Hughes has made it clear in his more recent writings that his definition of *apocalyptic* described a broad sense of cultural separation rather than the acceptance of premillennial theories, he argued in *Reviving the Ancient Faith* that the defection of the premillennialists robbed the churches of Christ of much of their apocalyptic vision. The expulsion of the premillennialists was critical: "It represented a rite of passage from the culturally pessimistic, separatist mentality that had characterized the Stone-Lipscomb tradition in the nineteenth century to the culture-affirming, patriotic mentality that would increasingly characterize the mainstream Churches of Christ in the twentieth century."[95] In the bitter war over premillennialism, Hughes argues, the majority wing of the churches of Christ shed its "apocalyptic, counter-cultural perspectives" and "deliberately sought acculturation into the mainstream of American life."[96]

According to Hughes, Foy E. Wallace, Jr., the militant pro-war, anti-premillennial crusader, became the standard bearer for a new mind set in the churches of Christ. He replaced the "cultural separatism" of the churches of Christ with a "denominational exclusivism."[97] Wallace, Hughes says, thrust the churches of Christ into a friendly engagement with American society through his patriotic support of war and at the same time used a legalistic, sectarian formula to drive out premillennialism and redefine the churches of Christ. Thus, Hughes concludes, Wallace evicted the radical separatists from the churches of Christ and set the majority that remained on the road to becoming a denominational, worldly church.

Hughes's interpretation is filled with important insights. He throws revealing light on the dual basic assumptions in the churches of Christ restoration vision, a common-sense hermeneutic that demanded adherence to scriptural patterns and a visionary self-image as a kingdom called out of the world. Hughes argues persuasively that David Lipscomb's thought was the quintessential combination of these two ideals. In identifying these ideas, and tracing them to Lipscomb and back to Barton W. Stone, Hughes has clearly tapped into the mother lode of restoration thinking. Prior to World War II, most members of churches of Christ would have imagined that they were being faithful to both of these foundational concepts.

It is less clear, however, that the premillennial controversy was a watershed that siphoned off the tradition of cultural separatism in the churches of Christ. While some premillennial leaders, including Harding and Armstrong, had a strong sense of cultural alienation, in general, premillennialists in the 1920s and 1930s were the group most in touch with the nation and the world. Dispensationalists viewed the future as dark and ominous, but they were intensely interested in the unfolding of world events. Premillennialists within the churches of Christ were clearly more engaged with the outside religious world; they parroted the views of American fundamentalists and, on occasion, participated in prophetic conferences. Hughes acknowledged that "Boll provided a concrete demonstration of his own rejection of the sectarian exclusivism of Churches of Christ when he routinely ran articles from . . . early fundamentalists . . . in the pages of his journal. Many viewed Boll's fraternization with fundamentalists as nothing short of scandalous."[98] Some dispensationalists came to identify more easily with Baptists and Pentecostals who shared their millennial hope than with their attackers in churches of Christ; several premillennial missionaries in Asia who were supported by churches of Christ defected to the Seventh Day Adventist church and Pentecostal groups. This outward-looking spirit did not escape the attention of their antagonists. In 1935, Roy E. Cogdill, repeating an oft-heard criticism, charged that premillennialists "fellowshipped Baptists in preference to brethren in Christ" because of their common "false theories."[99] Of course, Cogdill's remarks could be attributed to what Hughes called the spirit of "denominational exclusivism," which owed little to the sense of cultural separation. Objections to "mingling with the sects" far predated the premillennial debate, however, and they were usually part of the broader sense of cultural alienation that permeated the early restoration movement.

In fact, the premillennial division had a character of its own. Many avid foes of premillennialism, such as Homer Hailey, embraced pacifism and other counter-cultural beliefs. The churches of Christ after the premillennial debate of the 1930s remained a complex amalgam of religious ideas. At least for a time, the premillennial fight tended to creedalize dogma, but cultural separatism remained alive and well in all wings of the churches of Christ, as did Lipscomb's theories concerning war and civil government.

Peculiar People

The debate over pacifism and the division over premillennialism overlapped, but did not define, an important nexus of underlying, often covert, assumptions in the churches of Christ that are best described as a sense of alienation and distinctiveness, a sense of being a peculiar people. The clearest product of this mind set was a pervasive disinterest in worldly affairs. Richard Hughes sought to capture this broader sense of alienation with the word *apocalyptic*. Hughes's word and his descriptions of the churches of Christ sometimes seem to make the yearning for separation from the world so dependent on millennial ideas that the ubiquitous presence of a more general and less theologically grounded sense of alienation is obscured. Nonetheless, Hughes argued that the basic "apocalyptic" vision that he described as the "Stone-Lipscomb worldview" included "the themes of apocalypticism, separation from the world, and reliance on the power of God rather than on human wit and ingenuity."[100] This broad and loose set of assumptions is, indeed, at the center of the restoration psyche, and whiffs of the ideas could be detected in every niche of the movement.

The general sense of cultural separatism so evident in the churches of Christ was partly intellectual and theological; for some, the feeling was intellectually anchored by Lipscomb's opposition to civil government. On the other hand, the general sense of alienation was related to a sectarian disdain for denominations that was widespread in the early twentieth century, a separatism that kept the churches of Christ out of the organized fundamentalist movement and triggered hundreds of debates with their denominational neighbors. Historian Robert E. Hooper correctly points out that the churches of

Christ were a classic American example of "religious outsiders," regarding themselves as "a distinct people."[101]

The sense of alienation and distinctiveness felt by members of the churches of Christ in the first half of the twentieth century was social and cultural as well as theological; in a 1964 article in the *Journal of Southern History*, David E. Harrell dubbed the group "the spirited offspring of the religious rednecks of the post bellum South."[102] Richard Hughes captured the social isolation of the first half of the twentieth century: "For most of their history, Churches of Christ had been poor and socially marginal, standing over against other Christian denominations as well as the larger culture and typically viewing themselves as sojourners in a strange and foreign land."[103] It is safe to say, with Hughes, that such a forlorn social heritage fostered a mind set that was "fundamentally *pessimistic* about human possibilities."[104] This generally pessimistic and despairing view of the world, which members of churches of Christ shared with many of their poor Pentecostal and Fundamentalist neighbors, seeped throughout the movement with scant regard for variations in theological belief. The social and intellectual discontent of the first half of the century had a life of its own and all debates about theology or practice were seasoned by cultural prejudices.

Hughes's "sojourner" image perhaps best captures the sense of spiritual separation that permeated the churches of Christ into the 1940s, reinforced by Depression poverty and the continued dominance of a rural mind set. Such a mentality gave credence to David Lipscomb's views on civil government and pacifism, and was easily appropriated by premillennialists, but it existed quite apart from these debates. Otherworldliness in the churches of Christ, a sojourner mentality, was manifest less by positions taken than by positions not taken. The dominant mood in the early years of the century probably had less to do with Lipscomb's theology of world separation than a widespread disinterest in world affairs. Momentous world events and great stirrings in other religious bodies often went unnoticed by devoted cultural separationists—those intent on saving souls, restoring the church, and escaping the corruptions of the world. Most members of the churches of Christ felt separated from the world to some degree, but their sense of estrangement was general rather than specific; it rested on self-evident assumptions rather than theological arguments. To most church members, the affairs of the world lay remote from and irrelevant to their lives as New Testament Christians.

The Origins of the Institutional Debate

Premillennialism was the most divisive issue debated during the 1920s and 1930s, and, in many ways, pacifism most seriously tested the commitment of members of churches of Christ to cultural and spiritual separation, but, in the long run, other questions were more schismatic. Most important was an assortment of issues combined under the label "institutionalism." After decades of discussions, a number of well-defined positions had been articulated about the proper relationship between local churches and educational and benevolent institutions.

In the early nineteenth century, most Disciples, including Alexander Campbell and Barton W. Stone, clearly taught that local churches were autonomous and less consistently taught that missionary societies could not be supported by churches. Much of the early criticism directed at missionary societies argued against abuses rather than raising scriptural objections. Loose associations of churches, some of them inherited along with Baptist congregations that defected to the restoration movement, continued to exist all through the nineteenth century in the Disciples of Christ. The founding of the American Christian Missionary Society in 1849 raised the issue of church organizations to a new level of visibility and debate, and, after a half century of discussion, opposition to the society was one of the issues that defined the Christian Church–churches of Christ division. The missionary society debate forestalled the rise of official organizations in the churches of Christ, but the discussion did little to clarify the relations between churches and independent institutions such as schools, orphan homes, and papers.[105]

In the early years of the restoration movement, some churches financially supported educational and benevolent organizations, including Alexander Campbell's Bethany College and David Lipscomb's Nashville Bible School.[106] In 1936, Foy E. Wallace, Jr., observed that an institutional framework had evolved in the churches of Christ more or less without notice. As the institutions grew in size and number, Wallace became more alarmed: "The institutional idea is no longer a trend—we are institutional already. No week passes that churches are not circularized by 'our institutions.' True, 'we' did not start them but they were left on our doorstep for adoption, tagged, 'your institution, support it.' As a doorstep child, the only alternative is adoption or death. Too kindhearted to let any of them die, the 'brotherhood' adopts them all." Wallace offered no solution in 1936, but he believed that some "sober thinking is needed here," and he advised that "stress needs to be put on the independency of the local church."[107] At the time, according to the Bureau of the Census, members of churches of Christ were supporting seven "Bible, or Christian colleges, with 184 teachers, 2,206 students and with property valued at $2,610,974." In addition, churches and individuals supported several academies, seven orphanages, and two homes for the aged.[108]

Before Wallace's article, church papers included only sporadic articles questioning the relationship between churches and institutions, partly because of the high visibility of the premillennial debate. However, some influential preachers including F. B. Srygley and C. R. Nichol consistently opposed church support of institutions.[109] As early as 1922, in a speech in Cordell, Oklahoma, Wallace stated the noninstitutional view quite clearly: "We have pointed out the central thought of the subject, namely, the school is an auxiliary to the home.

This being true it is not the business of the church to run it. The church is not in the school business. The only way the church can scripturally do its work is through the elders of the local congregation. Appeals made to the churches, therefore, in behalf of the schools are wrong . . . and ought to be stopped."[110] In 1936, C. A. Norred sketched the borders of a noninstitutional position that would be fleshed out a decade later. He protested that the church "is not a glorified relief agency" and insisted that local churches had no responsibility for founding or funding "eleemosynary institutions." Rather, congregations should use their resources to promote "spiritual values."[111]

In the early 1930s, the institutional debate was foreshadowed, and to some extent muddied, by a furor over the Morrow Bible and Testament Foundation, a corporation formed in 1932 in Nashville by businessman S. F. Morrow to distribute Bibles. The foundation was immediately attacked in the *Firm Foundation* by editor G. H. P. Showalter and by James A. Allen, a former editor of the *Gospel Advocate*. Foy E. Wallace, Jr., who at the time was serving as editor of the *Advocate* and was a member of the Morrow Foundation board, found himself in the unusual position of being attacked as a liberal who was participating in an arrangement that paralleled the missionary society. The *Firm Foundation*, always ready to censure the *Gospel Advocate*, charged that the foundation was the "pet child of the Gospel Advocate" and that Wallace's participation raised questions about his "soundness." Wallace replied with characteristic gusto, charging that the *Firm Foundation*'s "outburst" was the "latest sample of [Showalter's] editorial hysteria."[112] Wallace was distracted by the matter throughout much of 1933, giving a few months of respite to premillennialists, but the issue slowly vanished. While the confrontation raised many of the issues that were subsequently a part of the noninstitutional debate, the Morrow Foundation was simply not significant enough to fuel wide interest.

Inevitably, because of their importance, the colleges operated by members of churches of Christ became the center of the institutional debate. By the 1930s, several well-defined views existed about the scriptural relationship of churches and colleges. A fairly small minority, mostly in the North, questioned the existence of religious colleges. Generally called Sommerites, because their view was associated with Daniel Sommer and his magazines, the *Octographic Review* and the *American Christian Review,* they argued that colleges operated by members of the churches of Christ were de facto church institutions. Sommer opposed "the church going into the school business," insisting that such institutions robbed the church of its proper glory.[113] Sommer was sometimes misrepresented and he mellowed through the years; in 1933 he visited Nashville, spoke at David Lipscomb College, and left persuaded that the school was not a church institution. Veteran *Gospel Advocate* staff writer F. B. Srygley believed that he and Sommer had reached a meeting of the minds; Sommer recognized that schools had a right to exist and Srygley agreed that churches should not contribute to their support.[114]

Sommerite objections aside, in the 1930s all of the colleges associated with the churches of Christ survived in an atmosphere that ranged from suspicious to openly hostile. College administrators found the going rough in a movement filled with preachers who distrusted education in general and who bridled at suggestions that preachers needed special training. Any hint that a college was harboring an evolutionist or modernist (unlikely as that prospect was in the 1930s) unleashed a deluge of criticism. In such an environment, distrust was endemic, and by the 1940s many older preachers feared that "scholarship, not faith is made to govern in the selection of Bible School teachers."[115]

In his inaugural editorial in the *Gospel Guardian* in October 1935, Foy E. Wallace, Jr., decried the tendency of Christian schools to "vie with the standards of worldly schools."[116] Three years later, having met resistance in most of the colleges to his premillennial purge, Wallace was even more critical: "They have harbored teachers of error; they have promoted a spirit of worldliness; they have manifested an air of superiority; they have conducted campaigns among the churches to affiliate church and school which will eventually, if continued, result in college domination and control in the church."[117]

Influential editors and preachers constantly scrutinized the colleges for signs of laxity. In 1946, after students at George Pepperdine College danced a Virginia reel while performing a play about the life of Abraham Lincoln, President Hugh M. Tiner answered a shower of attacks with the assurance that he had "preached for twenty years against the evils of the modern dance."[118] In the minds of some, the craze for football symbolized the rising secularism on campus. In 1936, G. H. P. Showalter reported that he had heard from "good authority" that an unnamed college (most likely Abilene Christian College) had "lost $6,000.00 on its athletics." He urged banning athletics on the campuses, and his suggestion was widely supported by letters from readers.[119] In 1937, Abilene Christian College drew fire from the *Firm Foundation* when a preacher, after visiting the campus, reported that a "pep rally and bonfire were allowed to conflict seriously with a mid-week prayer service." Isaac E. Tackett was taken aback by the behavior of the students: "I have seen political rallies, with their wild frenzies; I have observed banquets and mobs; but the wildest gathering I have ever attended was the pep rally. . . . [There were] young men going to a Christian College, to educate themselves to become quiet-minded, even-tempered gospel preachers; young ladies from quiet Christian homes, periodically turning themselves into a group of wild, yelling hyenas, exceeding that of a band of Comanche Indians; and a group of quiet, sensible teachers and gospel preachers looking on with pleasure and complacency, and aiding the exercise!"[120]

During the 1930s and 1940s, discussions of the "college question," like the earlier debate about missionary societies, engendered unstable alliances between those who objected to abuses and others who opposed church support for colleges as a matter of principle. Foy E. Wallace, Jr.'s attacks on the colleges were aimed fairly consistently at abuses. Writing in 1938 in the *Bible Banner,* he insisted that he was not opposed to colleges, rather, "we are simply opposed to the extremes to which the colleges in question have gone, to their worldliness, to their tendency toward ecclesiastical control, to their doctrinal weakness, and to their general departures."[121] Wallace's dislike for colleges clearly was both doctrinal and personal—college administrators challenged his tactics in the premillennial campaign, they exercised a power over churches that offended him, and they were a general source of doctrinal and moral softness.[122]

While charges of abuse kept college administrators on their toes, the doctrinal questions about how the colleges should relate to local churches of Christ was in the long run more critical. Everyone agreed that the colleges operated by members of the churches of Christ should not be considered denominational schools (although Sommerites charged that they were de facto denominational institutions), but there was little consensus about precisely how schools should be operated and controlled.[123] In 1930, Abilene Christian College tried a novel scheme, announcing that the elders of the College Church would begin "directly supervising all of the [Bible] teaching done and every religious service otherwise" conducted on the campus. Many Texas preachers in the 1930s flirted with the idea that religious institutions should exist only under the supervision of the elders of a local church; however, that idea never gained broad support. R. L. Whiteside warned that the Abilene experiment "is just as sure to kill A. C. C. as there is a God in heaven." He asked, "If the college as such is not to do any more Bible teaching, on what grounds can they appeal to the brethren for financial assistance?"[124]

Slowly, the institutional debate drove toward the central issue: how were colleges to be funded? Most schools operated by members of the churches of Christ received irregular contributions from local churches. When asked in 1931 if it was scriptural for a church to contribute to a college, the respected C. R. Nichol replied in the *Firm Foundation*, "No, it is not right to take the money contributed by the church of Christ . . . and use it for schools."[125] During the decade this issue was discussed discursively and indecisively. Generally, college administrators tried to straddle the fence, offering assurances that they did not solicit funds from churches, but acknowledging that "when the elders and members of a local congregation desire to contribute to the college, the college does not attempt to dictate to the elders how these finances should be handled."[126] In fact, Abilene Christian College sought contributions from churches at least as early as the 1930s.

Grover Cleveland Brewer, an influential preacher living in Lubbock, Texas, became the most visible promoter of church contributions to colleges in the early 1930s. In 1931, in a speech at the Abilene lectureship program, Brewer urged his "preacher brothers" from all over Texas to encourage their congregations to support Abilene Christian College.[127] Brewer triggered a broader discussion of the question when he issued an impassioned appeal for church contributions while speaking on the lectureship program in 1933. In 1933, Foy E. Wallace, Jr., while editing the *Gospel Advocate*, urged Brewer to write a series of articles defending church support for colleges. Brewer believed that the invitation signaled an endorsement from Wallace; in later years he cited an editorial letter to him stating that "your articles have our approval."[128] Wallace vehemently denied that he had ever approved of Brewer's position. He insisted that he simply wanted to air both sides and pointed out that the *Gospel Advocate* had published articles opposing church support of colleges written by John T. Hinds, C. R. Nichol, and F. B. Srygley.[129] Wallace repeatedly stated during the 1930s that he considered the question of church support to colleges "debatable," refusing to come down firmly on one side or the other.

Wallace's unclear stance on church-supported institutions

in the early 1930s was probably affected by the Morrow Foundation dispute and the attack on him by the *Firm Foundation* and former *Advocate* editor James A. Allen. The iconoclastic Wallace momentarily became a defender of the status quo, an opponent of "hobbyism" and bitter "diatribes" that called into question the soundness of one's own brethren.[130] By 1936, Wallace was the deposed editor of the *Gospel Advocate,* and he had resumed his crusade against premillennialism and other signs of digression. G. C. Brewer stepped directly into Wallace's line of fire when he made a renewed appeal for church contributions to Abilene Christian College at the 1936 lectureship. Speaking as a replacement for Wallace on the lectureship program, Brewer infuriated Wallace by denouncing the harsh treatment that had been heaped on premillennialists and calling for moderation.[131] In an article in the *Firm Foundation* replying to Brewer, Wallace reasserted his opposition to church contributions to colleges, a position he had voiced off and on since the 1920s: "For many years the majority of our strongest preachers in these parts have opposed affiliating the church with the school and putting the college in 'the budget' of the church."[132] He was probably correct. That was where the matter rested in 1940; the institutional debate was largely squelched by the outbreak of World War II. After the war, the institutional controversy reappeared, but by that time, the balance of power had shifted.

The Postwar Crisis: Missions and Sponsoring Churches, 1945–1950

World War II changed the Churches of Christ. In the first place, the great patriotic campaign badly damaged the pockets of pacifism that had survived World War I, thus drying up one of the tributaries that fed broader separatist feelings. More important, the war changed the economic standing and self-image of many of the small congregations that had appeared in lower-middle-class neighborhoods and in the rural

South. War-time prosperity boosted both the financial capabilitics and the social aspirations of many members of the churches of Christ; by 1945, they were better able to support large projects and were more ambitious to gain the respect of their friends and neighbors.

It was the potential to evangelize the world that most fired the imagination of church leaders in the 1940s and 1950s. After World War II, the prostrate nations of the world lay open to American influence and to American churches; in the early forties, enterprising preachers dreamed grand dreams and drafted ambitious plans. According to Robert E. Hooper, the churches of Christ supported about a dozen foreign missionaries at the time of the separation from the Christian church and still supported fewer than fifty in 1946. However, by the end of the 1950s that number had risen to more than seven hundred.[133] Two decades later, the churches of Christ were supporting about a thousand missionaries in sixty-five countries.[134] Historian Earl West captured the euphoria of the late 1940s: "With the return of peace, foreign mission work leaped forward in giant strides. The church stood optimistic and relatively harmonious when the clouds lifted, and the world seemed to be beckoning for American evangelists."[135] However, the postwar missionary fervor would add a new dimension to the institutional controversy in the guise of sponsoring churches.

The two men most responsible for fueling the missionary vision of the postwar churches of Christ were G. C. Brewer and Otis Gatewood.[136] In February 1943, Brewer wrote a landmark article entitled "Evangelizing the World in the Post War Period."[137] The article announced that the Broadway Church of Christ in Lubbock, Texas, where Brewer was preaching, would "sponsor" the evangelization of Europe in the wake of the war. Brewer urged churches of Christ around the country to start setting aside funds to be used for postwar evangelism, investing in "government bonds and thus helping the government and at the same time saving money for the work of the

Lord."[138] Brewer's initial plan was somewhat vague, and in a later article he explained that "it was never the purpose of the Lubbock church to act as agent for anybody and we did not want money sent to us." Rather, he explained, he intended to urge each congregation to begin saving to sponsor its own missionaries when the war was over. Brewer noted that his article had elicited "tremendous response." While all replies were "not complimentary," on the whole, the "enthusiasm for the plan" was great.[139]

Month after month, support built for Brewer's missionary vision. George S. Benson, a former missionary in China, believed that the "churches of Christ in America" had more to contribute to worldwide "Christian unity" than any other religious communion "because we have done more thinking along this line."[140] While some preachers cautioned that the proposed schemes would pool power in the hands of large congregations and violate biblical patterns, others scorned such concerns: "We have grown so accustomed to fighting any organization larger than the local congregation until the thought of congregational cooperation is as dead as faith without works."[141] By the end of 1945, scores of churches and individuals had become clearing houses for contributions to various missions and benevolent enterprises abroad.[142]

The center of the postwar missions thrust was the Broadway Church of Christ in Lubbock. Long a "mission minded" congregation, during the war the church supported Otis Gatewood in a concentrated effort to establish churches in Mormon Utah.[143] A group of mission enthusiasts discussed plans at a Yosemite camp retreat in 1942 that resulted in Otis Gatewood's being selected by Brewer and the Broadway Church to lead the postwar evangelization of Europe. In 1943, Gatewood began studying German to prepare to enter Germany as soon as possible when the war ended.[144] Brewer was succeeded as minister at Broadway in 1944 by one of the most skillful younger advocates of change in the churches of Christ, M. Norvel Young, and the church continued its leadership in the area of postwar missions. In July 1945 the elders of the Broadway Church announced that they were preparing to send Gatewood on "a survey trip to Europe as soon as passports and accommodations can be obtained." The elders revealed that "several thousand pounds of clothing" had been sent to them by other congregations and individuals, and they requested a moratorium on further shipments "until the prospect for immediate shipment are brighter."[145]

In June 1946, Gatewood and Paul Sherrod, one of the deacons of the Broadway Church, began a grand tour of Europe to develop a missions strategy; the church announced that "forty missionaries are now ready to go into Germany."[146] In June 1947, Gatewood and Roy Palmer were finally admitted into Germany, and they began "the huge task of evangelizing that area and preparing the way for further efforts to be made when other missionaries are allowed to enter."[147] Once in Germany, Gatewood began preaching and gathering food and other relief "for the starving and undernourished."[148] By 1950, twenty-eight American missionaries and their families had joined Gatewood in Germany, and they reported that more than a thousand converts were meeting in "nine congregations of the Lord's people." In addition, a "Bible training school . . . set up to train young Germans for service in the kingdom" had enrolled twenty-three students.[149]

In 1946, the Broadway Church hosted a lectureship on missions; the meeting turned into a bandwagon campaign promoting sponsoring churches and congregational cooperation. Several speakers complained about past anti-institutional prejudices and called for more "centralization of church work," noting that "our brethren have been so afraid in some cases of two or more churches working together. Brethren, that is one thing that has hindered our mission program."[150]

By the end of 1946 the rush toward concentrating funds in the hands of large congregations to sponsor missions had become a stampede. In August 1947, the elders of the Union Avenue Church in Memphis announced that they would sponsor mission work in Japan. The elders dispatched the congregation's minister, E. W. McMillan, on a tour to explore the potential for such work.[151] The elders reported that, should they decide to undertake the work, Homer Hailey had "expressed his willingness to go in the same capacity with Brother McMillan."[152] The Highland Church in Abilene quickly agreed to sponsor Hailey on a trip to Japan, because he had "formed numerous contacts with Japan during his work in Honolulu," and the church announced that he had agreed to undertake a survey trip to Japan.[153] Hailey did not go, and in later years he had no recollection of being asked to accompany McMillan. He believed that a casual expression of support on his part had been viewed by those sponsoring the work as a means of linking his reputation with the project.[154] In a promotional technique that became widespread in the 1950s, the Union Avenue Church in Memphis advertised in some of the leading papers asking "churches in rural sections, as well as larger congregations in towns and cities . . . to make monthly contributions" to Union Avenue to help build a school in Japan. The Memphis-sponsored work in Japan, they believed, was "the greatest opportunity the churches of Christ have ever had to teach a nation the word of God."[155]

Soon the air was filled with announcements by other local churches that they would sponsor large missions projects. In March 1948, the church in Brownfield, Texas, agreed to sponsor missionary Cline Paden in Italy to preach, distribute food and other relief, and oversee the construction and operation of an orphanage.[156] By the end of the 1940s, sponsoring churches were directing programs in Japan, China, Korea, Italy, the Philippines, Germany, Holland, and France.

The theme of the Abilene Christian College lectureship in 1947 was "World-Wide Missions," and the program attracted huge crowds.[157] In 1949, the lectures included reports from missionaries in China, the Philippines, Australia, New Zealand, Canada, England, Germany, and Holland. Few people escaped the missions contagion. After the 1949 lectures,

G. H. P. Showalter, the venerable editor of the *Firm Foundation,* reminded readers that it was important to uphold "the sound doctrine of Christ," but, he added, "at the same time, we have hundreds and up into the thousands of gospel preachers, well grounded in the faith and in the sound doctrine of the Lord Jesus Christ, who are qualified to go to many places and teach the glorious truth of the gospel. These should be sent, upheld and supported in the proclamation of the gospel."[158]

In practice, there was nothing new about the idea of a local church assuming the responsibility for a specific mission undertaking, or for some other kind of work, and requesting funds from other churches to help support the project. Early in restoration history, Alexander Campbell approved of such cooperation, complaining that a few Disciples showed "too much squeamishness about the *manner* of cooperation." He insisted that there was no "model" in the New Testament concerning how churches could work together, and he condemned those who would "do nothing right lest they should do something wrong."[159] In the early twentieth century, many cooperative schemes were supported by the churches of Christ. In Texas, and elsewhere, groups of churches frequently cooperated to sponsor an evangelist, rotating the responsibility for overseeing his work among the contributing congregations. The Preachers Meetings and congregational lectureships so common in the first half of the twentieth century generally featured the pooling of congregational funds under the direction of one eldership or a representative board.[160] During the 1930s many congregations participated in sponsoring-church arrangements to support radio programs.

A few people cautioned against sponsoring-church arrangements. David Lipscomb opposed some sponsoring-church projects, but at other times he participated in them.[161] During the mid-1930s, when most militants were engaged in fighting premillennialists, O. C. Lambert, writing in Foy E. Wallace, Jr.'s *Gospel Guardian,* raised the question of whether a "congregation has the right to assume more than it can do." Lambert warned, "If the Lord had intended that his work be done on a bigger scale than can be handled by the local church he would have designed a bigger organization."[162] After 1950 the debate over sponsoring churches escalated because of the unprecedented size of the new projects and the tone and scope of the solicitations for contributions by sponsoring churches. Recognizing that congregations had long used sponsoring-church arrangements, Wallace observed in 1950 that the "Broadway Plan" had "slipped up on us all" and had "developed into something that was not expected."[163] By that time, it was too late to stem the tide.

The Postwar Crisis: Colleges and Orphan Homes, 1945–1950

Like sponsoring-church arrangements, colleges and orphan homes also grew in size and number in the years immediately after World War II.[164] In the two decades after the war, the number of colleges operated by members of the churches of Christ tripled to twenty-one and the number of orphanages increased from seven to forty.[165] In the postwar mission euphoria, many local churches of Christ, basking in the growing respectability of colleges such as Abilene Christian College, left behind any remaining doctrinal squeamishness about institutionalism and began sending financial support to colleges. The "college question," wrote William E. Wallace, "had been dormant, waiting in the wings while the premillennial and war issues were debated," but a "full blown controversy" became inevitable in 1946 when N. B. Hardeman wrote a series of articles in the *Gospel Advocate* urging church support for schools.[166]

College administrators identified easily with a rising tide of denominational pride in the churches of Christ, readily assuming the task of furnishing the churches with "more and better qualified men to preach." The colleges also positioned themselves at the heart of the missions outburst. Postwar opportunities, one administrator wrote, called "for a multiplied number of trained Christians to carry out this missionary program."[167] In 1943, Abilene Christian College announced "plans to train missionaries in a world-wide program."[168] In the fall of 1944, Otis Gatewood joined the faculty of Pepperdine College, a new school established in Los Angeles in 1937, to "teach missionary training."[169]

Glutted with veterans and inundated with calls to supply missionaries in the aftermath of the war, the colleges increasingly eyed churches as sources of financial support, and the boldness of college fund-raising reached unprecedented levels in the postwar years. When Abilene Christian College launched a campaign headed by fund-raiser Robert M. Alexander to raise a $3 million endowment in 1947, specifically appealing to churches for support, the debate widened.[170] No longer satisfied with a half-hearted settlement in which colleges had no "connection with the church as an organization," many college administrators prepared to campaign for local churches to "support these schools."[171]

Several older preachers immediately protested. W. W. Otey, long the most consistent opponent of church support for colleges, urged college administrators, "for the sake of peace and unity," to "keep the support of their schools out of the Lord's treasury."[172] Otey had sounded a noninstitutional alarm for sixty years; as the colleges expanded, others joined in to warn that "it is time to throw on brakes."[173] Cranky old J. D. Tant informed the postwar noninstitutional vanguard that they were too late: the "Bible colleges got control of the churches" thirty years earlier, and they had turned out a generation of "preachers to entertain the sects."[174]

By the late 1940s, the "institutional" controversy had become clearly defined.[175] Once the premillennial issue had begun to subside in the late 1930s, Foy E. Wallace, Jr.'s *Bible Banner* had turned its attention to institutional issues. Wallace collected around himself a talented group of younger men eager to lead a campaign. Among the most aggressive was a young Houston lawyer-preacher, Roy E. Cogdill, who in 1946 formed a printing business for the express purpose of helping "Brother Foy E. Wallace keep the Bible Banner alive so there would be at least one medium through which issues that disturb the church could be fairly discussed."[176] In March, Cogdill became the publisher of the *Bible Banner;* Foy and Cled Wallace remained as co-editors and the paper's main theme was anti-institutionalism. It featured the writing of such old-timers as C. R. Nichol, W. Curtis Porter, R. L. Whiteside, and Early Arceneaux and a stable of younger men that included Cogdill and James W. Adams.

The postwar institutional controversy in the churches of Christ was notable for several reasons. First, it surpassed the premillennial discussion both in scope and in the amount of attention given to the debate in all of the movement's papers. G. C. Brewer sprang to the defense of contributions to colleges by churches, and he was joined in February 1947 by N. B. Hardeman. W. W. Otey continued to voice opposition in the *Firm Foundation,*[177] and, more portentous, Foy E. Wallace, Jr., thrust the *Bible Banner* into the discussion, printing articles attacking Brewer and Hardeman written by himself, his brother Cled, Roy Cogdill, and James Adams. The elated Otey wrote to Wallace: "It gave me a thrill of encouragement, that you have called N. B. Hardeman's hand on putting colleges in the church budget. I have spearheaded this opposition for you. . . . I began the fight sixty years ago."[178] Soon most of the papers read by members of churches of Christ bristled with articles on the subject.

Some hoped to find a middle ground in the college dispute. In 1947, Showalter announced that he would open the columns of the *Firm Foundation* to discussion "because I want those who are running the colleges to know what the brethren are thinking of them." Assuring everyone that he was not an "alarmist or a pessimist," Showalter stated his belief that the issue could be resolved and that neither "the colleges will be ruined" nor "the church will be divided."[179] Glenn L. Wallace defended Abilene Christian College, urging individuals to support the school and indirectly attacking Foy Wallace, but, at the same time, he insisted that only a "few" people believed that colleges should solicit funds from church treasuries.[180] In 1947, it appeared that Glenn Wallace was occupying a middle ground that would have broad support. Showalter predicted that after the controversy subsided "there will be far less effort of any of the schools to seek support from the budgets of the churches, even where they have regarded it [the doctrinal debate of the issue] as of indifference."[181] Several of the new colleges begun after World War II, including new schools in Oklahoma and Florida, announced that they would not accept contributions from churches.[182] When young James R. Cope became president of Florida Christian College in 1948, he announced that the school would "neither ask nor accept contributions from churches of the Lord," not wishing "to be a parasite upon churches." Some might think this decision "strange," Cope acknowledged, "but to those who are watching the horizon it is safe."[183] However, Cope badly misread the signs on the horizon.

Partly, the institutional debate quickly reached an impasse because of the unusually bitter personal direction that it took. The exchanges on the subject injected embarrassing new journalistic lows in personal recrimination and invective. In 1940, G. C. Brewer had come to the conclusion that the "cantankerous crowd" that supported Wallace comprised mostly "hysterical and schismatic preachers" obsessed with "inciting the brethren" to divide.[184] Those opposing contributions from churches to colleges were derisively termed "antis," and many progressive leaders were unwilling to let an unreasonable and obstreperous minority block the advancement of the churches of Christ. On the other hand, noninstitutional leaders labeled those who approved of church support of institutions "liberals," accusing them of abandoning the restoration plea. By 1950, the possibility that sponsoring churches and congregational support for colleges would remain in the realm of expediency was rapidly disappearing.

A third development that hardened lines in the late 1940s was a broadening of the debate to include church-supported orphan homes. Colleges had long been suspect in the anti-intellectual atmosphere of the churches of Christ, but before World War II few people questioned the right of churches to support the handful of orphan homes then in existence. Probably no more than a dozen preachers in the 1930s overtly questioned churches supporting orphan homes, although that number included the likes of C. R. Nichol, F. B. Srygley, and John T. Hinds.[185] In his 1933 defense of church support for colleges, G. C. Brewer sensed that a linkage between colleges and orphan homes provided a powerful defense: "It will be admitted by all that it is a part of the work of the church to care for orphan children, unless some radically 'apostolic' brother wants to contend that this is wholly an individual matter, and that the church as such is exempt from practicing pure and undefiled religion. Such an argument from *such a brother* would not surprise us, but we believe that *such brothers* are vastly in a minority."[186] Brewer was undoubtedly right; only the most militant anti-institutional preachers had spoken against orphan homes. In 1933, Foy E. Wallace, Jr., discredited former *Gospel Advocate* editor James A. Allen as "disgruntled" and "obstreperous" by pointing to Allen's opposition to all institutions: "Let it be observed by all that Brother Allen has come out in direct and unqualified opposition to Bible schools and orphan homes. He says that he, and others, *would like to see them all suspended and abolished!*"[187]

In his 1947 defense of church contributions to colleges, N. B. Hardeman seized the orphan home argument, noting that support for colleges and the homes "must stand or fall together." Hardeman reiterated his long-held prejudice against churches putting "schools in the church budget and thus binding them upon the church," but he stressed that he had "always believed that a church had the right to contribute to a school or an orphanage if it so desired."[188] Increasingly, those who favored church support for colleges tried to shift the battleground to the orphan homes, understanding quite well that there was much broader sympathy in the churches for orphan homes than for colleges.

The injection of orphan homes into the institutional debate reshuffled the balance of power. Hardeman pressed Foy E. Wallace, Jr., and other institutional critics to "come on out and condemn the right of the church to give to an orphan's home or a home for the aged."[189] In 1947 and 1948 people scrambled to find a consistent position in the boiling institutional controversy, and many changed loyalties. Some, like G. H. P. Showalter, remained skeptical of church contributions to colleges but argued that eleemosynary institutions were the work of a local church and could be operated under the oversight of an eldership.[190] On the other hand, Foy Wallace and his supporters drifted toward accepting the unpopular position that Hardeman and Brewer thrust upon them. Wallace believed that the orphan home was "a passive, harmless thing" that in no way posed the threat of dominating churches that colleges did, but he begrudgingly added orphan homes to the list of institutions he opposed, and many of the staff writers for the *Bible Banner* relished the opportunity to develop a full-blown and consistent noninstitutional argument.[191] In doing so, they developed a more consistent ideology, but at the same time accepted the status of a schismatic minority.

Personality Types and Personality Cults

In the absence of denominational organization, the churches of Christ, more than most religious groups, has been molded by the personalities of powerful editors, college presidents and professors, and preachers. Much of the interminable turmoil in the churches was inspired by influential leaders rallying supporters, either for their views or as personal devotees. "An underlying sense of competition lay hidden in each preacher's heart," wrote historian Earl West; these feelings sometimes erupted in "a contagion of jealousy."[192] In 1948, in an article exploring the "dangers" facing the churches, G. H. P. Showalter coupled "egotism" with "dogmatism" as the most ominous threats to unity. "The spirit of rivalry" seemed irrepressible; those who "desire prominence and preferment above the Lord" often savaged local churches to satisfy personal ambition.[193] Writing in 1947, as the institutional debate degenerated into bitter personal feuding between N. B. Hardeman and Foy E. Wallace, Jr., young James R. Cope acknowledged that "some of our most venerable men and scholarly brethren are not in perfect agreement on every point," but insisted that these clashes should not deter Christians from "seeking the truth on any issue." Too often, Cope ruefully observed, doctrinal issues were used as tools for personal self-aggrandizement by those "battling among themselves over places of prominence in his service." The end result could be disastrous: "Shall we surrender our plea for Christian unity upon the soils of division? Shall we shatter our hopes for the future upon the rocks of envy and pride? Shall we sectarianize an unsectarian body? Shall we be Campbellites or Christians, Stoneites or disciples, sectarianized sinners or sanctified saints?"[194]

For better and for worse, during the 1920s and 1930s, no individual contributed more to defining the doctrinal direction of churches of Christ and caused more instability than Foy E. Wallace, Jr. He was, in the words of historian Earl West, "both popular and unpopular in the superlative degree."[195] Immensely talented, Wallace was the premier debater (though he only held ten formal debates) in a movement that admired debaters. In 1934, at Wallace's debate with the famous Fort Worth Baptist fundamentalist J. Frank Norris, the audience included an estimated five hundred "preachers of the church of Christ" each evening. They listened hypnotically to a discussion that G. H. P. Showalter believed would "go down as one of the great debates of this generation."[196] At age thirty-eight,

Foy E. Wallace, Jr., had become a model for a generation of preachers in the churches of Christ. Wallace left an imprint on the generation of preachers who rose to prominence in the 1930s and 1940s; long after Wallace was estranged from men like Fanning Yater Tant and Roy E. Cogdill, they continued to reverence him.

In his mature years, Wallace specialized in "skinning the sects"; his preaching was calculated to "draw blood."[197] Wallace's McCarthy-like gift for intimidation and personal attacks on his opponents established a reign of terror during the premillennial debate. One of the board members of the magazine the *Christian Leader,* which was vigorously attacked by Wallace in the 1940s, charged that Wallace was a master of guilt by association and pejorative labeling. Ever the heresy hunter, in his last years Wallace closed many of his articles with a formula declaration: "I shall not surrender to them—and they shall not pass!" An enigmatic character, Wallace was his own worst enemy. He engaged in repeated acrimonious exchanges with a long list of respected preachers, and, on occasion, he shifted his position on important issues.

Wallace reached the zenith of his reputation in 1930, at age thirty-four, when he was appointed editor of the *Gospel Advocate.* The son of a well-known Texas preacher who was the father of six preachers, Foy E. Wallace, Jr., became a legendary preacher in Texas and the West while still a teenager.[198] Wallace had preached very little east of the Mississippi before becoming editor of the *Advocate,* and he had written almost nothing, but his reputation and his talents brought him to the attention of the paper's owner, Leon B. McQuiddy, and some of the editorial staff. The editor Wallace replaced was James A. Allen, a raw-boned and rambunctious old-time preacher who specialized in attacking Baptists and whose style echoed back to earlier decades.[199] McQuiddy felt that the *Advocate* needed a more sophisticated and charismatic leadership and chose the young westerner. In addition, McQuiddy had long tried to expand the influence of the *Gospel Advocate* into the

West, where the *Firm Foundation* remained the most widely read paper, and he believed that Wallace's fame would make the paper more competitive in the West.[200]

Having risen to the editorship of the *Advocate,* the most visible platform for a preacher in the churches of Christ, Wallace assumed the demeanor of a moderate and peacemaker, poised to lead the churches of Christ down a less stormy road. Wallace collected around him a group of influential staff writers, including two men who later became targets of his antipremillennial wrath: E. H. Ijams, president of David Lipscomb College, and Charles H. Roberson, a respected professor at ACC. Among his other trusted staff writers were men he later judged to be dangerous liberals, including B. C. Goodpasture and G. C. Brewer. In his study of Wallace, Terry J. Gardner concluded that he "closed 1931 with his personal popularity at an all time high."[201] Subscriptions to the *Gospel Advocate* reached an all-time high and young editor Wallace seemed poised for a more irenic career as a consensus builder.

It must have rubbed against the grain for Wallace to pursue a noncontroversial course; he soon was engaged in bitter battles with adversaries ranging from former editor James Allen to *Firm Foundation* editor G. H. P. Showalter. By the end of 1933 his friend (at the time) G. C. Brewer wrote to deny charges that the magazine was "full of contentions, strifes, bitter wranglings, and personalities."[202] Many were becoming disillusioned with Wallace the editor. Wallace's editorship of the *Gospel Advocate* came to a "sudden and unexpected end" in April 1934, apparently triggered by his financial problems.[203] He returned to Oklahoma City to preach and declared bankruptcy, a step, noted Terry J. Gardner, that "was considered almost sinful in 1934."[204]

Wallace was back in the editor's chair the next year when the *Gospel Guardian* was launched in October 1935. The new paper, Wallace announced, was not intended as a "competitor with other papers," but it would be in the vanguard of those militantly defending "truth against all errors and isms."

The *Guardian* was founded to be "controversial—doctrinal to the core," and it boasted an impressive panel of associate editors: N. B. Hardeman, Cled E. Wallace, Early Arceneaux, and John T. Lewis.[205] The *Gospel Guardian* was doomed by a continued pattern of insolvency and Wallace's seeming inability to meet editorial deadlines. After nine issues the *Gospel Guardian* merged with the *Firm Foundation* because the expense of publication became "a burden too heavy" for Wallace.[206] Some preachers, Wallace noted, celebrated "the jubilee" when they heard the news. Wallace became a staff writer for the *Firm Foundation,* apparently reconciling differences with G. H. P. Showalter, but that arrangement lasted only two years.

In 1937 N. B. Hardeman spearheaded an initiative to once again make Foy Wallace the editor of the *Gospel Advocate,* but the maneuver failed. However, *Advocate* owner Leon B. McQuiddy did agree to back a new paper to be published in Texas that would compete with the *Firm Foundation.*[207] In July 1938 Wallace launched the *Bible Banner,* a journal that continued publication for eleven years, with occasional lapses. Wallace biographer Terry Gardner judged that Wallace "was now in his prime," and it is true that Wallace's papers were at the heart of every major controversy in the churches of Christ,[208] but by 1940 his influence was greatly diminished. By the end of the 1940s Wallace was under attack from a number of quarters, most vitriolically by a young group of Texas preachers who wrote for the *Christian Soldier,* a magazine established by Ira Y. Rice, Jr., in 1939. They dubbed Wallace "Fuhrer Foy," commander of a "galaxy of gospel gangsters from coast to coast."[209]

Under attack from a variety of enemies by 1949, Wallace ceased publication of the *Bible Banner,* at the same time endorsing the founding of a new *Gospel Guardian*. That venture quickly soured and ended with the permanent estrangement of Wallace from his old friends Yater Tant and Roy E. Cogdill. Wallace founded yet another magazine in 1950, *Torch.* He wished the *Gospel Guardian* "happy voyage" but coolly stated,

"I prefer . . . to be entirely free to write in my own way . . . [to have my work] presented as I write it."[210] In the 1950s he influenced a loyal but small group of church leaders.

Well before the outbreak of World War II, Wallace's personal power was waning while the influence of other editors, college leaders, and preachers was growing. In 1941, he received a confidential letter telling him: "Just in case you have not heard it, your goose is cooked, and is now ready to be served by courses. You are doomed. . . . You are surrounded as completely as the Dago army in Libya."[211] By the late 1940s, when Wallace engaged N. B. Hardeman and G. C. Brewer in the beginnings of the anti-institutional debate, he had become a somewhat marginal figure. His enemies had come to far outnumber his friends. Hardeman summed up Wallace's predicament: "[First,] Brother Foy has broken connection with all of our schools and he can not endorse any of them. [Second, he] has severed connections with all of our papers and editors except the Bible Banner and he is at variance with both Cled and Roy in it. [Third, he] has broken relations with many of the oldest and most influential preachers in the brotherhood [including] G. H. P. Showalter, Jim Allen, John T. Lewis, H. Leo Boles, G. C. Brewer, and B. C. Goodpasture. . . . Truly the whole army is out of step and only Foy is in line. Too bad."[212] G. C. Brewer charged that Wallace was a "double-minded" man who had reversed himself on both the war question and on church support for colleges: "Brother Foy's radical changes, his personal attacks, abuses and insults, with a disposition to count every man who does not agree with him his personal enemy, are indeed unfortunate."[213] In 1945, one Houston congregation refused to cooperate in a Wallace campaign in the city because of his "general reputation and tactics, as they are well known throughout the brotherhood."[214] When Wallace deserted the noninstitutional cause in the 1950s, he abandoned the collection of fighting preachers who most admired his style and leadership.

After he lost the powerful tool of painting his enemies with a premillennial brush, Wallace's personal faults made him extremely vulnerable. In 1981, his old friend and admirer James W. Adams cataloged Wallace's flaws:

> (1) He found it difficult to forgive and forget injuries real or imagined. . . .
> (2) He was utterly intolerant of a point of view different from his own. . . .
> (3) If you were his friend, his enemies must be your enemies. . . .
> (4) He was intellectually arrogant. . . .
> (4) [*sic*] While a speaker of great talent, his unreasonably long preaching in his later years destroyed much of his influence and effectiveness.
> (5) His pulpit disposition, especially his public rebukes to young mothers in his audiences, did as much to impede the progress of the truth in later years as his knowledge and brilliant presentation of it did to advance it. He became better known for his pulpit disposition than he did for his preaching.
> (6) His undependability was reflected by his closing practically every meeting he conducted prematurely by reason of some emergency. . . .
> (7) His absolutely indefensible management of his personal finances. . . .
> (8) He would rationalize his conduct in almost all matters. . . . In a word, I firmly believe that Brother Wallace often deceived himself.[215]

When Wallace joined battle with N. B. Hardeman in 1947 over church contributions to colleges, he was an extremely vulnerable warrior. His financial problems had never been completely hidden from view and had on occasion been front-page news in the papers.[216] Hardeman and Wallace had been close friends, and the Freed-Hardeman College president was intimately acquainted with Wallace's record of financial irresponsibility. When he became the target of Wallace's acid pen in 1947, Hardeman skewered his tormenter, exposing the details of "Foy Wallace's sinful extravagance and utter lack of business judgement [that] forced him to take an oath of insolvency and to hide from his creditors behind the bankrupt law." Hardeman recounted the kindnesses he had shown the financially distressed Wallace and charged that Wallace had turned on him because he had refused to support World War II.[217] According to his friends, Hardeman later regretted his bitter personal assault on Wallace, believing that he had sullied himself in the process.[218] After nine months of replying to the "Bible Banner boys," Hardeman in his concluding article apologized "to the brotherhood" for allowing himself to be lured into a mud-slinging contest and promised never again "to descend to such low levels."[219] Wallace was at his caustic worst during the controversy, charging that Hardeman was "a cheap politician" and "a hypocrite," who was guilty of "deliberate and unmitigated falsehood," "dishonesty, deception, perversion, and prevarications," "demagoguery," and "stupid duplicity."[220] The Wallace-Hardeman exchange was "shocking to many"; Wallace's son, William, recalled that the episode left his father "deeply depressed."[221] Determined to lower his visibility, Wallace wrote no more in the *Bible Banner* after the January 1948 issue and he encouraged Yater Tant and Roy E. Cogdill to take leadership of the anti-institutional fight.[222]

While Foy E. Wallace, Jr., was the most irrepressible, and the most lethal, leader in the churches of Christ in the 1930s and 1940s, his popularity was challenged by several other preachers. Nicholas Brodie Hardeman was the most highly respected preacher in the churches east of the Mississippi River. A successful businessman and breeder of Tennessee walking horses, Hardeman was a powerful political force in the state of Tennessee.[223] In 1959, at age eighty-five, Hardeman's friends honored him with a banquet that included among its guests Governor Buford Ellington and Senator Albert Gore of Tennessee, and Senator Lyndon B. Johnson from Texas. He was an eloquent speaker; in 1920 fifty Nashville congregations sponsored a union meeting in famed Ryman Auditorium that showcased Hardeman's old-time oratory. In 1922, the Nashville churches once again sponsored Hardeman in a series of meetings, this time in the War Memorial Building. That meeting turned into a massive churches of Christ rally; Nashville's two newspapers printed the full text of his sermons, and Hardeman's name became a household word among the churches of Christ.[224] Hardeman returned to Nashville for city-wide meetings in 1923, 1928, 1938, and 1942 and he conducted similar campaigns in other cities. Historian Michael Casey noted the symbolic relevance of Hardeman's rise to fame and the Nashville meetings: "The Tabernacle Sermons clearly announced, first to Nashville, then to Tennessee, and finally to the whole South that the Churches of Christ had arrived. They had achieved respectability, and the church was going to be a religious force in the South for years to come."[225] Hardeman was conservative and militant and he participated in several debates, but his style was far more elegant and humane than Wallace's, with the latter's penchant for brawling. Wallace's comrade in the fight against premillennialism, Hardeman, a college president himself, refused to follow Wallace's lead in the war on church institutions.

Grover Cleveland Brewer was generally regarded as the third of the triumvirate of leading preachers in the first half of the twentieth century. His only service as an editor came when he for a time after World War II edited a semipolitical magazine named the *Voice of Freedom,* and he was never an educator, although he was a favorite of many college administrators and was given honorary doctorates by both Harding College and Abilene Christian College. Brewer's fame came mostly as a preacher, and he preached at several of the largest and most influential local churches in the country, including the Union Avenue Church in Memphis and the Broadway Church in Lubbock.[226] In many ways, Brewer's persona and modus operandi seemed much like those of Wallace, Hardeman, and other leading preachers—he wrote widely in the papers, he spoke on lectureship programs (more often for the prestigious Abilene Christian College Lectures than any other person), and he conducted scores of debates with sectarian enemies. However, Brewer was always on the cutting edge of rethinking the most separatist assumptions of the movement, embracing those on the fringes of the movement, including premillennialists, and he became the mentor of a generation of forward-looking church builders in the war years. While he was often attacked by Wallace, at the time of his death in 1956 Brewer's influence far exceeded that of Wallace.

The man who finished the task of isolating Foy E. Wallace, Jr., emerged as a major figure in the 1940s. Benton Cordell Goodpasture became the editor of the *Gospel Advocate* in March 1939 and held that position until his death in February 1977. Goodpasture had worked briefly as the magazine's circulation manager in 1919 and became a staff writer in 1931. He was a successful preacher in Atlanta before becoming editor of the paper, but he was not so widely known as most of the former editors. Goodpasture was the protégé of H. Leo Boles, a commanding figure in the churches of Christ in Tennessee who had succeeded David Lipscomb as president of Nashville Bible School in 1913 and had at times served both as president of David Lipscomb College and as editor of the *Gospel Advocate*. Leon B. McQuiddy, the publisher of the *Advocate,* depended largely on the advice of H. Leo Boles in the appointment of Goodpasture. To give assurance to those unacquainted with Goodpasture, McQuiddy chose a committee of "twelve reliable men" to advise him.[227]

B. C. Goodpasture was a superb businessman and manager and in the 1950s he turned the *Gospel Advocate* into a dominating force in the churches of Christ. In the 1970s, one of his contemporaries judged, probably correctly, that "no other preacher except David Lipscomb has been so honored by his own brethren." His admirer believed that Goodpasture's stature arose because he "is sound in biblical scholarship, is articulate in speech, and has a literary flow in the written language." Actually, Goodpasture wrote very little while editor of the *Advocate,* but he was unswervingly astute in using others to argue his cases. Whatever his editorial abilities, the surpassing talent of B. C. Goodpasture was his ability to "soundly and accurately appraise the issue of the brotherhood."[228]

Goodpasture opened his editorial tenure with a promise "to stand foursquare for the propagation of truth," but to eliminate from the magazine "all slurs, insinuations, and innuendo." Foy E. Wallace, Jr., took Goodpasture's editorial as a "broadside frontal attack . . . which cannot be conscientiously ignored."[229] In 1940, Wallace observed that Goodpasture was "a princely man, a gentleman, and a friend of mine just as long as he wants to be," but he regretted that the *Gospel Advocate* had "succumbed to the sweet strains of soft-pedalism."[230] The two sparred through the war years because Goodpasture refused to repudiate the Lipscomb pacifism that he had embraced under the influence of H. Leo Boles. According to historian Earl West, Goodpasture "did what he could to promote the non-combatant positions during the war,"[231] and Goodpasture's hand was behind the unleashing of attacks by Brewer and Hardeman on the *Bible Banner* immediately after the war. By the time Goodpasture and Wallace resolved their personal differences in 1952, Wallace was a spent force. In the years from 1945 to 1960 the suave and mild-mannered Goodpasture proved to be a formidable enemy to the noninstitutional movement and the consummate architect of the postwar churches of Christ.[232]

Though not as visible as the leading preachers and editors, the leaders of the five colleges supported by members of churches of Christ—Abilene Christian College, David Lipscomb College, Harding College, Pepperdine College, and Freed-Hardeman College—formed another formidable locus of influence in the movement. In 1936, Foy E. Wallace, Jr., warned of the power of the colleges: "Remember that it was the colleges, not the societies, that swept the church into the digression. The colleges were before the societies and far more powerful in their influence. Their original intent was right, but they later became the hotbeds for innovation, compromise and all forms of digression."[233] Many of the college presidents in the years before and after World War II, such as Hugh M. Tiner and M. Norvel Young at Pepperdine, N. B. Hardeman of Freed-Hardeman, H. Leo Boles and Athens Clay Pullias at David Lipscomb, and Batsell Baxter, who headed several different colleges, were also well-known preachers, and their voices were particularly influential because of their positions as educators.

In the years just before and after World War II, a new generation of presidents appeared, all of them ambitious to build the prestige and influence of their institutions. George Benson became president of Harding College in 1936, and he quickly aligned the college with business interests and conservative political causes; Don H. Morris was named president of Abilene Christian College in 1940 and skillfully moved the school toward accreditation; Athens Clay Pullias rose to the presidency of David Lipscomb College in 1946; in 1957, in a move designed to realign Pepperdine University with its historic relationship with the churches of Christ, M. Norvel Young moved to California to assume the presidency of that institution. The only college that remained in the hands of a first-generation preacher in the early 1950s was Freed-Hardeman, the small school in Henderson, Tennessee, headed by the venerable N. B. Hardeman.[234] By 1950, the colleges had trained a substantial percentage of the church's preachers, and these college-trained preachers formed a self-conscious elite who, with a degree of open disdain, put distance between themselves and the rough-and-ready preachers of the previous generation. The annual lectureships conducted by most of the colleges showcased this new talent and came to be surrogate denominational conventions. Most preachers and church members became lifelong friends of their alma maters, and of their professors. While the colleges were careful to ward off charges of heresy, they were autonomous enclaves capable of protecting professors like Charles H. Roberson who were suspected of premillennial leanings or of other heterodox beliefs, even from the assaults of Foy E. Wallace, Jr.

The Diverging Minds of the Churches of Christ

The personality factions in the churches of Christ in the 1930s and 1940s mirrored far more than the personal whims and partialities of church members. The personality clusters faced one another across intellectual fissures that were constants in the mind of the movement. On the left and the right, the fringes of the churches of Christ were occupied by antithetical personality types. Wallace was the hero of one extreme—the fighters. He led a hard-nosed, debating, sect-battering vanguard of old-time preachers. Pioneer preacher Joe S. Warlick, who died in 1940, conducted 399 debates during his lifetime, and hundreds of other formal debates during the thirties and forties featured a gallery of preachers that included G. C. Brewer, N. B. Hardeman, C. R. Nichol, W. Curtis Porter, and J. D. Tant.

Foy E. Wallace, Jr., believed that "courage was an essential quality of the man who preached the gospel" and that it was courageous preaching that had saved the churches of Christ from the Christian Church digression and had rebuilt the group in the thirties and forties. By the 1930s, Wallace and many of the fighting preachers instinctively sensed that "preaching is heading in the wrong direction." "We would not assume (far be it) a hypercritical, holier, wiser, better-than-thou attitude," Wallace sarcastically wrote in 1936, "but there has been too much 'method-of-approach' preaching" instead of "straight live-coals-from-the-altar gospel preaching."[235] In 1933, young Roy H. Lanier, Sr., bemoaned a tendency among some "devout brethren" to be critical of "fighting preachers and debaters." The result was churches filled with members who "courted denominational approval," having been "brought up on soft moral lectures."[236] Sometimes the fighters drew the circle of orthodoxy very small. In 1934, Cled Wallace "concluded that there are less than a dozen preachers in the whole church who can be depended upon to preach the gospel like it ought to be preached." Teased the editor of the *Firm Foundation,* "Anyway, as long as it takes all his fingers to count them, maybe we will escape the fate of Sodom."[237]

On the other extreme were those who consciously sought a more respectable image and objected to the crude methods of the fighters. Many members of the churches of Christ never approved of the tactics of Foy Wallace; some doubted the efficacy of debating altogether. G. H. P. Showalter acknowledged in the 1930s that "some very good-meaning people dislike any and all forms of controversy—specially religious controversy."[238]

Several developments in the 1930s uncovered a deeper resentment against the Wallace faction. In 1936, Claude F. Witty, who preached at the Westside Church of Christ in Detroit, joined with Christian Church leader James DeForest Murch to propose a series of "unity meetings." The first meeting convened in Cincinnati in 1937 and later conferences met in Detroit, Indianapolis, Akron, Los Angeles, and Columbus, Indiana. The Cincinnati gathering featured speeches by J. N. Armstrong and George Benson from Harding College, as well as an address by an aged and mellowed Daniel Sommer; the Indianapolis meeting in 1939 featured speeches by E. W. McMillan and H. Leo Boles from the churches of Christ and such Christian Church leaders as James DeForest Murch and Edwin R. Errett.[239] The unity campaign was both impolitic and chimerical. Witty undermined his credibility with most members of churches of Christ by calling for a "restudy" of the instrumental music issue; neither side in this recent division was seriously ready to revisit that debate. The conference organizers had hoped that G. C. Brewer would deliver a keynote address, but he declined, apparently reluctantly, reminding them that "we cannot unite by agreeing to disagree."[240] Foy Wallace had a field day in attacking the unity meetings, charging that Witty was willing to compromise on a variety of doctrinal fronts, including premillennialism.

More significant was an undercurrent of dissatisfaction with the policies of all of the movement's most influential papers. Many preachers and college leaders were uncomfortable with the raucous brawling so common in the papers.[241] In February 1937, in a letter to J. N. Armstrong, S. H. Hall, a Nashville preacher and staff writer for the *Gospel Advocate,* expressed the mood of discontent: "It seems that our papers have lost all sense of justice and fairness. I've tried and tried and tried till my soul is almost worn out to get Leon [McQuiddy, publisher of the *Gospel Advocate*] to take a firm hand and see that our paper here stays on a high plane. But in spite of all this he lets the old heads slash at this one and that one, and then they edit your replies and make you say what they want you to say in reply."[242] The next year Hall met in Nashville with a group that included G. C. Brewer; J. N. Armstrong; E. H. Ijams, president of David Lipscomb College; E. W. McMillan, minister of Central Church of Christ in Nashville; Jesse P. Sewell; James F. Cox, president of Abilene Christian College; and New York businessman Clinton Davidson to discuss beginning a new paper. The spiritual leader of the movement was Sewell, a genteel and respected preacher and educator who served as president of both Lipscomb and Abilene Christian colleges, who was determined to bring "a more positive thrust in Christian journalism among Churches of Christ."[243]

Learning that the *Christian Leader,* a journal that had been published for fifty-two years by John F. Rowe and his descendants, was for sale, Davidson secured the financial backing to buy the paper and E. W. McMillan was named editor.[244] The new *Christian Leader* was launched in January 1939 with an illustrious editorial board. The new *Leader* was slickly produced and had an air of professionalism, even pretentiousness, and it was a landmark experiment. The paper featured articles by some of the most progressive preachers in the churches of Christ, as well as such visible ACC faculty members as Walter H. Adams, Charles H. Roberson, and Paul Southern. The paper studiously avoided controversy and some believed that it "set a new high standard in religious journalism."[245] Sewell envisioned a magazine that would be both attractive and solidly biblical, filled with "constructive teaching so thoroughly in harmony with the word of God that, every time they [Wallace and his supporters] strike, the blow will react against them."[246] In an unprecedented departure intended to thwart Wallace and his cohorts, the paper was copyrighted.

The new *Christian Leader* was never a circulation success and it lasted for only two years; in December 1940 Davidson withdrew his financial support and the paper merged with the *Gospel Proclaimer,* a magazine published by G. H. P. Showalter. Some blamed the high-pressure tactics of Clinton Davidson for its failure. Davidson had been reared in Kentucky and attended Potter Bible School in Bowling Green, where he was deeply influenced by James A. Harding and J. N. Armstrong. On the other hand, he was virtually unknown in churches of Christ when he began to exert his influence in the late 1930s. In 1936, having made a modest fortune as a financial consultant in New York City, he visited Armstrong and George Benson at Harding College and offered to help the struggling school. In the late 1930s, Davidson funneled money to the college and aspired to recast the image of the churches of Christ. George Benson at Harding College was the most receptive of the presidents to Davidson's ideas, and in the long run, the two men left an imprint on the churches of Christ by linking Harding College to business interests and conservative politics. However, the new *Christian Leader* also left the mark of Clinton Davidson on the churches of Christ.[247]

The Achilles heel of the new *Christian Leader* was the magazine's unclear sound on premillennialism. The paper betrayed the same kind of passive sympathy for premillennialists and resentment against Wallace that typified J. N. Armstrong and Harding College, and most churches of Christ were unwilling to tolerate such laxity in 1938. In 1940, editor McMillan announced that the magazine would publish a discussion on premillennialism featuring R. H. Boll and G. H. P. Showalter, but the debate never appeared and McMillan offered only vague explanations for the delay. More serious, in the spring of 1940, Clinton Davidson delivered two speeches at Abilene Christian College that clearly marked him as a premillennialist. Jesse P. Sewell "felt betrayed" by Davidson and backed away from the magazine, as did E. W. McMillan. McMillan resigned as editor, insisting that he had no premillennial sympathies, and curtly noted that Davidson would have to answer for himself.

Seemingly, the new *Christian Leader*'s venture into noncontroversial journalism was a flop, and Foy E. Wallace, Jr., gleefully announced in 1941, "The Davidson-Leader movement is dead." Wallace had leveled a withering barrage on the "Christian Leader Digressive Boys" that no doubt had an effect. In a letter to Wallace, C. B. F. Young, a Birmingham chemical engineer who had made a fortune in New York City and was one of the *Leader*'s board members, protested that there was not a "digressive" on the board and chastised Wallace for his name-calling: "How would you like to be called 'Foy-somebody-else-pay-his-bills-Wallace.'"[248] But the businessmen who had launched the new paper to change the image of the churches of Christ offended many besides Wallace. When the influential H. Leo Boles wrote to Clinton Davidson asking a series of questions, Davidson replied that he was "rather surprised to receive a letter from a total stranger asking me for rather personal information regarding my religious life."[249] Boles was clearly miffed and curtly replied, "I seem to be a 'total stranger' to you. I will let the public decide whether this is a reflection on me or on you."[250] In spite of the short-term resistance to the paper, Richard Hughes correctly concluded that "in the long run they succeeded"; in fact, the short-lived new *Christian Leader* was "pivotally important" to the future of the churches of Christ. Hughes wrote, "The new *Christian Leader* had pioneered a kind of journalism—and a kind of theology—that would increasingly characterize the progressive wing of Churches of Christ for the remainder of the twentieth century. The new journalism and associated theology would move Churches of Christ further and further away from the sectarian mentality of the nineteenth century and would increasingly celebrate the values of conservative Protestant culture in the United States."[251]

The *Gospel Proclaimer,* which absorbed the *Leader* in 1941, had been founded in 1939 by G. H. P. Showalter to fill the "distinctive" need for a noncontroversial paper that could be given to "some one who is not a Christian."[252] By 1941 the paper had a substantial circulation of eighteen thousand. Even more symptomatic of the new demand for more positive journalism were two other extremely successful publishing ventures launched in 1938 and 1946. The *Twentieth Century Christian* began publication in Nashville in October 1938 under the editorship of J. P. Sanders, the respected preacher of the Hillsboro Church of Christ. Its editorial board included Dean Hugh M. Tiner of Pepperdine; Athens Clay Pullias, vice-president of Lipscomb; and educators M. Norvel Young, James D. Bales, and George DeHoff. The new journal was inspirational rather than polemical; the editors abandoned "the battlefield that Foy Wallace claimed as leader and watchdog."[253] Even more striking was the dramatic post–World War II success of the *Christian Chronicle*. Founded in 1946 by Olan Hicks, the *Chronicle* was a newsy, upbeat paper that soon far surpassed in circulation all other publications edited by members of the churches of Christ. Its formula for success was a chronicling of the unity and success of the churches of Christ.

In 1937, as a prelude to launching the new *Christian Leader,* Clinton Davidson conducted a poll of "average ministers" in the churches of Christ soliciting their views on Christian journalism.[254] In 1938, the *Leader* published the results of the poll. The survey was far from scientific, but the results were eye-opening. Only three percent of those polled approved of papers in which "one writer criticizes another writer" by name. Sixty-seven percent of the preachers polled by Davidson believed that "religious papers" were "used unfairly to subject them to unnecessary criticisms or to injure their chances of being called to churches or to hold meetings."[255] The survey was tainted because of Davidson's connection with it, as well as by its dubious sampling method, but it did reveal a festering dissatisfaction among a substantial number of preachers. Foy E. Wallace, Jr., knew that much of the discontent was directed at him. He charged that the new *Christian Leader* was "little short of an official organ, or mouthpiece for certain colleges," operated by the "most underhanded, ignoble personalities that have ever been imposed on a brotherhood."[256] Because of the paper's copyright policy, Wallace dubbed its financial backer "Copyright Davidson." Wallace insisted that the poll was rigged and collected the names of two hundred preachers who had not received Davidson's questionnaire, but none of that changed the main point revealed by the survey; that is, that many found Wallace's style offensive. No preacher or college wanted to be tarred by Wallace's brush, but there was a growing effort to try to neutralize his influence on the churches.

Most people in the churches of Christ in the thirties and forties embraced neither the siege mentality of Wallace nor the noncontroversial ideals of the new *Christian Leader*. Most people sought a moderate middle course. "We should have more positive teaching," wrote G. H. P. Showalter in 1942, because "the beauty of truth will attract those people who have good and honest hearts." On the other hand, he insisted that preachers should not "neglect to oppose the teaching that is false." Showalter probably voiced a widely held sentiment when he concluded that "severity may be in place at times, but this method of teaching is not usually effective."[257] Even among the most conservative preachers in the movement, many deprecated the caustic personal attacks that were so common. One of the patriarchs of noninstitutional views, W. W. Otey, repeatedly pled for a measure of fairness and reason: "Many subscribers have been alienated and strife stirred both by 'airing' questions that should never have been introduced into our papers, and more especially by the spirit of bitterness and even hatred manifested by the disputants. . . . We start by professing our admiration for our 'good brother's high intelligence,' and our unbounded 'love for him.' Then we proceed to show our readers that he is anything else than 'intelligent.' . . . We simply take the 'hide off.'"[258]

More than any other editor in the wake of World War II, B. C. Goodpasture clearly grasped the yearning for a constructive journalism. Most of the men responsible for founding the new *Christian Leader* applauded Goodpasture's appointment as editor of the *Gospel Advocate*.[259] Jesse P. Sewell and the other principals of the *Leader* coalition had hoped in 1937 that *Advocate* publisher Leon B. McQuiddy would abandon the conservative circle headed by Wallace and Hardeman, but McQuiddy continued to support the fighters, bankrolling Wallace's *Bible Banner* in 1939. The inauguration of the *Leader*, however, pushed McQuiddy toward the center, opening the way for the selection of Goodpasture as editor.[260]

By the end of World War II, most moderate leaders in the churches of Christ believed that they had found in Goodpasture a man capable of neutralizing Wallace and returning the *Advocate* to the "high standards" of journalism that had characterized the paper under David Lipscomb and Tolbert Fanning.[261] In his opening editorial, Goodpasture appealed to the memory of Fanning and Lipscomb: "These venerable men exalted principles above persons, and sought to be free from personal bitterness and recriminations. Their example is worthy of our consideration and emulation."[262] Wallace regarded Goodpasture as a "panty-waist editor," and "quite simply . . . Wallace accused Leon McQuiddy and the *Advocate* of selling out to pressures from Clinton Davidson."[263] In short, by 1939 the *Gospel Advocate* began shifting ground; in the years after World War II, Goodpasture would be joined by a new editor of the *Firm Foundation,* Reuel Lemmons, in seeking a journalistic balance that would eliminate the incessant internal bloodletting without embracing doctrinal laxity.

The widening rift in the churches of Christ in the early 1940s, which found its most visible expression in the journalistic wars between the fighters and the builders, was more than a matter of style and taste. Underneath the sound and fury over methods were real doctrinal differences. For the most part, however, the theological divergences had to do with emphasis rather than content, with mood rather than belief. Richard Hughes and Michael Casey juxtaposed two competing ideologies during the years before World War II—on the one side was a "sectarian mentality" associated with Foy E. Wallace, Jr., which embraced a legalistic definition of "primitive Christianity" as the "foundational myth" of the churches of Christ, and, on the other side was a "spiritual, irenic, grace-oriented, culture-transforming tradition of preaching," which, Casey concluded, "has been present in the Restoration Movement for as long as the debate tradition."[264]

In short, historians Hughes and Casey described serious theological rifts among the most articulate preachers by the 1930s, centering on the meaning of grace. Although some early leaders in the churches of Christ, most noticeably T. B. Larrimore, developed the concept of grace in their preaching, Casey discovered a distinct "lack of grace in the debating tradition."[265] The preacher most noted for his exploration of the theme of grace during the 1930s, Kenny Carl Moser, was generally shunned as a heretic because his views called into question long-accepted notions about the basic "plan of salvation" that was a cornerstone doctrine in the churches of Christ. Moser was defended by G. C. Brewer, and near the end of his life Moser came to be something of a hero among more progressive elements in the churches of Christ, but, in fact, a serious theological debate over grace did not occur in churches of Christ until the 1960s.[266]

It was not so much traditional, evangelical concepts of grace that had a legitimate claim to a place in the progressive restoration intellectual heritage as it was a softer, less judgmental attitude that viewed the concept of restoration contextually rather than propositionally. Grace had always been preached in the restoration movement insomuch as it stood for defining "primitive, nondenominational Christianity in spiritual and practical terms, largely divorced from the legal and rational understanding that informed the doctrinal controversies of their age."[267] This "heritage of grace," embraced by people like Brewer and Sewell, had little to do with evangelical notions of grace, but it did, indeed, signify a less legalistic and less propositional understanding of the meaning of restoration.[268]

Even though it is possible to identify two opposite foundational poles in the churches of Christ—one a rational, propositional, and relatively closed notion of primitive Christianity and the other a more open, tolerant, and grace-oriented quest for the substance of being a New Testament Christian—the concepts were neither clear-cut nor necessarily conflicting. Most members of churches of Christ instinctively embraced both ideologies and most leaders gave lip service to both. Sometimes the two modes of thought materialized in unexpected ways to support both conservative and progressive doctrinal beliefs. The restoration movement survived with a degree of tension and an unspoken ambivalence about these general principles; danger became most acute when factions within the churches came to believe that others had abandoned completely one or the other of these principles.

Impasse

In addition to highlighting the intellectual fissures in the churches of Christ, the institutional controversy that gripped the churches of Christ in the 1950s was rooted in profound social, economic, and educational changes that had transpired by the end of World War II. However, in 1950 the issues continued to be discussed largely in doctrinal terms. Most of the doctrinal issues that would separate a small minority of non-institutional churches of Christ from the mainstream by the beginning of the 1960s had been defined and discussed for many years, but few people envisioned that these issues would cause an open rupture. W. W. Otey, who had an uncanny insight into the sociological tensions in the churches of Christ, pondered the question of schism in 1946 and judged that the movement was not quite ready to divide again, as it had early in his life, but predicted that a splintering was not far away. A "powerful leadership is taking form" in the colleges, Otey warned, and this new leadership would move the churches of Christ either toward Rome or Jerusalem. Otey feared that it would be toward Rome.[269] Still, in 1950, the old veteran observed that there was as yet "no actual breaking of fellowship" in the movement, and he hoped schism would be avoided.[270]

Whatever the other divisive social and intellectual pressures at work in the restoration movement, all debates ended in discussions of the limits of New Testament authority. During the decade of the 1950s both sides in the institutional controversy rallied scriptural arguments in an effort to build consistent positions. After more than a decade of debate the two sides would lose patience with one another. In 1948, W. W. Otey noted that the "tactic of error" that had made inevitable the churches of Christ–Christian Church division was the introduction of "quibbles" about "incidental" matters by Christian Church preachers who wished to obscure "plain commands." Division over institutionalism was becoming inevitable, he feared, because "we have men in high places who adopt the same tactics adopted by errorists who sponsored the same innovations a half century ago."[271]

In 1949, W. W. Otey insisted that there were only "two possible positions in religion." One required "faithfully making all things according to the pattern so plainly set forth in the word of the Lord." The other path led to "denominationalism." The aging warrior forewarned the younger generation: "Young man, you will have to choose which end of the road you will travel. One is easy, popular, and offers high rewards in positions of prestige, and cash salaries. The other is the road of hardship, self-denial, often poverty and being denounced as reactionary."[272] The decade of the fifties was a time of choosing. Both sides wearied of talking and listening. Some years before, in 1945, progressive preacher Ulrich R. Beeson had summed up the dilemma: "The preacher who writes or who stands in the pulpit and cannot see, in view of a vastly changing world, the needs of the youth of tomorrow is not entitled to a hearing."[273] When people in the churches of Christ tire of "hearing" one another, the movement is ripe for schism.

3

Consummating the Institutional Division

THE LAST ISSUE of Foy E. Wallace, Jr.'s *Bible Banner* in 1949 provided something of a landmark divide to close the first half of the twentieth-century history of the churches of Christ. Wallace's relentless attacks on premillennialism and other minority views, and his dreaded monitoring of the colleges and other institutions, had isolated him from many of the most influential leaders in the churches of Christ. Shaken in 1949 by N. B. Hardeman's withering attack on him and by the death of his father, Wallace became depressed and disinterested in the publication of the magazine.[1] In the early 1930s Wallace had been, without question, the dominant preacher and editor in the movement; by 1950 he was a vulnerable warrior and the *Bible Banner* had become a fringe publication.

In an effort to regroup the noninstitutional movement, which many regarded as Foy Wallace's legacy at mid-century, on May 5, 1949, the first issue of the *Gospel Guardian* was published in Lufkin, Texas. Edited by Fanning Yater Tant, the forty-year-old son of the irascible J. D. Tant, the *Gospel Guardian* was launched with Wallace's consent and blessing. Tant later reminisced about the origins of the magazine: "Foy said that his sharp controversy with G. C. Brewer (and N. B. Hardeman) had deteriorated to 'personalities' and he was fearful that *he* (rather than the real problem) was becoming too much the center of attack and attention. He wanted to

Fanning Yater Tant (1908–1995). The son of pioneer preacher J. D. Tant, Yater Tant was one of the primary publicists of the noninstitutional protest in the churches of Christ after World War II. A witty and prolific writer, Tant edited two magazines, the *Gospel Guardian* and *Vanguard,* and wrote several books. (Courtesy of the Center for Restoration Studies, Abilene Christian University.)

'fade into the back-ground' and let the discussion focus on the real issue . . . rather than him personally."[2] The paper's publisher was Roy E. Cogdill and listed as associate editors were Foy E. Wallace, Jr., Cled E. Wallace, R. L. Whiteside, and Cogdill. Tant and Foy Wallace had agreed on a stable of writers for the new magazine; the list included, in addition to the editors, C. R. Nichol, Early Arceneaux, W. Curtis Porter, O. C. Lambert, and James W. Adams.[3] G. H. P. Showalter welcomed the new journal, recommending Tant as a "capable," "safe," and "faithful" brother, but the *Gospel Advocate* ignored it.[4]

The first two issues of the *Gospel Guardian* included articles from the pen of Foy E. Wallace, Jr., that more or less defined the noninstitutional case. However, Wallace wrote almost nothing in the months that followed, even though his name remained on the masthead as an associate editor. Wallace had become angry with Tant before the first issue of the *Guardian* was published. In the final issue of the *Bible Banner*, a long article appeared under Wallace's signature announcing the beginning of the *Guardian* and heaping "lavish praise on Yater Tant."[5] Tant had liberally edited an article given to him by Wallace, adding personally complimentary material from letters that Wallace had written to him. Tant believed that Wallace, who was notoriously unable to meet publication deadlines, had authorized him to edit his work, but Wallace angrily wrote to his son that "the entire middle and main part [of my article] had been lifted out—the editor had written the middle section himself, about himself and stuck it into the article with my name on it."[6] Because of this and other misunderstandings, by 1950 Wallace was permanently estranged from both Tant and Cogdill.[7] In July 1950, he launched yet another small magazine, *Torch*, but only twelve issues were printed before it ceased publication in December 1951. Wallace became "very, very bitter" against Tant and Cogdill and increasingly backed away from the noninstitutional attack.[8] Although many of his noninstitutional friends recalled sermons by Wallace well into the fifties denouncing sponsoring churches, he later denied that he had ever taken any of the positions espoused by the *Guardian*.[9] Wallace's defection from the noninstitutional campaign was a serious loss, but the course of the *Gospel Guardian* was set and in 1950 the battle was joined in earnest.

The "Rock Fight" Triggers a Division

In January 1950, the *Guardian* fired the shot that opened the final phase of the institutional controversy. In that issue, Cled Wallace, in his typically swashbuckling and irreverent style, criticized a sponsoring-church venture in Italy. Several of the postwar missions sponsored by American churches of Christ had encountered difficulties with local authorities and, particularly in Italy, with the Roman Catholic Church. Predictably, the aggressive evangelistic tactics of Cline and Harold Paden irritated many Italian Catholics.[10] In 1949, the relationship between the Padens and the Italian government reached an impasse, and in December 1949, they were given a "Catholic inspired" order by the government to cease distributing food and to close the orphan home that they had established.[11] During one of the church's public meetings, a rowdy crowd disrupted the services and threw rocks at the Padens. The Paden brothers were a hot-headed pair, and the situation worsened. In February, the Italian government forbade them to hold public meetings in Rome. These incidents sparked a storm of protest from American churches of Christ; preachers organized rallies supporting the evangelists, churches published paid protests in newspapers, and members of the churches of Christ flooded congressmen with demands that the Padens be protected.[12]

The Padens' predicament quickly became a minor cause célèbre in churches of Christ in America. A minister in Texas informed the press that the group's hundred and fifty thousand members in that state were "pretty indignant" about the mistreatment of their missionaries. A Houston preacher orchestrated a mass prayer meeting and urged members of the churches of Christ to send telegrams to President Truman. About seven hundred people in the Dallas–Fort Worth area staged a rally and began collecting signatures for a mass telegram to be sent to the president.[13]

In January 1950, on the front page of the *Gospel Guardian*, appeared Cled Wallace's article entitled "That Rock Fight in Italy." Cled, whose acerbic wit and provocative pen won him the reputation of being the "ace writer" in his brother Foy's stable, dryly noted that the Padens recently had been on the "receiving end of some rock-throwing." He then presented the Italian point of view: the Padens were in the country on tourist visas (rather than waiting to be admitted as missionaries) and the Italian government had charged that the young Americans had "attacked the Holy See—as well as other Protestant religions—with ill-advised words." Wallace dismissed the whole affair with barbed sarcasm. He had known several preachers who had been "whipped in this country," he quipped, and "the preachers involved have been behaving better ever since." He ridiculed the public outcry in the churches, calling it "half-cocked." Noting that thousands of telegrams had been sent to the president, Wallace concluded that at least "they decided not to bother the Lord with it until things got more serious."[14]

It was unthinkable to most members of the churches of Christ that Cled Wallace had sided with Roman Catholics against the persecuted Paden brothers. Letters of protest poured in to Yater Tant, and the *Gospel Guardian* came under intense pressure to apologize. Even the usually unflappable Cled Wallace was nonplussed by the furor. He asked, almost meekly, "When did it come to pass that any project or movement among the brethren becomes such a 'holy cow' that it cannot be criticized, if somebody thinks it needs it?"[15] Wallace remained on the defensive for months as he tried to turn the argument toward a serious consideration of the sponsoring-church arrangement. In March, he begged for everyone to "calm down, quit asking me to apologize and quit insinuating that I am not a Christian, long enough to show me . . . that sponsoring churches [existed in the New Testament]."[16] A month later, he outlined his objections to the arrangement: "The elders of one church have no right to form themselves into a missionary board to get hold of the money and direct the work of other churches in preaching the gospel."[17] Cled was under such duress that Foy E. Wallace, Jr., agreed to write a defense of his brother for the *Guardian*. Once again, he was incensed by what appeared in the magazine, charging that editor Tant "changed it, deleted it, rewrote it," and he never again wrote for the magazine.[18]

Most of Cled Wallace's friends agreed that his "rock fight" article was crude, ill-timed, and needlessly disrespectful of the young Americans in Italy. It damaged the noninstitutional cause, giving substance to the charge that the movement was composed of irresponsible hypercritics with little interest in building churches. By 1950, the day of intimidating opponents through personal attacks and ridicule was coming to an end.

On the other hand, Cled Wallace's article gouged a critical nerve exposed by the postwar changes in the churches of Christ. While it may have been a "judgmental error," recalled James W. Adams, it was "wholly justified from the standpoint of the facts of the case." The Padens were "never in danger," Adams believed, and the whole affair had been little more than a "ploy to raise more money."[19] The Italian episode highlighted the growing denominational pride that in the years ahead would nurture a proliferation of institutions and sponsoring-church arrangements. During the public posturing surrounding the Italian crisis, the supporters of the Padens boasted about their numbers, exaggerated their influence, and clothed themselves from head to foot in the stars and stripes. They were outraged that a foreign government would dare persecute a church as important as the churches of Christ. Cled Wallace's article was a visceral reaction against such posturing. Crude though it may have been, Cled Wallace was restating the movement's historic dogma of cultural separation.

A Decade of Noninstitutional Attack

Despite the acrimonious exchanges that followed the "rock fight" article, there was no clear-cut sense of division in the churches of Christ at the opening of the 1950s. Throughout the decade, a wide-ranging debate raged in the major papers read by members of the churches of Christ. In 1950, the *Gospel Guardian* stood "alone among the papers in the 'brotherhood' in questioning the scripturalness of one church becoming the equivalent of a 'missionary board.'" Editor Yater Tant urged the *Firm Foundation* and the *Gospel Advocate,* both "riding the crest of a wave of popularity," to "awaken from their lethargy" and to "begin to condemn and warn against and oppose the popular tide."[20]

After 1950, noninstitutional preachers in the churches of Christ began building a case to prove that sponsoring churches were unscriptural, though nearly all of them had participated in such arrangements during the thirties and forties. The situation at the beginning of the decade remained fluid; *Gospel Guardian* editor Tant refused to commit himself unequivocally on the issue, especially in the midst of the "high hysteria" caused by Cled Wallace's "rock fight" article. Tant simply urged that "certain doctrinal aspects to the whole foreign mission program need a very careful and earnest study."[21]

Tant's plea for further study was far too late. In 1948, E. W. McMillan had accepted an appointment as a full-time promoter of the "work of preaching the gospel to the world" under the sponsorship of the Union Avenue Church in Memphis. According to McMillan, a few dozen sponsoring churches were doing in 1948 "more missionary work than all of our congregations combined thirty years ago." He acknowledged that "some among us have seemed to have fears—not many, but a few." However, he insisted, most people in the churches of Christ were ready to move ahead: "Brethren are realizing that the best way to kill factions and overcome lethargy is to load the congregations down heart and pocketbook in good works."[22] By 1950, a majority were prepared to ignore the gainsayers.

Nonetheless, the *Guardian* attack was relentless in the first half of the fifties, and it often turned biting and personal. The *Guardian* boasted that its policies encouraged publishing both sides of controversial issues, as opposed to the one-sided editorial policies of its chief adversary, the *Gospel Advocate,* but it became the indefatigable organ of the noninstitutional movement. After the publication of an article by G. K. Wallace in 1949 that defended orphan homes under the supervision of church elders, the *Guardian* was a committed and, for a time, a more or less single-issue, noninstitutional magazine.[23] The paper was so stigmatized by the early fifties that any preacher identified with it risked his reputation and his job.

The defection of Foy E. Wallace, Jr., and subsequently of Cled Wallace, were blows to the prestige of the *Guardian,* but by the mid-1950s Tant could still assemble a formidable and well-known group of preachers to write articles for him. In the spring of 1956, he put together a "Unity Special" that featured articles written by fifteen men who believed that "only one thing can save the church from disaster: AN UNQUESTIONING ACCEPTANCE OF BIBLE TEACHING." The roster was a representative collection of leaders in the noninstitutional movement. Among the "hoary heads" in the group were C. E. W. Dorris, an eighty-five-year-old resident of Nashville who had been a writer for the *Gospel Advocate;* John T. Lewis, the patriarch of the churches in Birmingham, Alabama, and a former student of David Lipscomb; C. D. Plum, another former *Advocate* staff writer; and W. Curtis Porter, one of the most widely known debaters in the churches of Christ. These older men were joined by a group of preachers who, along with Tant, had been in the forefront of the noninstitutional fight since the end of World War II: Roy E. Cogdill, the publisher and associate editor of the *Guardian;* James W. Adams of Beaumont, Texas, "one of the keenest thinkers and reasoners among us"; A. Hugh Clark of Baytown, Texas, "one of the ablest preachers of the age"; Cecil B. Douthitt, whose barbed pen rivaled that of Cled Wallace; Robert H. Farish, an independent thinker who had preached widely in the Southeast; Marshall E. Patton, a highly respected preacher in Alabama and Tennessee; George P. Estes from St. Louis, who specialized in restoration history; Robert C. Welch, "one of the most logical thinkers to contribute to the study of current problems"; and Bryan Vinson, Sr., a pious and studious man who had won great respect in Texas churches. The youngest writer in the issue was Charles A. Holt, a brilliant and creative thinker who quickly became one of the premier debaters of institutional questions. Perhaps the most unexpected contributor to the special issue was Tant's old friend Homer Hailey, commended by the editor as "one of the finest Bible teachers ever to conduct a class."[24]

Tant acknowledged that the participation of the writers did not "mean they necessarily agree with the policy of the *Gospel Guardian*."[25] Indeed, Hailey's article, "The Church and Human Organizations," began with something of a disclaimer: "This article is submitted in the hope that it may contribute something toward a better understanding of the scripture teaching of matters before us today. It is presented in a non-partisan spirit and in the interest of love and unity among the brethren." Nonetheless, Hailey's conclusion marked him: "It is the conclusion of this writer that human organizations through which men seek to do the Lord's work are condemned."[26]

The *Gospel Guardian* remained the major vehicle for noninstitutional ideas throughout the 1950s. The paper featured brusque and ponderous onslaughts by Roy E. Cogdill, studious and detailed attacks from James W. Adams, cutting sallies by Cecil B. Douthitt, and a steady diet of noninstitutional argument written by scores of other preachers. The paper's most widely read author was unquestionably editor Yater Tant. Tant's prickly wit, encased mostly in his highly readable "Overflow" column, was often sarcastic, occasionally raucous, and very often aimed directly at B. C. Goodpasture.

The leadership of the noninstitutional movement became more diffuse in the 1950s with the appearance of several new papers. A second magazine taking the noninstitutional position, the *Preceptor,* was launched in November 1951 by a group of men associated with Florida Christian College. The panel of editors was James R. Cope, Clinton D. Hamilton, Pat Hardeman, Bill Humble, and Homer Hailey, but Cope was the leader of the group. The name of the new magazine was suggested to Cope by Foy E. Wallace, Jr.[27] Less combative than the *Gospel Guardian,* the *Preceptor* added a dimension of serious discussion to the controversy. A third journal, *Truth Magazine,* edited by Bryan Vinson, Jr., began publication in 1956. The paper was needed, Vinson wrote, because "we need a paper allowing Christ-like controversy." It was unfortunate, he wrote, that "other publications have swerved to the . . . extreme of controversy filled with bitterness, slander, and jealousy."[28] During its early years, Vinson tried to position *Truth Magazine* in "the middle of the road," refusing to "appease those who make the current issues a personal hobby."[29] Florida Christian College administrators Jim Cope and Clinton Hamilton became staff writers for *Truth Magazine,* and the journal also provided a platform for the thoughtful voice of Robert F. Turner, a widely respected preacher whose noninstitutional vision of the nature of the church left a deeper imprint on the noninstitutional churches of Christ than the thought of any other individual.[30] Finally, in 1960, two Florida preachers, H. E. Phillips and James P. Miller, began publishing *Searching the Scriptures,* a magazine that had a large circulation in the Southeast. William E. Wallace observed that by 1960 the noninstitutional revolt "could no longer accurately be called the *Guardian* movement."[31]

Most of those in the front ranks of the noninstitutional movement believed, in the words of Charles A. Holt, that "controversy is needful and right."[32] Many welcomed the idea that they were a detached, pure remnant that had freed itself from an apostate majority. Despite his reputation, Yater Tant was not one of those who coveted division. In 1951, he optimistically observed that "the clouds of doubt, misunderstanding, and suspicion are being blown away," and for several months in the early 1950s tempers did seem to cool, but the de-escalation was short-lived.[33] In spite of the *Gospel Guardian's* slashing style, Tant insisted that division could be averted if "we can continue the open, general type of discussion, with articles, sermons, and face to face conversations." In the meantime, he conjectured, "the right side is *gaining ground.*"[34] Throughout the tumultuous fifties, Tant seemed to believe that all would ultimately come to their senses and that some last-minute resolution of differences would forestall a division. In 1956, Tant backed a chimerical scheme that he saw as the "lesser of two evils": "Instead of the elders taking funds from the church treasury for such support [contributions to institutions], let them put up a box in the church vestibule, clearly marking it for whatever project they desire, and let those who want to contribute to that work do it on an individual basis, and not compel those who oppose to support the institutions." Tant's suggestion was put into practice in a few churches, but it was generally ridiculed by both friends and foes.[35] However, the idea stood as a tribute to Tant's desire for reconciliation: "We are trying with all our heart and strength to persuade brethren NOT to break fellowship over present issues, but rather to study them through with the determination to arrive at *Bible teaching,* and be united upon that basis."[36]

The Issues Joined: Responses from the Mainstream

The maturing of the institutional crisis can more or less be gauged by the editorial policies of the most widely circulated magazines in the churches of Christ during the fifties. In 1950 and 1951 both the *Gospel Advocate* and the *Firm Foundation* continued to publish articles on both sides of the issues written by such old-time preachers as W. W. Otey, John T. Lewis, G. C. Brewer, and G. H. P. Showalter.[37] In 1950, James W. Adams, a staff writer for the *Gospel Guardian,* wrote articles in the *Firm Foundation* questioning sponsoring-church arrangements.[38] Increasingly, however, the *Advocate* and the *Firm Foundation* offered only rebuttals to the stinging noninstitutional attacks that appeared in the *Guardian*. Responding to a derogatory series of *Guardian* articles, E. W. McMillan admonished, "It is good to be conscious of the danger of departures. But it is dangerous to be so danger-conscious that we do little but find fault with other people's efforts. What inspiring work has the Gospel Guardian done in a missionary way?"[39] W. W. Otey, who had written for the *Firm Foundation* for many years, complained that the editor would not publish his response to McMillan's article. He labeled Showalter's decision "about as arbitrary a piece of censorship as I have ever known."[40] Showalter disagreed with his old friend Otey, replying that he was disturbed by "this new idea [that] just started a year or so ago and on which they are threatening to divide the church." The new schismatic rhetoric was dangerous and had "no counterpart in the work of the churches sixty or seventy years ago," Showalter warned; he was determined not to aid the cause of wrecking the churches of Christ.[41] By 1952, no paper offered more than one point of view on institutionalism.

B. C. Goodpasture cautioned in 1950 that "seldom in modern times has the church been more jeopardized by 'partisans, cliques, quarrels, critics, and self-righteous snobs,' reactionaries and radicals than at the present time." The heat of the debate edged up throughout the decade as leaders on both sides grew more and more suspicious of one another's motives. G. C. Brewer characterized the *Guardian* and its writers as the "kingdom of crankdom" ruled by "defeated and frustrated preachers." Roy E. Cogdill, the publisher of the *Guardian*, replied in kind, observing that Brewer thought of himself as "one of the original twelve seated on a throne judging Israel."[42] Goodpasture became more and more convinced that "the 'anti-movement' was started by disgruntled preachers who did not get the attention they thought they deserved."[43] In a letter to B. C. Goodpasture, N. B. Hardeman, who was a world-famous horseman, observed that "Yater seems to be 'A degenerate son of a noble sire.'"[44]

Hundreds of local churches suffered through vitriolic and ugly disputes and divisions in the decade of the fifties, but none was worse than the 1951 split in the Fourth and Groesbeck Church in Lufkin, Texas, a schism that pitted Cled Wallace against Roy E. Cogdill. The two ostensible allies in the noninstitutional cause and personal friends locked in a fierce battle over the congregation.[45] Both the *Firm Foundation* and the *Gospel Advocate* published accounts of the local church squabble written from the point of view of the congregation's elders who disfellowshipped Cogdill. William E. Wallace noted that Goodpasture was "apparently delighted to receive the information and departed from his stated resolve not to publicize local church divisions to give priority to coverage of the Lufkin division."[46] Goodpasture twitted the *Guardian*, urging editor Tant to "pick up his 'versatile and pungent pen' and give us a racy account of happenings in 'East Texas'—'1951 Style.'"[47] In a letter to William E. Wallace, Tant insisted that he did not "want to argue the Lufkin trouble" and had "avoided it as much as possible." However, he acknowledged that as a result of the incident "both Foy and Cled think the *Guardian* is so compromised in the eyes of the brotherhood as to have destroyed its usefulness."[48]

For several months a stream of personal acrimony surrounding the local church division was splashed in both the *Gospel Advocate* and the *Gospel Guardian*. Cogdill charged that Goodpasture was determined "to disparage, slur, belittle, and otherwise discredit the *Gospel Guardian*, her editor, her publisher, and a number of her writers." He warned, "Be not deceived, Brother Goodpasture. Your slimy tactics will not succeed."[49] Goodpasture classified Cogdill's rhetoric as "typically Cogdillian . . . bombastic, blusterous and bitter."[50] Month after month charges and countercharges filled the two papers, ever broadening beyond the Lufkin dispute. In an article entitled "The Advocate Editor Can't Take It," Cogdill leveled a sweeping, and unlikely, accusation that the *Advocate*'s Bible school literature was "full of modernistic teaching."[51] By the end of the year, Goodpasture washed his hands of the matter, concluding that "Cogdill stands before the bar of brotherhood justice and truth, discredited and condemned as a convenient and willing medium for the circulating of gossip and slander."[52] As early as 1951, N. B. Hardeman, remembering his own ugly confrontation with Foy E. Wallace, Jr., urged Goodpasture to back away from the fight: "If you answer his

[Cogdill's] tirade, the Guardian will rejoice over personalities. They made the first personal attack and you gave such a reply that has stirred up all the venom, envy and jealousy of which they are capable. I know full well the temptation to make full reply. I had such an experience with Foy. My suggestion is that only a brief statement—or none at all—be made."[53]

To his credit, *Guardian* editor Yater Tant repeatedly tried to get the institutional debate off of personalities and back on the "principles of truth which the *Guardian* defends."[54] While neither side was able to eliminate personal vendettas from the discussion, people on both sides did try to clarify the doctrinal issues at stake. Beginning in June 1950 the *Firm Foundation* published a long and courteous series of articles written by James D. Bales, a respected Harding College professor, that challenged the noninstitutional attack on the sponsoring arrangement for missions employed by the Broadway Church in Lubbock. Bales insisted that the Gospel Guardian Corporation was a more questionable religious institution.[55]

The institutional debate reached its most substantive level in the summer of 1951. Cecil N. Wright from Denver, Colorado, began a series of nine articles that appeared in both the *Gospel Advocate* and the *Firm Foundation*. Wright had earlier written two articles charging that the noninstitutional arguments published in the *Gospel Guardian* were filled with "inconsistencies and absurdities," and he pointed out that Roy E. Cogdill had himself defended a sponsoring-church arrangement in a city-wide meeting sponsored by the Norwood congregation in the Houston City Music Hall in 1945.[56] In his long series of articles on the subject, Wright believed he had proven six points: "[First,] That the sponsoring church method of cooperation in mission work, which the Guardian has been fighting . . . is eminently scriptural. [Second,] That the Guardian itself also editorially endorsed it as scriptural as late as only eight months before it charged it with being a 'new digression" . . . [Third,] That the Guardian's charge of its being 'new' is absolutely false. [Fourth,] That the Guardian's charge of its being 'digression' . . . is equally false. [Fifth,] That the Guardian's editor and publisher have themselves made concessions that allow the very thing they have been fighting . . . [Sixth,] That the Guardian's fight . . . has not only been palpably wrong, but consummate folly."[57]

Editor Tant reviewed Wright's long series in the *Gospel Guardian*. Tant complained that Wright had used "half-quotations, plucking words and phrases out of their context" and that his articles were laden with "sarcasm, ridicule, and irony." Wrote Tant, "This type of journalism we regret and deplore." Tant had some difficulty defending the past use of sponsoring-church arrangements by Cogdill and others, but he continued to insist that the *Guardian* had no desire to divide the churches and that all he wanted was an honorable and thorough discussion of the issues.[58]

All in all, the Wright articles, combined with the strong opposition voiced by Goodpasture, clearly put the noninstitutional preachers (most often called "antis") on the defensive. Goodpasture reported that the "devastating articles . . . by Cecil N. Wright" had mortified Cogdill. "And why not?" asked Goodpasture. "One of his former writers [allegedly Cled Wallace] is quoted as saying, 'Cecil had knocked the ball out of the park. If the other boys want to go look for it, they can. I am not going to.'"[59] In the judgment of William E. Wallace, after the counterattacks of 1951, "the dissent against brotherhood projects became a minority movement carrying the burden of unfortunate images, labels, and prejudice."[60]

The vigorous defenses of institutionalism in 1951 smoothed the way for the blossoming of many programs. In the fall of 1951 the Fifth and Highland Church in Abilene began negotiating with several networks for a national radio broadcast that would feature James D. Willeford as the speaker. By the end of the year the congregation had agreed to sponsor a broadcast called the "Herald of Truth"; the first program was aired on thirty-one ABC stations in February 1952. The program was expensive and the church circulated an "urgent appeal" for aid from other congregations.[61] Because of its scope and the amount of money solicited, the "Herald of Truth" captured the hopes and fears of both sides in the sponsoring-church controversy. The program brought criticism from a number of influential preachers who had not been identified with the noninstitutional attacks of the *Gospel Guardian*, including Glenn L. Wallace and Foy E. Wallace, Jr. Glenn Wallace protested that the "Herald of Truth" clearly created an organization larger than a local church and Foy Wallace warned that the Fifth and Highland elders had presumed to become a "brotherhood eldership."[62] The *Guardian* attack on the "Herald of Truth" began with a thoughtful warning written by Robert H. Farish.[63]

The "Herald of Truth" was an enormous success among those interested in boosting the image of the churches of Christ. Its success was aided by the fact that the preacher at Fifth and Highland, Ernest R. Harper, was a man with impeccable conservative credentials and a personal friend of many of the noninstitutional leaders. Harper recalled standing with the "great army of men" who "fought together on the vital issues" during the premillennial struggle. "I have loved those men, and have understood their manner of thinking more than many who have criticized them," Harper wrote. However, those who had "so valiantly fought the battles of the church during the past twenty years" had lost the respect of the people because "too many of you boys have changed your positions too many times on too many things."[64] Harper was soon locked in a written exchange with Yater Tant, and the two subsequently conducted formal debates in Lufkin and Abilene, Texas.

Debating was a long and respected tradition in the restoration movement, and the institutional issues triggered a number of large and small debates on a variety of propositions. The first debate was held in Indianapolis in 1954 between Charles A. Holt and W. L. Totty. It was followed by a flurry of others.[65] The Harper-Tant debates in 1954 and 1955 on the question of congregational cooperation were auspicious occasions. "I fear the outcome of this debate," wrote Reuel Lemmons in the *Firm Foundation* before the 1955 discussion. "I believe we are seeing history made in the church right now. . . . This is the time for all good men to keep their heads and their senses."[66] The two men had an appreciation for the importance of their public discussions. Harper acknowledged that if the issues were not "settled *here,* it bids fair to rend the church of our Lord asunder."[67] As Lemmons predicted, the debates widened rather than narrowed the chasm in the churches; Tant was so dissatisfied with the editing done on the published volume that he labeled it "an undying monument to the trickery, deceit, and dishonesty of the modern 'promoters.'"[68]

The most noted debate on church support of orphan homes, and thus of the broader question of the relationship of congregations to independent institutions, was conducted at Phillips High School in Birmingham, Alabama, in November 1957. Roy E. Cogdill and Guy N. Woods debated both church support of orphan homes and the sponsoring-church arrangement of the "Herald of Truth."[69] The debate was published by both the *Gospel Guardian* and the *Gospel Advocate* and the two men were soon at odds about the accuracy of the other's publication.[70] Scores of other debates on the various institutional issues took place during the decade. The most noted defenders of institutional practices were Woods, Totty, Thomas B. Warren, and G. K. Wallace, and, in addition to Holt, Tant, and Cogdill, the most prominent noninstitutional debaters were W. Curtis Porter, James P. Miller, Lloyd Moyer, and Cecil B. Douthitt.

While the debates were often attended by hundreds of people and no doubt changed the minds of some in the 1950s, for the most part, they simply demarcated and solidified the two camps. Probably more important in the long run was the steady stream of articles published in the papers. Many preachers stepped forward to offer serious as well as frivolous defenses of the methods used by the churches in the 1950s. In 1954, Guy N. Woods wrote a seven-article series in the *Gospel Advocate* defending church-supported orphanages: "The Scriptures enjoin upon us the care of the fatherless and the widow; they bid us to remember the poor. They do not descend to particulars in designating *how* this work is to be done. We are thus left to our own judgment in following the procedure which appears to be most effective."[71] In 1955, Thomas Warren authored an exhaustive series in the *Advocate* on "cooperation between New Testament churches." The articles were filled with jargon-laden and complex prose, but Warren insisted that he had constructed a watertight case: "The Scriptures teach that one church may (has the right to) contribute to (send funds to) another church which has assumed (undertaken) the oversight of a work to which both churches sustained the same relationship before the assumption (undertaking) of the oversight." Warren fashioned a "syllogism" that affirmed that "all total situations the constituent elements of which are scriptural are total situations which are scriptural" and argued that eight constituent elements found in the New Testament authorized the types of congregational cooperation being practiced by churches of Christ.[72]

In hindsight, probably the single most serious effort to resolve, rather than win, the debate over institutionalism was the book *We Be Brethren,* written by Abilene Christian College Bible Professor J. D. Thomas in 1958. Thomas confessed that "all of us share to some degree in the responsibility for the tensions that exist in the BROTHERHOOD," and he urged everyone to take a new and unbiased look at the issues.[73] Thomas correctly diagnosed a hermeneutical dissonance underlying much of the rhetoric in the debate and called for a "more thorough study of interpretation."[74] Thomas's book was an essentially conservative effort to uncover the logical rudiments in restoration thinking. His most critical contention was that examples of New Testament actions were lawfully binding only when common sense determined that they were a part of

God's divine will. He believed that this important hermeneutical insight would help clarify one of the very fuzzy premises in restoration thinking and could help resolve the debate over institutional practices. Thomas torpedoed serious consideration of his hermeneutic in noninstitutional ranks by arguing that most of the current practices of the churches passed his test for New Testament authority.

Yater Tant welcomed the publication of Thomas's book, commending the author for "seeking a dignified, intelligent, and *scriptural* justification for present practices."[75] However, Roy E. Cogdill soon began an extensive review of the book, which he correctly saw as a direct challenge to his own book on hermeneutics, *Walking by Faith*. Cogdill insisted that the institutional issues were not hermeneutical, rather they were "due to a difference in attitude toward the Word of God and divine authority." Furthermore, no matter how plausible Thomas's rhetoric, his conclusions were unsatisfactory: "He accepts all that the *Gospel Advocate* and the *Firm Foundation* and the most radical among the 'Institutional' brethren advocate. His position is liberal enough to suit the most liberal among them. He disagrees with many of them in arguments made and positions taken in his effort to justify his conclusions but he reaches the same conclusions they reach, one way or another."[76]

The Vanishing Middle Ground

By the middle of the fifties the older papers circulated among the churches of Christ had formed a fairly solid front against the *Gospel Guardian* and the noninstitutional preachers. The *Firm Foundation* tried to retain contact with moderate noninstitutional preachers, though by 1955 the paper's editor, Reuel Lemmons, had endorsed the right of a church to "engage in a work larger than its local capacity."[77] Lemmons chided the "inconsistency of anti-ism," pointing out that "almost every brother" who opposed sponsoring churches and the support of institutions had in the past engaged in the practices themselves. Comparing the "antis" to such "hobbyists" of the past as proponents of the non-class movement, Lemmons urged elders to "throw off encroaching anti-ism."[78] At the same time, Lemmons consciously sought a middle ground in the increasingly intense atmosphere of the fifties. He appealed to the restoration slogan that "in opinions, liberty must be maintained" and to the equally revered principle of local autonomy. He wrote: "The same verse that speaks of 'Brotherhood Institutions' speaks also of 'Brotherhood Issues.' If brethren who are so anxious to reduce institutions to congregational size were as anxious to reduce issues to congregational size perhaps we would have made a step in the right direction. Consistency, thou art a virtue!"[79]

The *Firm Foundation* came close to carving out a middle ground in the institutional debate in 1957 when Roy H. Lanier, Sr., for many years a staff writer for the *Gospel Advocate,* proposed that all orphan homes operate under the management of a local church—as some did. Lanier wrote: "The work being done, caring for the needy, is a church work. All work of the church should be done under the oversight of the overseers of the church. But these homes under boards insist and persist in doing under the oversight of a board what should be done under the oversight of elders."[80] Reuel Lemmons endorsed Lanier's view, saying that it reflected an old Texas belief "in the all-sufficiency of the church to *do* what God commanded the church to *do.*"[81]

The Lanier articles, combined with Lemmons's endorsement, sent shock waves through the churches of Christ. In the *Gospel Advocate,* Guy N. Woods expressed "astonishment and sorrow" at the publication of Lanier's articles, constituting as they did "an attack on the position which the *Advocate* throughout its one hundred years' existence, has held and propagated touching the management and operation of homes for the care of fatherless and destitute children." If the *Firm Foundation* was seeking a new position in the middle of the road, Woods warned, the paper had occupied "the middle of the *wrong* road."[82]

In the eyes of most of the leaders in the churches of Christ who had sought to minimize the damages done by noninstitutional critics whom they regarded as fanatics, the worst fallout of the *Firm Foundation*'s new proposal was the aid and comfort it gave to the "antis." Woods warned: "Radicals and extremists among us will gleefully hail it as evidence of divided sentiment among those who have hitherto presented a solid phalanx against these troublers in Israel."[83] Woods was correct. Yater Tant boasted that the Lanier articles signaled a "hopeful turn of affairs." He wrote, "We believe it will have considerable effect in dampening any wholesale 'quarantine' campaign and give time for brethren to calm down a bit and agree to further studies and discussions. Our congratulations to both the *Gospel Advocate* and the *Firm Foundation*—each for exposing the fatal weakness in the other's position."[84] However, Tant's hope that the orphan home tiff signaled a major rift in the ranks of the enemy turned out to be wishful thinking. In May 1958 Woods announced in the *Gospel Advocate* that there had been a "meeting of minds" between the two papers. While significant differences did remain, the two papers closed ranks once again against the *Gospel Guardian*. Woods concluded, "Further usage of such phrases, by the *Guardian* and its writers, as 'the *Gospel Advocate*' position, and 'the *Firm Foundation*' position, based on the assumption that there is any basic difference between the two, will properly be attributed to a lack of information; or, deliberate disregard of facts."[85] In later years, some noninstitutional leaders concluded that "we made a terrible tactical mistake" in not pressing the breech between the *Advocate* and the *Firm Foundation*.[86]

Even after the "meeting of the minds," however, the *Firm Foundation* writers continued to display a softer attitude toward their noninstitutional brethren, holding out hopes for a compromise that would diminish tensions. The *Firm Foundation* had retained the support of many staunchly conservative western preachers who rejected the noninstitutional case. Men such as Roy H. Lanier, Sr., Eldred M. Stevens, and Johnny Ramsey had no soft side for compromise. In 1958, Lemmons wrote to Yater Tant, "I am interested in doing everything within my power to alleviate the hard feelings that have arisen in the immediate past. The heat of controversy, I feel, has produced extremes as dangerous as any of the issues involved. It is high time for something constructive." The two editors exchanged articles, published in both the *Gospel Guardian* and the *Firm Foundation,* that were forthright and friendly, though Tant's "suggested solution" to the crisis—that no one try to "activate the universal church"—was rejected out of hand by Lemmons as a semantical straw man.[87]

Lemmons allowed a number of noninstitutional preachers, including Bryan Vinson, Sr., Robert F. Turner, and Harry W. Pickup, Jr., to argue their cases in the *Firm Foundation* long after the *Gospel Advocate* had closed its pages to noninstitutional writers. In a striking series of articles in 1960, Turner delineated his highly nuanced understanding of the nature of the church universal and explained his belief that a local congregation was "God's plan for collective action of Christians."[88] Lemmons and Turner engaged in a brief and refreshingly civil exchange on the heated questions of the day. Lemmons commended Turner as "a conscientious and good man." He wrote, "We count him our friend. This does not, however, keep us from concluding that he has drawn an extreme conclusion regarding congregational cooperation and is striving hard to justify it. If brethren want to hold these views as opinions we believe they may do so, although we would not care to hold the same opinion at all. But when these opinions are taught as doctrine they must be opposed. . . . Brother Turner is a good thinker and a good writer and we are glad for the Firm Foundation readers to hear him, and urge that you give fair and unprejudiced consideration to his articles."[89] For his part, Turner was courteous and sensitive, though he believed that Lemmons missed his point that "the issue that is before us today" was not "cooperation versus non-cooperation," but "collective action versus concurrent independent action." "May God help us to study His Word carefully and prayerfully," Turner urged, "and show the full measure of love for our brothers and sisters in Christ."[90]

Five years after his exchange with Turner, Lemmons published an article written by Harry Pickup, Jr., entitled "Institutionalism: A Virulent Cancer." Echoing Turner's charge that institutional-minded Christians had come "to view the church of God as an organization rather than a relationship," Pickup forcefully defended the noninstitutional case.[91] Once again, Lemmons was touched by Pickup's argument and his manner, but he rejected the noninstitutional conclusion: "Many warnings administered by good brethren would do us lots of good if we would heed them, but when those who would warn us go too far and make charges and draw conclusions that do not fit what we are doing, nor the direction in which we are going, they do harm instead of good."[92]

All through the early 1960s Reuel Lemmons continued to insist that "we like it in the middle of the road."[93] Partly, Lemmons was frightened by the swiftness of the changes in the churches. While wholeheartedly approving of the idea that "the church is on the march," Lemmons warned, "It would . . . be a tragedy if in our marching we quit looking where we were going. We might march right off the battlefield!"[94] He was frightened by the emergence of an aggressively liberal fringe that had arisen under the leadership of Leroy Garrett, publisher of the *Restoration Review,* and Carl Ketcherside, editor of *Mission Messenger.*[95] Most of all, Lemmons wanted to "keep the door open," believing that "all shades of thinking among us have much in common."[96] He repeatedly urged everyone to stop the "narrow sectarian line drawing." He warned, "Extreme brethren seem to think that the way to fight other extremes is to cancel meetings, advise elderships against those on the other side, pack college lectureships with handpicked extremists of a given persuasion, and brand everybody not on their extreme as being with the other extreme, and fit for nothing but to be marked, branded, and if possible annihilated. Such is sheer gangsterism—not Christianity."[97] By 1960, however, Lemmons was whistling through the graveyard; the middle of the road had pretty well disappeared.

B. C. Goodpasture and the Quarantine of the "Antis"

By 1960 B. C. Goodpasture had committed the full force of the *Gospel Advocate* toward marking and quarantining the troublesome "antis." All through the 1950s the *Gospel Advocate* engaged in a campaign to limit the influence of noninstitutional preachers. The paper vacillated between ignoring the *Gospel Guardian* and publishing frontal assaults. In addition to the defenses written by Cecil N. Wright and Guy N. Woods, in the fifties, the *Advocate* featured a scholarly series by Abilene Christian College professor J. W. Roberts that explored the practices of New Testament churches and a belligerent defense of the "Herald of Truth" written by E. R. Harper.[98]

Goodpasture himself wrote little about anything, but he worked quite effectively to isolate those whom he regarded as church wreckers. The most persistent theme in Goodpasture's own writings was that the *Advocate* had continued down the trail blazed by the revered David Lipscomb and Tolbert Fanning. In 1953, for instance, he collected the writings of past editors in an article he entitled "Colleges and Orphan Homes—Who Has Changed?"[99] Goodpasture, who was an excellent student of restoration history, repeatedly reprinted the articles of former editors, including David Lipscomb and H. Leo Boles, supporting church contributions to schools and orphan homes.[100] Beyond his excursions into restoration history, Goodpasture did little to advance the debate; mostly, he parried the barrage of personal charges leveled against him by the *Guardian*, repeatedly accusing Tant and Cogdill of "unscrupulous conduct."[101]

One charge that Goodpasture did directly answer was the

Benton Cordell Goodpasture (1895–1977). Goodpasture edited the *Gospel Advocate* for thirty-eight years and probably wielded more influence over the churches of Christ than any other person for three decades after World War II. A master of church politics, Goodpasture skillfully isolated the critics of institutionalism in the 1950s and 1960s, believing them to be embittered and irresponsible fanatics. (Courtesy of the Disciples of Christ Historical Society.)

accusation that he had closed the columns of the *Advocate* to all writers who opposed his views, essentially quarantining all dissent. A few moderate opponents of institutionalism, including James P. Miller, Franklin T. Puckett, Benjamin Lee Fudge, Homer Hailey, Clinton Hamilton, and James R. Cope, sustained a strained relationship with the magazine until near the end of the decade, sending in occasional reports and writing infrequent articles. Nonetheless, in the 1950s the *Advocate* never pretended to have an open editorial policy. In 1953, Goodpasture defended the paper's editorial policy: "It is not the policy of the Gospel Advocate to print everything that is sent to its offices for publication. . . . We do not feel that we are obligated to furnish a medium for radicals and hobbyists to ventilate their hobbies, nor are we obligated to become an agency for the dissemination of error. . . . When the farmer gets ready to sow a bushel of wheat, it is not necessary for him to sow a bushel of weeds in order to be fair."[102]

In the 1950s, B. C. Goodpasture blossomed as a man with masterful managerial skills. In November 1954 Goodpasture published in the *Gospel Advocate* a letter from a well-known elder suggesting that a "quarantine" be leveled against all preachers who "are sowing the seeds of discord among the brotherhood."[103] Goodpasture embraced the idea and the *Gospel Advocate* began to exert immense pressure on preachers to renounce "antism." In September 1957, historian Earl Irvin West announced that after two years of "re-studying" the issues, he had concluded that he could not "prove that the type of cooperation represented by the Herald of Truth violates a New Testament principle." Goodpasture praised West's "forthright pronouncement of his convictions" and hoped that his "example will encourage others to make similar announcements."[104]

In the months that followed, the *Advocate* published a deluge of confessions from preachers well-known and little-known, including Charles H. Lucas, G. F. Raines, Hugo McCord, W. C. Anderson, Charles E. Crouch, John Cox, Rex Turner, and Jack Meyer, Sr. Goodpasture relished each dispatch from "these good brethren who have been courageous and clear in their statements concerning their change of convictions." Sometimes the exchanges seemed to offer a quid pro quo. When Charles E. Crouch's renunciation of "antism" appeared, Goodpasture noted that Crouch was "one of our best young preachers" and added, "Any congregation needing an able and successful preacher would do well to get in touch with Brother Crouch."[105]

The coup de grace in the *Gospel Advocate* series labeled "confessionals" by noninstitutional preachers came with the publication of a statement written in March 1958 by Pat Hardeman. Hardeman, who had recently resigned from the faculty of Florida Christian College, was one of the ablest and most acclaimed young preachers among the noninstitutional churches. Goodpasture commended Hardeman as "one of the most gifted young men in the church today," assuring readers that the charges of "modernism" that had been leveled against him were false. Hardeman ended his personal statement with an appeal: "I entreat my brethren associated with the *Gospel Guardian* with whose views I formerly agreed and for which I formerly contended, to restudy the criteria for binding examples and to realize the presumptuousness of binding where God loosed. . . . I also hope that many of my former colleagues of Florida Christian College . . . will abandon their extreme views which have caused them dwindling support from members of the church."[106] Goodpasture savored the defection of Hardeman and gave him free reign to attack the school in the *Gospel Advocate.*[107] After a second article by Pat Hardeman appeared in the paper, his uncle, N. B. Hardeman, wrote to Goodpasture: "Pat has scored again. His article of Sept. 4th will cause Tant and Cope no little trouble. It may turn out that it was good for him to have been one of them and now knows whereof he speaks."[108]

Pat Hardeman's second article was a scathing denunciation of the "dogmatism" of the *Guardian,* but he quickly became a liability to the *Gospel Advocate.*[109] Hardeman's flight from his former conservatism was so rapid that by the time his second article appeared in the *Gospel Advocate* he had become a minister in the Unitarian Fellowship. At that point, Goodpasture was forced to retract his earlier assurances that Hardeman was no "modernist."[110] Goodpasture noted the change in the *Gospel Advocate* because "we have carried articles by Brother Hardeman and commended him for his renunciation of the hobbies which have caused disturbances in some sections of the country." "We cannot say," Goodpasture concluded, "how much the persecution of his erstwhile companions in hobby-ism contributed" to his "present condition."[111]

Hardeman's defection in particular, and the inauguration of the confessional column in general, turned up the heat in the institutional crisis. James P. Miller, a widely known evangelist who worked with the Seminole Church in Tampa, criticized the *Advocate* for championing Pat Hardeman's "cause against every loyal preacher and congregation in the city of Tampa." Goodpasture answered Miller with a blatant political warning: "Churches which have been using him [Miller] with some misgivings as to his stand on the hobbies will now know where his heart is. Some of the FCC teachers have had twelve or fifteen meetings canceled on account of their hobbies. Miller need not be surprised if he shares their experience. If he does, he will have the satisfaction of knowing how he brought it on himself."[112] Noninstitutional preachers were outraged by Goodpasture's calculated exercise of political power. Cecil B. Douthitt wrote in the *Gospel Guardian,* "The proof that a great host of timeservers and moral cowards will follow Goodpasture down the broad road of popularity regardless of how crummy his logic (?) may be is so abundant that it cannot be denied successfully. . . . To see turncoats like Earl West, John Cox, Rex Turner and several others bow down in Goodpasture's 'confessional', kiss his toe . . . is more than nauseating."[113] By the end of the 1950s, most noninstitutional preachers marked Goodpasture and the *Gospel Advocate* as the chief culprits in drawing lines and splitting the churches of Christ. Roy E. Cogdill charged that Goodpasture thought he was the "pope" of the churches of Christ and that he had used the "quarantine" to "intimidate all the preachers of the brotherhood who refused to 'line up' on the institutional issues."[114] From the perspective of the other side, the "bitterness, wrath, anger, and clamor" of Douthitt's and Cogdill's articles marked noninstitutionalism as a narrow, divisive and self-destructive movement.[115]

From B. C. Goodpasture's point of view, his actions were a

reasonable and responsible effort to save the churches from the pillaging of radicals and extremists. Goodpasture came to view the noninstitutional clique as a cancer to be excised. He delayed for years before criticizing a few popular preachers who quietly held noninstitutional views, including Homer Hailey and James P. Miller, but by the end of the decade, his patience was exhausted. In 1959, G. K. Wallace summed up the *Advocate* policy on the front page of the paper: "To my knowledge, there is not a single preacher who holds to these divisive doctrines who will agree to refrain from teaching what he believes *publicly and privately*. By agreeing to abstain from preaching his hobby in the pulpit he is simply agreeing to forbear his false doctrine at a *certain time*. The false teacher is not so much concerned as to the *time* he may spread his divisive teaching as he is the opportunity to teach it *some time*."[116] Despite the temporizing of Reuel Lemmons in the *Firm Foundation*, Goodpasture was ready to draw lines. In 1958, the *Advocate* published a "restrictive clause for deeds to meetinghouse property." The creed-like document included two general statements of loyalty to "the teaching and practice of the New Testament" and three telltale statements that highlighted Goodpasture's understanding of the historic divides in the movement: "[Three,] No mechanical instrument of music shall be used in the worship. [Four,] The support of such organizations as care for orphans, dependent children, aged and sick, shall not be opposed or forbidden. [Five,] The doctrine of premillennialism shall not be taught, or otherwise approved or encouraged."[117]

In 1958 a new militant paper, the *Spiritual Sword,* began publication, marking another landmark in the move to seal off noninstitutional critics. Edited by Thomas Warren, who at the time was preaching in Fort Worth, the paper's purpose was stated in the first issue: "At the present time, the *Spiritual Sword* is especially concerned with the creed-making being done by various brethren in the realm of church cooperation and orphan homes. The staff of this paper is vitally concerned with the way men have divided churches, alienated brethren, and sought to hinder good works of churches helping one another in the preaching of the Gospel and of churches sending funds to orphan homes so that the needs of children might be adequately supplied."[118] Goodpasture was elated that Warren had taken up the task of bashing the "antis"; he lavishly commended the staff that would be writing for the new paper: William S. Banowsky, Roy C. Deaver, A. G. Hobbs, M. Lloyd Smith, Bill L. Rogers, and E. R. Harper. Goodpasture urged churches to distribute the new polemical journal: "Congregations would do well to buy a supply of each issue of the *Sword,* especially if they are being disturbed by the 'Antis.'"[119]

The Dynamics of Division

Whatever the intentions or desires of moderates and middle-of-the-roaders, by 1958 a division over institutionalism was inevitable. When Reuel Lemmons opened the 1958 volume of the *Firm Foundation* with the statement that "this great brotherhood of Christ is not about to have a doctrinal division," Yater Tant asked incredulously, "Is the man blind to the facts?" Even though many, including Tant, remained "keenly interested in trying to avoid any such possibility," the *Guardian* editor admitted that "a 'major division' seems certain."[120]

Many people were saddened and disillusioned by the prospect of division. In the late 1950s preachers came under intense pressure to decide which side they would support. "Politics and pressure will subdue the vitality of the Lord's Army," warned Johnny Ramsey in the *Firm Foundation*. Disgusted by the coercion from both sides to conform to an "unwritten creed," Ramsey plaintively longed for better: "I keep hoping that there will always be a place for those of us who are neither 'anti' nor 'anti-anti.' Either of these camps spends too much time on issues and not enough on Christ. To summarize we simply say: The church needs more back-bone and fewer promoters. Fewer crusaders and contenders; more peacemakers and humble servants of God."[121] But it was not to be.

The ties between the two wings of the churches of Christ were extremely fragile by the end of the decade of the fifties. Wishing to use the papers to help him gather biographical information for a new directory of preachers in churches of Christ, which was published in 1959, Batsell Barrett Baxter wrote to Yater Tant, "If you can see fit to include the enclosed announcement [requesting preachers to register] in a forthcoming issue of the *Guardian* both Norvel Young and I (editors) will appreciate it. We do not wish—in this publication, or elsewhere—to draw a line, excluding our brethren with whom we do not agree on certain brotherhood issues." Tant published the announcement, seeing the offer as "a useful move in counteracting the influence and efforts of those who are seeking to promote a 'quarantine.'"[122] However, few noninstitutional preachers returned biographical information for the revised directory.

As the lines of division became clearer in the early 1960s, the noninstitutional movement probably included slightly more than ten percent of the membership of the churches of Christ. Many of the more progressive leaders in the churches of Christ willingly sloughed off the "antis," who had become an embarrassing fringe. They believed that the noninstitutional movement would implode and wither away. However, others recognized that the division was weighty, including as it did the defection of Florida Christian College and, in the words of B. C. Goodpasture's biographer, J. E. Choate, "some of the finest preachers of this century."[123]

The division was followed by a predictable period of finger-pointing and assessments of blame. Noninstitutional preachers laid the blame on the *Gospel Advocate* and Goodpasture's quarantine campaign. Increasingly, mainstream leaders used prejudicial rhetoric to marginalize the noninstitutional camp, branding them as cranks. In 1960, Robert F. Turner complained that "prejudicial name-calling and 'straw-man' argumentation" had become the order of the day. He wrote, "Many brethren today have been so frightened by the name 'Anti' that they will disown their brothers and sisters in Christ rather than risk being called this 'bad name'!! . . . If you can't answer the argument, call him 'Anti!' If you covet their members, call the congregation 'Anti!' MAY GOD HAVE MERCY UPON OUR SOULS."[124] Indeed, by the end of the fifties the *Gospel Advocate* linked noninstitutional arguments with every eccentric schism that had occurred in the churches of Christ. Ira Y. Rice, Jr., was master of the art of tarring the "antis" with a brush of guilt by association: "I care not what phase of church function you bring up, from *anti-women-teachers* to *anti-teaching-the-Bible-in-classes* to *anti-more-than-one-container-in-the-Lord's-Supper* to *anti-Bible-colleges* to *anti-special-songs* to *anti-orphan-homes* to *anti-standing-when-you-pray* to *anti-paid-preachers* to *anti-this* or *anti-that*—you name the function, and we in the churches of Christ can name a faction that has risen up among us during the past one hundred years contending it had to be done *just one way* to the exclusion of all other ways."[125] Robert C. Welch, replying to charges that noninstitutional preachers were "drawing lines," protested: "We 'iconoclasts' are . . . recognizing the line which they have already drawn."[126]

For all of his moderation, Reuel Lemmons believed that it was the noninstitutional group, led by "Yater Tant and the Gospel Guardian," that wanted to establish a "faction" and sever "fellowship with the body of Christ." He wrote, "We get sick of self-righteous brethren referring to themselves as 'the Loyal Church,' or announcing 'the only faithful church' in a city filled with churches. It is nauseating when some brother announces that he is going to a place filled with churches of Christ to start a 'faithful church.' If these people are the only ones faithful to the Lord, then the Lord started a vicious, sarcastic, egotistic, self-centered and divisive thing, and what he bought with his blood was so ugly it certainly can lay no claim to being a beautiful bride."[127] Disgusted by such church-splitting tactics, moderates like Lemmons felt that they had no choice but to isolate the rabble rousers and minimize the damage.[128]

By 1961, Yater Tant was ready to accept the division, believing that it had "weeded out" the "time-serving, self-seeking, materialistic element" in the churches. He wrote, "Brethren who are concerned for the purity of the church may well feel a deep gratitude toward brethren Guy N. Woods, E. R. Harper, B. C. Goodpasture, and others who have been so vigorous in applying the 'financial pressure' argument to compel preachers to 'line up' behind their institutions. Under the providential hand of God such measures will have purified the church, getting the self-seeking time-servers into one group, and leaving men of true consecration to go about the task of re-building the broken churches."[129] Beginning in the 1960s most members of noninstitutional churches of Christ began to refocus on building new congregations, more often than not leaving the local churches they had attended for many years to begin anew.

In the midst of the debating and recrimination of the 1950s, it was difficult to focus on the broader pressures that had caused such severe stresses in the restoration movement. Reuel Lemmons insisted that all churches of Christ in the 1950s still adhered to "the same attitude toward the authority of the Scriptures," that "the saints all still believe the same things," and that the noninstitutional division should not have reached such an impasse.[130] Tant labeled Lemmons's statement an "incredible assessment,"[131] and it was clearly a flawed reading of the mind of the movement. Major divisions in churches of Christ do not occur when the movement is of one basic mind, even though people harbor serious disagreements about applications of the restoration principle. Most of the doctrinal issues involved in the noninstitutional split had been debated for decades. Why, Lemmons wondered, could like-minded brethren no longer live together civilly discussing these matters as they had in the past? The answer, which became clearer in the sixties, was that Lemmons's assumption that "the saints all still believe the same things" was quite incorrect.

Changing Leadership Styles

Lemmons certainly had reason for judging that the essential unity of the churches of Christ remained intact in 1960. On the surface, throughout the fifties, all leaders in the churches of Christ appeared to honor the basic truths preached by earlier generations. Earl West described the ideological unity of the decade: "The Christians of this period . . . worried about liberal theology moving into the church. They believed in the Bible as the source of God's religion. They held the view that Bible knowledge was supremely important and that it was attainable with diligent study."[132] For two decades after the end of World War II, a vast majority of the members of churches of Christ seemingly embraced both the past and the movement's mushrooming array of programs and institutions.

If the rhetoric heard in churches of Christ had a familiar ring in the fifties, attitudes had changed dramatically. The churches of the postwar years basked in the glow of a growing recognition and respectability and exuded a self-confidence bordering on euphoria. As in most American churches in the prosperous and conservative Eisenhower era, the membership of churches of Christ swelled and congregational budgets rose precipitously. The leaders of the postwar churches that embraced institutionalism were a different breed who mouthed old slogans in new and softer styles.

Clinton Davidson's survey of ministers in 1937 uncovered a deep generational gulf among the preachers in the churches of Christ. Eighty percent of the preachers polled believed that articles in religious journals should be written by people "trained specifically to write such articles, articles that will favorably affect those who are not already Christians."[133] By 1945, many congregations employed college-educated preachers, paying them comfortable salaries, and a generation of pioneer preachers found themselves being patronized by a new breed.

Tensions between the older pioneer preachers and the more professional new breed had been brewing for years. In 1930, J. D. Tant observed that the Apostle Paul would have been out of place in the company of the rising generation of "located ministers, having beautiful homes, fine cars, [and] two or three hundred dollar salaries each month."[134] Tant, who ended most of his articles with the warning "We are drifting," regularly scored the younger generation. In a typically prickly notice in the *Firm Foundation* in 1940, Tant announced that he had been farming all year and wished to hold six meetings during the summer. He listed his limitations, in case some congregations were interested in his services:

> I don't hope to hold big meetings, as I note quite a number of big preachers begging for work through each issue of the Firm Foundation. If any old time church of Christ, run down at the heels and sticking out at the toes would appreciate an old time gospel meeting, the kind I have had for the past fifty years, I would be glad to help you. Don't expect to get any calls from big churches who want college preachers, for I don't belong in that class. I suppose the reason I haven't a college education and a degree is the fact that I was a first class gospel preacher and debater eight years before we set our first preacher incubator to hatch our college preachers wanting located jobs. . . . But if we have no such churches I can still have work in the cotton field and hold a position that none of my brethren would desire.[135]

Even J. D. Tant's friends marked him as "a rantankerous [*sic*] old maverick." It was all right to "love him," warned Cled Wallace, but one should "approach him from the fore, not the rear, as you would a mule, or else he'll kick you clear over the corral."[136] However, Tant's apprehensions about "college preachers" were shared by an entire generation of his peers. In 1941, sixty-nine-year-old H. D. Jackson of Fort Smith, Arkansas, published a notice in the *Firm Foundation* that he was "looking for work." Noting that he was "old, but not too old yet, to be active in debate," Jackson identified his "class" of preachers: "I have never been in the 'high priced preacher ranks.' So should you be in need of a preacher in my class for a summer meeting, regardless of where, or what your financial condition may be, I may be available."[137]

Economic and cultural prejudices mingled easily with doctrinal concerns in the minds of those who felt the church was becoming soft. In his opening volley in the *Gospel Guardian* in October 1935, Foy E. Wallace, Jr., warned, "Our preachers are becoming mere pastors, presidents of Ministerial Associations, stage performers and star actors at worldly clubs."[138] When he launched the *Bible Banner,* Wallace focused on the "general softness" that was "pervading the church": "Firm and plain preaching, once universal and unanimous among those devoted to the ancient gospel, are now yielding to the persuasions of the plush-mouthed and velvet-tongued moderns among us who piously admonish us to 'speak the truth in love.'"[139] G. H. P. Showalter agreed that "commercialized professionalism" among preachers was one of the clearest dangers facing the churches by the end of the 1930s.[140] At the other end of the spectrum, always in guarded language, college spokesmen defended upgrading the quality of preachers. In 1933, H. Leo Boles, president of David Lipscomb College, stated the college case in the *Gospel Advocate:* "Surely no one can afford to become the champion of ignorance and plead for unlearned men to enter the pulpit and become very inefficient leaders and preachers of the gospel."[141]

By the 1950s the balance had clearly tilted toward better training for preachers; most believed, with Glenn L. Wallace, that "in this day of increased missionary efforts and membership with better educations," preachers should no longer "continue to repeat in unaltered form what our frontiersmen-fathers set forth as the full gospel," but rather they should "shift to a new emphasis in our preaching and thinking."[142] The colleges quickly grasped the influence they gained by being the source of "college trained preachers." In 1947, Abilene Christian College fund-raiser Robert M. Alexander estimated that "Christian colleges" had trained ninety-five percent of those preaching. Even those who had not had the "advantage of training in a Christian college are able to see that they have missed much and are therefore inefficient from the lack of proper preparation," Alexander concluded in a fit of hyperbole.[143]

By the decade of the fifties the churches of Christ were led by a new generation of preachers and educators who, in the words of historian Robert E. Hooper, were "men with a new vision."[144] Younger men such as M. Norvel Young, Batsell Barrett Baxter, Willard Collins, and Ira North "possessed different qualities, including a wider worldview," attributes appreciated by the powerful editor of the *Gospel Advocate*, B. C. Goodpasture.[145] In his study of preaching in the churches of Christ, Michael W. Casey found that during the decade of the fifties, "the 'hard' gospel of the debaters—the 'truth-oriented' approach—changed into the 'soft' gospel that is more person-centered."[146] A new generation of preachers who had received "speech training" at the colleges from "homiletics teachers trained in the neo-Aristotelian method of rhetorical criticism" transformed the preaching in churches of Christ.[147] Baxter, "the master of the relaxed style, which played so well on television," became the model for the new generation of "soft" preachers. His book, *Speaking for the Master*, published in 1954, was a manual for those who wished to put the churches of Christ before their neighbors in a more favorable light.[148]

The Changing Social Profile of Churches of Christ

Historian Robert E. Hooper captured the triumphalist mood during the postwar expansion of the churches of Christ: "The fifteen years ending with 1965 were indeed tremendous for the growth and development of churches of Christ. During the decade and a half, churches of Christ became more visible than ever before across the United States and around the world."[149] It was a time to cherish, wrote Reuel Lemmons: "The church is no longer smothered in insignificance. Brethren are forced to cease their praying thus: 'Lord, comfort the faithful few.'"[150]

During the two decades after World War II, the churches of Christ grew rapidly, as did most religious groups in America. In 1951, the *Yearbook of American Churches* estimated the membership of the group at one million in 14,500 congregations, noting that the churches of Christ "do not collect or furnish statistics."[151] By 1970, Frank S. Mead's *Handbook of Denominations* estimated that the group's membership had risen to 1,500,000 members in 10,000 congregations. According to Mead, the churches of Christ had "emerged as one of the top ten non-Catholic bodies in America."[152] These estimates of church membership were largely subjective guesses by church leaders and there was a good deal of boosterism in the soaring numbers, but the hundreds of reports by evangelists heralding thousands of additions to the churches during the years from 1930 to 1970 were more than mere embellishment.

M. Norvel Young, a notable preacher and, after 1957, president of George Pepperdine College, was one of the leading publicists of the church's successes. In a 1957 article about the churches of Christ written for the *Encyclopedia Britannica Yearbook,* Young estimated that one thousand buildings had been constructed or enlarged during the preceding year. In the same article Young judged that the membership of the churches of Christ had reached 1,650,000 people in 15,500 congregations. While Young's estimates may have been inflated, his projections buoyed enthusiasm and reflected the growing denominational spirit in the church.[153] Others fueled the speculation about church growth. In 1959, B. C. Goodpasture estimated that the churches of Christ had two mil-

M. Norvel Young (1915–1988). Young was one of the great builders in the post–World War II churches of Christ. In 1950, while he was serving as minister of the Broadway Church of Christ in Lubbock, Texas, that congregation built the largest sanctuary constructed by a local church of Christ up to that time. Young encouraged a church building boom all over the country. In 1970 he became president of Pepperdine University where he supervised the building of a spectacular new campus in Malibu, California. (Courtesy of the Center for Restoration Studies, Abilene Christian University.)

lion members;[154] by the mid-1960s the membership of the churches of Christ probably reached about 2,350,000.[155]

While all of these estimates of church growth were anecdotal, it was clear that the churches were booming. Each year the papers reported thousands of baptisms and hundreds of new congregations being planted, and the budgets of some of the large congregations soared into hundreds of thousands of dollars. By 1953, the budget of the Broadway Church in Lubbock had passed two hundred thousand dollars and several other congregations, including Central in Houston, Hillsboro in Nashville, and Skillman Avenue in Dallas, passed one hundred thousand dollars.[156] Interest in foreign missions soared after the war, and the number of workers supported outside the United States ballooned from fewer than fifty in 1945 to about eight hundred by the 1970s.[157]

On the basis of this evidence, demographers generally cited the churches of Christ as one of the fastest-growing religious groups in the nation. In a prominent series of articles published by *Life* magazine in 1958, Union Theological Seminary President Henry P. Van Dusen included the churches of Christ as a part of the conservative religious revival in America, which he labeled the "third force in Christendom." The fifties religious boom, Van Dusen argued, was spearheaded by a highly visible revival among evangelicals symbolized by Billy Graham's crusades, by an unnoticed surge of Pentecostals exemplified by Oral Roberts's healing campaigns, and by the rapid growth of such conservative groups as the churches of Christ and Mormons.[158] When Dean Kelley wrote *Why Conservative Churches Are Growing* in 1972, the day of unbridled growth in conservative churches, which paralleled the political conservatism of the 1950s, was probably past, but the phenomenon he chronicled was real and the churches of Christ shared in the general expansion of conservative religion during the fifties and sixties.[159]

No one better captured the ebullient spirit in the churches of Christ in the postwar years than Ira North, minister of the Madison Church of Christ in suburban Nashville for more than thirty years.[160] Under North's leadership, which began in 1952, the Madison Church grew from four hundred members to more than four thousand; in May 1982 the congregation celebrated a record attendance of 8,410. The Madison megachurch sponsored numerous teaching and benevolent programs and in 1971 launched a national television broadcast called the "Amazing Grace Bible Class," which was aired in 265 markets throughout the country. North was flamboyant and dynamic, earning the nickname "Firey Ira"; in 1959, he wrote a manual celebrating church growth, *You Can March*

Ira North (1922–1984). North became the minister of the Madison, Tennessee, Church of Christ in 1952 and built it into the largest congregation in the nation. Nicknamed "Fiery Ira" because of his flamboyant style, North was the personification of the "on the march" mood of the fifties. (Courtesy of the Center for Restoration Studies, Abilene Christian University.)

for the Master.[161] Often a target of ridicule from conservatives, North refused to be diverted from his goal of building a large and tranquil church, and he earned the plaudits of many church leaders. Reuel Lemmons chided North's critics: "Most such remarks are made by those who are neither on the march nor willing for the Lord's people to be. The Madison church has literally marched off and left its critics."[162] North, a consummate promoter and showman, fostered an ongoing contest during the 1950s between the Madison Church and the Broadway Church in Lubbock, Texas, for the title "biggest church of Christ in the world." "Bigness is the hallmark of the North touch," reported the *Christian Chronicle* in an article about the Madison congregation. North was the "spark plug" of the church growth crusade of the fifties, a man whose "innovative ideas" were both effective and controversial.[163]

In many ways, "bigness" defined the institutional boom in the churches of Christ in the 1950s. Unconsciously, people on both sides of the institutional division recognized it. The "on the march" mentality clashed sharply with noninstitutional thinking that still contained a sharp sense of cultural dissonance and world separation. Cleon Lyles complained that such negativism reflected poorly on the image of the churches of Christ: "When brethren air their difficulties before the world they are obscuring the greatness of the church because of their littleness. . . . We may not ever make such an impression on others as we would like, but the one thing within the reach of all is bigness."[164]

Another highly publicized church-building project of the 1950s that symbolized the dynamics of growth in the churches of Christ was a campaign to provide a building for the congregation meeting on Manhattan Island. Well-known preacher Burton Coffman became "minister of the Manhattan Church of Christ" in 1955 and immediately launched the "Manhattan Church of Christ Expansion Program," requesting congregations around the country to "put Manhattan . . . in your budget." Coffman sought to make the Manhattan church building a test of the commitment of the churches of Christ to growth and respectability. Noting that the "oldest Church of Christ in Manhattan has less than seventy-five members and still worships in a converted residence," Coffman warned, "There is no cheap way to win for Christ in the skyscraper canyons of Gotham. To succeed, we must pray and work night and day, weep for the lost multitudes, and buy our way with gold." Reuel Lemmons commended the Manhattan campaign in the *Firm Foundation:* "New York is a mighty city. The people of New York, like the people of Washington, or any other great city, are hard to reach and hard to impress from the confines of a rented upstairs room, or the side room to a beer parlor! Must the Lord appear to them in rags? Even for the morale of the Saints who labor there respectability is a 'must.' We can hardly expect to reach the people with the gospel until we have respectable means of reaching them."[165] Others agreed. George Benson, president of Harding College, urged churches around the country to "put the work in New York City on the map." G. C. Brewer made it clear that "brotherhood" pride and respectability was on the line in New York City: "No 'brotherhood' can remain permanently unaffected by an inferior status in a world center like New York City. Either, we shall rise and develop stronger congregations there, or the failure to do so will eventually cast a shadow over the entire church."[166]

No one did more to encourage the building of new buildings in the postwar years than M. Norvel Young. While he was serving as the minister of the Broadway Church of Christ in Lubbock, Texas, the congregation completed in 1950 an impressive auditorium that would seat twenty-one hundred people. Young urged congregations across the country to adopt positive, growth-oriented ideas. At the Abilene Christian College lectureship in 1947, Young conducted a workshop on the building of church buildings, urging postwar churches not to select building sites on the basis of "low cost" but rather to choose locations that would give the congregations the "highest visibility."[167] In 1957 Young and James Marvin Powell published a celebration of the building boom in the churches of Christ, *The Church Is Building,* in which they reported the construction since 1940 of one thousand new church buildings valued at $147 million. Many of these new buildings were equipped with the latest technology and included kitchens and other recreational and social facilities to accommodate a growing array of social activities.[168] Each week during the 1950s, papers featured pictures of the parade of new church buildings from around the country.

Church-sponsored institutions and programs, having survived the attacks of the noninstitutional minority, were both agents of change and symbols of the booming denominational pride. M. Norvel Young's 1965 entry on the churches of Christ in the *Encyclopedia Britannica Yearbook* told mostly of the successes of "large evangelistic campaigns," the "intensified" use of radio and television, and the "increased enrollment" in the movement's "five major colleges, the three graduate schools, and the 16 junior colleges operated by members of the churches of Christ."[169] The older church-supported colleges continued to grow in size, wealth, and prestige, and the number of schools supported by churches multiplied during the fifties and sixties. In 1950 five colleges (excluding Florida Christian College) were being supported by American churches, though the amount of money contributed by churches was always small. By 1965 the number had grown to seventeen colleges in the United States, two in Canada, and one in Japan.[170]

No cooperative, sponsoring-church venture had a deeper impact on the churches than the "Herald of Truth" radio and television broadcast. The dream of James Walter Nichols and James D. Willeford, the national radio program began airing in the fall of 1951 under the sponsorship of the Fifth and Highland Church of Abilene. In 1954, the "Herald of Truth" television program was launched on twenty stations. Fairly conventional in its early years, the program reached a new level of sophistication and visibility in 1959 when Batsell Barrett Baxter became the featured speaker. Robert E. Hooper's assessment of the significance of the "Herald of Truth," which by the mid-sixties was aired on about 150 television stations, captured the relevance of the program to many members of churches of Christ: "By 1965, Herald of Truth and Batsell Barrett Baxter were well established on the national scene, giving greater visibility to churches of Christ."[171]

Baxter, who was head of the Bible Department at David Lipscomb College, had received a doctoral degree in speech from the University of Southern California and a bachelor of divinity degree from the Divinity School at Vanderbilt University. One of the most widely known preachers among churches

Batsell Barrett Baxter (1916–1982). The son of a noted educator, Baxter was the speaker on the "Herald of Truth" radio and television programs from 1960 to 1981. His conversational style and irenic nature were well suited to present the churches of Christ to the nation in a less confrontational manner. A speech and Bible teacher at David Lipscomb University, Baxter influenced a generation of preachers. (Courtesy of the Center for Restoration Studies, Abilene Christian University.)

of Christ, Baxter spoke with dignity, moderation, and quiet fervor. While Baxter used language that was easily recognizable to the average member of the churches of Christ, Richard T. Hughes argued that, in time, "the content of the preaching changed much." Increasingly, Baxter and others associated with the "Herald of Truth" embraced "the sort of 'peace-of-mind' piety that had dominated the national religious landscape for more than a decade." The program "focused on issues pertaining to self-esteem, anxiety, marriage and the family, and the like," eschewing traditional doctrinal preaching. The national broadcast had immense influence throughout the country, begetting, in the words of Hughes, a generation of "electronic bishops" in the churches of Christ. As the emphasis of the broadcasts turned more irenic and toward social consciousness, "pulpit preachers throughout the fellowship of Churches of Christ quickly followed suit."[172]

The "Herald of Truth" was a consummate triumph for the booster mentality of the 1950s. As early as 1954, Reuel Lemmons had grasped the denominational significance of having a national radio program: "I am happy to be a member of the church of Christ. I am glad to see it grow until the most powerful radio networks on earth regularly carry the plea of religious liberty and religious unity for which I stand."[173] The dream grew in the years ahead. In 1959, "Herald of Truth" fund-raiser Paul Hunton announced that the two-million-strong churches of Christ had the ability to "preach the gospel to every creature in our generation." Hunton was ecstatic about the potential of television: "The Lord willing, 100,000,000 souls can hear the gospel each week. . . . The cost is nominal. One hundred dollars a month from a church will preach the gospel to 75,000 people each week. One dollar will reach 3,000. A potential audience of 100,000,000 can listen to the gospel each week in 1960 for $1,461,068.32."[174]

The Upswing in Denominational Consciousness

The spread of institutionalism and the growth of denominational pride were companion pieces. As Richard Hughes put it: "By the early 1950s, Churches of Christ were not only establishing institutions to serve a variety of causes but were establishing the church itself as a formidable institution on the religious landscape."[175] The rhetoric of church leaders made it quite clear that the explosive growth of churches and institutions in the churches of Christ after World War II was accompanied by an overt denominational consciousness and a conspicuous sense of self-importance. Paul Hunton's appeal for support for the "Herald of Truth" in 1959 noted that Billy

Graham spent $2 million each year on television and radio, that the Lutheran Church spent $2.2 million and that the Roman Catholic Church produced 598 "film episodes for the armed services alone."[176] It was time for the churches of Christ to learn "that we can do great things for the Lord." Joe K. Alley wrote in the *Gospel Advocate,* "For years we watched our religious neighbors build fine church buildings. We saw them send their preachers by the score to foreign fields. We listened to their coast-to-coast broadcasts. Now *we* know that they are not the only ones who can do these things. *We* can, too. . . . An inferiority complex is a miserable thing. It seems that there was a time when the church had such a complex. But now we see that we have the ability, the resources, the faith and everything else necessary *to do* great things."[177]

By the 1950s the churches of Christ had become richly heterogeneous. Still comprising mostly lower-middle-class working people, urban congregations included growing numbers of successful businessmen and professionals and a few Texas oil tycoons. "Even twenty-five years ago," wrote the editor of the *Christian Chronicle* in 1946, "we had very few substantial church buildings and the most of those we had were located on back streets of the cities and towns." After the war, things changed: "We now have substantial buildings located on important streets in many cities" and "a number of orphanages have been established." He urged the generation of postwar preachers to awaken these "lazy churches," now housed in "splendid buildings," to a grander vision of the future.[178]

In 1946, when the Census Bureau began collecting data for a census of religious bodies in the United States, which was never completed, M. Norvel Young urged small congregations to return the forms mailed to them by the government and to provide the Census Bureau with the names of additional congregations that had not received forms, which he believed numbered in the thousands. Young and other knowledgeable leaders in the churches of Christ believed that the 1936 census had badly underestimated the membership of the churches of Christ. Young insisted that there was much to gain by being fully counted: "We know that some kind of picture of the churches of Christ will be given in this Census and we believe that a reasonably correct and complete picture will be a great encouragement to those who are pleading for a restoration of New Testament Christianity, and that it will make it possible for gospel preachers to gain more time on the radio and more consideration from the government in regard to mission work in foreign lands and in many other ways in the next ten years."[179] The Broadway minister reminded the churches that there was "power in numbers."[180]

In the minds of progressive church leaders, the new standing of the churches of Christ and the rising social status of the church's members presented opportunities and required changes. "We have found it easy to give recently," wrote the editor of the *Christian Chronicle,* "because we had plenty."[181] In 1945, Little Rock minister Ulrich R. Beeson urged the churches to build "bigger buildings" because the returning veterans would "expect larger and better built classrooms and auditoriums to which they can take their friends without embarrassment." "Bigger budgets" were needed, Beeson argued, so the churches of Christ could "send more preachers out into the world."[182] When the Broadway Church decided to sponsor the postwar evangelization of Europe, the aim of the elders to "help increase the vision, strengthen the faith and prepare the hearts of the Lord's people" had as much to do with the church's self-image as with missions.[183]

The opportunities of the postwar years, Ulrich R. Beeson argued, made it imperative to oppose the old spirit of negativism and bickering. He believed that the churches must simply ignore the "grand, elderly ministers" who represented the antiquated "ways and means of yesteryears." "While old Brother 'Snickelfritz' is up in the pulpit expostulating on which churches of Christ cannot scripturally cooperate with one another in developing financially this better and better environment," Beeson concluded, "the modest, intelligent business man and church leader on the back seat is slipping out of the old ramshackle meeting-house with the young people."[184] In 1947, a Georgia minister urged churches to "get into the school business in earnest" as a part of the Great Commission, noting that it would take "ten billion years to evangelize the world" unless the "ideas of our people" changed.[185]

The "rock fight" episode was a measure of the pervasive new denominational pride that had developed in the churches of Christ. Cled Wallace's sarcastic article infuriated members of the churches of Christ who felt they deserved the respect of the United States government and who perceived that they had a strong political influence in the state of Texas. The whole incident bristled with denominational consciousness. Nothing offended the majority more than Wallace's lack of optimism "over the prospect of persuading the President and the State Department to bomb the Vatican" because "it is doubtful that 'our' denomination is that popular in Washington at the present time."[186] To those aspiring to a degree of recognition and respect, denigrating "our denomination" was in distinct bad taste. By the end of the 1940s most leaders in the churches no longer felt a deep sense of alienation from their culture; indeed, they had become breast-beating American patriots. In 1943, the churches of the Dallas area sponsored a city-wide meeting featuring N. B. Hardeman. The aim of the sponsors of this meeting, and of many others during these years, was to present the "church before the citizens of the region in a favorable light."[187]

By the 1950s churches of Christ no longer displayed a "sojourner" mentality, argued Richard Hughes; rather, they had "settled into their cultural environment and felt increasingly at home in the world in which they lived."[188] Nothing marked this transition more clearly than the diminishing influence of the apolitical world view long defended by David Lipscomb and other conservative preachers. During the postwar years, Hughes noted, the "progressive wing of Churches of Christ" moved "further and further away from the sectarian mentality of the nineteenth century and would increasingly celebrate the values of conservative Protestant culture in the United States."[189]

Michael Casey judged that G. C. Brewer was "the key person to introduce the political pulpit" in churches of Christ.[190] Of course, most members of churches of Christ had never been totally apolitical; they had voted in the past in large numbers on issues such as the prohibition of alcohol and gambling.[191] During the 1920s Brewer took up the cause of protecting the public schools from the teaching of evolution and dubbed himself "the Bryan of the West." By the mid-1930s, he had become fixated by the threat of communism, and he was one of the founders in 1952, along with B. C. Goodpasture and Batsell Barrett Baxter, and named the first editor, of an anti-Catholic, anti-communist paper, the *Voice of Freedom*. Symbolically, the inaugural issue of the journal included an emotional appeal for support for Italian missionary Cline Paden.[192] The most purely political of all twentieth-century publications edited by a member of the churches of Christ, the *Voice of Freedom* reached a record distribution with its October 1959 issue of about a hundred thousand copies, a testimony to the politicizing influence that World War II and the conservative fifties had wrought in the churches of Christ. L. R. Wilson, editor of the magazine at that time, tapped into the deep fears rising from the impending presidential race of Roman Catholic John F. Kennedy and urged members of the churches of Christ to join a political crusade along with conservative Protestants: "When we lose our freedom, the Protestant denominations will lose their freedom. . . . Remember that we stand or fall together in our fight for freedom. If we cherish our present way of life, and want to preserve it, it will cost us all money, hard work, sacrifice, and self-determination."[193]

A second center of rising religious/political activity was the campus of Harding College where President George S. Benson, in league with entrepreneur Clinton Davidson, led the struggling school from debt to prosperity in partnership

Grover Cleveland Brewer (1884–1956). Brewer was one of the most influential preachers in the churches of Christ before and after World War II. Brewer tried to moderate the attacks on premillennialists and clashed with Foy E. Wallace, Jr. A strong supporter of the colleges and other institutions supported by churches of Christ, and one of the chief architects of the postwar missions boom, Brewer correctly foresaw the path the movement would take in the 1950s. (Courtesy of the Center for Restoration Studies, Abilene Christian University.)

with powerful business connections and a right-wing political agenda.[194] Benson became one of the national leaders of the religious right of the 1950s and transformed the college into "a bastion of Americanism and anti-Communism" that brought it to the attention of the national media.[195] Benson won over many of those who had formerly held apolitical views. James D. Bales, who had opposed "meddling in politics" before becoming a leading anti-communist writer himself, "swung over" to Benson's political and economic conservatism in 1944, persuaded that "we do have something at stake. If we lose the battle for economic freedom, we lose the battle for religious freedom. . . . How much money have you got for evangelism, if the government takes it all?"[196]

In his history of the churches of Christ, Richard Hughes found it ironic that it was the "progressive" wing of the churches of Christ, the less dogmatic and more irenic leaders such as Brewer and the founders of the new *Christian Leader,* who fathered the world-affirming, patriotic, right-wing churches of Christ of the 1950s. Even more ironic was the transformation of J. N. Armstrong's school, the last link to the apocalyptic heritage of the nineteenth century, into a nationally recognized center for pro-business, right-wing politics. With this, Hughes believed, these progressives "unwittingly launched an assault on their own religious heritage," and as surely as the Wallace forces who used a bludgeoning legalism to crush premillennialism, they destroyed the separatist ideology that was the movement's intellectual heartbeat.[197] Thus, by the 1950s, the former "sojourners" had become "settlers," captured by the self-serving political agenda of the American right wing.

Historian Robert E. Hooper challenged Hughes's interpretation with the observation "that churches of Christ have not changed as much as some might think."[198] Repelled by the revisionist notion that the churches of Christ in the fifties and sixties were little more than an adjunct "to the Republican establishment," Hooper argued that the movement's leaders were better portrayed as "populists" whose political causes were "radical" and issue-oriented rather than consistently conservative. Thus, in the postwar years, leaders in churches of Christ supported "the party that support[ed] their issue."[199] Therefore, Hooper insisted, "the distinctive characteristics, both religious and political, associated with churches of Christ should not be so quickly dismissed." Their commitment to "dissent" continued to be strong and many were satisfied to occupy an "outsider position" at the end of the twentieth century.[200]

The meaning of the transition that occurred in the two decades after World War II had less to do with the form of politics embraced by church leaders in the fifties—whether right-wing, as Hughes disapprovingly argued, or erratic and radical as Hooper believed—than with the sweeping nature of the marriage of religion and politics. The critical change that had transpired had to do with the degree to which the churches of Christ had become a part of the American culture in which its members lived. The leaders of the 1950s were far removed from the generation of poor, alienated farmer-preachers of the first half of the twentieth century who felt that the affairs of civil governments had little to do with their own well-being or that of the kingdom of God. By the 1950s, churches were filled with upwardly mobile, successful Americans who yearned for recognition for themselves and their church. They built their denomination, they advertised their successes, and they set out to prove to their fellow Americans that they were worthy of a place under the canopy of America's patriotic civil religion.

A Sociological Interpretation of the Institutional Schism

In hindsight, clear sociological, as well as theological, tensions had surfaced in the churches of Christ in the 1950s. Historian David Edwin Harrell, Jr., wrote a substantial corpus of historical literature in the 1960s and early 1970s that highlighted the sociological dimensions of the Christian church–churches of Christ divisions of the nineteenth century.[201] In a 1964 article in the *Journal of Southern History,* Harrell suggested that the institutional division in the churches of Christ was following the same pattern: "The Churches of Christ have not remained an economic and cultural unit since 1906. The sociological and economic elevation of a portion of the membership of the church, especially since World War II, has motivated a large part of the church to begin the transition toward denominationalism. The result is that the movement is once again dividing along sociological lines. Conservative appeals in the movement in the 1960s have a distinctive lower class and anti-aristocratic flavor, while the centers of liberalism are in the areas where the church is most numerous and sophisticated."[202]

The emergence of an educated and middle-class elite was quite apparent by the end of World War II. Richard Hughes wrote, "The battle over institutionalization was thus in many ways a struggle involving class distinctions. . . . To some extent, their [noninstitutional leaders'] protest against institutionalization was an expression of their opposition to the growing power of those with more wealth and education. But it was also a lamentation over the demise of a way of life they long had identified with the primitive Christian faith."[203] Michael Casey discussed the growing economic gulf of the postwar years: "After World War II, the church entered a new phase of prosperity and change. A new South emerged that was more homogenized with the rest of America, and the Churches of Christ were part of that new, modern South."[204]

While most members of churches of Christ in the 1950s and 1960s saw the debate over institutionalism as no more than another trial in the effort to define orthodoxy in an intellectually open movement, underneath lay more general, amorphous discontents rooted in changed social realities. At some level, almost all noninstitutional leaders sensed that a social chasm had developed in the movement, and a few saw this new economic and cultural diversity as more ominous than the raging doctrinal debate. To some extent, a sociological divide had been visible before World War II. In 1936, in the midst of his jousting with educators and more irenic preachers, Foy E. Wallace, Jr., advised, "If history repeats itself in the rise and the fall of empires and in the destinies of nations, it is none the less true in the development and the declension of the church."[205] Of course, Wallace was mouthing a sociological truism—all institutions and organizations do change—and his premonitions of decadence and liberalism were clearly premature in the 1930s, but he and others did see signs on the horizon.

If the fears about encroaching liberalism and the loss of the separatist vision were premature in the 1930s, by the 1950s, the lamentations of the prophets were firmly rooted in reality. In 1948, W. W. Otey pointed to "undoubted evidence of 'trends' toward apostasy," even though he recognized that those who "sound warnings" would be dismissed as "alarmists," "soured," and "old and senile."[206] He put his finger on the growing sociological divide that had appeared in his lifetime: "That the church is passing through a transition in becoming adjusted to the complex, highly organized social age, is recognized by a number of educators. . . . Big things are proposed and performed, denominational 'plans and successes' are cited to inspire liberality. The simplicity of the church of the Lord is not a suitable instrument for entering upon a centralized undertaking of such magnitude. Great centralized associations are unknown to the ancient order of things."[207]

Few of the leaders of the noninstitutional movement had a grasp of the meaning of the division comparable to that of Robert F. Turner. Writing in 1965, Turner pointed back to G. C. Brewer's 1943 article in the *Gospel Advocate* advocating a "new plan" for postwar mission work and to the opposition voiced in the *Bible Banner* as the "early rumblings" of the noninstitutional division. After the war, he complained, grandiose plans "swept the brotherhood, but God's word has not changed a line."[208] The debate of the fifties, Turner believed, had more to do with denominational posturing and boosterism than with proof-texting and syllogisms.

The boosterism of the fifties seemed ridiculous to many old-time preachers, and it drew a barrage of ridicule. Harold Dowdy of Jacksonville, Florida, zeroed in on the pretentious claims of the "Herald of Truth," which he characterized as a "three pound chicken laying a five pound egg." Observing that the promoters of the program claimed to "reach more people than it would take our pulpits to reach in 74 years," Dowdy wryly ribbed, "If one week of HOT equals 74 years of preaching by cornfield preachers, and assuming that HOT has at least 'the very best preachers,' and throwing in gratis all the unimportant work of non-HOT preachers, what do you think we have? Due to the work of HOT everyone in the United States should have been a 'Church of Christer' by September 17, 1961. And BY NOW there should be 314,000,000 converts in the United States."[209]

Noninstitutional leaders viewed the estimates of growth in the churches of Christ in the years immediately after the war as exaggerated products of an unhealthy denominational mentality. Yater Tant complained in 1958, "For more than a decade now we have been deluged with 'statistics' from 'on the march brethren' blowing and boasting as to how the church is growing. Figures appeared as if by magic, out of the thin air, claiming 1,000,000 members for the Churches of Christ, and 12,000 congregations. Then in less than two years time that figure had jumped to 1,500,000 members and 15,000 congregations. And last year, we saw confident reports suggesting that an estimate of 2,000,000 members was not over optimistic and 18,000 congregations was quite within the realm of possibility."[210] Noting that *The World Almanac* reported a 481 percent growth in the churches of Christ between 1948 and 1958, a Mississippi preacher wrote, "In the present day apostasy there is an amazing CRAZE about 'bigness,' and anything with a flavor of 'bigness' about it is accepted with eagerness."[211] Tant chastised the "wild-eyed optimists" responsible for such reports: "Brethren everywhere were getting drunk on their own 'figures,' heady with the feeling of bursting seams and irresistible growth. We were hailing ourselves as 'the fastest growing religious body in America' and the 'on the march' philosophy seemed to be taking the day."[212] Bryan Vinson, Sr., labeled the rage for growth in the 1950s "the birth of a denomination."[213]

In a perceptive article written in 1958, George T. Jones of

San Antonio detected the larger sociological issue. Disturbed by the ballyhoo surrounding a Dallas Youth Rally that featured budding movie star and alumnus of David Lipscomb College Pat Boone, and attracted ten thousand people, Jones wrote, "Our trouble is not institutionalism. Institutionalism is only a symptom. . . . Our trouble is disrespect for the authority of Christ, along with boredom for the simplicity that is in Christ. Add to this the denominational pride that fills the hearts of so many brethren and the stage is set for men to attempt the very thing these are seeking to accomplish: to change the church of Jesus Christ."[214] Noninstitutional critics hammered away at the "on the march" mentality that symbolized the denominational spirit. In 1962, Hoyt H. Houchen of Abilene, Texas, wrote, "The pied piper promoters of brotherhood elderships and other big scale plans are playing the fanciful tune of 'big things in a big way.' They are being followed by a large segment of zealous, ambitious, but uniformed and gullible brethren who are shouting with glee to the tune of the flutes, disregarding the warnings of honest and thoughtful brethren who see eminent dangers ahead."[215]

In a 1959 article in the *Gospel Guardian,* Ed Harrell, then a doctoral student in history at Vanderbilt University, argued that institutional division was rooted in an unprecedented "social gospel" emphasis in those churches intent on improving their denominational image. Emphasizing the role of the church in this world, the progressive "social gospelers" had abandoned the other-worldly separationist ideology of the restoration movement. While few institutional preachers embraced the theological liberalism of nineteenth-century social gospelers, Harrell maintained that the churches of Christ had in subtle ways become a world-embracing rather than a world-rejecting religious body.[216] J. W. Roberts and J. D. Thomas of Abilene Christian University challenged Harrell's article because it prejudicially implied that institutional churches were interested in "*only* a social gospel."[217] In the judgment of Richard Hughes, "most leaders of mainstream Churches of

Christ never fully comprehended the issues that the noninstitutional people sought to raise. They remained convinced, in spite of all their concessions to modernization, that Churches of Christ persisted unscathed as the twentieth-century embodiment of primitive, nondenominational Christianity."[218] Hughes was probably correct, also, in his judgment that most noninstitutional leaders thought fairly narrowly in their opposition to the series of innovations that appeared in the fifties. He wrote, "The anti-institutional people gave little evidence of having recognized that the issue of modernization and institutionalization had taken a critical new turn with the emergence of 'Herald of Truth.' They typically combated the 'Herald of Truth,' by focusing on the shop-worn issue of the 'sponsoring congregation.'"[219] Nonetheless, the 1959 exchange over the social gospel did put the noninstitutional division in a sociological framework, as many subsequent observers also did.[220]

A more far-reaching sociological interpretation of the nature of the institutional division was presented by Harrell in a series of three lectures delivered at the Florida College Lectures in 1961. These sociological lectures were published in several papers and subsequently printed by the *Gospel Guardian* in a tract entitled "The Emergence of the 'Church of Christ' Denomination."[221] Using established sociological models of the sect-to-denomination process, Harrell theorized that the institutional division in the churches of Christ in the 1950s paralleled the Christian Church–churches of Christ schism at the beginning of the twentieth century. He noted that both divisions had a demonstrable social and economic base and that each was less about "issues" than a general divergence in the "mind of the movement." He said, "As the kinds of people who were members of the church began to diversify, it was inevitable that theological 'issues' would arise between the sociological groups. What those issues happened to be is really accidental. The church is not really dividing over the relationship of the local congregation to an orphan home. . . . It could have been something entirely different; other areas of friction will surely arise in the future. The church is dividing because there are two basic kinds of people within the movement who are demanding two very different kinds of religion."[222] Harrell predicted that in the years ahead the churches of Christ would break into three segments, as the restoration movement had in the late nineteenth and early twentieth centuries. He believed that the sloughing off of the noninstitutional churches of Christ fit a repetitious pattern in the American restoration movement.

For the most part, recent historians have agreed that divisions in the churches of Christ were both theological and sociological.[223] Douglas A. Foster's sociological interpretation of the tensions in the churches of Christ in the last three decades of the twentieth century saw the noninstitutional division and the premillennial controversy as relatively minor "disturbances," both of which "resulted in relatively small divisions."[224] However, Foster's interpretation dismissed too lightly the powerful social stresses in the churches of Christ in the 1950s that separated a noninstitutional segment of about the same size as the churches of Christ at the division of the restoration movement at the beginning of the twentieth century.

Richard Hughes offered the most nuanced reading of the institutional division in the churches of Christ, describing the controversy in a chapter entitled "The Fight over Modernization."[225] Basically, Hughes believed that the two primal pillars of restoration thought—an essentially hermeneutical commitment to "the primitive church of the apostolic age" and a more cultural vision of "the apocalyptic kingdom of God"—had "all but collapsed" by the 1960s.[226] He contended that in the premillennial purge the churches of Christ lost the "apocalyptic orientation of the Stone-Lipscomb tradition" and in the institutional division the group discarded its "democratic and legal biases," thus opening the door to embrace wholeheartedly a denominational self-image and a worldly religion.[227] To some extent, Hughes saw the noninstitutional movement as an exaggeration of the "legal dimension" of restorationism "because of its emphasis on the Baconian hermeneutic. Noninstitutional arguments rendered the Scripture undiscriminatingly flat and binding at every point."[228] Citing Roy E. Cogdill's ponderous briefs as evidence, Hughes presented an argument that seemed well-taken; on the other hand, many of the defenders of institutionalism were at least equally committed to the "Baconian hermeneutic," for instance, J. D. Thomas and Thomas B. Warren. Hughes was closer to the mark when he noted that noninstitutional people instinctively believed that "to shift from democratization to institutionalization would be to abandon the entire primitivist vision upon which Churches of Christ based their very reason for existence."[229]

In short, the theological debate over institutionalism often turned legalistic and narrow, as all doctrinal disputes in the restoration movement did. The common-sense, Baconian hermeneutic was a part of the arsenal of disputants on all sides of every argument. While this hermeneutical approach more or less totally defined the commitment of some people, and was regarded as a necessary evil by others, almost no one would have jettisoned the idea of common-sense Biblical proof-texting. On the other hand, the commitment to a more amorphous sense of alienation and world rejection, of cultural dissonance, which Hughes called "apocalyptic," was direly threatened by the new social realities of the 1950s. Noninstitutional people instinctively grasped and embraced the vision of a separated people in the 1950s and some of the leaders of the noninstitutional movement—Robert F. Turner, Harry Pickup, Jr., Ed Harrell, Homer Hailey, and Sewell Hall—were more likely to appeal to cultural commentary than to textual argument in their criticisms of the "on the march" mentality.

By the middle of the 1960s the "antis" were pretty well separated into churches of their own, rallying around Florida Christian College in Tampa and the magazines that had led the fight against institutionalism. To the majority, the noninstitutional movement seemed destined to be an isolated and insignificant minority, while the future of the mainstream churches of Christ seemed bright. However, the noninstitutional churches of Christ in the 1960s and 1970s displayed a strong camaraderie as they went about the task of building new churches. They enjoyed two decades of uncommon unity and good will. Homer Hailey lived the second half of his life in the environs of the noninstitutional churches of Christ, increasingly isolated from his former friends and brethren.

4

The Mainstream Becomes a Divided Stream

MOST MEMBERS of the churches of Christ in the fifties and sixties believed that "before them . . . lay a glorious future marked by striking growth, upward social and economic mobility, and increased participation in the mainstream of American life."[1] They welcomed the notion that they were the mainstream of an important American religious body. However, this optimistic veneer hid serious fault lines in the large group of churches that had rejected noninstitutional thinking. On one extreme of the mainstream were old-time debaters who throughout the sixties continued to wage war against the opponents of institutionalism on a hermeneutical battlefield that looked much like the historic restoration landscape. On the other extreme, scattered radical voices challenged some of the most basic assumptions of restoration thinking. In the fifties and sixties their protests seemed quirky and marginal; but, in contrast with earlier discontented preachers who left the churches of Christ in disgust, a few serious critics of restoration ideology remained in the church, biding their time, nurturing a younger generation who would take seriously their revisionist ideas.

The Legacy of Foy E. Wallace, Jr.

Nothing troubled noninstitutional leaders more than the defection of Foy E. Wallace, Jr., who spent the last decade and a half before his death in 1969 disassociating himself from the crusade he had done so much to encourage.[2] Wallace's journey back into the mainstream began with an article in the *Firm Foundation* in 1955 that affirmed that he had "no connection at all with the present 'Gospel Guardian.'"[3] In an important article in 1959 he again disassociated himself from the *Guardian* and warned, "The course of the current controversy has made it clear that the church is in a squeeze between liberalism and extremism, both parties radical and both parties wrong." The "antis" were condemning others for doing "things in which they recently engaged," Wallace wrote, and he insisted that the whole noninstitutional argument hung on "vague and intricate processes."[4] In a 1964 article in the *Firm Foundation*, Wallace again vigorously denounced the noninstitutional movement: "The unscrupulous conduct, wicked deeds and fallacious issues have been and are the cause of my own rejection of these men and their agitation movement."[5]

To noninstitutional leaders, including his son William, it appeared that Foy E. Wallace, Jr., in his last years "labored and struggled in trying to demonstrate that he had made no change, seeking to explain away what he had written in the 1940s and 1950s against sponsoring churches and church support of institutions."[6] William Wallace insisted that it was his father who had in the 1950s convinced him that the "Herald of Truth" was unscriptural.[7] Foy Wallace continued to honor and respect some of his old friends in the noninstitutional movement, such as Homer Hailey, Franklin Puckett, and W. Curtis Porter, but he remained extremely bitter toward Roy Cogdill and Fanning Yater Tant.[8]

Wallace's heralded rehabilitation in the mainstream was marked by a string of "appreciation dinners" and "plaudits" from former enemies, including honorary celebrations at such unlikely places as Harding University and Pepperdine University and tributes from such improbable people as B. C. Goodpasture and George S. Benson.[9] In the estimation of his son, the wounded warrior "worked to reestablish himself in the broader majority interest of churches of Christ."[10] While many judged in the 1960s that Wallace was a "has-been" with little influence among the mainstream churches, Goodpasture and other moderate leaders welcomed his repudiation of "antism" and his willingness to rally around him a group of like-minded conservatives to continue the battle against damaging noninstitutional raids on the churches. Wallace's stand against "antism" no doubt had some impact. Years later, Yater Tant estimated that "if Foy had 'stayed hitched' to his basic convictions as set forth in Torch," his "influence might conceivably ha[ve] made the division much more nearly fifty-fifty."[11] At any rate, by the 1960s, Goodpasture had chosen to ignore the troublesome "antis," and he happily relinquished the rear guard skirmishing to a cadre of two-fisted battlers who embraced the legacy of Foy E. Wallace, Jr.

Discontent on the Left

In the late 1950s, a murmur of dissenting voices could be heard on the left, but it seemed no more than a minor nuisance to those enchanted by the successes of the church on the march. The most influential and resourceful of the new liberals were two gifted editors who urged a rapprochement with the Christian churches, Carl Ketcherside and Leroy Garrett.[12] Early in his life, Ketcherside had been associated with the schismatic iconoclasm of Daniel Sommer, but by the 1950s he concluded that he had neglected the central restoration message of Christian unity, a conclusion that Leroy Garrett had also reached. Ketcherside was irenic and persuasive, and Garrett, who earned a doctorate in the philosophy of religion from Harvard in 1957, was acerbic and confrontational; together, they were a formidable team. In 1957, Ketcherside's magazine, *Mission Messenger,* which had begun as a Sommerite journal in 1939, adopted the theme of "unity based on love." It grew to a peak circulation of about eight thousand.[13] Garrett published *Bible Talk* from 1952 to 1958 and in 1959 began editing a long-running journal called *Restoration Review*. Ketcherside and Garrett offered extensive critiques of what they regarded as the denominational bigotry and hermeneutical shallowness of the churches of Christ, and they attracted a small circle of supporters. More important, they emboldened a generation of younger preachers who in the 1960s became uncomfortable with the leadership of the mainstream churches. Carl Ketcherside died in 1989, but Leroy Garrett remained an observer and critic of the churches of Christ up to the end of the century, an iconoclast and maverick whose sword cut in all directions.

Looking back from the 1990s, some conservative preachers saw Garrett and Ketcherside as "the first wave of digressions which were later to plague the Lord's people."[14] Richard T. Hughes agreed that "there is a sense in which the progressive tradition among Churches of Christ . . . was founded by Carl Ketcherside and Leroy Garrett."[15] When Leroy Garrett attended the lecture programs at the various church-related colleges in the late 1950s and 1960s to spread his message of unity in diversity, he was forced to hold underground meetings with students and on a number of occasions was legally restrained from entering dormitories. Not until the 1990s did the views of Ketcherside and Garrett find much of a platform in the churches of Christ. After attending the 1996 Abilene Christian University Lectures, Garrett wrote, "I was stunned, for I saw it as an excellent summary of what Carl Ketcherside and I have been saying all these years. That was confirmed when old friends said to me afterwards, 'Leroy, I didn't know you were here. I thought of you.'"[16]

Garrett and Ketcherside were prophets before their time; their role in the churches of Christ was much like that of the lonely liberals in the Disciples of Christ in the 1870s, men such as George Longan and Alexander Procter whom David Lipscomb labeled the "Missouri rationalists."[17] On the other hand, while Ketcherside and Garrett were withering critics of the foibles of the mainstream churches of Christ, they did not explore many of the themes that would become central to the progressivism that arose in the eighties and nineties. As Richard Hughes noted, Ketcherside and Garrett labored within a context that showed little interest in contemporary scholarship, and they were not a part of the network of university-trained theologians who were the architects of the progressive movement of later years.[18]

A second protest that was more disruptive to the mainstream churches of Christ in the 1970s was a "discipling movement" that proved to be very successful in recruiting young people. The movement borrowed from campus evangelism ideas developed in the 1960s, as well as from a controversial and divisive "discipling movement" that flourished among charismatics.[19] Begun at the Crossroads Church of Christ in Gainesville, Florida, and led by its minister Charles H. Lucas, the discipling movement soon caught the attention of religious sociologists who, because of the tight controls that the church placed on the private lives of young converts, labeled it a cult.[20] The Crossroads congregation grew from a membership of 175 to more than a thousand in the early 1970s and became a model for scores of other churches. Guy N. Woods estimated that more than 250 congregations were divided by the teachings of the movement during the seventies.[21]

The discipling movement flourished partly because it offered a revitalization ideology that counteracted the growing lethargy in the mainstream churches. A few noninstitutional leaders, including the venerable Yater Tant who spoke at the Crossroads congregation, viewed the movement as an effort to return the churches of Christ to an evangelistic mind set, moving away from the social agenda and denominational breast-beating of the fifties. By the end of the seventies, however, the discipling movement had become much more than an orthodox effort to revitalize the churches of Christ. The leadership of the movement had passed by then into the hands of Kip McKean, a student convert at Crossroads who established a highly successful congregation in Boston. In one decade, the Boston church, which met in Boston Garden, grew from a membership of fifty to thirty-two hundred. In the 1990s the church recorded crowds of more than sixty-five hundred and it was one of the largest churches of Christ in the world. Under McKean's firm guidance in the role of "world evangelist," by the 1990s the Boston church had established more than one hundred congregations around the world, all of them tied together in a centralized ecclesiastical hierarchy controlled by McKean, who in the 1990s moved to Los Angeles. Called the International Church of Christ, the movement continued to expand rapidly in the 1990s.

While some demographers still view the discipling movement as a part of the churches of Christ, in practice the International Church of Christ was a separate entity by the mid-1980s. The collection of churches headed by McKean and the Boston church had ventured far from the primitivist vision of the nineteenth century, particularly in matters of church organization. For the most part, the Boston movement, including its leaders, was made up of first-generation members of the churches of Christ, people unversed in and uncommitted to the broader principles undergirding restoration thinking. Driven by a rigid acceptance of the traditional "plan of salvation," which culminated in baptism for the remission of sins, and by concepts of "total commitment" borrowed from discipling literature, the International Churches of Christ had limited continuity with the historical tradition of the churches of Christ. When "20/20" produced a program on the movement in 1993, host Hugh Downs made it clear that "the Boston Church of Christ was to be distinguished from the denomination also known as Church of Christ."[22] Historian Robert E. Hooper saw the International Church of Christ as a "conservative movement" that had "given up on churches of Christ."[23] The discipling movement was, in fact, an aberration that, like the Christadelphians of the nineteenth century, drifted far from restoration moorings and came to have a life of its own.[24]

By the late 1960s, other fountains of reform were bubbling that would have a far more lasting impact on the churches of Christ. During that decade, a progressive coterie of younger preachers and college professors reached the conclusion that "the theological house that Churches of Christ had built for themselves in the nineteenth century had all but collapsed."[25] They were deeply concerned by both the doctrinal inconsistencies and the cultural malaise in the churches of Christ. Carl Ketcherside published in 1966 a collection of critical assessments entitled *Voices of Concern* that included articles by the editor, Robert Meyer, and by Pat Hardeman and Logan Fox. Echoing the charges made by noninstitutional critics, the rebels writing in *Voices of Concern* concluded that "all our protestations to the contrary not withstanding, *we are a denomination*."[26]

The pioneers of dissent within the mainstream churches in the 1950s and 1960s were a few students and professors in the colleges.[27] Graduate "theological education" began in the churches of Christ with the founding by W. B. West of graduate programs at Pepperdine and Harding College in 1944 and 1952.[28] By the 1960s most of the colleges aspired to higher levels of professionalism and sheltered young professors fully engaged with modern scholarship. Inevitably, such environments elicited evaluations of the churches of Christ from intellectual perspectives outside of the restoration context. Most significant was the core of professors who taught religion at Abilene Christian University led by LeMoine G. Lewis, who returned to the college in 1949 as professor of church history and subsequently completed a doctorate at Harvard. In the same year, Frank Pack returned to Abilene with a doctorate from the University of Southern California in New Testament studies and J. D. Thomas joined the faculty with a doctorate in New Testament studies from the University of Chicago. Several of Lewis's students at Abilene Christian completed advanced degrees and then returned to join the faculty, including Everett Ferguson and Abraham Malherbe. Writing in *Mission,* Donald Haymes summarized the impact of Lewis on the generation of the 1960s: "He returned to his alma mater . . . as a man seized by a mission, and the fruits of his labor are visible on the faculties of several major American universities, as well as the Christian colleges. . . . It is his almost single-handed creation of a new *tradition* of scholarship that will remain his legacy."[29] Others, including Thomas H. Olbricht, believed that J. D. Thomas and J. W. Roberts had been equally influential in encouraging a generation of students to seek advanced degrees. In 1957, two Lewis students, Abraham Malherbe and Pat Harrell, launched the journal *Restoration Quarterly* to "create a community of scholarly discourse" in the churches of Christ. The new quarterly, the first effort in the churches of Christ by scholars to publish an academic journal, "specifically sought to redirect the theology of Churches of Christ."[30]

More significant at the popular level was the 1967 launching of *Mission* magazine under an editorial board led by Abilene theologian Thomas Olbricht and by Frank Pack, J. W. Roberts, Roy Bowen Ward, and Walter Burch. The early supporters of the new magazine included the most visible of the young and discontented in the churches of Christ: Dwain Evans, John Allen Chalk, William S. Banowsky, Wesley Reagan, J. W. Roberts, Donald Haymes, and Gary Freeman. Its founders wanted to establish "a journal that would 'speak to contemporary man in vital, energetic language' with 'a message of renewal.'"[31] A part of the socially conscious generation of the sixties, some of the *Mission* rebels, particularly Haymes and Freeman, "took Churches of Christ to task for their preoccupation with fine points of doctrine to the neglect of social justice."[32] However, the magazine also challenged the churches of Christ doctrinally; in 1965, Roy Bowen Ward, an innovative thinker who for a time served as editor of *Mission,* questioned the "traditional restoration hermeneutic" in an article that anticipated a divisive debate that erupted in the eighties and nineties.[33]

By the end of the sixties, the volume of progressive literature in the churches of Christ demanded notice. In 1969, Foy Ledbetter began editing *Integrity* in an open effort to encourage self-analysis and change in the churches of Christ. Gary Freeman, who wrote a regular column in *Mission* entitled "Balaam's Friend," skillfully satirized the leadership of the mainstream churches; in 1969, Harper and Row published Freeman's popular book, *A Funny Thing Happened to Me on the Way to Heaven,* which lampooned his experiences as a student at Abilene Christian College. Richard Hughes summarized the mood at the end of the sixties: "Many in the younger generation, well educated and driven by the social agenda of that period, found the traditional concerns of twentieth-century Churches of Christ inadequate and irrelevant to the world in which they lived. As a result, they seriously questioned almost every aspect of their tradition, from the Baconian hermeneutic to the way church leaders had formulated the restoration vision."[34]

One of the forces at work in the churches of Christ in the sixties, as in American society in general, was a "generational crisis" that isolated "young people from the thinking of their elders."[35] While the countercultural youth revolt of the sixties had a limited direct impact on the churches of Christ, the younger generation of preachers were keenly aware of the social convulsion. In the late 1960s, Jim Bevis and John Allen Chalk began an organization called Campus Evangelism that, modeled on Bill Bright's Campus Crusade, "placed more emphasis on a personal relation with Jesus than on the institutional church, and . . . sought to present the gospel in language that would speak to America's youth."[36] In 1968, Chalk preached a controversial series of three sermons on the "Herald of Truth" entitled "Three American Revolutions" that reflected an interest in evangelical theology and a commitment to social activism. Campus Evangelism attracted little support from church leaders, however, and died in 1970 from a lack of funding.[37]

The innate conservatism of the churches of Christ that sheltered the group from the shrill rebellion of the counterculture also shielded it from the booming charismatic movement in the sixties and seventies. Scores of debates with Pentecostal preachers in the years before World War II had established firmly in the churches of Christ the orthodox Protestant notion that miracles and the gifts of the Holy Spirit were limited to the New Testament age. However, in the late 1960s two highly visible encounters with the charismatic movement caused ripples. Dwain Evans, who led the popular Exodus Movement that founded the West Islip Church on Long Island in 1963, fell from grace in 1966 when he delivered a lecture at Abilene Christian University that appeared to be open to a Pentecostal understanding of the gifts of the Holy Spirit. Though he later clarified and toned down his remarks, his flirtation with the charismatic movement essentially ended his promising career as a leader.[38]

Even more disconcerting to most members of the churches of Christ was the 1969 defection of Pat Boone to the charismatic movement. Boone, the premier celebrity in the churches of Christ in the 1960s, was introduced to the charismatic movement by Clinton Davidson, who had befriended Pentecostal luminary David Wilkerson in the 1950s. When Boone and his wife, Shirley, reported that they had received the baptism of the Holy Spirit and spoken in tongues, they were ostracized by their former admirers. A few small bands of charismatics survived in the churches of Christ, but the movement remained a very hostile environment for Pentecostal ideas.

The ephemeral impact of the Ketcherside-Garrett unity movement, the discipling movement, and the charismatic movement demonstrated how effectively the leaders of the churches of Christ were still able to quarantine dissent in the 1960s.[39] During the sixties, even those progressives working within the structure of the church's institutions were more or less marginalized. Richard Hughes complained that "the mainstream and the conservative wings of Churches of Christ either resisted or rejected practically every new idea, every new institution, and every new periodical that reflected the concerns" of the young progressives.[40] Such influential mainstream leaders as Batsell Barrett Baxter, M. Norvel Young, and Ira North "declined to lend active support to *Mission,*" and Reuel Lemmons, still hoping to find a moderate center that would fend off division, labeled the progressives "a far-out liberal movement in the church."[41] Conservative pressure on the colleges forced the resignation of some faculty members from the magazine's board in the 1960s "in order to escape the scrutiny that severely diminished the delight of college teaching," though these conservative victories did little to change the future direction of the educational institutions.[42]

Nonetheless, at the end of the sixties, dissent remained uncomfortable, even dangerous, in the churches of Christ. Many of those who wrote articles in *Voices of Concern* left the churches of Christ for friendlier environs. Richard Hughes described the flight of the 1960s: "As time went on, increasing numbers of these young people abandoned Churches of Christ for other more socially concerned, more ecumenical, and more spirit-filled Christian traditions. Many left organized Christianity altogether."[43] Even in the 1990s, serious rebels pondered whether to remain a part of the churches of Christ or to leave and serve "God within another fellowship." Editor Denny Boultinghouse of *Image* magazine advised a young liberal in 1996, "I really hope you will be able to stay with us on the journey. It may be selfish, but we need more people like you."[44]

Many young progressives did stay in the 1960s and 1970s and they ultimately dramatically influenced the churches of Christ. At the end of the sixties, Richard Hughes saw three groups within the mainstream: a broad center that "embraced some diversity" but sought to "preserve the dominant vision of the 1950s"; a group of "progressives who challenged that vision"; and a "group of conservatives" who "absolutized the historical vision of Churches of Christ" and "claimed to understand absolute truth absolutely."[45] The stage was set for a new struggle for the soul of the churches of Christ.

Resurgent Conservatism

The conservative flank in the mainstream churches of Christ was largely occupied in the fifties and early sixties with banishing the heretical noninstitutional extremists. When that job was completed, the tested warriors who had fought the "antis" turned their attention to the new deviants on the left. This large and vocal group of preachers, composed of "men who were deeply concerned with biblical authority, law, rationality and order," had seemed almost dormant to many in the mainstream churches, because their batteries had been aimed at the noninstitutional camp. They again "rose to prominence in the sixties" because the target of their fire was the new enemy within.[46]

While the older papers in the churches, such as the *Gospel Advocate* and *Firm Foundation,* tried to find a nondivisive middle ground that would not disrupt the onward march of the churches of Christ, the reoriented conservatives of the sixties were born of the fighting tradition. In 1967, Roy Hearn of Memphis and Franklin Camp of Birmingham launched a journal called the *First Century Christian* to stem the liberal threat. In the long run more significant was the legacy of Thomas B. Warren, who, having led the fight against the noninstitutional movement, in the mid-1960s began to attack "middle-of-the-roadism." In 1969, Warren, who received a doctorate in philosophy from Vanderbilt University and was a professor of Bible at Freed-Hardeman College, resumed publication of the *Spiritual Sword,* which he had published for a short time in the 1950s to attack the noninstitutional movement. Assisted by one of his students, Rubel Shelly, Warren declared war on "the threat of liberalism" and set on a crusade to save the churches of Christ from the rebellious left wing.[47] The *Spiritual Sword* became the most important voice for those seriously concerned about the growing boldness of progressives in the churches of Christ.

The "most flamboyant and sensational" of the new conservative journals established to fight the progressive threat was *Contending for the Faith,* edited by Ira Y. Rice, Jr., a longtime missionary in Singapore who returned to Nashville in 1970.[48] In the 1960s Rice published a series of books attacking liberalism entitled *Axe at the Root,*[49] and in 1970 he launched *Contending for the Faith*. Rice predicted that a new division was on the horizon that would "make the 1946 Anti-Cooperation Movement seem insignificant by contrast."[50] Rice was adept at the attack style made famous by Foy E. Wallace, Jr., "routinely identifying 'heretics' in print 'by name, rank, and number.'" He roamed throughout the movement identifying liberals, warning particularly that a "Trojan Horse" had transported dangerous liberals into many college Bible Departments.[51]

Nothing more clearly demarcated the widening gulf in the churches of Christ in the 1970s than the emergence of a set of alternate institutions, including a cluster of schools of preaching founded by conservatives to train preachers. By the middle of the 1960s, many conservatives believed that they were being excluded from policy decisions in the colleges and given no voice in the schools' prestigious lectureships, so they founded a parallel set of institutions. Commenting on the schools of preaching in 1996, a reporter in the *Christian Chronicle* observed, "These institutions can be best classified as seminaries, a term not in the common parlance of churches of Christ. They offer undergraduate and graduate degrees in Bible and related fields only, but no general education curriculum."[52] The Sunset Church of Christ in Lubbock, Texas, founded the first school in 1964 to train preachers to work in Spanish-speaking countries; in 1965, three new schools of preaching were launched, including the Nashville School of Preaching, headed by the conservative Roy Hearn, and the Brown Trail

School of Preaching in Hurst, Texas, which under its first head, Roy C. Deaver, became a prototype training school. In 1966, the influential Memphis School of Preaching opened. In 1970, Batsell Barrett Baxter estimated that ten schools of preaching were training about twenty-five percent of the preachers in the churches of Christ.[53] While founders of the schools of preaching generally cited a growing shortage of preachers as the reason for their existence, the new institutions clearly signaled dissatisfaction with the older colleges. As historian Robert E. Hooper put it, the schools were candid "warnings . . . directed at the mainstream churches of Christ."[54] The conservative magazines, schools, and lectureships that appeared in the late sixties provided a network to counter the powerful institutional nexus controlled by the older periodicals and the schools. They gave a voice to those whose conservatism, combativeness, or lack of academic credentials made them personae non grata at the older colleges. In short, by the 1970s an alternate institutional network was in place that would provide a framework for a division in the decades that followed.

In the 1970s, the warriors who believed that they had preserved the mainstream churches of Christ from the ravages of "antism" were stunned that the churches they had saved had been infiltrated by a group who appreciated neither their victories nor their methods. In an article written in 1993, Hugo McCord seemed bewildered by the progressives' disregard for biblical patterns: "Long ago the digressives split the body of Christ by speaking where the Bible does not speak, by refusing to respect the silence of the Scriptures. Now some gospel preachers are not following the pattern. If one is not bound by the silence of the Scriptures he cannot oppose infant baptism, nor dancing in the worship, nor clerical vestments, nor candles . . . nor non-prescription drugs, nor lotteries and other gambling."[55] While the attention of the conservatives had been focused on fighting the "digressives," some very disconcerting ideas had crept in unawares.

The dissident voices of the sixties were disruptive, but they were a muffled warning of the war that lay ahead in the 1980s and 1990s. Looking back, conservative preacher Roy H. Lanier, Jr., surmised that in the sixties and seventies progressives "craftily . . . infiltrated several teachers into our colleges who no longer believed in the inerrancy of the Bible," but that these infiltrators kept their views undercover.[56] The drift toward a more open theological stance in the Bible Departments of the church-related colleges was more a product of rising academic aspirations than of calculated conspiracy, but it did have a cumulative effect on the churches of Christ. The progressives of the sixties and seventies proved that it was possible to hold deviant views and remain in the churches of Christ and, particularly in the colleges, to rise to positions of influence and power.

The range and ferocity of the debate that erupted in the mainstream churches of Christ in the 1980s and 1990s, and the de facto division of the movement in the 1990s, paralleled those of earlier sociological schisms in the movement. In a book deploring the strife-ridden condition of the churches, *Will the Cycle Be Unbroken*, Abilene historian Douglas A. Foster paralleled the impending division in the churches of Christ and the churches of Christ–Christian Church schism of the early twentieth century.[57] In fact, the splintering of the churches of Christ at the end of the twentieth century was more akin to the division between the Independent Christian Churches and the Disciples of Christ in the 1930s, a split that was a second wave of division that followed the shedding of the churches of Christ in 1906.[58] Similarly, the shedding of the noninstitutional churches of Christ in the 1950s was followed by a second wave of division that delineated two distinct groups within the mainstream.

Much changed in the mainstream churches of Christ in the decades following the euphoric fifties and early sixties.

In 1996, the editor of the *Christian Chronicle,* acknowledging that the churches of Christ were in the midst of an "identity crisis," elaborated on the sociological changes that had occurred since World War II: "The church is no longer a splinter group which meets on the other side of the tracks and has poorly educated preachers and ministers. The members of the churches of Christ are not part of the lower middle class committed to rising economic and social standing." The churches of Christ, he reported, had become a diverse group, whose members ranged from people with "old family money" to "welfare families," and the strain was showing.[59] A study conducted by the Center for Church Enrichment at Abilene Christian University in the early 1990s confirmed that the churches of Christ were a sociologically diverse group. The group included many substantial congregations, and twenty percent of the churches employed more than one minister; 66.3 percent of the ministers had bachelor's degrees and 31.6 percent held graduate degrees. Predictably, those with higher educational credentials preached in the larger churches. The average income of pulpit ministers was $37,418; one in five received salaries of more than $55,000 per year; one in twenty more than $75,000.[60]

The power structure in the churches of Christ also had been seriously altered by the end of the seventies. The transformation, Richard Hughes noted, amounted to "the dismantling of an old, entrenched power structure that had resided for years in the 'editor-bishops.'"[61] Throughout most of the sixties and seventies the "on the march mentality" and the boosterism that followed World War II captured the headlines, and most church members basked in their newfound image of respectability. During those years, recalled the editor of the *Christian Chronicle,* "most church members could name dozens of preachers and members were acquainted with the people and works of congregations all around them. The *Herald of Truth* and Ira North's *Amazing Grace Bible Class* were known by almost all church members. Both of those programs promoted the image of the churches of Christ as a unified, successful fellowship."[62] However, as church growth slowed and then turned downward in the 1970s, these cherished icons lost appeal. By the mid-1970s, optimism waned and the churches of Christ began a public discussion of the malaise that Batsell Barrett Baxter called "the crisis."[63]

The progressives of the sixties, joined by a new generation of university-trained preachers and professors, lay the blame on the spirit of philistinism that had captured the churches of Christ. The rampant institution-building of the two decades after World War II was born of a vacuous, traditional, denominational mentality. In the last three decades of the twentieth century, the progressive voice had a sharper edge; a self-conscious, educated elite often spoke with condescension and disparagement about their church's past and were contemptuous of the doctrinal conservatives who resisted change and self-analysis. In 1995, a young rebel summed up the militant mind set of the new generation of progressives: "The seeds of anti-intellectual fundamentalism planted earlier in the century are bearing fruit in a number of frightening ways today. I am hearing about a young group I'll call 'hybrid extremists.' They are an odd mix of the 'brotherhood regulator' mentality . . . and Generation X pessimism. They have an immediate audience among older generation 'church-'n-society-goin'-ta-hell-in-a-handbasket' handwringers. Recite the state of American moral decline, throw in a few founding fathers and Christian Coalition quotes, hammer the abortionists, and presto, you are on the circuit. The milder ones see themselves as sort of last-of-the-breed survivalists, proudly waving the Remnant Shall Return flag. The more militant ones still have a dream of purging the Church of Christ and sternly go about their prophetic mission like Rush Limbaugh, minus a sense of humor."[64]

There were many direct links between the aggressive progressives of the 1990s and the older generation who had voiced their concerns through *Mission* and *Integrity*. In 1973, in a symbolic act of defiance, Lynn Anderson, a bright and respected young minister, pronounced from the pulpit of the Fifth and Highland Church in Abilene that the church of Christ was a "big, sick denomination."[65] In the years ahead, many of the most talented preachers in the churches of Christ laid siege to the church, picturing it as a bigoted, sectarian, politically conservative, and materialistic denomination. It was the church into which they had been born, however, and they had decided to stay. They believed that the movement had lost its way and its distinctiveness. Mike Cope wrote, "Religious restoration movements (and there have been many!) begin with a hunger to search God's word, to seek God's favor, and to live as God's counter-culture. . . . But at some point the 'movement' stops. Calcifies. Petrifies. People start assuming everyone knows what their identity is: they are the 'true' New Testament Church."[66]

In the 1980s and 1990s a series of historical studies sought to define and redefine the churches of Christ. The progressive reassessment of the churches of Christ found its consummate expression in Richard Hughes's richly nuanced history of the churches of Christ, *Reviving the Ancient Faith,* published in 1996 by William B. Eerdmans. Hughes's interpretations were complemented by Abilene Christian University historian Douglas Foster's book, *Will the Cycle Be Unbroken: Churches of Christ Face the Twenty-First Century,* published in 1994, and by Pepperdine professor Michael W. Casey's book, *Saddlebags, City Streets and Cyberspace: A History of Preaching in the Churches of Christ,* published in 1995.

In his study of the churches of Christ, Hughes deftly portrayed a movement adrift from its moorings, a post–World War II church mesmerized by its success and sense of self-importance. The theme that Hughes most valued in the restoration storehouse of ideas was "apocalyptic primitivism." He believed that this prophetic dimension had been replaced by sterile denominational legalism. Hughes, Foster, and Casey all grasped the sociological, as well as the theological, dimensions of the twentieth-century history of the churches of Christ and, in differing ways, reflected on the cultural captivity of the group in the postwar years.

In the minds of these historians, the heroes of the postwar years were the younger generation who in the eighties and nineties demythologized the churches of Christ, determined to drag the group, kicking and screaming, into the twenty-first century. Hughes believed that it was the modern progressives who retained the countercultural, apocalyptic commitment that was the essence of the churches of Christ: "Therein lies the final irony of the tradition: the older generation characterized the younger generation as deviant, liberal, and subversive when in fact the younger generation upheld many of the sectarian ideals of the nineteenth century, especially the ideal that had descended from the Stone-Lipscomb tradition that their parents had rejected."[67] C. Leonard Allen, a member of the Bible faculty at Abilene Christian University along with Hughes in the 1980s, also explored dissenting traditions in the churches of Christ. The most notable of Allen's historical works, published in 1993, *Distant Voices: Discovering a Forgotten Past for a Changing Church,*[68] focused on such issues as race, women's rights, and the role of the church in addressing social injustice.

In 1985, a new magazine, *Image,* was launched to promote progressive ideas. *Image* was founded and edited by Denny Boultinghouse; in its early years Reuel Lemmons also served as an editor, having been forced to leave the *Firm Foundation* when it was bought by conservative interests. After Lemmons's death, Boultinghouse continued to edit *Image,* until it merged in 1996 with *Wineskins,* a publication begun in 1992 by Mike Cope, Rubel Shelly, and Phillip Morrison.[69] *Wineskins* was more dauntless than *Image* in its iconoclasm; the editors announced in the inaugural issue that they were "committed to the stimulation of bold but responsible change in the church of God." They wrote, "The very title is taken from Jesus's parable about the ever-fresh gospel, and its always-frail containers.

He warned against putting 'new wine in old wineskins' lest the skins burst and waste the contents. In his metaphor, the skins are the culturally-conditioned and time-bounded experiences of the people who form the covenant community of God. When those receptacle-carriers of the heavenly message become fixed and inflexible, they no longer serve God's purpose effectively."[70]

Image and *Wineskins* became visible symbols of the strength of progressives in the 1980s. *Mission* ceased publication in 1987, its leaders convinced that the mantle of reform had passed into competent new hands.[71] While the aims of the new progressives were similar to those of the rebels of the sixties, they labored in a much less hostile environment. "In the 1960s," recalled Richard Hughes, "Churches of Christ largely resisted the kind of renewal that *Mission* sought to achieve, thereby relegating *Mission* to the status of gadfly to the mainstream tradition."[72] In the eighties and nineties the progressives competed for the hearts and minds of the churches of Christ. In 1989, Nashville progressives, led by Rubel Shelly, began to sponsor an alternate lectureship program called the Nashville Jubilee. Hosted by a number of Nashville congregations, the "celebration" in the early nineties attracted more than twelve thousand people who participated in innovative classes and nontraditional worship.[73]

Conservative Counterattacks in the Eighties and Nineties

Given the new forthrightness of the progressives, by the 1990s, heated skirmishes filled the landscape. In 1992, Abilene Christian University professor Andre Resner set off a firestorm with an article in *Wineskins* entitled "Christmas at Matthew's House." In a stunning piece of iconoclasm, Resner wrote that Matthew's genealogy of Jesus "begins with sexual scandal and it ends in political power plays. Before he can tell the scandal of Mary's 'immaculate conception,' he has to subtly remind us of other scandalous women."[74] Such twitting of the traditional beliefs of members of the churches of Christ (and, indeed, of most orthodox Christians) unleashed bellows of outrage. Freed-Hardeman historian William Woodson wrote, "A sickness of heart arises and lingers that a brother in Christ could and would so write of Jesus and his mother! How could responsible editors allow such disrespectful words to appear in their columns?"[75]

The furor over Resner's article was only the most visible of a stream of heated exchanges in the 1980s and 1990s between progressives, many of whom taught in church-related colleges, and an increasingly irate conservative opposition. Two journals, the *Spiritual Sword* and the *Firm Foundation,* desperately tried to contain the inroads of the progressives. In 1983, the *Firm Foundation* fell into the hands of conservatives, resulting in the unseating of its editor since the 1950s, Reuel Lemmons, and his replacement by H. A. (Buster) Dobbs. Dobbs, who was cut from the same cloth as Foy E. Wallace, Jr., was incensed by the growing boldness of liberal pronouncements and the apparent irreversible capitulation of the colleges to the cause of progressive change. He quickly gave notice that he intended to revitalize the church's tradition of honorable controversy: "A far greater danger is in developing the foolish notion that all controversy is sin. . . . Jesus did not back away from altercation. . . . He was an accomplished logician and master apologist. He never walked away from an argument."[76] The *Firm Foundation* under the leadership of Dobbs became the watchdog that hounded every indiscretion by a college faculty member or editor and alerted its readers to the danger. The magazine bristled with attacks on the "watered down" Christianity of the "ease-off, cool-down, rein-in, pull-up, gloss-over, type—the type so broad minded that it makes one's brain fall out."[77]

There was a softer side to the conservatism of the eighties and nineties. Sometimes conservatives waxed nostalgic remembering the heyday of the churches of Christ in the 1950s and 1960s. During those years the church had prospered, wrote Alan E. Highers, editor of the *Spiritual Sword,* because "the churches of Christ [were] . . . largely untouched by the ravages of liberalism." In that idyllic era, before the raucous cacophony demanding change, Highers recalled, "we were content to believe and preach the scriptures as the word of God. Our pulpits rang out with 'book, chapter, and verse' and 'thus saith the Lord.' Rare indeed were the preachers or professors who advocated a 'new hermeneutic' or questioned biblical authority."[78] In 1995, the *Spiritual Sword* published an issue on the theme "precious memories," reminding the younger generation of "the way things once were, with particular emphasis on the peace and unity which characterized the church as a whole, even when issues arose among brethren and long before the current company of critics invaded our ranks to sow the seeds of discord, division, and dissatisfaction."[79]

Boosterism died hard and many rued the destruction of the "brotherhood" that the postwar generation had built. Harvey Porter wrote in 1993, "According to Mac Lynn in the *Churches of Christ in the United States,* there are more than 8,000 mainline congregations in the United States and hundreds overseas. . . . We hear the church being labeled 'out of touch,' 'non-progressive,' 'uncaring,' 'too conservative' and 'too liberal.' Articles and books are being written that bash the church and predict her demise within a few years. In a religious world that has not recognized congregational autonomy, we might have emphasized it to the detriment of 'loving the brotherhood.'"[80] While challenging the "liberal tendencies within our great brotherhood," some conservatives still hoped to find a middle ground, avoiding the "radical reactionism" that injected "personality" issues into every dispute and made "issues out of non-issues."[81] Many of the older preachers who had built the churches of Christ seemed befuddled by the tidal wave of discontent and criticism. Leroy Brownlow expressed the consternation of the older generation: "The Restoration plea is a proven winner. No doubt about it. . . . We became the fastest growing religious body in America. . . . Just think how big we could be today if the body of Christ had not suffered from digressions. . . . In spite of Holy Scripture and glorious success, it appears that history is now attempting to repeat itself. Hence, our number one challenge today is to hold the line against the forces of apostasy. . . . If we lose here, we lose everything."[82]

Some of the older preachers who were distraught by the pace of change in the churches of Christ by the 1990s still loved the colleges and the other institutions that had been captured by the progressives and tried to believe the best of these cherished organizations. On the other hand, the leaders of the colleges tried to stay out of the firing line, though they were the favored targets of conservative heresy hunters.[83] Abilene Christian University president Royce Money did his best to keep open lines of communication with all segments of the churches of Christ, though in his inaugural address he issued a firm warning to zealots on both sides: "As a Christian university, ACU is not for sale. Not to the right or to the left. Not to sectarian spirits who set themselves up as standards of orthodoxy or to any spirits who would have us sell our religious birthright."[84] In a 1993 speech at the Abilene Christian University Lectures, Money tried to position himself "squarely in the broad middle of our movement to restore New Testament Christianity," eschewing both "the ultra-conservative, legalistic mindset" and the "progressive, most liberal mindset."[85]

President Money and others discovered that the middle of the road had become very narrow by the 1990s. Conservatives ridiculed his nonpartisan claims, pointing out that such liberals as Rubel Shelly and Bill Love were regulars at the Abilene Christian University Lectures while conservatives had been boycotted for years.[86] In a clear effort to embarrass Abilene administrators, in 1995, conservatives requested permission to host a "seminar on the New Testament Church," which would have caused serious unrest on campus. Conservatives were sure their request would be refused, but they made their case:

Royce Money (1942–). Money became president of Abilene Christian University in 1992. A skilled administrator, Money tried to find a middle path that would make the growing university useful to churches of Christ and faithful to the vision of its founders while at the same time striving for excellence in an environment of academic freedom. In spite of his efforts, Money and Abilene Christian University were the frequent targets of mainstream conservatives. (Courtesy of the Center for Restoration Studies, Abilene Christian University.)

"We simply want ACU to give equal time, attention, and status to the expression of a diametrically different viewpoint of the doctrinal stance of the New Testament church from that which was voiced by Rubel Shelly and others . . . which was sponsored by ACU. We believe that it is a grave sin to use instrumental music in worship as well as to enter into fellowship with those who do so, as Shelly and others at the Unity Forum advocated."[87] It became increasingly clear that President Money and other college leaders would not be able to respond adequately to the constant barrage of charges leveled by conservatives, nor was there any likelihood that the widening breech would narrow.

Some moderates in the 1990s still hoped that the lines of communication could be kept open in the churches of Christ; the *Gospel Advocate* frequently published articles appealing for calm. In a 1993 editorial Gregory Alan Tidwell urged moderation: "Many sweep all differences under the rug and attempt to gloss over the problems we are facing as a movement. Others approach all differences in a militant, almost vicious manner. Both approaches are a danger to our spiritual well-being."[88] Generally unwilling to identify with the most militant foes of liberalism, the *Gospel Advocate* nonetheless tilted to the right in the 1990s, concerned about the drift away from the "ancient landmarks." Month after month in the 1990s, old-time preachers warned against the encroachments of "the liberalist" in the churches of Christ, particularly in the colleges.[89] A few months before his death, James D. Bales, who had been vigorously attacked by conservatives in the 1970s because of his views on marriage and divorce, asked in the *Gospel Advocate,* "What shall we do when men arise and would lead us from Christ and His church as set forth in Scripture?" He warned that another division lay on the horizon and that those loyal to the churches of Christ "must not let personal friendships keep us from contending for the faith once for all delivered to the saints (Jude 3)."[90] In 1993, *Gospel Advocate* editor F. Furman Kearley, generally noncontroversial, warned that "the Bible teaches repeatedly that Christians must exalt truth above error, principle above peace, purity above corruption."[91]

In his history of the churches of Christ, *A Distinct People,* Robert E. Hooper, long associated with the History Department at David Lipscomb University, portrayed a broad mainstream constantly under barrage by "insurgency" movements on the left and the right. This guerilla warfare was the natural result of the inherent tensions between faith and opinion in the restoration plea.[92] In spite of these tensions, Hooper believed that the "broad middle" that had been so clearly demarcated in the 1950s, before coming under withering attack in the 1970s and 1980s, continued to survive, resisting the shrill clamor on both extremes. By the mid-1980s, Hooper believed, the mainstream churches of Christ had stanched the decline in membership in the United States and shown marked increases in membership outside the United States.[93] The church's missionary zeal was at an all-time high and many of the cooperative programs launched in the fifties remained healthy and productive.

Hooper's middle clearly did exist in the 1990s; in a movement as amorphous as the churches of Christ it would be an oversimplification to imagine that only two networks existed at the end of the millennium. In truth, many complex and uneasy configurations waxed and waned within the movement and many individuals and churches found it difficult to position themselves.[94] Nonetheless, by the 1980s, two alternate networks of fellowship had taken shape in the mainstream churches of Christ. Every congregation and every person within the churches of Christ was obliged to identify with one of the two loci of papers, schools, lectureships, and preachers. No one could write articles in both the *Firm Foundation* and *Wineskins*. If a broad ideological center did still exist within the movement, its institutional nucleus had vanished.

The New Hermeneutic

Richard Hughes concluded that the progressive-conservative confrontation in the churches of Christ that began in the sixties and escalated in subsequent decades was "profoundly theological in character," but "also grew out of long-standing cultural, educational, and demographic rifts."[95] The theological debate was less about specific issues, however, than it was a "hermeneutic crisis" in which many college professors and younger preachers, some of them trained in postmodern thought, demanded "nothing less than a reevaluation of the traditional hermeneutic of Churches of Christ—that is, how they understood the Bible."[96] The cultural crisis, which was equally unsettling, questioned historic assumptions about the undenominational nature of the churches of Christ. In short, the battle lines at the end of the century cut across two basic assumptions of restoration thought—that doctrinal correctness was based on a common-sense reading of the New Testament and that the churches of Christ were the undenominational church of the first century.

In a general way, the theological openness of the progressives signaled a willingness to rethink old doctrinal questions that had long been a part of the movement's settled dogma; for instance, evangelical concepts of grace and Pentecostal understandings of the gifts of the Holy Spirit. Pat Boone was compelled to leave the churches of Christ in the 1960s when he embraced the charismatic movement, but by the 1980s, progressives in the churches of Christ felt free to reexamine the Holy Spirit. While not endorsing charismatic theology, in an article in *Wineskins* in 1996, Randy Harris urged members of the churches of Christ to "re-study and re-think the concept of the reign of God and what that might mean in our day." That subject, Harris believed, like others long considered taboo, should be open to discussion without impugning "each other's faith, motives, or spirituality."[97]

Many progressives felt that the churches of Christ had long been held captive by a dry rationalism that belittled piety and subjective insight. Lynn Anderson pled for more tolerance of the "right-brain Christians in a left-brain church." In the past, he wrote, "many restorationists limited the Holy Spirit to the status of retired author and worship to five acts—stacked heavily on the left-brain side."[98] Appealing for a balance between objective and subjective approaches in 1996, the editor of the *Christian Chronicle* wrote, "Today we see a growing rebellion in the church against a logical, factual approach to worship and doctrine and in favor of a 'feeling' and totally grace-oriented approach. This can be expected, eventually, in any movement that has been overbalanced toward religion of the head, more than that of the heart. Yet, these who insist on change, may carry it to the point at which the pendulum will swing to the devotional extreme, with little room for the basic Bible doctrine."[99]

More portentous than such excursions into personal piety and spiritual insight was the eruption of a full-scale hermeneutical debate. The person who gave impetus to the "new hermeneutic" was Thomas H. Olbricht, chairman of the Relgion Department at Pepperdine University, who in the eighties described a "paradigm shift" in which "church members concerned themselves not so much with biblical pattern for the church as with a more meaningful relationship with God and the members of his body."[100] In a 1996 book, *Hearing God's Voice: My Life with Scripture in the Churches of Christ,* Olbricht described a Bible-centered hermeneutic that seemed far from radical, but his ideas set off and encouraged an academic debate that had a far-reaching impact on the churches of Christ.[101] A young group of scholars, most of whom were familiar with postmodernist and deconstructionist ideas, insisted that the Bible must be read contextually and subjectively, rather than according to a mechanical and legalistic formula inherited from the nineteenth century that demanded literal obedience to commands, apostolic examples, and necessary inferences. Gary D. Collier of Abilene Christian University, one of the most outspoken of the young scholars calling for a reevaluation of restoration hermeneutics, followed iconoclastic presentations at Christian Scholar's Conferences on the campuses of Pepperdine University and Abilene Christian University in 1987 and 1989 with a 1995 book outlining a new mode of interpretation: "The law of God must never be read apart from who God is as he has shown himself through his actions, nor apart from the reasons God gave the law in the first place. . . . Jesus shows that the real issues of understanding the Bible go beyond being focused on the words of the text or even the context. We must instead focus centrally on the heart of God as it reaches out from behind the words and contexts to people."[102] A number of other books published in the 1990s explored alternatives to the traditional hermeneutical approach used in churches of Christ, including C. Leonard Allen's *The Cruciform Church: Becoming a Cross-Shaped People in a Secular World,*[103] Bill Love's *The Core Gospel: On Restoring the Crux of the Matter,*[104] and a book by Rubel Shelly and Randy Harris, *The Second Incarnation: A Theology for the Twenty-First Century Church.*[105] While decrying the preoccupation with hermeneutical debate even as "the world's crises mount," young Darryl Tippens proposed a series of innovative tests that should guide Bible interpretation, such as "understanding the Bible in its original language," reading "in the light of the community's collective wisdom," and considering "the practical effects of the interpretation."[106]

While hardly typical, Rubel Shelly's personal journey from the right wing to the left wing of the churches of Christ in the last four decades of the century was a parable of the journey made by a generation of progressive leaders in the movement. A star pupil of Thomas Warren in the 1960s and a co-founder of the *Spiritual Sword,* Shelly swung sharply to the left in the 1970s; in 1984, in a book entitled *I Just Want to Be a Christian,* he cut himself loose from the denominational loyalties that had previously motivated him.[107] By the 1990s, Shelly had embraced a new hermeneutic and he urged others to "get past the petty infighting and shouting about hermeneutics to the real issue involved. Bible study that is redemptive follows a 'guiding principle' that is offered in the Scripture itself." That "principle," Shelly believed, was "the life of Jesus." He concluded: "Devoting all of one's energy to the minutiae of textual and grammatical-historical criticism may reduce him to a dry academic who lacks the fire of personal spirituality. . . . Read the Bible to discover Christ."[108] In 1985, in a Preachers and Church Leaders Forum hosted by Freed-Hardeman College, Shelly defended his new beliefs and challenged his old

Rubel Shelly (1945–). In the 1960s Shelly was a rising star among the conservatives in the mainstream churches of Christ, but in the 1970s he moved to the opposite extreme of the movement. Questioning the traditional restoration hermeneutic, in 1992 Shelly was one of the founding editors of *Wineskins,* a magazine that quickly became the voice of the left wing in the churches of Christ. (Courtesy of the Center for Restoration Studies, Abilene Christian University.)

comrades to face the fact that "the task of this generation is the serious topic of hermeneutics." So long as people were "looking at the Bible differently," they were destined to repeat over and over again the restoration movement's tragic history of bickering and division.[109]

Conservatives readily acknowledged the centrality of hermeneutics in their controversy with the progressives. By the 1990s, the *Firm Foundation* and the *Spiritual Sword* repeatedly alerted readers to the dangers of the new hermeneutic.[110] Roy H. Lanier, Jr., warned that the hermeneutic crisis was not just another doctrinal skirmish that would cause "upsets but no general division," because by the 1990s, differences were "no longer being discussed on the basis of biblical teaching."[111] Buster Dobbs complained, "Deconstruction and postmodernism show us that words do not mean anything. Feeling is what matters—not words."[112] Reacting to a speech delivered at the Abilene Christian University Lectures by William S. Banowsky, Dobbs warned that discussion was becoming impossible because, for progressives, "logic is a bugaboo"; they had retreated to the obscurantist notion that "he who follows his mind has no heart, and he who follows his heart can forget about reason."[113]

The Cultural Church

The average church member had little interest in the subjective and often obtuse arguments supporting a new hermeneutic; on the other hand, most people instinctively understood that the church's relationship with American culture had changed dramatically. The cultural issue was joined in 1988 with the appearance of *The Worldly Church,* a book written by C. Leonard Allen and Richard T. Hughes, both then at Abilene Christian University, and Michael R. Weed, who taught at the Institute for Christian Studies in Austin, Texas. Their assessment of the churches of Christ sounded much like that of noninstitutional critics three decades earlier: "We often *behave* like a civic club with religious overtones. . . . One current trend in building programs is to hire financial consultants from outside the congregation who teach us how to orchestrate a secularly based 'fund-raising campaign' in the body of Christ. . . . Is it any wonder that evangelism is a low priority item for many members of Churches of Christ?" The authors complained that the churches of Christ had lost sight of "our biblical identity and offer the world only basketball and aerobics, counseling and therapy."[114] In 1996, the editor of the *Christian Chronicle* agreed that the social emphasis in churches of Christ had caused them to lose vitality and cohesion. Echoing *The Worldly Church,* the editor charged that many viewed "the church as just another social agency," leaving behind concerns about "the saving of souls."[115]

The progressives faulted the worldly church on a second, somewhat contradictory, ground. While disapproving of the church's identification with the conservative political and cultural agenda of the fifties, they deplored the lack of interest in other social concerns such as racial equality and women's rights. In his 1993 book, *Distant Voices: Discovering a Forgotten Past for a Changing Church,* C. Leonard Allen probed the history of the churches of Christ in search of "softer, fainter voices" of social protest that had been drowned out by powerful majorities.[116] Richard Hughes concluded that "the historic theology of Churches of Christ left them unprepared, by and large, to deal with issues of social justice and racial equality."[117] The social agenda of the progressives was pretty much that of American liberalism. After a more or less unsuccessful effort to integrate white and black churches of Christ in the 1960s and 1970s, the most visible social cause of the 1980s and 1990s was women's rights. At the end of the century, Hughes judged that questions about women's roles in the churches were "far from resolved"; most progressives continued to call for rethinking the limitations placed on women in the church's activities.[118]

Conservatives reacted angrily to the worldly church charges, "filled with disgust for the likes of Rubel Shelly, Douglas Foster, and Richard Hughes who profess love for the churches of Christ which they dishonor by reducing the churches to the status of another Protestant denomination."[119] Such attacks heaped "dishonor on the biblical traditions of the conservative churches of Christ," seeking to replace them with a "new jerry-built denomination . . . which is not yet on the drawing board."[120] Most denied that they were denominational, insisting that they trusted in the "Lordship of Jesus Christ, not in restoration traditions."[121]

The most effective conservative rebuttal to the cultural captivity indictment was the countercharge that the progressives were themselves politically correct clones of secular academics who were much more given to destroying than to building. F. LaGard Smith, a maverick law professor at Pepperdine University whose background was in the noninstitutional tradition, attacked the agenda of the progressives in a widely read book entitled *The Cultural Church.*[122] His book stated the obvious: the hermeneutical arguments and cultural causes of the progressives (particularly their embrace of "women's issues") marked them as the most overtly culturally captive group in the churches of Christ. Smith was not alone in sensing that the progressives had an Achilles heel. Alan E. Highers, editor of the *Spiritual Sword,* saw them as faddish dilettantes: "That is the reason . . . why *Wineskins* advocates new worship styles, expanded roles for women, soft-pedaling of doctrine, ecumenical attitudes toward denominationalism, and abandonment of the restoration plea. *It is responding to the demands of the marketplace!*"[123]

Debating Fellowship—Again

The substantial disagreements in the churches of Christ in the 1990s sparked a new discussion of the question of what constituted fellowship and schism in the churches of Christ. On a broader level, progressives looked again at their relationship with their evangelical neighbors. Having reconstructed the churches of Christ as simply one of many denominations that had set out on a restoration journey, and having acknowledged that their heritage was as filled with flaws as most others, progressives were ready to reopen the lines of communication with the religious neighbors. At a second level, as conservatives and progressives in the churches of Christ became more and more disdainful of one another, they looked at the limits of fellowship within their own movement. A new generation mouthed old arguments, striving to understand the process by which, without denominational apparatus, the churches of Christ divide.

Progressives in the 1990s rediscovered the power of the restoration slogan: "We are Christians only, but not the only Christians." Speaking at the Highland Church of Christ in Abilene in 1997, Mike Cope announced that he wanted to "come clean" and acknowledge that he believed that many people in various denominations were "God's people, even though they're not a part of my little group." Cope, like many other young progressives, was moved to his confession by the participation of the popular devotional writer Max Lucado in the Promise Keepers rally in Washington in 1995: "One evening Max Lucado, former member of this church and now minister of the Oak Hills Church of Christ in San Antonio, spoke on unity. He called on Christians to quit building walls between denominations, but to let those walls come down. . . . To quit thinking that we're the only little one in Christianity. It was a valiant call for unity."[124] Lucado was a hero to the most open-minded progressives. Douglas Foster, noting that Lucado was "the most widely-known and respected member of Churches of Christ among American evangelicals," was pleased that his stature "undoubtedly had a positive effect on the way many others see us."[125] A generation of preachers in the churches of Christ had grown up reading the writings of evangelical scholars and admiring the work of Billy Graham and other evangelical preachers, and they joyously embraced the idea that they could have Christian fellowship with them. In this respect, and in other important ways, the new progressives left behind the earlier generation that had founded *Mission* magazine and energized the nonconformist thinking of the 1970s.

Many of the younger progressives wondered whether the churches of Christ had any relevance in such a broader community of Christians. Some decided to leave, but others, for reasons of style or personal commitment, were content to stay.

Max Lucado likened the fellowship dilemma to the situation on an embattled ship manned by a diverse and quarrelsome crew: "There is a common deck on this boat on which we can all stand. We can 'bunk' with whomever we choose—probably those who are like us—but when the Captain calls all hands on deck to battle the enemy, it's time to leave opinions and personal preferences behind and stand together."[126]

Such thinking was pure heresy to the conservatives in the mainstream churches of Christ. *Firm Foundation* editor Buster Dobbs wrote, "Real unity is the result of accepting the truth, all else is sham and pretense. Truth, by its nature, can only teach one thing. . . . The essential oneness of truth is a self-evident and a universally recognized maxim."[127] The progressives, Wayne Jackson warned, had "egregiously perverted the teaching of the New Testament in an effort to accommodate an ecumenical agenda."[128] For conservatives, the guidelines for fellowship remained simple: "God desires that we search the scriptures to find the biblical ground, and when that heavenly path is found to brotherhood and fellowship, then we are expected to stay with it. . . . May we resolve to forsake the false ways of the denominations and the teachings of man and follow the teaching which is as old as the New Testament but is forever new."[129]

Some thoughtful members of the mainstream churches of Christ sought for definitions of fellowship broad enough to slow the rush to schism. James S. Woodroof, an irenic and respected moderate preacher, explored the issue in a book that acknowledged that the church was "in transition" and needed to learn "how to differ without dividing."[130] "Love is not the best way to achieve unity," Woodruff urged, "it is the only way."[131] Cecil May, Jr., the conservative and reflective president of Magnolia Christian College, suggested that "levels of fellowship" existed "even among faithful Christians," thus allowing a degree of tension within the movement, though he balked at extending fellowship to the unbaptized who were "not children of the Father."[132]

F. LaGard Smith posited a full-blown theory about levels of Christian fellowship in a book entitled *Who Is My Brother?*[133] Smith defined five levels of "fellowship" engaged in by all Christians. *Universal fellowship* acknowledged the "brotherhood of man" and was shared by all people; *faith fellowship* described the kinship between those who "share our faith in Jesus Christ but who have not experienced rebirth according to the biblical pattern." Smith used the term *Christian fellowship* to describe the relationship of those who had been baptized into Christ (and thus were in fellowship with Christ); this group constituted the Christian's "extended family." *Conscience fellowship* separated those who had been baptized into "enclaves of special 'close family' fellowship among groups of congregations" that allowed "elbow-room for the exercise of individual and collective conscience." Finally, *congregational fellowship* was the "immediate family of Christians who work and worship together in local congregations."[134]

Smith's categories, and his book, were both an effort to describe the types of distinctions that governed the behavior of members of churches of Christ and an effort to find a reasonable balance between doctrinal correctness and mindless factionalism. He was unwilling to abandon his distinctive identity as a separated baptized believer. Widely known in evangelical circles, Smith acknowledged that some with whom he shared a faith fellowship were "like family and may even be closer to us in many respects than brothers and sisters in Christ"; but, he added, "sadly, frustratingly, almost unthinkably—they are not a part of the family of God."[135] He appealed to his friend Max Lucado not to carelessly bridge the divide that separated the churches of Christ from the evangelical world: "Keep that great heart of yours, Max. And keep the vision of Christian unity alive. . . . But I beg you to tell our 'Christian' friends about redemptive, saving baptism. It's you, of all people, they'll listen to!"[136] At the same time, Smith's Christian fellowship and conscience fellowship categories were efforts to give a kind of legitimacy to the loose and disconnected fragments of the restoration movement that littered the religious landscape by the end of the twentieth century.

Whatever the theology of separation, in fact, the churches of Christ at the end of the century had again divided into quite distinct communities. By the 1990s, these two groups of mainstream churches were again sorting out the methodology of separating. In 1993, President Emeritus E. Claude Gardner of Freed-Hardeman University, "out of a troubled heart," explored the untidy technique of dividing the churches of Christ. Having lived through another cycle of "stolen colleges, stolen papers, stolen church buildings," Gardner lamented, "we have no alternative but to begin 'marking' those who have espoused false teaching." He outlined seven needed correctives that fairly well described the way in which churches of Christ separate into distinct communions: "[First,] It is time for elders to remove preachers and other employees who are advocates of restructuring the church by changing doctrine. [Second,] It is time for a number of youth ministers to be 'reined in.' . . . [Third,] It is time for Christian colleges . . . to quit inviting to campus the glib and personable teachers who are on public record for teaching error. . . . [Fourth,] It is time for any member of a board of trustees who believes in restructuring . . . to resign. . . . [Fifth,] It is time for any member of a congregation who becomes divisive . . . to leave, and if not the church should withdraw fellowship. [Sixth,] It is time for congregations to quit using as study materials the Bible class books prepared by the change and restructuring set. [Seventh,] It is time for any administrator, faculty or staff member of a Christian school who is not in sympathy with the purpose of the founding of it . . . to resign posthaste."[137]

In the 1990s members of churches of Christ were, of necessity, defining the institutions and papers that they would support and ideologically purifying the congregations that they attended. Irked by the nontraditional methods used at Nashville's Jubilee, conservatives launched the sort of congregational marking that signals the last days of a division in the restoration movement. J. E. Choate wrote in the *Firm Foundation*, "The elders of Trinity Lane Church of Christ in Nashville served notice to the Woodmont Hills church elders that they no longer could 'recognize' Woodmont Hills Church of Christ as a faithful congregation and would not support or endorse the Jubilee agenda."[138] In a decentralized and purportedly undenominational movement, the process of division was completed when churches delineated parallel lists of "faithful congregations" and when they would no longer "support or endorse" one another's nonchurch organizations.

Looking for Roots

In February 1996, William Banowsky delivered a stunning address at the Abilene Christian University lectureship program. He was nearing the end of a highly successful career that had taken him from preacher of the Broadway Church of Christ in Lubbock, to the presidencies of Pepperdine University and the University of Oklahoma, to a lucrative career in business, and, finally, back to the pulpit. In 1996, Banowsky was returning to the town of his birth and to a "deeply troubled brotherhood." His lecture, entitled "The Christ-Centered Church," was a lucid and predictable defense of progressive ideas; he called for new hermeneutical approaches, the lowering of sectarian boundaries to fellowship, and a jettisoning of the image of the secular church. Most arresting was Banowsky's appeal to the past. Again and again he quoted or used the names of the heroes of earlier generations: Batsell Baxter, G. C. Brewer, Cled E. Wallace, M. C. Kurfees, E. W. McMillan, Hall L. Calhoun, and Jesse P. Sewell. Over and over he appealed to the sense of fairness and moderation they had exhibited. He reminded his listeners of G. C. Brewer's words: "Even if a man teaches error, it would have to be very heinous to be as great a sin as the sin of division." Banowsky went on to quote E. W. McMillan—"Let us know that we, too, are susceptible to all of the errors religious thinkers have ever made"—and Jesse P.

Sewell, one of the chief architects of the Abilene Christian University lectureship program: "The importance of our plea does not consist in the particular truth we now practice, but rather in our attitude toward all truth. If we ever allow ourselves to become satisfied, our usefulness will be ended. Our minds must ever be kept open."[139]

Conservatives bridled at Banowsky's effort to link himself and the progressives of the nineties with such hallowed names from the past. Alan Highers replied to the speech in a *Firm Foundation* article to which Buster Dobbs appended an admonition (as he often did): "Read the following slowly, carefully and taste every word—it is most important." Highers was particularly perturbed that Banowsky had cited Brewer and Sewell, two men whom he had known when he was a young man. Sewell's appeal for openness did not imply that he would have fellowship with denominations, and Banowsky knew it, Highers charged. As for Brewer, Highers cited his statement that he was "forced to work apart from all who will not abide within the doctrine of Christ." "I knew G. C. Brewer," chided Highers, "and, brother Banowsky, I can tell you, you are no G. C. Brewer." He concluded, "It is disappointing to see the words of the pioneer preachers wrested from their context, misappropriated by modern thinkers, and twisted to teach things they never taught and never believed. That such could be accomplished from the platform of ACU is doubly disappointing."[140]

Such squabbling over the past highlighted the complexity of the intellectual heritage of the restoration movement. In fact, it laid bare, once again, the sometimes enigmatic and always varied mixtures of ideas that lay buried in the minds of members of the churches of Christ. On one end of the spectrum lay the common-sense, Baconian legalism of the debaters and on the other lay a broad, culturally alienated, commitment to search for the essence of New Testament Christianity. In between, people embraced millions of individual mixes of those two ideas.

Historians like Richard Hughes, Michael Casey, and Douglas Foster have probably best understood the at times complementary and at times contradictory suppositions undergirding all thought in the churches of Christ. Hughes is something of a personal case study in the ambivalence and contradiction felt by most members of the churches of Christ who tried to reconcile all of the themes they valued from their religious heritage. In a 1997 article assessing the "strengths of our heritage," Hughes praised the churches of Christ for being "a people of the Book." At the same time, he thought that the "best moments" in the church's past came when people were "not bound by inflexible creeds and opinions but, instead, have remained open to a change in perspective if we find that change warranted by the biblical text." While Hughes praised progressive ideas and the desire for Christian unity, including being open to dialogue and fellowship with other religious groups, he also expressed gratitude for "the sectarian dimensions of our heritage." Hughes knew that such statements were "likely to be misunderstood," but he felt a deep personal commitment both to the new progressive vision of the churches of Christ and to the countercultural, prophetic ideology that he found heroically weaving its way through the history of the churches of Christ.[141]

While nearly every member of the churches of Christ would give allegiance to both of these ideas, they existed together in a state of tension. People tended to slip toward one end of the spectrum or the other, particularly when social stresses confirmed their sense of difference. On the conservative extreme were those whose understanding of the churches of Christ was, at best, propositional, based on a common-sense reading of the Scriptures. At worst, it was strongly creedal and sectarian, arbitrarily mandating the boundaries of "brotherhood" fellowship. The idea of a general, open-ended quest for restoration seemed to them a repudiation of the truth inherited from the past and an open door that abolished the rule of law in the churches. Progressives, on the other hand, embraced with open arms the plea for a nonsectarian quest. "We live in a *postdenominational world,*" wrote an exultant Rubel Shelly. "One would think that such a world—without denominational loyalties—is ideal" for the churches of Christ, because the group was based on a "passion for nonsectarian faith."[142] Shelly insisted that this open, dynamic vision was the genius of the spirit of the restoration movement: "The restoration of New Testament Christianity will always be a goal to be sought and never an accomplishment to be applauded and defended."[143] All of these rhetorical forays, on both the left and the right, resonated with the restoration past. The ideas became schismatic only when juxtaposed against one another, when used to justify dramatically diverse visions of the church.

Searching for a usable past in the 1990s, conservatives and progressives found appropriate heroes. It was fitting that the conservatives sought to resurrect the spiritual legacy of Foy E. Wallace, Jr. In 1996, in an article published in the *Firm Foundation* and republished as an advertisement in the *Christian Chronicle,* Noble Patterson of Fort Worth, Texas, eulogized the memory of Wallace: "His life was without blemish, nothing to avoid, explain or extenuate. . . . The brotherhood, probably, has not produced an individual more perfectly rounded—intellectually, physically, and morally—than that presented to us in the person of Foy E. Wallace, Jr." Wallace's legacy, Patterson believed, would withstand the debunking of the younger generation: "Modern revisionists and 'change agents' state their intention to restructure the church and change the past and lay blame for current problems on the older preachers, but they are mistaken!"[144] Editor Buster Dobbs conceded that Wallace was "not perfect," but he was neither "weak nor unsure" and consequently he "was the great Alps and Andes of the living world." "His massive knowledge of God's word made him an enemy of error and sin," Dobbs wrote wistfully, "and even today heretics tremble at the mention of his name."[145]

Reuel Lemmons became the hero of the progressives of the

1990s. In his Abilene speech in 1996, William Banowsky recalled that "Lemmons started out, as most of us did, with the idea of an identifiably exclusive church," but, in later years he came to believe in a "universally inclusive church." Lemmons moved toward a broader faith, Banowsky adroitly observed, because he despised the narrow "sectarianism" so often found in the churches of Christ.[146] For many years Lemmons occupied the middle of the road, trying to listen to and communicate with individuals to both his left and right. Thomas Olbricht recalled, "Because of his middle-of-the-road stand, Reuel was often attacked from either side of the spectrum and accused of inconsistency. He was well aware of this criticism." Near the end of his life, Lemmons summarized his longtime commitment to open-minded discussion and toleration: "As a young preacher, I was sure that I knew what I knew. As I grew older, I wasn't so sure about some things. . . . It takes a while, seemingly, to learn that what appeared as black and white isn't always pure black and white. There are many points of view and many shades of black and white upon closer examination. It takes a while to recognize the rainbow."[147]

Winners and Losers

It is still a bit early to pronounce winners and losers in the churches of Christ at the end of the twentieth century. In 1995, a conservative leader insisted that most congregations remained orthodox and that a firm opposition to instrumental music in worship "is the viewpoint of probably 95 percent of the leaders of the churches of Christ throughout the nation."[148] On the other hand, most conservatives were reconciled to the fact that they had no control over the older educational institutions in the churches of Christ. In 1996, *Firm Foundation* editor Buster Dobbs lamented, "The tragedy of all this is that schools for which good people have sacrificed are now turning against restoration principles—against their founders and benefactors. Our schools—ACU, Pepperdine, Harding—are now going the way of Bethany, College of the Bible, and TCU. History repeats and repeats and repeats."[149]

The best empirical evidence about the current trends in mainstream churches of Christ was offered in a survey conducted in the early 1990s by Mel Hailey, Douglas A. Foster, and Thomas L. Winter through the Center for Church Enrichment at Abilene Christian University. They asked pulpit ministers and youth ministers in churches of Christ a variety of questions, and the answers revealed a growing generational rift in the churches. Asked to define themselves as "fundamentalist," "conservative," "moderate," or "liberal," nearly sixty percent of the pulpit ministers chose the label "conservative" and only thirty-one percent described themselves as "moderate." However, among youth ministers, the answers indicated that fifty percent considered themselves "moderates" and only 35.9 percent "conservative." The authors of the study concluded that the leadership in the churches of Christ held "surprisingly diverse" views on many historically charged doctrinal issues. They reported, "While affirming the importance of a capella singing in worship, our ministers are cautious in prescribing judgment about this issue."[150] The two camps in the mainstream churches of Christ remain fairly evenly matched at the end of the twentieth century, but time and youth seem to be on the side of the progressives.

PART III

Homer Hailey and the Noninstitutional Churches of Christ

1925–1999

5

Texas Preacher and Professor

Homer Hailey enrolled in Abilene Christian College in the fall of 1926 at age twenty-three. He soon cast his lot with the churches of Christ and over the next twenty-five years he became a respected and widely known preacher, writer, and college teacher. Like most members of the churches of Christ, Hailey was rarely at the center of the swirling controversies that often seemed to consume the movement; not until late in his life did he become a focus of controversy during a skirmish over marriage and divorce in noninstitutional churches of Christ. Until that time, the cycle of Hailey's life, like that of most preachers, was filled not with debate and argumentation, but with preaching, baptizing, and studying the Bible. He was one of the foot soldiers who built churches in thousands of cities and villages throughout the United States.

Abilene Preacher Boy

When Homer Hailey entered Abilene Christian College, the twenty-year-old, unaccredited school had a student body of fewer than five hundred students. It was, in fact, little more than a Bible Institute; it had remained a junior college until 1920. ACC was founded in 1906 after the trustees of several small Texas schools decided that "a greater work would be done by combining the efforts of the educationally inclined among the churches of Christ in one great school."[1] During its first session in 1906, the "school began daily with a spelling match held in the largest classroom" and then convened for chapel services. The mission of ACC, engraved on the cornerstone of the administration building, was terse and explicit: "We believe in the divinity of Christ, and in the inspiration of the holy scriptures. Contend earnestly for the faith once for all delivered to the saints." Asked the president of the board of trustees, "If we teach the student this, and similar things found in the Bible, will he or she not be a better boy or a better girl upon leaving here?"[2] The students were "country kids," mostly the children of Texas and Oklahoma ranchers and farmers who were members of churches of Christ.[3] Academic standards were slipshod. Paul Southern recalled teaching a course in journalism while still a student; he enrolled in the course and awarded himself an *A* for his outstanding work.[4]

The editor of the *Firm Foundation* occasionally encouraged "conscientious Christians interested in the cause of the education of their children or of the rising generation in a general way" to aid ACC, but the college was always underfunded and subject to the constant scrutiny of the crusty preachers who had built the churches of Christ in Texas, most of whom were neither college educated nor overly fond of institutions.[5] Every ACC appeal for funds began with a hypothesis that was by no means settled in the 1930s: "If Abilene Christian College has a right to exist . . . "[6] Most of the instructors preached part-time and raised cattle to help feed their families and supplement their meager salaries.[7]

Hailey funded his first year at ACC with the inheritance of nearly five hundred dollars that he received from the estate of Grandfather Hailey and his part of the money he and his brother Rob received when they sold their share of the Willcox store. Homer, his cousin Sybil, his mother, Mamie, and his sister Ruth set up housekeeping in Abilene in the fall, but the arrangement proved to be too costly and in December Mamie returned to Hallsville where Roy had been living with his

Abilene Christian College administration building, circa 1930. (Courtesy of the Center for Restoration Studies, Abilene Christian University.)

uncle Roger Collins; Ruth went to Arizona; Sybil found another apartment; and Homer moved into the dormitory. Ahead of him lay "four great years," years of hard work and notable accomplishments. He graduated third in the class of 1930 and was vice-president of the senior class; his life's work as a preacher was already well under way, and he had plans to marry a few months after graduation.

After moving to Abilene, Hailey immediately sought a home congregation. Still almost totally ignorant of the decades of controversy and debate that had divided the Christian Church and churches of Christ, he first visited the First Christian Church in Abilene. He was disappointed. The Christian Church in Abilene was far more liberal and pretentious than the little group in Willcox. "We didn't know what liberalism was in Willcox," Hailey later recalled. Exposed to the more "fashionable" Christian Church in Abilene, Hailey instinctively felt out of place, as he had when he visited the campus of Texas Christian University.

Hailey soon began attending the College Church of Christ that met on the campus. Most of the students attended the congregation, and several soon challenged Hailey to defend the use of instrumental music. Hailey readily admitted that he was unprepared to discuss the question either pro or con. Some of his fellow students were abrasive; others, particularly Glenn L. Wallace, a member of the celebrated family of preachers who later preached at the College Church, studied patiently with Hailey. As was typical for Hailey when sufficiently prodded, he withdrew and studied the question for himself. He checked three books out of the library: O. E. Payne's defense of instrumental music, *Instrumental Music Is Scriptural;* M. C. Kurfees's attack on the use of instrumental music in worship, *Instrumental Music in Worship;* and a published debate between I. M. Boswell and N. B. Hardeman, *Discussion on Instrumental Music in Worship.*[8] After Hailey had finished reading the three books, he was convinced that instrumental music was unscriptural. He never again questioned that judgment. It was a typical Hailey problem-solving scenario—he delayed studying until circumstances forced him to do so, he studied privately and intensely, he made up his mind, and he never looked back.

Before his first quarter at ACC ended, Hailey had placed his membership at the Northside Church of Christ, where a blunt and conservative Englishman, Frank B. Shepherd, was the preacher. Hailey's move from the Christian Church to the churches of Christ was unceremonious; he never made a public acknowledgment that he had changed. During the 1930s, thousands of people moved informally between the two groups. Some educated and affluent members of churches of Christ joined Christian churches; a much larger number of people, mostly working people who felt ill at ease in the upwardly mobile Christian churches, joined Homer Hailey in an exodus that swelled the ranks of churches of Christ. A generation later, some churches of Christ balked at such easy passage from the Christian Church, demanding a formal confession acknowledging one's former sinful beliefs. However, such barriers formed slowly within the restoration movement. In the 1920s, the Christian Church and churches of Christ were estranged brethren, not separate churches, and Homer Hailey and thousands of others moved easily from one wing of the movement to the other, having little sense that they had changed churches.[9]

Homer Hailey often demonstrated that he was a man with tunnel vision. As a student, he was "interested in one thing, and that was the Bible."[10] He endured courses in psychology and science. In English, he never learned the difference between "syntax" and "sin tax"; "Greek took him." His speech teacher was a "monkey in class . . . who wasn't prepared." None of that was of much importance, however. He had enrolled at ACC to learn the Bible. He had come to the right place. "We teach literature and other subjects," noted the president of the board of trustees, "but it is all done that we may teach the Bible more perfectly."[11]

Hailey quickly developed a formidable campus reputation as a student of the Bible. He and his classmate Paul Southern, another older student who decided to become a preacher after working as a reporter for several years, set a formidable standard for study and academic achievement. Walter H. Adams, later the distinguished academic dean of ACC for many years, remembered teaching Southern and Hailey in his Sunday morning Bible class at the College Church: "Even then they knew more Bible than I did."[12] Hailey was disappointed with some of his Bible teachers: the "sorriest Bible class I ever had in my life" was taught by the flashy and personable preacher at the College Church, E. W. McMillan. However, he savored the instruction of R. C. Bell, a modest and studious man who made his students love the Bible. Bell was somewhat controversial because of his emphasis on grace. "When you talked about grace back then, you were a Baptist," recalled Hailey. However, he inspired a fierce loyalty among his students, including Homer Hailey.[13]

Hailey's single-minded focus on Bible study fairly well determined the limits of his activities. He tried to play football, and participated in a couple of games, but his skills were unimpressive and his heart was not in it. He maintained his interest in physical fitness and boxing, however. He formed a close friendship with ACC's young English teacher and track coach, J. Eddie Weems, and the two of them sparred regularly. Hailey relished the "sting of the leather" and the self-confidence that boxing gave him.

None of the students at ACC had much money; most of their entertainment was provided by on-campus plays and parties. The administration permitted "social clubs," more or less surrogate fraternities and sororities, but Hailey shunned them as elitist. He rarely dated; during his first year in Abilene his sole date came when a coed invited him to a banquet. Not until his senior year did he allow his attention to waver from his goal of becoming a preacher long enough to begin to think about the possibility of marriage.

Hailey's outside activities, like his studies, were mostly spiritual. He was most active in the Missions Study Class, a group composed of those students "deeply interested in the spread of the Gospel and the salvation of souls."[14] During his junior and senior years, Hailey was the leader of the group, scheduling appearances by "various missionaries who pass through Abilene" and directing the students in local evangelical activities.[15] In 1929 and 1930 the Missions Study Class, under Hailey's direction, organized "classes for the colored people of Abilene" on each Monday afternoon.[16] Assisted by three other students, Mildred Caricker, Gertrude Pettigrew, and Mary Ethel Tackett, Hailey directed a "negro school" throughout the year, enrolling about thirty students for worship and Bible study.[17]

Hailey began to preach regularly in nearby churches during his junior year. He delivered his first real sermon in January 1927, while still a freshman, traveling with Eddie Weems to Buffalo Gap, a small community just south of Abilene where

Weems preached regularly. Hailey spoke on the topic of hope; he later recalled that the effort was "sort of hopeless." He had prepared to speak for forty minutes, but he was out of material in eighteen.[18] By the fall of 1928, however, Hailey had won recognition as one of the "preacher boys from Abilene Christian College who go far and wide to proclaim the gospel."[19] The 1928 group included several young men who later became widely known preachers: Paul Southern, Glenn Wallace, Don H. Morris, and Hailey. The "preacher boys" commanded great respect from their fellow students.[20]

Hailey preached in several different places during his sophomore and junior years; by the end of 1928 he had established a circuit of small churches that he visited once each month.[21] His regular appointments took him to nearby Hamby; to Gustine, about 135 miles to the east; to Santo, about halfway to Fort Worth; and Lamesa, a town 150 miles to the west. While the compensation was meager, ranging from twenty-five dollars per Sunday in the larger churches to ten dollars in the small ones, Hailey earned nearly a hundred dollars each month, a sum that went far toward paying his college expenses.

Hailey's preaching skills grew with practice; at the beginning of his senior year in the fall of 1929, he was widely regarded as a "good speaker." In the spring, he won the "annual Cox extempore contest," having finished second to Paul Southern the previous year. Hailey won twenty-five dollars for a speech on the Good Samaritan;[22] he used the money to purchase his first "preaching suit." In April he was invited to deliver a sermon at the eleven o'clock service at the College Church. Preaching on "our calling," Hailey concluded with the homey admonition: "The latch string is on the inside and Christ is on the outside knocking at the door. We have to open the door ourselves if we are to hear the call of Christ."[23] At ACC's graduation ceremonies in the spring of 1930, Hailey's friend J. Eddie Weems, who had been the class sponsor, delivered the commencement address, and Hailey and Paul Southern "were chosen . . . to preach the sermons for the senior class Sunday June 1 before the college congregation."[24]

Hailey and Paul Southern often car-pooled to their preaching appointments. Shortly after midnight on the morning of January 28, 1929, as the two arrived at the campus in Homer's little roadster, they discovered that the school's administration building was in flames. They turned in the alarm, and soon the campus was alive as "boys and girls began scampering out of their beds to watch the spreading, leaping flames as they completely destroyed the old building."[25] Fortunately, the college already had a new campus under construction, intending to move the next year. The loss of the building was largely sentimental, "because of the sort of folks who have studied and taught, labored and loved each other under its leaking roof."[26]

Each summer while he was a student at Abilene, Hailey scrambled to earn enough money to fund his next year's studies. During the summer of 1927 he secured a job at the Swift Packing House in Fort Worth, but he lasted only two weeks working in the dark interior of the packing house. He collected his pay and hitchhiked to Willcox. There he spent the summer working a construction job on a dude ranch in the Chiricahua Mountains. Each Saturday evening he drove into Willcox to stay with the Huffmans and to preach on Sunday in the Willcox Christian Church. He had lost his suitcase on the way to Arizona and arrived without suit, Bible, or sermon notes, but the women of the Christian church presented him with a new American Standard Bible, the version that he would use the rest of his life.

At the end of the summer of 1927, Hailey conducted a gospel meeting for the Willcox Christian Church, the first he had ever held. Although he had decided that instrumental music was wrong, the church continued to use a piano during the summer and during the meeting. The next summer Hailey returned to Arizona, working at odd jobs, including escorting a trainload of cattle to Los Angeles, and again held a meeting in the Willcox Christian Church at the end of the summer. This time, he asked that the instrument not be used; the members were willing if Hailey would lead the singing. He preached and led the singing each evening. His song leading, he later judged, provided "the best argument for the use of instrumental music that could have been made."[27]

During the summers of 1929 and 1930 Hailey held gospel meetings, having gained confidence as a preacher and a modest reputation in Arizona. They were "great summers," crammed with wholesome activity and good companionship. In 1929 Hailey traveled with his friend and fellow ACC "preacher boy" Alton Wimbish. The two had only a few meetings scheduled when the summer began, and no promise of financial support, but they began the summer in Tucson, with Homer preaching and Alton leading the singing, and then proceeded to Tempe and other little churches in Arizona as they received impromptu invitations, baptizing scores of people along the way. Hailey and Wimbish traveled all summer in Homer's Model T Roadster, camping out in the evenings when not housed by one of the brethren. Mamie Hailey met the two young men after their meeting in Tempe, and the three of them camped out at the Grand Canyon. Hailey ended the summer back in Texas; he held a meeting near Hallsville at a rural church known as "Across Cyprus," baptizing twenty-nine people. By the time Hailey and Wimbish returned to Abilene for the opening of school in the fall, they had accumulated scores of lifelong remembrances and had harvested scores of converts. For school expenses, they had earned a net profit of about one hundred dollars each.

In the summer of 1930, immediately after his graduation, Hailey set out again for Arizona, this time with quite a few meetings scheduled in advance. He was accompanied by fellow students Alton Wimbish and Paul Simon. Once again, the young men departed "without any assurance of support"; Frank B. Shepherd, then preaching at the College Church of Christ in Abilene, reported that Hailey had gotten an advance on his winter's salary and that the other two young men left Abilene with seven dollars between them.[28] At age twenty-seven, newly graduated from college, Homer Hailey had become the apostle to Arizona. The three young men reported their progress all through the summer in the columns of the *Firm Foundation*. Hailey began the summer in Tucson in June, proceeded to Tempe for a three-week meeting, and then met Alton Wimbish in Coolidge. Hailey reported that Coolidge was a "new town of about nine hundred inhabitants." The two young men rented the hall of the Woman's Club and flushed out a few members of the churches of Christ. Five of the Christians they discovered were "faithful members," but they also uncovered "several others whom ice would blister."[29] "It is usually found," reported young Hailey, "that people coming to this country from other parts leave their religion at home." After three weeks in the "mission meeting" in Coolidge (meaning they received no compensation), Hailey reported, "We closed a three weeks meeting here last night. Alton Wimbist [*sic*] was with me the first two weeks leading the singing, but left at the end of that time for Payson. . . . Seven were added by baptism, and about fifteen members gotten together from around here. So we are leaving a congregation of between twenty and twenty-five members. Brother Jones, an old time gospel preacher, was responsible for the meeting, and is a capable leader to carry on the work."[30] From Coolidge, Hailey went to Wickenburg for a three-week meeting, living with Dr. and Mrs. Copeland, a physician and his wife who were much "praised for their work and effort." Six were baptized in Wickenburg and Hailey departed for Gilbert for a tent meeting.[31] In October, the newly formed Gilbert church reported that five had been baptized during Hailey's meeting, including "a man 73 years of age." The "brethren are meeting regularly for worship," the report boasted, and they had started a building fund.[32]

All in all, it was a remarkable summer. Hailey wrote an extended report for the *Gospel Advocate* describing the state of the churches of Christ in Arizona.[33] In the fall of 1930, he knew them more intimately than anyone else. Phoenix had three congregations, Hailey reported, but only "one of these can be said to be really progressive and active." Tempe had a "wonderful little congregation" with a stucco building and seventy-five members, a number of them baptized by Hailey during his two summers of preaching there. Besides Tucson and Tempe, Hailey reported, Arizona had only scattered congregations with twenty-five or fewer members; there were about six hundred active members in the entire state. Hailey appealed for other preachers to help spread the message in Arizona: "Brethren, the fields are white, but the laborers are few. What are we going to do with this field at our door? You will find that the brethren in this country are not able to pay big money for preaching, but they will always take care of you, and see that you do not go away hungry, and that you will get to the next place." It was a strikingly self-sacrificial summer, one filled with the kind of single-minded devotion to the cause of Christ that endeared Homer Hailey to a generation of church members in Arizona and elsewhere. Frank Shepherd commended Hailey and Wimbish, noting that the two young men planned to return to Arizona in the summer of 1931; he judged that "it would be a worth-while investment for some strong congregation to finance their activities."

Hailey returned to Abilene in September 1930 to become principal of the small elementary and high schools operated by ACC and to wed Lois Manly. The two had become engaged just before their graduation. Both had been popular students. Because Homer was vice-president of the senior class (Paul Southern was president) and Lois was secretary, they sat next to each other at chapel each day, in seats assigned to the class officers in the front row. They became friends; Lois had poor vision and they began to study together for a history class, and Homer invited her to the Junior-Senior Banquet. As graduation approached, Hailey for the first time allowed his mind to turn to thoughts of marriage. He thought that Lois would make "a mighty good wife"; he proposed and she accepted. It was not entirely a cold-blooded decision, there was "chemistry" in it, but the marriage occurred because the time was ripe.[34]

It was, in many ways, a good match. Both Homer and Lois were serious, devout, and talented. In other ways, it was a curious match. Lois was president of the Ko Jo Kai Club, "one of the traditional social clubs composed of co-eds whose purpose [was] to broaden their views of life through happy associations." Lois and the Ko Jo Kais sponsored "many feasts, parties, luncheons and dinners," including an "annual banquet given in the spring term at the Hilton Hotel."[35] Aside from being a social leader on campus, Lois was most noted because of her talent for dramatics. In 1928, as a sophomore, she was elected secretary of the Dramatic Club and played Juliet in a performance of "Romeo and Juliet" that became legendary on the ACC campus.[36] She was in demand to give dramatic readings at various social functions on campus, and, according to the student newspaper, received "a Bachelor of Oratory from Simmons University" in the summer of 1930.[37] Homer, on the other hand, actively disliked the social clubs. He had won recognition as a "preacher boy," the leader of the Missions Study Club, and the president of the James A. Garfield Scholarship Society, an organization drawn from the top ten percent of the junior and senior classes dedicated to promoting "school loyalty."

Mrs. Dennis Manly obviously had higher aspirations for her daughter than marrying preacher-boy Homer Hailey. Dennis Manly and his brothers were successful pioneer ranchers in the Abilene region; Dennis's brother, Hollis, was a member of the ACC board of trustees for many years. Lois and her cousin, Roma, the daughter of Easton Manly, were the cream of the social crop at ACC. In 1929 the school paper, the *Optimist,* noted that the Manly girls had treated the Ko Jo Kais to a recent "outing." The young people had "motored to Cobb Park" where "they gathered around a table filled with delectables."[38] In the spring of 1930, shortly before Homer proposed to Lois, the *Optimist* reported another social event: "Miss Lois Manly entertained a group of young people with a '42' party at her home on North Third Street Saturday night. Violets decorated the rooms, and were used to carry out the purple and green theme. After two hours of '42' a refreshment plate of Strawberry mousse and date loaf cake was served." The guest list did not include Homer Hailey.[39]

Lois was an adopted daughter; her natural mother was a family black sheep, little discussed by the family, who allowed the Manlys to adopt Lois. Serious and sensitive, she never shared the social aspiration of her adoptive mother. Her marriage to Homer Hailey increased the tensions that had grown through the years between Lois and Mrs. Manly. Despite these undercurrents, the two young people were married in the Manly home in Abilene on December 20, 1930. The Manlys treated Homer and Lois generously through the years, but the relationship between Mrs. Manly and Lois remained strained throughout their lives.

Hailey's Arizona preaching companion, Alton Wimbish, was his best man. Homer borrowed thirty dollars to buy a wedding band. Frank Shepherd performed the ceremony and Homer paid him with a five-dollar gold coin he had saved for many years. Shepherd handed the coin back to Lois after the wedding. The couple made a quick trip to East Texas to visit Mamie Hailey before returning to Abilene, where Homer had already assumed his responsibilities as principal of the ACC Academy.

Hailey began his job in the fall. With fewer than two hundred students in its elementary grades and high school, the academy provided education mostly for the children of the ACC community and a few children from the more prosperous homes in the area. The appointment was an honor for Hailey. "Hailey has not applied for the place," explained ACC President Batsell Baxter when the appointment was made, "but I had watched his record the entire time he had been in Abilene

Homer Hailey and Lois Manly Hailey, shortly after their marriage in 1930.

Christian College and decided that he would be the man for the place."[40] Hailey's spiritual fervor and his growing stature as a preacher had called him to the attention of the leaders of the Texas churches of Christ.

As principal of the academy Hailey was a jack-of-all-trades—teacher, administrator, and chief disciplinarian. Under his reign, students learned something about frontier justice. A young man who made "immoral comments" to a female student at the school received a Hailey-administered whipping that "lifted him off the ground." After the whipping, there was "no trouble from him." Another young man who was repeatedly tardy and absent received an unexpected home visit from the principal. When the student told Hailey that he was sick, Hailey replied that if he was sick, he needed medicine. He provided the money and dispatched a student to the drug store to purchase a bottle of castor oil. When the student returned, Hailey took off his belt, "and holding it in one hand and the bottle of castor oil in the other, I told him he had a choice: the belt or the castor oil." The youngster chose the castor oil. Hailey told him that he probably needed to stay around his house that day, but after that the student's health, and his attendance record, improved dramatically. Hailey was favorably impressed by some of his students at the academy, especially Batsell Barrett Baxter, the son of the president, who would become one of the most illustrious preachers in the history of the churches of Christ. On the other hand, Hailey expelled the son of prominent Nashville insurance millionaire A. M. Burton.[41]

All in all, Hailey did not like the principal's job. He continued to preach in area churches every Sunday, but he and Lois felt that his preaching "was slipping." They agreed that he had been a better preacher while still a student because his job placed such restraints on his study time.[42] During the spring he told President Baxter that he would not return the next year, and he and Lois made plans to move to Arizona to begin his life as a preacher.

From Preacher Boy to National Evangelist: 1931–1942

The Haileys departed for Arizona in the summer of 1931 in the midst of the deepening Depression. Lois was several months pregnant with their first child, and they had no clear-cut plans for the future. In June, they stopped in Junction, Texas, and Homer preached in a meeting. After ten days of preaching, Homer reported four baptisms and "one restored to his first love." He added to his report a sentence that was new and filled with pride, and one that he would rarely be able to repeat in later years: "My wife is accompanying me." With regard to future plans, he could only report that they would journey from there to Hanover, New Mexico, where Alton Wimbish had settled, and "we go from there to Arizona to do work."[43]

After two and a half weeks in New Mexico, the Haileys arrived in Tempe in mid-July. For three weeks Homer toiled nightly in the brutal heat. He and Lois were shuttled from house to house, living in whatever accommodations the church members were able to provide—the trip had turned into a nightmare for the pregnant Lois. Nonetheless, Homer's report from Tempe was upbeat. Four had been baptized, "two of them coming from the Mormon church and one from the Methodist." The church in Tempe was "doing well," he cheerfully concluded.[44]

From Tempe, the young couple moved to Wickenburg for a three-week meeting. There they were comfortably housed by the pillars of the small Wickenburg church, Dr. and Mrs. Copeland. After the meeting, Homer headed out to complete his scheduled Arizona preaching appointments and Lois remained with the Copelands. Just after services were concluded one evening during his next meeting in Gilbert, he received a telephone call from Wickenburg telling him that Lois was in labor. He sped the seventy-five miles back to Wickenburg and arrived in time to witness the birth of his first daughter, Roma, on September 20, 1931. Homer remained for two days and then returned to finish the meeting, extending it to three and a half weeks. The results were impressive: "Seventeen were added, eleven by baptism."[45]

Hailey's summer meetings stretched into the fall. After preaching for the church in Coolidge where he and Alton Wimbish had collected a small group the previous year, he concluded his summer schedule with a three-week meeting in Tucson. "The church was greatly strengthened," reported local preacher Ira L. Winterrowd, "besides two were baptized, two received from the Christian church, one restored and one came for membership." The meeting ended on a high note with "new faces in the audience every service, and the interest good both on the part of members and also the visitors." The three weeks, Winterrowd judged, had put the Tucson church "on the map in a better view than heretofore."[46]

Hailey had chosen to leave his secure job in Abilene at an inauspicious time from an economic point of view. By 1931 the nation was reeling toward a total economic collapse, and the Great Depression had begun. The little churches of Arizona, made up mostly of the working poor, could provide meager support for preachers. Nonetheless, in September, Homer, Lois, and Roma moved to Tempe, where he had been invited to preach three Sundays each month for a salary of thirty dollars. One Sunday per month Hailey drove to Gilbert to preach, for which he received an additional twelve dollars. He had saved one hundred dollars from his summer's meetings, and with that nest egg the couple rented a small house, paying six months in advance. They then settled in to trying to survive on forty-two dollars a month. During the winter, one of Hailey's former students at the academy died, and he traveled to Abilene to preach the funeral. The family paid him one hundred dollars, a financial windfall that kept the Hailey family eating through the winter.

The months in Tempe tried the mettle of the young preacher and his family. Roma required a special formula that cost ten dollars each month. The Haileys became intimately acquainted with "hard times." But they were young and resilient. At Christmas, the two sat down to a dinner of soup and beans. Homer began to offer thanks, but before he had finished they erupted into laughter. However, they were thankful, and they survived. More than once they got down to their last dime, but, Hailey recalled, they never spent it—they were never dead broke.[47]

In spite of the tough times, Hailey later looked back on the stay in Arizona as a "good year." In February, he reported to the *Firm Foundation* that the "work here is doing nicely."

He continued to look after the interests of the churches throughout the state, seeking information about "brethren in Flagstaff, Prescott, Williams, Winslow, and Willcox," and he planned another schedule of mission meetings for the summer.[48]

The area around Tempe was strong Mormon country, and Hailey spent the year studying Mormon doctrine. He aroused a furor in Gilbert when he referred to Mormonism as "a damnable doctrine." Challenged by an elderly Mormon bishop, Hailey offered to debate the proposition that "Joe Smith was an imposter, and the Book of Mormon is a fraud." The Mormons accepted and several hundred people attended a two-night discussion. Hailey never esteemed himself to be a great debater, but he felt that his Mormon opposition was fairly weak. The "wonder," he later recollected, was that he "didn't get shot."[49]

The Haileys' financial situation in Arizona grew worse and worse, and Homer "saw that we were going to starve." So, in the summer of 1932, Homer loaded Lois and Roma in his car and headed for Abilene and Hallsville, holding meetings along the way. In May, they stopped in Willcox and stayed for two weeks; Homer reported three baptisms and noted that he would hold "a mission meeting or two" before going to Hanover, New Mexico.[50] They spent "three great weeks" with Alton Wimbish in Hanover in June, reporting that "twenty-eight were baptized and about ten confessed their waywardness." Homer then took Lois and Roma to Texas to visit their families and returned to Arizona to preach, touring such old haunts as Gilbert and Coolidge. In October he reported in the *Firm Foundation* that his winter address would be 314 Graham Street in Abilene.[51]

The Fifth and Highland Church of Christ in Abilene had invited Hailey to become the congregation's regular preacher. The congregation was made up of a remnant of the College Church that had remained in the old location when ACC moved to its new campus in 1929. By 1930 the group had

Homer Hailey, around 1936, at the Manly home on a ranch outside Abilene. He was the successful preacher at the Fifth and Highland Church of Christ in Abilene and a part-time instructor at Abilene Christian College.

grown to about three hundred members and had announced plans to build a thirty-five thousand dollar "modified Gothic" auditorium that would be "the newest and one of the prettiest buildings in Abilene." The ACC student newspaper described the plans with a tinge of pride: "Art glass in the auditorium windows will add to the dignified atmosphere created by the architectural design."[52] Unfortunately, the Depression struck full force in 1930, and the church canceled its building plans and began meeting in an unfinished basement. Frank Shepherd was the local preacher at Fifth and Highland from 1929 until 1932. Lois's uncle, Amos Manly, was a member of the congregation, and because of his influence and because Hailey was Shepherd's close friend, the twenty-nine-year-old Hailey received the invitation to return to Abilene. The church furnished the Haileys with a four-room house and paid him a salary of seventy dollars per month.

The Hailey family thus began eleven "great years" at Fifth

and Highland. In 1934, the congregation gave him permission to assume a three-fifths teaching load at ACC and each summer he took three months off to hold meetings.[53] Fifth and Highland struggled through the Depression trying to pay off the forty-five hundred dollar debt the church had accumulated building its basement auditorium. "They were kind of whipped," Hailey recalled in later years, but the young preacher's enthusiasm was contagious, and the church soon began retiring its debt.[54]

Fifth and Highland began to grow noticeably in 1938, both in numbers and financially. The church reinstituted its building plans and completed its auditorium in September 1938. "Various congregations of the city" participated in a "praise and thanksgiving" service to dedicate the building.[55] The church grew steadily, adding new members almost every week, reaching a membership of about five hundred by the time Hailey resigned in 1943. Hailey believed that the congregation had been "built solidly, upon a true foundation, that stands the test." He had tried to make his preaching "varied and balanced."[56] When Hailey left, the elders reported that for eleven years the church had "enjoyed a wonderful unity among its members, with . . . no whisper of dissatisfaction." On the last Sunday that Hailey preached, the congregation retired "the last of its indebtedness of every kind."[57]

Hailey had become a powerful preacher, but his success at Fifth and Highland, and elsewhere, was probably more attributable to his transparent "dedication."[58] He was no social butterfly. Hailey went daily to his office in the church basement to study; he informed the congregation that he was open for business but that he did not intend to waste time just "shooting the breeze." On the other hand, he was frenetically active, teaching "classes somewhere nearly all the time." He was, indeed, a workaholic. Lois once told her husband that Roma had not seen her father for six weeks.[59]

Hailey became noted during his years at Highland as "one

of the most ardent exponents of evangelism in the church today."[60] That reputation was well deserved. Hailey conducted hundreds of "cottage meetings" in private homes that resulted in scores of baptisms. During his years at Highland he was pressed by Lois's uncle, Hollis Manly, to conduct a class with Dennis Manly, the one Manly brother who was not a member of the churches of Christ. Homer conducted the study, unsuccessfully. However, the experience made him wonder why all Christians were not effective teachers. He asked Hollis Manly, who was an insurance executive, to lend him some books on salesmanship. He came to believe that "Jesus followed the same principle in his teaching" that good salesmen did, and he drafted a manuscript adapting those principles to conducting Bible classes. In 1951, the Christian Chronicle Publishing Company published Hailey's ideas in book form; the work was called *Let's Go Fishing for Men,* and it further identified Hailey's name with personal evangelism.[61] In the 1940s, according to his old friend Harry W. Pickup, Jr., Hailey's emphasis on "cottage meetings" put him well "ahead of his time in personal work."[62]

Hailey's growing fame rested most of all on his effective and tireless work as an evangelist. Each summer Hailey left Abilene for three months of meetings. He was never compensated by Fifth and Highland during the summers, nor was he ever during his career given a paid vacation by a local church. Fifth and Highland did support him in "mission meetings" in "many near-by places," as well as in Arizona, California, Oregon, and Montana. The elders reported, "Whenever the church sent out its preacher to destitute and hard places, the church would sympathetically follow him in the work with their prayers and interest." For Hailey, summer after summer brought the same routine. He left home, as he had in 1929 and 1930 while a student, going wherever he was invited, to churches large and small, preaching in buildings and in tents. He was fearless, guileless, selfless, talented, and single-minded. Hailey often rode the train to his meetings and usually stayed with people in their homes, enjoying the hospitality and conviviality. However, he was not there to socialize or play golf, just to preach.

Years of preaching sped by, filled with adventures and misadventures, triumphs and flops. Hailey sent a stream of reports to the *Firm Foundation,* as did other western preachers. In 1933, he reported five baptized in a two-week meeting in Gilbert, Arizona; from there he proceeded to Casa Grande, where he and Wallace Layton spent two weeks, baptized ten, and reported "a number of members were gotten together who promise to carry on the work." He finished the summer back in Texas, baptizing four in a two-week meeting at Gustine, one of the little towns where he had preached as a student. Five more were baptized in a ten-day meeting at Nugent; the "visible results" at "Gordon School, ten miles south of Slaton," were three baptisms. Hailey concluded his summer's work at "Cross Road, south of Merkel."[63]

Year after year the cycle went on, but there were subtle changes as the years passed. As Hailey's reputation grew, he was invited to preach in bigger and more prestigious congregations, and he wandered farther and farther away from his familiar territory in Arizona and Texas. In 1934 he held a ten-day meeting for the University and Walnut Street congregation in Wichita, Kansas, where his former classmate G. K. Wallace was "doing an excellent work."[64] In 1935 and 1936 he preached in California, and in the summer of 1937 he preached in Dodge City, Kansas, on his way to Oregon, where he conducted a series of meetings. The summer in Oregon was a memorable one for Hailey; Lois accompanied him, along with Roma and their three-year-old adopted daughter, Mary Lois. They stayed with the Roy Goodwin family, friends from their days in Tempe who had migrated to Oregon at about the same time that Homer left for Texas. "Oregon presents a wonderful field for evangelistic work," Hailey reported cheerily to the *Firm Foundation.*[65] He returned many times to preach in the congregations of the state in later years.[66]

As Hailey's meeting schedule expanded, so did his circle of friends and acquaintances. He worked with the "new and growing" Park Hill Church in Denver in 1938 where "Yater Tant, a most faithful and energetic worker, is preaching and working."[67] Three years later, he worked with Tant again, this time at the Northwest Church in Chicago. Hailey reported that Tant was "doing a splendid work" and that the "future of this congregation looks bright."[68] Hailey regularly preached in the growing churches in Oklahoma; he liked the church in Altus, returned repeatedly to the church in Maud, where he usually reported ten or more baptisms, and held meetings at churches where Curtis Camp and C. E. McGaughey preached in Oklahoma City.[69] After a two-week meeting with the Tenth and Francis Church in Oklahoma City, Hailey was impressed: "This is one of the most aggressive and zealous congregations to be found anywhere. It stands squarely for 'the faith,' and insists upon firm and straight preaching always." In Missouri, Hailey was particularly impressed by the Flora congregation in Kansas City and by the local preacher, C. Roy Bixler, a "tireless and faithful worker."

Even as his reputation grew, however, Hailey returned with striking regularity to preach in the small churches of Arizona and Texas. Establishing a pattern that marked his entire life, Hailey scheduled summer meetings three to five years in advance, always accepting invitations as they came without regard to the size or reputation of the congregation. He never showed a "preference," taking meetings anywhere in the order that they were requested.[70] In Texas, Hailey's meeting schedule came to include the more prestigious congregations in the state: the College Church in Abilene, Pioneer Park in Lubbock, and the largest congregations in Galveston, Dallas, Brownwood, Fort Worth, and Houston. However, year in and year out, Hailey also wrote reports from the little churches where he had worked as a "preacher boy": Gustine, Hallsville, Hawley, Albany, and Roby.[71] And over and over he returned to the country churches, to "Cross Roads, south of Blair," and

"Gordon School, south of Slaton," and "Wilson church, a few miles south of Lamesa," one of the "finest country congregations I know of."[72] As Hailey became a nationally celebrated preacher, his visits to Arizona were less frequent, but he returned to Tempe to help that "little band" in 1934 and baptized nine. In addition, he held several meetings in Willcox during the 1930s, baptizing four in 1934 during a ten-day meeting, noting that "lots of preaching is needed in this country."[73] After a meeting two years later, he reported that another twelve had been baptized in Willcox.[74]

While much remained the same in Hailey's summer ritual of preaching, there were slow but discernable changes in his reports. Three-week meetings largely disappeared from his schedule, despite Hailey's protest after visiting Willcox in 1934 that "two-week meetings are entirely too short." By 1940, ten-day meetings had become standard fare. More and more of Hailey's meetings were in established churches that had local preachers, and they frequently featured special song leaders hired for the occasion: Andy Ritchie from Nashville, Earl McCord of Arkansas, and Norman Jones of Kansas City, whom Hailey dubbed "one of the best."[75] Even country and small-town congregations frequently had "efficient and zealous" local preachers.

Most noticeable was the declining number of baptisms reported in Hailey's meetings. Almost every meeting still reported some baptisms, but the number increasingly fell from double figures to four or five, and occasionally Hailey's cryptic reports ended with the notation, "no additions" or "no visible results."[76] Still, many of his meetings were very successful; twelve were baptized in Hailey's 1938 meeting in Maud, nineteen during his meeting with the College Church in Abilene in the same year, and eleven in 1940 in Kansas City.[77] Additionally, his reports almost always included notices that some had "returned to the Lord," or been "restored to the faith," or "restored from sin."[78] Hailey occasionally reported that a church had gained "several from the Christian church."[79] Finally, during his meetings Hailey sometimes helped to "set in order" a local church, assisting in the appointment of elders.[80]

"I was in demand everywhere during those days," Hailey later recalled. "I was young. I was vigorous. I was studious. . . . I fought sin and tried to lead people to the Lord. . . . I was very popular and had lots of invitations to go places."[81] By the early 1930s Hailey's preaching style had matured; his lessons were crammed full of scriptural quotations, delivered, in the words of G. C. Brewer, in such a way that "there was a spark between your heart and his heart."[82] He impressed his peers. Sixty years after hearing Hailey preach a sermon in Hallsville, Texas, James W. Adams still remembered the sermon and continued to "use one of his illustrations."[83]

Hailey's growing stature in the churches of Christ was exemplified by his appearance on numerous lecture programs during the 1930s and early 1940s. He spoke at the Abilene Christian College Lectures first in 1934. The college lectureships were designed to showcase the most talented and respected preachers in the churches of Christ, and they assumed a quasi-political status. The 1934 ACC lectureship theme was "The New Testament Church in History." Hailey, speaking on the subject "The Church in the Ante-Nicene Period," delivered a summary of the period based largely on a reading of Philip Schaff's *History of the Christian Church* and concluded with a typical Hailey admonition: "We should learn the lesson about the ease and patience with which apostasy creeps upon the 'faithful'; and the absolute necessity of 'speaking as the oracles of God'; retaining the simplicity, beauty, and purity of Christianity, as delivered by the apostles, guided by the Holy Spirit."[84]

Hailey spoke at the ACC Lectures again in 1937, when the theme of the lectures was "The Church and Its Great Mission: To Preach the Gospel to the Whole Creation." Hailey preached on "How They Went in the First Century," a subject that would be widely debated a decade later. In 1937, he showed little insight into the nuances of the simmering debate, staying with the more practical themes close to his own experience. He urged individuals to go sacrificially to preach the gospel in difficult places, a call he had answered himself.[85] Hailey returned to the lectures again in 1939, joining a roster of speakers that included such well-known older preachers as Jesse P. Sewell, P. D. Wilmeth, and G. C. Brewer and a number of young men destined to play important roles in the decades ahead such as Fanning Yater Tant, Guy N. Woods, C. E. McGaughey, and Roy H. Lanier, Sr. Hailey's assigned topic, "Stewardship of Time," lent itself to the type of noncontroversial teaching that had come to be expected of him, but his lecture also included a trademark Hailey warning: "Our pioneers met most faithfully those issues of yesterday, but it is now our responsibility to meet those of today, of the 'now.' Those confronting us today are error outside and inside the church, sin, and infidelity. Tomorrow these will have become deeply rooted, bearing fruit of ungodliness in our children and children's children."[86]

In addition to his appearances at the Abilene Christian College Lectures, Hailey preached frequently at lectureships sponsored by local congregations. The lectureships, sometimes called "preacher's meetings" or "united evangelistic campaigns," were common occurrences in the 1930s and 1940s. Generally sponsored by a number of congregations in a city or area, the lectureships were often coordinated by the "senior elders" of certain congregations.[87]

Hailey participated in several debates during these busy years. In the rough-and-tumble religious environment of the thirties and forties most preachers were presented occasionally with an opportunity, and sometimes with the necessity, to debate. In the early 1930s Hailey met a seasoned Baptist debater in Gustine, accepting the challenge even though he "knew nothing of Baptist doctrine." Had it not been for the help of his moderator, A. R. Lawrence, an elder at Fifth and Highland who had preached part-time for many years, Hailey felt that he would have "lost my shirt in the debate." Under the circumstances, he judged his effort to have been only "fairly acceptable." In the spring of 1943, while conducting a meeting in Douglas, Arizona, Hailey and a Christian church preacher, Percy Krewson, met "in a public discussion of the scriptures and instrumental music in worship." Once again, Hailey was not entirely pleased with his efforts.[88] In the summer of 1943 Hailey debated a Seventh-Day Adventist in Oklahoma City. This time Hailey spent several months preparing for the debate, but his adversary turned the debate into a farce. His opponent, Hailey reported to the *Firm Foundation,* would "neither affirm Adventist doctrine, nor attempt a reply to an argument. He contented himself with a bunch of Sunday school boy 'orations.'" On the final two nights of the debate, the Seventh-Day Adventist did not show up, so Hailey spoke to large audiences on the errors of premillennialism and Sabbatarianism.[89] Hailey greatly admired the skilled "professional debaters" among the preachers of his generation, and he would always accept a challenge if confronted, but by the end of the mid-1940s he had concluded that he was "no debater."[90]

Hailey's reputation as a fervent evangelistic preacher was reinforced by the strong missions program of the Fifth and Highland Church. During Hailey's eleven years at Highland the church sponsored a variety of projects, using methods that Hailey would later repudiate. The congregation sponsored Miss Hettie Lee Ewing in Japan for a number of years, "with the cooperation of the church in Cleburne, together with other churches and individuals."[91] Fifth and Highland also contributed to works in Africa, Mexico, and among the "negroes in Abilene."[92] In the early 1940s, the church began to sponsor the work of James E. White, a Sioux Indian, "among the Oneida tribe of Wisconsin" and that of Harry Johnson in Provo, Utah. Hailey was particularly pleased that the congregation had become White's sponsor. The Indian preacher had formerly been "under the supervision of the Murray Hill congregation" of Flint, Michigan. When Fifth and Highland became White's "overseer and helper," Hailey earnestly solicited "the aid of any and all congregations in this matter." Hailey regularly reported on the funds secured from other congregations in the papers circulated in the brotherhood, including the magazine edited by arch-conservative Foy E. Wallace, Jr., the *Bible Banner.*[93]

Abilene Christian College: 1934–1943

In the fall of 1934, President James F. Cox invited Hailey to teach a three-fifths load in the Bible Department at Abilene Christian College. Hailey's growing reputation among the churches was clearly an asset to the school. President Cox proudly reported in 1934 that the "opportunities for Bible training" at ACC were "unusually good": "Such outstanding teachers as Batsell Baxter, Chas. H. Roberson and Homer Hailey, who are well able to give instruction in the bible text—the thing that Abilene Christian College emphasizes most of all—guarantee safe and very thorough instruction in the Book of books." The school existed, Cox emphasized, to "put Christianity first in the thoughts and activities of the student body."[94] The ACC at which Hailey began teaching in 1934 was still largely a Bible school. In addition to the various extracurricular spiritual activities that most students participated in, all students attended daily chapel services to hear "inspiring talks by faculty members and visitors." Parents were assured that "student life is kept free from worldliness and contaminating influences" and that "young men and women who are not amenable to such an environment are soon weeded out."[95]

Religion, rather than academic attainment, was the critical qualification for faculty members; the college bulletin assured that "only men and women of sterling Christian character are permitted to teach here." President Cox's credentials included bachelor and master of arts degrees in education from the University of Texas and "three years in a one-teacher rural school; two years principal of a village school; four years President of Lingleville Christian College; two years tutor of Public Speaking at University of Texas."[96] Dean of Students Walter H. Adams completed a doctoral degree in secondary education at Columbia University in 1932 and Howard L. Schug received a doctorate from George Peabody College for Teachers in 1933. Otherwise, the faculty had few academic attainments. A number of teachers, including Hailey, had only bachelor of arts degrees from ACC. Hailey's faculty blurb read, "B. A., Abilene Christian College, 1930. Minister and evangelist in Arizona, New Mexico, Kansas, Texas, 1930–'34."[97]

In most respects, Hailey's relationship with ACC was a marriage made in heaven. It lasted for nearly a decade. In 1934, the Fifth and Highland Church was struggling to pay Hailey seventy dollars a month, and his teaching job allowed him to supplement his salary while at the same time it provided cheap labor for ACC. In January 1938, when the work at Fifth and Highland began to expand and the church entered a building program, Hailey resigned his teaching position, but he rejoined the faculty in the fall of 1939.[98] Hailey was most at home teaching freshman Bible courses, offering the students well-researched, but practical, common-sense expositions of biblical texts.

Hailey left a mark on ACC students for a decade. "His whole countenance was so wholesome, human, and patently sincere" that he had "a great appeal," remembered Garvin Beauchamp.[99] Both male and female students were "crazy about him," recalled Georgia Deane Cope in later years, but he was especially close to the "preacher boys."[100] Hailey the teacher was drawn to the same types of campus activities that had occupied him when he was a student. He was a fixture in the meetings of the "Evangelistic Forum," speaking on "Reasoning and Persuading with Sinners," advising the preacher boys about sermon topics, and giving them practical advice about "located work." "Do not visit too much," he told the prospective preachers in a 1937 address, "and do not visit more frequently those with whom you have most in common." Hailey also warned the preacher boys to "be careful about the choice of a wife," reported the student newspaper: "Selfish, nagging, and talkative companions were named as the least desirable. Patience in dealing with individuals, pointedness in address, he highly extolled."[101] Hailey tried to instill in the students the sense of calling harbored deep in his own psyche. He told the Missions Study Class in 1938, "The consciousness of providential working should make every Christian feel that he is not insignificant, but any humble ability might be turned into a great power by the hand of God."[102]

Hailey had a particularly close relationship with the campus athletes. An experienced body builder by the mid-1930s, he worked out regularly in the gym and was a whiz on the punching bag. His skills and his physique impressed the athletes. "He was a specimen," recalled one student, "He had big muscles." Hailey was a man's man, and there was a natural camaraderie between him and the football players, whom he frequently tutored privately. After the family moved to the Manly ranch in 1936, the Haileys often invited students out for an evening. Homer and the boys would shoot prairie dogs while Lois prepared an old-time western feast. He was, as Garvin Beauchamp put it, "a friend of ours."[103] Hailey was the faculty sponsor for the class of 1938 and was the baccalaureate speaker in May 1938.[104] In April 1938, Hailey conducted a meeting at the College Church. He preached each morning on "moral principles, stability in the faith and elements of proper growth" and in the evenings discussed the "plan of redemption." Because of his "effective straightforward manner," reported the student newspaper, Hailey was able to "hold the attention of large audiences each day."[105] The meeting was long remembered in Abilene; nineteen were baptized, including eleven members of the ACC football team.[106]

Many ACC students visited the Hailey home on the ranch at one time or another. It was an ideal setting for picnics, hay rides, and wiener roasts. Lois was a good cook and Homer enjoyed treating the students to cake and fresh milk from his cow. Most of all, Hailey relished hosting "chuck wagon dinners," like the ones he and his brother Rob had enjoyed when they worked in Arizona roundups as teenagers. Around campfires on the ranch, the ACC students feasted on steak, beans, and chili and were regaled with frontier tales of Willcox and ranches and cowboys.[107]

Hailey's financial circumstances improved slightly in Abilene, and in 1934 the family purchased a small house on Meander Street for twenty-one hundred dollars. Two years later Mr. Manly gave the couple a 130-acre farm, and they moved into the old family ranch house. Homer liked living on the ranch, but the conditions were primitive and housekeeping was difficult for Lois. In 1939, Mr. Manly gave them a thirty-three-acre plot just three miles away from the ACC campus, and in 1941 Homer built a house on the land and the family moved back into town.

The Hailey family continued to grow. Both Lois and Homer wanted more children, and in 1934 they adopted a five-day-old baby girl, Mary Lois, through a Baptist placement agency. In 1939 Lois became pregnant again; she had so much difficulty in carrying the child that Homer had to return home during the summer from Oregon where he was preaching in meetings. Rob, the Haileys' first son, was born October 14, 1939; a second son, Dennis, was born September 17, 1941.[108]

By 1942, Hailey had decided that he needed to make a change in his life. He was certain that he wanted to be a college teacher, and ACC, under the leadership of Dean Walter Adams, was pressing to gain accreditation from the Southern Association of Colleges and Schools. Several members of the faculty had earned doctoral degrees by the end of the 1930s, and just a few had only bachelor's degrees. The pressure was on to secure credentials, and at the end of the 1942 academic year, Hailey resigned from the faculty. He continued to preach at Fifth and

Highland for another year, giving notice that he intended to leave in the summer of 1943 to pursue a graduate degree.

Another personal matter induced the Haileys to consider shuffling their pattern of life in Abilene. Lois's health deteriorated. She had always been nervous, and by the end of the 1930s, Lois's health caused her to become more and more reclusive. After her death in 1954, an autopsy revealed that she had been born with a rare and incurable brain tumor that grew larger and larger throughout her life. In hindsight, she was an incredibly courageous woman. In spite of her serious physical disability, she tried to attend to the needs of her growing family, and she carried more than an equal share of the day-to-day responsibilities for rearing the children.

Homer and Lois grappled to find a solution to the "nervous problems" that made her take to her bed for long periods. At Homer's insistence, Lois consulted a nutritionist when they lived in Arizona, but she received no relief. In Abilene, Homer and Lois decided that her condition might be related to the tensions between Lois and her adoptive mother, Mrs. Manly.[109] They agreed that a move might help.

Diversion to Dallas, Houston, Los Angeles, and Hawaii: 1943–1949

Having resigned at Fifth and Highland and at ACC, Hailey conducted his regular schedule of meetings during the summer of 1943. Fifth and Highland supported him in "mission meetings" in Douglas, Arizona, and Helena, Montana. Hailey long remembered his visit to Montana, where he conducted "probably the first meeting held in the city of Helena by our brethren." The meeting was held in a "large down-town theater building." Even though the local members ran a blitz of newspaper advertisements, the largest crowd during the two weeks was twenty-three people. After two weeks of hard labor, teaching every day from house to house and preaching in the evenings, Hailey baptized two people. The Helena church had been organized two weeks before Hailey's arrival with eight members, mostly servicemen. Two soldiers were transferred while the meeting was in progress, leaving eight members when Hailey departed. Hailey later remembered the Helena experience as the "toughest two-week meeting I ever conducted." However, some months later, he read an item in the *Christian Chronicle* reporting the baptism of an American soldier in the waters off Anzio Beach during some of the fiercest fighting in World War II. The soldier recounted that he had "learned the truth" during a meeting in Helena, Montana, conducted by "a Homer Hailey."[110]

From Montana, Hailey proceeded through his round of summer meetings. Seven were baptized during ten days with a "fine congregation" in the "little oil town" of Denver City, Texas. Next came a two-week meeting with the Sunset Church in Dallas, followed by a trip to Lubbock where three churches "cooperated in a fine way with the Avenue T congregation" in a meeting, and then he moved onward to Durham, Oklahoma, and Abilene and Odessa, Texas.[111]

All through the summer, as he conducted his meetings, Hailey pondered where he should go to graduate school. He considered going to the University of Chicago, but the idea seemed entirely impractical. While in Dallas, he visited Southern Methodist University and liked the school. Clearly, attending SMU would make the separation from his family less burdensome, and he was offered a job earning fifty dollars a week preaching at the new Shamrock Shores Church in Dallas. Hailey began working with the church on September 15, 1943, and enrolled in the Perkins School of Theology at Southern Methodist University.[112] Two other young ACC faculty members were SMU students at the time, J. D. Thomas and Carl Spain.

Lois lived in Abilene with the children, and Homer moved into a boardinghouse in Dallas not far from the SMU campus. He ate nightly at Wyatt's Cafeteria, longing for some good home cooking. He made an occasional trip to Abilene during his nine-month stay in Dallas, and Lois and the children visited him a few times. Homer continued his regimen of exercise, working out daily in the university gym, but mostly he studied, intent on finishing his master's degree in nine months because "I had to do it to get home." It was a "hard year on all of us," Hailey later recalled; one of his old friends remembered him as the "most homesick person I ever saw."[113]

Hailey's foray into graduate education was not motivated by a keen desire for a degree, or by any strong sense that he needed one, but by his desire to teach at the college level. In his preaching, he often warned others about the dangers of higher education; he entered SMU with some "apprehension about the effect it might have on me." By the time he completed his course work, however, he had concluded that "those men didn't have a thing in the world." "If you are solid to start with," he later declared, "you come out stronger." His theologically liberal professors were "awfully nice to me," Hailey recalled, but they did not dent his practical common-sense faith in the Bible.[114] Asked to speak in chapel not long before his graduation, Hailey did not pussyfoot around; he laid his beliefs on the line in a speech entitled "Why We Exist as a Religious Body Separate and Distinct from All Others." He later recalled that "it was well received by some, but not by others." In January, he took aim at his professors in a lecture on "modernism" during the "Fourth Annual Dallas Lectures," sponsored by five Dallas churches.[115]

At SMU, Hailey majored in church history and minored in Bible. His favorite teacher was Dr. Hicks, a scholarly man with a deeply "reverent attitude toward God." Even so, Hicks did not believe in "the miracles" and, like Hailey's other teachers, did not have "a right attitude toward the scriptures." Hailey had little respect for some of his professors. He studied the book of John under a widely known theologian and concluded that his professor "didn't know one thing about John." Hailey finished his class work and thesis in nine months. He wrote a thesis on the leaders of the early restoration movement, reading widely for the first time the writings of Alexander

Campbell, Barton W. Stone, Moses E. Lard, and James W. McGarvey.[116]

Lois and his son Rob attended Homer's graduation in June 1944, then he departed immediately for his round of scheduled meetings. By mid-summer he learned that Abilene Christian College did not intend to rehire him as a teacher. Hailey was surprised and deeply disappointed; he had fully expected to return to Abilene in the fall. His surprise revealed a streak of naivete in his character that surfaced repeatedly during his life.

Hailey had deeply offended the longtime head of the Bible Department, Charles Heber Roberson, and Roberson had vetoed Hailey's return. Roberson was a formidable man to cross, and the unpolitical Hailey had committed the offense almost without knowing it. Roberson had taught in several small Christian colleges in Texas in the 1920s and 1930s and arrived at ACC in 1932. He became head of the Bible Department in 1935. Roberson was courtly, and, in the judgment of his fellow teachers, a "proud fellow," "one of those people who was right."[117] Walter Adams, who regarded Roberson as his mentor, remembered that Roberson was "very exact," he "quoted Greek a great deal," and "he would correct me on things I would say in chapel."[118] Roberson came to Abilene with master's degrees from Georgia Roberson Christian College in Henderson, Tennessee, and from Texas Christian University; while in Abilene he was awarded an honorary doctor of laws degree in 1940 by ACC. Roberson was a respected figure in the Texas churches of Christ and was generally regarded as an important Greek scholar. To a large degree, Roberson's reputation rested on his book, *What Jesus Taught,* a 752-page compendium on "subjects taught by our Saviour." When it appeared, the *Firm Foundation* labeled Roberson's book "unique, pretentious, comprehensive."[119]

What Jesus Taught, published in 1930, catapulted Roberson and ACC into the midst of the furious premillennial controversy that raged all through the decade. Foy E. Wallace, Jr.'s

Charles Ready Nichol (1876–1961) and Charles Heber Roberson (1879–1953). Nichol was a noted preacher and debater, and Roberson was the head of the Bible Department at Abilene Christian College from 1936 to 1951. Foy E. Wallace, Jr., pursued Roberson as a premillennialist in the 1930s, a charge he denied. Roberson escaped with his job, but he deeply resented those who had been involved in calling him to account, including Homer Hailey. In 1944, he vetoed Hailey's appointment to a position in the Bible Department at Abilene Christian College. (Courtesy of the Center for Restoration Studies, Abilene Christian University.)

crusade was forging full steam ahead when Roberson's book was published, and before the decade was over the pompous professor inadvertently was thrust into the boiling argument. The chapter on the millennium in Roberson's celebrated book was lifted almost word-for-word from evangelical Bible study literature that was explicitly premillennial. Paul Southern, Roberson's protege and successor as the head of the Bible Department at ACC, surmised that Roberson was "in poor health" while preparing the book, and that while "under lots of stress," he "let some things get in that he would not have allowed."[120]

By 1940, Roberson was clearly in the sights of Foy E. Wallace, Jr., and his militant anti-premillennial cohorts; it appeared that Roberson would be compelled to confess either that he was a premillennialist or a plagiarist. Paul Southern believed that Roberson could have averted much of the trouble that followed had he "acknowledged that he made a mistake," but "Brother Roberson was a very proud sort of a person, and he was not going to admit any kind of error on his part."[121] At the Abilene Christian College Lectures in 1940, the assault on Roberson took a public and ugly turn. President-elect Don Morris, in an obvious effort to assure anti-premillennial crusaders that ACC was sound, invited questions from the floor during an open forum at the lectures, including "criticisms of A. C. C." A free-for-all erupted when J. L. Hines charged that Charles H. Roberson "is a premillennialist if he believes the chapter on the 'Millennium' as it appears in his book." Roberson was present; he arose and dismissed the charge and "undertook to justify his use of the word 'millennium.'" Hines later charged that Roberson, when approached privately after the forum, "shouted at me and pounded on my chest." That evening, Roberson asked for permission to speak, and he delivered an emotional address. Charging that his "integrity had been called in question," he asked all those who had studied in his classes to raise their hands. According to the account of the incident reported in Wallace's paper, "When this show of egotism came to an end," Hines took the podium to remind the audience that he had not attacked Roberson personally, but had only charged that Roberson's writings were premillennial and needed to be corrected. Many of Roberson's supporters began to file out of the auditorium as Hines tried to extend the debate, and "Brother Paul Southern arose and said; 'Let's sing.'"

Following the stormy session, "Don Morris, Walter Adams, Harvey Scott, Homer Hailey, and some others, went to Brother Roberson's home for a conference" that lasted well into the morning hours. The next day, Morris, Adams, Scott, and Hailey met with Hines and some of his sympathizers. Hines insisted that Roberson "sign a statement repudiating the article in question or be dismissed from the college as an unsafe teacher." According to Hines, the four men "agreed with me that the article is premillennial, but said; 'Roberson does not believe premillennialism.'" The group drafted a set of resolutions on February 22, 1940, that they hoped would settle the matter. Roberson agreed to sign the following statement: "If in the past I have unconsciously taught premillennialism, I repudiate it now, and do not believe it. I have never believed such a false doctrine." Hines then signed a statement: "I accept the foregoing statement as a full explanation of the questions asked yesterday, and appreciate Brother Charles H. Roberson's attitude in the matter." Morris read the two statements before the lectureship audience and thanked Hines for "having brought this matter to light."[122]

In the months that followed, President Morris tried to save the reputation of ACC and to rescue Roberson. In January 1941, he circulated two statements aimed at distancing the college from any hint of premillennialism. The first was a somewhat longer explanation by Roberson. The Bible Department head admitted that his original essay was "susceptible of being understood as teaching pre-millennialism." He submitted a proposed sentence that would be added to any new editions of the book: "The doctrine of a future era of righteous government upon the earth, to last a thousand years, is nowhere taught in the Scripture." Finally, the Roberson statement added, "Almost daily in my classes I set forth in some form or other the fallacy of the heresy of pre-millennialism. I shall be glad to furnish this statement to anyone who had the book." The second announcement, signed by the entire ACC Bible Department—Charles H. Roberson, R. C. Bell, Paul Southern, James F. Cox, and Homer Hailey—read: "Each of us whose names appear below does not believe in premillennialism, has no sympathy for the doctrine, and is glad at every opportunity to teach against this false and unscriptural doctrine."[123]

The Roberson affair did not die easily. Morris thought the college had done all that it could; he agreed that Roberson's earlier statements were "unfortunate," but he believed that Roberson should be "allowed to withdraw them, and to restate his views more clearly."[124] Roberson, however, would never completely humiliate himself before the militants and admit his mistake. Immediately after the confrontation at the ACC Lectures, Roberson wrote a letter to Hines insisting that his writings had been "misjudged." When he did finally restate his position, Foy E. Wallace, Jr., charged that the teaching was still "premillennialism—his own brand of it, if not the Scofield brand."[125]

Neither were the militant anti-premillennialists willing to let the Roberson affair die. When Roberson rejected further concessions, Wallace went for the jugular. He wanted more than a confession that the language in Roberson's book was "susceptible of being understood as teaching premillennialism." He wanted a clear confession. Wallace was infuriated that Roberson had tried to "shift the blame to 'some' who, he says, 'have so interpreted' his language." Roberson's essay, Wallace argued, "is not susceptible to any other understanding." Furthermore, Wallace asked, why was Roberson unclear? When Roberson wrote the book he was nearly fifty years old, he was "educated," and he had "long been a college teacher." Why was he "misunderstood?" The only thing that would clear ACC's reputation with Wallace was the firing of Roberson. The colleges supported by members of the churches of Christ, Wallace reported, had "disclaimed premillennialism—but they have not purged their faculties of men whose records on the issues have not been and are not now above reasonable doubt and legitimate suspicion." Roberson, he insisted, must go.[126]

The Roberson affair was a serious embarrassment to ACC in the early 1940s, but Roberson had powerful supporters, and he weathered the storm and retained his position as the head of the Bible Department. Furthermore, despite the fulminations of Wallace and others, Roberson clearly had no sympathy with premillennial theories.

On the surface, Homer Hailey appeared in the Roberson affair in the role of peacemaker. However, by the late 1930s, everyone knew that Hailey was a strong supporter of Foy E. Wallace, Jr., and that he was a militant opponent of premillennialism. Hailey was the first ACC faculty member to detect the premillennial teaching in Roberson's book, having had his attention called to the matter by a student. Long before the confrontation at the 1940 lectures, Hailey, who had a hunch that trouble was coming, had approached Don Morris about the problem so that he would be prepared.[127] Morris discussed the issue with Roberson, revealing to him that Hailey had raised the question. Whatever the circumstances leading to the public confrontation in 1940, it was clear that Hailey's sympathies were with Wallace, and some suspected that he had been a conduit of information to the anti-premillennialists in the subsequent squabbling. At any rate, Roberson identified Hailey with his persecutors, and he vetoed Hailey's return to the campus in 1943.

Hailey was in the midst of his summer meeting schedule when he learned that he would have to rethink his career plans. The summer began with a meeting at the Sunset Church in Dallas, and from there he moved on to Ackerly, Texas; Elk City, Oklahoma; and then the West Coast where he held meetings in San Leandro and at the Central Church of Christ in Los Angeles.[128] Both San Leandro and Central were searching for a regular preacher, and both asked Hailey to become the local preacher. In September he accepted the job in Los Angeles, to begin in January 1945.[129] He then resumed his travels, holding meetings in Tucson, Tempe, and Yuma; in Dallas at Saner Avenue Church; in Irving, Texas; in Washington, D.C.; and in McAllen, Texas.[130]

At the end of 1944, many of Hailey's acquaintances thought that he looked drawn and tired. He had worked extremely hard to finish his degree at SMU; during the fall, he became seriously concerned about his health. Shortly after his graduation from SMU a large mole appeared on his neck and began to grow rapidly. A Dallas physician and member of the ACC board of trustees, Dr. John G. Young, diagnosed the growth as a cancer and urged Hailey to enter the hospital immediately. Hailey demurred, fearing that the cancer would "scatter" if he allowed surgery. On the other hand, he was told that he would not live for another year without surgery. Hailey delayed, however, having heard of a doctor in Houston who treated cancer in "a different way," with the application of "a chemical substance." When he completed his meeting schedule in December, he moved to Houston to begin treatments.[131]

For four months the Haileys lived in Houston while Homer received "extremely painful" treatments at a clinic. At the same time he put himself under the care of a nutritionist in Houston, Mrs. Purtee. She told Homer that he needed to "balance the chemistry of his body" and put him on a diet without sugar and pork. He ate mostly fruits, vegetables, and lean meat and took large doses of vitamins and minerals. Hailey was convinced that Mrs. Purtee's treatment "detoxified" his body; he remained a health-food devotee all through life.[132]

All in all, the months in Houston were a nightmare. The city was glutted with newcomers in the midst of World War II, and it was virtually impossible to find housing. Homer, Lois, and the children stayed in the small home of "a good old sister" until "she couldn't put up with us any longer." They then moved in with Hailey's friend, Basil Doran, who preached at the West University Place Church of Christ, and Homer helped with the preaching. Word spread quickly through the brotherhood about Hailey's health crisis, and he was flooded with "prayers on my behalf," "cards and letters," and "financial help."[133] He was not dismissed from the clinic until April; he left with a badly scarred left shoulder and in a state of near exhaustion.[134]

The Central Church in Los Angeles patiently waited for Hailey to finish his treatments. In April, Homer and the family drove to Los Angeles. "We are hopeful that the trouble is under control and that there shall be no recurrence of it," he reported to the *Firm Foundation*. Ever upbeat, he settled in to his new work with the Central Church, a "fine congregation" with a splendid building located in downtown Los Angeles. Hailey believed the congregation had "great promise of becoming one of the most outstanding churches in that growing city."[135] By the summer of 1945 he was again touring the country holding meetings, and he reported to the *Christian Chronicle* that his "health was returning completely." He believed that he was "completely cured."[136]

Hailey liked the people in Los Angeles, but a number of factors contributed to his leaving the church after one year. The work load was heavy, and Hailey had difficulty settling in to the routine of local preaching after his years of teaching at ACC. He also concluded that "I didn't fit a big city."[137] He told Lois, "Honey, I can't do the work here. I've got to get away." He felt that he was not "recuperating" as he should in Los Angeles; he remained weak from the treatments he had undergone in Houston. The atmosphere at the Central Church was far more liberal and experimental than the conservative environment around Abilene. Particularly troubling to Hailey was the growing tendency for California churches to give financial support to Pepperdine College. He was opposed to church support for colleges, but he did not want to begin a controversy over the question in Los Angeles.[138]

Hailey's most important accomplishment during his year in Los Angeles was the rewriting of his master's thesis and its publication by the Old Paths Book Club under the title *Attitudes and Consequences in the Restoration Movement*. Hailey's first book, the study was widely read. The book was not a definitive history of the restoration movement, but it was a perceptive interpretation of the Christian Church–churches of Christ division, and it was a useful overview of the intellectual foundations of the schism.[139]

In the spring of 1946, young Bill Patterson, a sailor stationed in Honolulu whose ship was berthed in Los Angeles, attended the services at Central and engaged Hailey in a fervent conversation about moving to Hawaii. Osby Weaver had just completed two fruitful years in Honolulu, sponsored by the church in Ferris, Texas, and the Hawaiian church had purchased and paid for a thirty-five thousand dollar building that served both as a meeting house and a preacher's residence.[140] Patterson told Hailey that he and several other Christian servicemen wanted to return to Hawaii after they were discharged. The two men fleshed out a plan for Hailey to begin a "Bible School" in which veterans could study the Bible supported by their GI benefits.[141] The idea intrigued Hailey. He and Patterson presented the proposal to Lois, and she approved of the move. Before spring was over, Hailey had canceled his 1946 schedule of summer meetings and was preparing for the trip. It was the first time since 1929 that he did not spend the entire summer preaching in meetings.

Just before the family planned to embark for Hawaii in April 1946, Lois was stricken by a severe "spell." She remained behind for two months, keeping Roma with her. Homer, Mary Lois, Rob, and Dennis departed as scheduled, accompanied by Mamie, who had agreed to keep house until Lois arrived. Hawaii proved to be an elixir for Hailey. He enjoyed the sun and swimming in the ocean, and he began to work out regularly at a Honolulu gym, gaining weight and his former vigor. On the other hand, Lois never recovered from her collapse in Los Angeles. Increasingly, she was physically unable to care for the family. More and more of the responsibility for shopping and looking after the children fell on Homer.[142]

Hailey later looked back on his years in Hawaii as "the two most productive and enjoyable years of any local work of my life."[143] The Central Church in Los Angeles supported Hailey in Honolulu, paying him four hundred dollars a month. He and Bill Patterson were soon joined by other workers. Haskell Chesshir was discharged from the navy in May and "voluntarily returned to Hawaii to do missionary work." Chesshir, his wife, and his car were transported to Hawaii by the El Cajon Boulevard congregation in San Diego, but he departed without any "church sponsoring." Upon the recommendation of Hailey, who commended Chesshir as "one of the most active workers and a most promising student," Central in Los Angeles agreed to act as a clearinghouse for funds going to Chesshir.[144]

Shortly after his arrival, Hailey won the approval of the Department of Education to teach courses for veterans, and he formally opened the Honolulu Bible School, offering two years of courses designed to "prepare the Christian to do personal work, to teach the Bible, and to preach the gospel of Christ." The school did not aim to teach secular subjects. Although the Bible School was really no more than Homer Hailey teaching a few young men, it listed a "faculty" that included Hailey teaching the Bible, Lee Ella Wallace teaching speech, and Robert Baker teaching chorus.[145]

In spite of the difficulties caused by Lois's poor health, Hailey's two years in Hawaii were a blur of activity. In early 1947, Hailey, Patterson, and Chesshir were joined by young Len Spencer, and the four men devoted "full time to house to house teaching, night classes, and personal calls." In addition, the teaching program was aided by Lee Ella Wallace, the daughter of Foy E. Wallace, Jr., described as a "beautiful young woman," who had come to Hawaii to teach school after her marriage collapsed. Hailey recollected that Lee Ella "did more to convert people than anyone." She kept the men supplied with prospects to teach.[146] By the summer their efforts began to produce results. In June, Hailey reported, "Eight baptisms during the past two months: Two white men and one white woman; one Filipino, one Chinese-Hawaiian, one Japanese, and two Korean women." "Whether a 'great door, and effectual' is opened to us or not, we hope to know by the end of our summer's work," Hailey informed readers at home, as he and his helpers began an intense series of summer classes.[147] At the end of the summer, Hailey reported that "only nine were baptized during these three months," but he also noted that four of the converts would enter David Lipscomb College in the fall, "two Chinese girls and two Japanese girls."[148] When he departed from Hawaii in 1948, Hailey had baptized eighty-two people, "forty-one anglos and forty-one natives."[149]

The two-year stay in Honolulu brought to the surface the core components in Homer Hailey's character. He relished working with the young zealots who joined him, and he was a master at teaching classes and persuading people to become Christians. In addition, for all the race prejudice that sometimes surfaced in Hailey's language, he adored native Hawaiians and worked with utter disregard for racial barriers, building a unique multiracial congregation in Honolulu. Hailey was particularly supportive of the native Christians, and he tried to train "local teachers and preachers" who would give the church a "more permanent status."[150]

Back to Abilene: 1948–1951

Hailey was less visible during his years in Hawaii, but he was not forgotten by the churches on the mainland. The widely circulated journal *Christian Chronicle* regularly published articles written by Hailey. He wrote mostly on noncontroversial, practical, biblical themes. In February 1947, Hailey returned to Abilene, having been accorded the honor of delivering the closing address in an annual lectureship with the theme of worldwide missions.[151] Hailey issued a passionate "appeal to all young men, especially veterans who have seen the carnage of war and the needs of the world for the Gospel, to offer their lives now in the service of Christ."[152] In the spring of 1948, Hailey announced, through the *Christian Chronicle,* that he would return to the mainland for a series of meetings that would take him to Los Angeles, Washington, D.C., San Antonio, and the Fifth and Highland Church in Abilene.[153]

At some point during the spring of 1948 Hailey decided to return to the mainland to stay. Lois's health remained poor, and, when the opportunity presented itself to return, she told him, "Homer let's go home. I can't take care of the children."[154] Hailey had two firm offers for teaching jobs, one at ACC and the other at a newly established school in Temple Terrace, Florida, Florida Christian College. Thus, in the late spring of 1948 he boarded a Matson Line ship to begin a flurry of meetings, leaving Lois and the children to follow when the school term ended. It was a beautiful journey home, but, as on his other sea voyages, Hailey was seasick the entire trip.[155]

After conducting a meeting in Washington, D.C., Hailey took a train to Tampa to visit the campus of Florida Christian College. In the absence of President L. R. Wilson, he was guided on a campus tour by Roland Lewis, later one of Hailey's most trusted friends. A few days later, Wilson flew to San Antonio, where Hailey was in a meeting, and urged him to move to Florida. Wilson told Hailey that he planned to leave the presidency after another year to return to full-time preaching, and he wanted Hailey to succeed him as president. That prospect was not a carrot to Homer Hailey. Hailey replied, "Brother Wilson, if that's what you want, you've said too much. I'm not going to be president of anything. . . . I'm not an administrator. . . . I'm a preacher and a teacher."[156]

Several factors tipped the scales toward returning to Abilene. Hailey still owned a home on the Albany Highway near the ACC campus, and he and Lois had deep roots there. In July he accepted a position as associate professor of Christian Education and agreed to work with the Graham Street Church as its preacher. In many ways it seemed as if he had never left. Hailey conducted the fall "revival meeting" at the College Church; the student paper observed that Hailey "probably knows and is known by more people of Abilene and vicinity than any other minister of the church of Christ." Roma entered ACC as a student in 1948 and Mary Lois, Rob, and Dennis enrolled at the "demonstration school" where Homer had been principal.[157]

A number of circumstances conspired to make it possible for Hailey to return to ACC. The college was bursting with a record enrollment of more than 1,650 students in the fall of 1948. Like other colleges around the country, it was teeming with returning veterans taking advantage of the GI Bill. The ACC enrollment had grown from around seven hundred in 1946 to over fourteen hundred in 1947. Dean Adams scoured the county searching for "teachers that are members of the church who have Master of Arts or higher degrees."[158] By 1948, Charles Roberson no longer had an uncontested veto on Hailey's return. Though he remained head of the Bible Department until 1951, Roberson was "pretty well out of it" during his last years on campus; some students irreverently dubbed him "whistlin' Charlie." In a move that bypassed Roberson, in 1946 President Don Morris appointed W. R. Smith as ACC vice-president and head of a newly formed Christian Education Department. Smith was "not a member of Dr. Roberson's team," recalled Paul Southern, and one of Smith's early objectives was recruiting Homer Hailey to come back.[159]

President Morris and other leaders at ACC knew that Hailey brought to ACC an impeccable reputation among the churches of Christ and a degree of legitimacy even within the strictest wing of the movement. Morris was ever alert to improving the school's standing with the churches; he customarily advertised the summer preaching itineraries of the fifteen members of the faculty who were "engaged in preaching the gospel."[160] ACC remained strongly identified with the churches of Christ; in 1947 the college reported that it had enrolled "approximately 300 preacher students" and that ninety percent of the student body came from churches of Christ.[161] In a half-page ad run in several periodicals, ACC announced that Hailey was returning "to give practical training in the work and worship of the church." "As a Bible student, evangelist, debater, writer, and Christian he ranks with the best," the college boasted. "The brotherhood know him as a sound, safe, and effective Bible teacher and preacher."[162]

Hailey was an invaluable link between the school and the churches. He continued to preach a hectic schedule of meetings each summer, reaching out to more and more distant places. The harvest was good in 1949; after a twelve-day meeting in Lamesa, Hailey reported "36 baptized and seven restored" in a church that had been made "ready for this meeting" by local preacher Paul McClung.[163] Late in the summer, in Lometa, Texas, where "brother C. A. Buchanan . . . had things in readiness for a good meeting," Hailey reported "eighteen baptized and several restored. . . . At least half were men between thirty and seventy."[164] Hailey was in demand; churches proudly advertised that their meeting would be held by the "well-known evangelist" Homer Hailey.[165] He preached frequently on lectureships. In 1950 he was one of the featured speakers in a program sponsored by "twenty-two co-operating churches in Fort Worth."[166]

Hailey was the anchor of the Department of Christian Education. He taught a variety of subjects, including a course in Christian Evidences, one in Denominational Doctrines, another on the Problems of the Preacher, and, his favorite, a course on Preparation for Mission Work. Hailey's practical, Bible-based courses were flooded with students, and he was a particular favorite of the young veterans, many of whom were filled with zeal to return overseas as missionaries. Hailey fed their fervor. In a chapel speech delivered to the students and faculty in December 1948, he urged, "Give yourself. Make this college a training ground for evangelists."[167] Because of his love for missions, Hailey formed a strong bond with the young men who studied with him during his three years in the Christian Education Department at ACC—probably the strongest he ever formed. Many years later he could still tick off their names—Bob Owen, Bill Fling, Robert Bolton, Tex Williams, Abe Lincoln; most of them remained devoted friends. Looking back many years later, Hailey concluded, "I did my greatest work there in those three years."[168]

In 1951, the Christian Chronicle Publishing Company published Hailey's second book, *Let's Go Fishing for Men*. A practical guidebook on personal evangelism, it summarized the principles of salesmanship that Hailey had learned while preaching at Fifth and Highland. The book was the product of "years of intensive personal evangelism and Bible study," boasted the publisher, and it would "give every member a guidebook to instruct and inspire him to become a real personal worker for the Lord."[169] By 1951 Hailey had become a prominent expert on "personal work," and he spoke frequently on the subject at lectureships.[170]

Hailey's departure from ACC in 1951 was hastened by the appointment of Paul Southern as Charles Roberson's successor as head of the Bible Department. A good campus politician (which Hailey was not and Southern was) could easily have predicted the appointment. Southern anticipated the growing pressures for academic respectability in Abilene, and in 1945 he took advantage of a faculty grant to begin work on a doctoral degree. He enrolled at the University of Chicago, but he quickly left that program and enrolled in the less demanding doctor of theology program at Southern Baptist Theological Seminary in Louisville, graduating in 1948.

Southern forged a good relationship with Charles Roberson. "I knew that some of his techniques and methods were not up to modern standards," Southern recalled years later, "but he had a big following and I was not about to raise a ruckus. . . . So we got along just fine."[171] As the new head of the Bible Department, Southern bemoaned the loss of Roberson's "great leadership and wise counsel," and he declared himself a team player: "I pledge my greatest loyalty and cooperation to the administration and the department of Bible."[172]

Hailey was chagrined that he had lost the job to his old friend and competitor. When he returned to Abilene in 1948 he asked President Don Morris whether he would be a candidate for the position when Roberson retired, and Morris assured him that he would. On the other hand, Southern was led to believe that he would be the next head when he completed his doctor's degree.[173] When Southern returned to Abilene with his doctor's degree in hand, the die was cast. Of course, Hailey's position was not threatened by Southern's appointment; he could have remained at ACC had he wished to do so. However, Southern's appointment was symbolic of a change in directions that made Hailey feel increasingly ill at ease.

By 1950, ACC was a college on the make. As Dean Walter Adams put it, during the early fifties the school "grew from a Bible College to an emerging university." ACC began a major fund-raising campaign in 1946 aimed at gaining accreditation. The college reminded its supporters that "as an educational institution, [ACC] is in competition with all other educational institutions in the land."[174] Guided by Adams, ACC gained full accreditation from the Southern Association at its 1951 meeting in St. Petersburg.[175] It had been a difficult struggle. The college had supported a number of faculty members with paid leaves to earn graduate degrees; in 1951 thirteen members of the faculty had earned doctorates.[176] Each year new faculty members joined the Bible Department with doctorates from major institutions. In this academic environment, it was no surprise that Hailey was passed over in the search for a new Bible Department head.[177]

ACC was also in a period of financial transition in the years after World War II. In 1943, President Don Morris announced that an eighteen-month fund-raising campaign had liquidated the "entire indebtedness of Abilene Christian College." Morris promised that "those in charge will continue to direct the school in the most business-like way they know."[178] The next step in the financial expansion of the school was a 1946 $3 million "expansion and endowment" campaign launched by "brethren in many communities of Oklahoma and Texas." The campaign paid for major physical improvements on the campus and provided permanent endowment funds for the graduate and undergraduate schools.[179] Successful business people and ranchers became increasingly visible on campus and were featured in the college's publications; perhaps most shocking was the appearance of a wealthy Oklahoma oil man and philanthropist as a chapel speaker even though he was not a member of the churches of Christ. "They had discovered outside money," observed Bob Owen, a student at ACC at the time, and in the eyes of some observers, including Hailey, ACC's administrators seemed willing to "close their eyes to some moral issues" if money was involved.[180]

These general changes, rather than any specific grievance, provided the backdrop for Hailey's growing dissatisfaction in Abilene. The emphasis on academic respectability, and the high-pressure fund raising, combined with a relaxation in the disciplining of students, fed Hailey's apprehension. Paul Southern remembered a faculty meeting in which Hailey "made a speech . . . expressing his uneasiness about the way things were going." "He wanted the 'i's dotted and the 't's crossed," his rival recalled, and he was direct and demanding. Southern was surprised that "they didn't fire him," but Hailey survived because everyone "knew that he was strong in his faith and was not a hypocrite."[181]

Many of the older preacher students were aware of the growing tensions on campus. "Homer was the Bible scholar," recalled Bob Owen, whereas some of the younger Ph.D.s joining the department had "come through the liberal theological schools" and were viewed by the conservative preacher boys as "tainted." "He knew more Bible than those Ph.D.s did when they came out," agreed Garvin Beauchamp.[182] Hailey's classes were crammed with preacher boys who felt they were "not getting anything in their other classes."[183]

Homer Hailey and ACC were headed in different directions. Hailey respected Don Morris and "esteemed his friendship highly." He admired Dean Adams "as an educator," though he never felt close to him, and he knew that Adams was the architect of the new academically respectable ACC. Hailey was comfortable in the Christian Education Department, feeling that he "fit in well in this department." However, overall, "I saw things coming at the school, and I didn't know how I was going to fit in there."[184] He was not going to fit in very well.

In 1951, Hailey was again invited to join the faculty of Florida Christian College, and he received several feelers from other new colleges that had been established after World War II. He had "seriously considered" moving to Florida in 1949, spending "almost an entire night praying about the matter," before deciding to remain in Abilene, mostly "because of the veterans who were older students." In 1951, most of those young men were nearing graduation, and, after the Bible Department job had been given to Southern, Hailey began to think of other possibilities. One of Hailey's preacher students, Bob Owen, had become his friend and confidant, and Owen, who had ties to Florida Christian College, became a recruiter for FCC. Knowing that Hailey was dissatisfied at ACC, Owen talked with him about the potential of the young, biblically oriented Florida school, and he informed FCC's new president, James R. Cope, that Hailey was considering a move.[185]

Lois was also ready to move in 1951. The family had grown to include a fifth child, Carol Ann, who came to live with them in 1950. Carol Ann was born in New York but her mother took her to Honolulu to live with the Hailey family. The Haileys hoped to adopt the baby, keeping her for more than a year before her mother changed her mind. Two years later, Carol Ann's mother once again contacted the Haileys and they adopted the little girl when she was about four years old. The burden of rearing five children bore heavily on Lois and her health continued to deteriorate. Her relations with her mother grew more and more strained after they returned to Abilene; once again, both Lois and Homer hoped that a change might help her health.[186]

Signaled by Bob Owen that Hailey had agreed to discuss moving to Florida, Cope flew to Abilene to offer Hailey a position as vice president and head of the Bible Department at Florida Christian College. He was a good salesman. After about three hours of discussion at his home, Hailey went into the kitchen where Lois was preparing lunch, and "after consulting her, we decided to move to Florida." Scheduled to leave the next day for his summer meetings, Hailey went directly to the offices of Don Morris and W. R. Smith to tell them of his decision. Later in the afternoon, Morris and Smith visited in Hailey's home for two hours trying to persuade him to change his mind, but Hailey was convinced that "with the change of the student personnel in ACC, I could do more good in a small school." Recruiting Hailey was a coup for Florida Christian College and Cope. The "well-known teacher, author and preacher" would bring much-needed prestige to the little school.[187]

The next day Hailey headed out once again for a summer of meetings, dropping back into Abilene from time to time. Lois sold their Abilene home, and the family packed while Homer conducted an August meeting at the Fourteenth and Vine congregation in Abilene. The Haileys left many memories behind in Abilene. Except for his brief sojourns in Arizona, at SMU, in Los Angeles, and Hawaii, Abilene had been Homer's home since he enrolled in ACC as a student in 1926. Lois was leaving her home, and her mother. They were headed toward a new life in Florida. Did he ever regret the move? Not Homer Hailey. He had learned to live without looking back during his youth on the Arizona frontier: "My policy through life has been that once a decision is made, never look back. So I have believed that it was according to God's providence, as have been all my decisions and moves."[188]

6

Hailey in the Eye of the Storm

The Florida Years

No individual fits neatly into the categories constructed by historians and social scientists. The personal journeys of members of churches of Christ through the labyrinth of faith and factionalism within the movement in the twentieth century were as varied as the personalities of the hundreds of thousands of Christians who lived and died within the church. Each person was a unique blend of belief and temperament. In the years before 1950, each individual not only held a distinctive mix of beliefs but also exhibited a personal level of patience. Everyone tolerated some degree of disagreement, and almost everyone held a minority view on some subject. Because churches of Christ were a self-conscious and tight-knit community, united by ties of kinship, friendship, and informal institutional networks, most individual biographies were filled with unexpected alliances and unpredictable twists and turns.

Anomalies and paradoxes abound in the personal stories of the twentieth-century seekers of the ancient order. For instance, W. W. Otey, who was a Sommerite as a youth and for decades spearheaded the noninstitutional cause, was a lifelong friend of J. N. Armstrong, the much-maligned moderate, premillennial sympathizer, and committed college builder. The irony was compounded by the fact that the arch-conservative Otey was "infatuated with politics" and a caustic critic of pacifists, and Armstrong, the suspected liberal, was a strong believer in David Lipscomb's views on world separation and suffered persecution because of his pacifist convictions. Their ties were personal; Otey lectured on four occasions at Harding and he respected Armstrong. Daniel Sommer chastised Otey for the relationship, ridiculing him for working "hand-in-glove with Prof. J. N. Armstrong of 'Bible College' fame."[1]

After Armstrong died, Otey wrote a brief tribute that was published in the *Firm Foundation*. E. R. Harper, Foy E. Wallace, Jr.'s ally who kept Harding College under surveillance, wrote a rebuttal attacking Armstrong, which editor G. H. P. Showalter refused to publish. Harper complained that Otey's praise for Armstrong called into question the tactics of the anti-premillennial crusaders. Otey curtly replied, "I still believe my statement true. You have attacked him bitterly and persistently for years, and many who are not premillennialists have a suspicion that it was part of a concerted plan by a number, to force Armstrong out of the college and elevate one of their choice to that position. I say many have suspected this. Now since he is dead you still want to pursue him with bitter attacks even to the grave, and ask me to aid in the attack. Once and for all, I have never, and never shall, become a collaborationist in this sort of unholy work. I did not agree with him in everything, but his memory will still be held dear when some of his bitter enemies who attacked him unjustly will be forgotten."[2]

A Personal Journey through the Maze of Faith

Like most people in the churches of Christ during the turbulent years surrounding World War II, Homer Hailey had mixed personal loyalties and was ambivalent about many of the issues that were heatedly debated. He knew and admired people who held widely divergent views. Hailey was first and foremost a preacher, and he focused on building churches. He was more interested in spreading the gospel and baptizing converts than in debating the controversial issues that divided the brotherhood and ravaged local churches. Always interested in missions, in the 1940s, Hailey wrote frequently for the *Christian Chronicle,* a journal more noted for ballyhoo and promotion than for strictness in doctrine.[3]

At the same time, there was no soft side in Hailey's personality or preaching. He left the Christian Church because of conviction, and he never lost his zeal for returning to the "old paths." Just out of college in 1932, Hailey, speaking on that topic in a lectureship, called on churches to clear away the "debris and rubbish of ecclesiasticism and ignorance."[4] Hailey returned repeatedly to the theme of restoring New Testament Christianity, highlighting the digression of the Christian Church and urging the churches of Christ not to follow the same pattern.[5]

If Frank B. Shepherd was Hailey's mentor, the man who captured his imagination, as he had that of so many other younger preachers of his generation, was Foy E. Wallace, Jr. Hailey attended Wallace's debate with J. Frank Norris in Fort Worth and went away convinced that they had been "in the presence of a great man." In 1945, he sat through Wallace's Music Hall Lectures in Houston; he was enthralled by Wallace's grasp of premillennial doctrine, and he remained convinced throughout his life that Wallace was "the greatest pulpit man I ever listened to." Hailey considered Wallace a "profound thinker" as well as "a master of the pulpit."[6]

Hailey devoured Wallace's writings on premillennialism, his admiration growing ever deeper, and by the mid-1930s the two were "pretty good friends." The premillennial issue pushed Hailey into the arms of Wallace. He had never studied biblical prophecy before he returned to Abilene to preach in 1932. By that time the topic was hotly disputed and "invariably came up" in conversation. A premillennial congregation had begun meeting in Abilene, and Hailey felt compelled to decide what he believed. He read diligently and concluded that the theory was "a materialistic view of the kingdom of God" that was false. Later a recognized expert on the prophetic writings of both the Old and New Testaments, Hailey was introduced to the subject through the premillennial issue. By the mid-1930s, Hailey agreed wholeheartedly with Wallace that premillennialists should be driven out of the churches.[7]

Hailey began writing regularly for the first time in Foy E. Wallace, Jr.'s *Bible Banner* at the end of the 1930s; most of his articles were biblical studies on noncontroversial topics. "Foy had a lot of respect for me," Hailey recalled, but "I stayed off the controversial subjects. . . . I don't like to fuss."[8] In 1940 Wallace listed Hailey as one of his "staff of writers whose names are known for soundness on all questions before the church."[9] During the war years, when Wallace became a superpatriot, Hailey disappeared from the pages of the *Bible Banner,* as did his fellow conscientious objector, Associate Editor John T. Lewis. Nonetheless, when Wallace founded *Torch* in 1950, Hailey wrote him a warm note of support: "Let me say that I am glad you are writing again. For a long time I have missed your writings. They have always been stimulating and thought-provoking. The monumental work in stemming the tide of premillennialism will ever be appreciated by those of us who love the truth and were helped by your work."[10]

While Hailey's articles in the *Bible Banner* were usually noncontroversial, he sometimes displayed the watchdog mentality of the magazine and occasionally used Wallace-like language. He forthrightly condemned the "general attitude" of "softness" and "straddle-the-fence-ism."[11] Hailey was wary of the "inner threat of softness" and urged his fellow preachers to "quit trying to find some ground on which we can fellowship sectarians in Ministerial Alliances, love feasts, and such; and a loop-hole through which we may encourage them in the belief that they are saved."[12] He insisted that "every Christian is called by Jesus to combat," and he reminded his fellow Christians that "the church won the fight in those early days because men had the courage to stand up and speak the truth, charge the sinners with their sins, and tell them what to do about it."[13]

Hailey never was very attuned to the political infighting that was an endemic part of the life of churches of Christ, but he was drawn into several skirmishes at Abilene Christian College. When Clinton Davidson visited the college in 1940, Hailey reported to Wallace that his speech attempted to "apologize for Boll, and to denounce the men who have fought the pernicious theory for the past few years."[14] Hailey also denounced Claude F. Witty's unity conferences in the *Bible Banner,*[15] and, of course, he played an important role in the Charles H. Roberson affair.[16]

Hailey's strong stance against premillennialism and his identification with Wallace's crusade delineated only one side of his religious character. He was never a debater and he was slow to study the intricacies of controversial questions. More important, though Hailey was anti-premillennial, he had a strong sense of cultural separation. No church, he believed, should court "favor with all the people."[17] The church was "a rock of refuge in the midst of the storm," the "preserver of faith and righteousness at all costs" in the "midst of a crooked and perverse generation."[18] In 1942, Hailey demonstrated his keen sense of cultural aloofness in an unpopular cause, denouncing "the disposition of gospel preachers to line themselves up with sectarian preachers in campaigns to outlaw alcoholic beverages." Hailey's arguments smacked of David Lipscomb: "Now certainly every Christian should hate alcohol as a beverage in every form. He should fight it with all that he has. But which is the divine mission of the church, to outlaw a thing by legislation, or by changing the hearts of men through the gospel? When gospel preachers begin trying to ride a thing out by the ballot and legislation, instead of by the gospel, does not that have a rather faint appearance of a 'new cart'?"[19]

Hailey's pacifism also placed him within the historic world-separationist stream. In the 1930s, Hailey was the pacifist leader on the Abilene Christian College campus, advising students to "bring your own passions, your own desires into submission to end all wars; the answer to our prayer this morning depends on your stand toward the future wars." Hailey argued that the "spirit of war," with its emphasis on "killing, crushing, destroying," could hardly be balanced with the "spirit of Christ" that demanded "humility, trust, faith, and equality."[20] During World War II, Hailey, like most other pacifists in churches of Christ, said little about the issue, but he was harshly criticized by the superpatriots in the church.[21] In 1950, when he returned to teach in Abilene, Hailey lectured the returning veterans about the Christian's responsibility to be a conscientious objector.[22]

In 1952, as Homer Hailey prepared to leave ACC to begin a new career at Florida Christian College, he, like most people in the churches of Christ, could not be neatly categorized. At Abilene, he was regarded as an arch-conservative, but he was much loved and respected, and President Don Morris was reluctant to see him leave. Hailey had no firm convictions about most of the institutional issues being hotly debated at the beginning of the fifties. He had long believed that churches should not contribute to colleges, but he had been employed by a college that accepted contributions. Many of the pioneer preachers he most admired had tolerated the same ambivalence. He liked fighting preachers, but he was hardly a rabble-rouser.[23] He thought Cled E. Wallace was a "loveable character," but he considered the "rock fight" article completely "out of order."[24] Hailey had never questioned the right of local churches to act as sponsoring agencies, and he had frequently participated in projects supported through congregational cooperation, but he was disturbed by the size and tone of the big missions programs begun after World War II.[25]

Like many other conservative-minded people, Hailey balked at noninstitutional attacks on the orphan homes supported by churches of Christ. He had long supported orphan homes; he and Lois adopted two children and he had a deep personal compassion for suffering children. He spoke on a number of occasions at the Tipton Home in Oklahoma. After a visit to the Maude Carpenter Children's Home in Wichita, Kansas, in 1949, Hailey wrote an impassioned appeal asking churches to support the orphanage, which was directed by his old friend G. K. Wallace: "Many congregations are wasting enough money on useless weekly bulletins, Sunday bouquets of flowers, and other needless expenditures, to make worthwhile contributions to the needs of these children."[26] In later years, after Hailey changed his mind on the subject of church-supported orphan homes, he observed that "it was as good an article as could be written without a passage of scripture."[27] Actually, he cited two passages, though neither addressed the questions raised by the critics of church-supported institutions.

Hailey drifted slowly into the noninstitutional camp in the 1950s. Like so many others in churches of Christ who were not much interested in controversy, he was forced by circumstances to make a choice. Hailey finally studied the institutional issues in the early 1950s, but he had long before committed himself to a path that led away from Abilene. Many people went in surprising directions when the lines of division hardened in the late 1950s, but Hailey's choices were eminently predictable.

Florida Christian College

Homer Hailey had long "dreamed of living in the South"; his move to Florida Christian College in Temple Terrace, Florida, did not disappoint him. Looking back, he surmised that his twenty-two years of teaching at the small college were the "greatest years of my life."[28] During their first year in Florida, the Hailey family lived in a dormitory apartment, sharing the crumbling old building with several other faculty families who had arrived in 1949, including Clinton and Margaret Hamilton, Jim and Bobbie Miller, and Pat and Deedee Hardeman. During that year, Homer purchased three lots facing the Temple Terrace golf course, and in 1951 the family moved into a western-style home, designed by Homer, where they lived for two decades. Always a shrewd real estate investor, Hailey built on two of his lots and sold the third in the booming Tampa real estate market for enough money to pay off his indebtedness.[29]

President James R. Cope lured Hailey to Florida Christian College by promising that he would have an opportunity to teach scores of serious young men interested in preaching and missions. From Cope's point of view, Hailey added critically needed maturity and experience to the young school's Bible faculty. Only thirty-two years old when he accepted the presidency in 1949, Cope was older than any other member of the Bible Department. In 1950, he began recruiting "some gray hair for the school." Cope persuaded Aaron W. Dicus to retire early from his position as head of the Physics Department at Tennessee Technological University to become dean of Florida Christian College and to teach Bible, and he also employed Harry W. Pickup, Sr., a respected Tampa preacher, to teach Bible courses. However, Cope still felt that the school needed a "Bible student and teacher" with a national reputation among churches of Christ to attract students.[30] Hailey fit that job description. In the years ahead, recalled Bob F. Owen, Hailey "set a standard for the Bible Division."[31]

Jim Cope triumphantly announced Hailey's arrival in Florida in the *Gospel Advocate:* "Homer Hailey brings with him a veritable storehouse of Biblical knowledge and classroom, pulpit, and personal evangelism experience. Now only forty-seven, he is in the prime of life with his best years yet ahead. His coming to Florida Christian College will give the school that richness which experience and maturity alone can produce in its fullness."[32] Hailey was the "star" the school needed as a "drawing card"; a number of ACC students followed him to Florida Christian College.[33] Bob Owen, Cope's successor as president of FCC, believed that Hailey's "presence had as much to do with Florida College making it as any other force." Hailey's "prestige" and his sterling reputation among the churches made him "a recruiting tool *par excellence.*"[34] Bill Humble, a young Bible teacher at the college when Hailey arrived, always considered Hailey's addition to the faculty to be Cope's "great achievement" as president of the school.[35]

When Hailey became the vice-president and head of the Bible Department at FCC in 1951, the school was five years old.[36] Located on 197 acres of prime real estate along the banks of the Hillsborough River in Temple Terrace, on the outskirts of Tampa, the five buildings that housed the college had been conceived as a part of a golfing resort during the Florida land boom of the 1920s. Before being acquired in 1945 by a board led by Tampa realtor C. Ed Owings and wealthy Jacksonville paper manufacturer Clifford G. McGehee, the property had served as the campus for an evangelical Bible school attended by Billy Graham. L. R. Wilson, a respected preacher and "school man," served as president of FCC for three years, resigning in 1948 because he was unable to "get preaching sufficiently out of my system to settle down indefinitely to routine school matters."[37] Owings reported that Wilson's departure filled the board with "fear and trembling," but in the spring the board proudly announced that it had hired as the college's new president the "distinguished evangelist and teacher of Henderson, Tennessee," James R. Cope.[38]

The men who founded Florida Christian College were conservative members of churches of Christ. In an address delivered to a public forum of supporters nearly a year before the school opened, L. R. Wilson assured the audience that "no effort will be made to place the school above the church" and that "no effort whatever will be made to dictate to the congregations, or to take over their work." Emphasizing that the school intended to be a serious Bible training center, the president announced that FCC would not "sanction commercial sports and 'rough and tumble' competitive athletics." The primary purpose of the school was to "strive to prevent our children from being swept away by infidelity in college."[39]

In a public meeting held shortly after Wilson's resignation, the FCC board of trustees tilted toward the noninstitutional position in the brewing controversy in the churches of Christ.

Owings outlined the college's policies: "I wish to say that our by-laws state that there will be no solicitation of funds from any church treasury for Florida Christian College. I assure you that this has never been done and never will be done, and I can go further in stating that henceforth funds from church treasuries will not be accepted."[40] The shift from nonsolicitation to nonacceptance of church contributions positioned FCC squarely in the camp of the noninstitutional churches of Christ.

The arrival of young Jim Cope was a defining moment in the history of FCC; Owings speculated that "it now appears that . . . God himself has provided just the man needed to fill the place so vital to our hopes for a real Christian college in Florida."[41] Cope had won considerable fame as an evangelist, and he had taught for five years in the Bible Department at Freed-Hardeman College. Many believed that he was being groomed to succeed N. B. Hardeman as president of that flourishing institution. E. H. Ijams, former president of David Lipscomb College, recommended Cope highly to the FCC board: "His leadership will attract other sound and able men to the institution he heads. Brother Cope is zealous, but not fanatical."[42]

Even though Jim Cope was a protégé of N. B. Hardeman, he apparently arrived at FCC convinced that the board's noninstitutional views were correct. Shortly after his arrival in 1949, he wrote in the *Firm Foundation*, "Being a human organization operated by individual Christians, Florida Christian College as an institution does not desire or expect to be a parasite upon churches. It will neither ask nor accept contributions from churches of the Lord."[43] Cope guided FCC for more than three decades. During those years, he and the college played crucial roles in defining the noninstitutional movement among churches of Christ.

The little college that Cope came to head was beset by financial and academic problems. An unaccredited institution with 149 students enrolled in college-level classes, the school's credits were transferrable "on the basis of merit." In 1950,

The trio of early leaders of Florida Christian College. *Left to right:* President James R. Cope, Vice-President Homer Hailey, and Dean Clinton Hamilton.

Cope reported that most in-state colleges would give full credit for hours earned from FCC, but he announced that the school had no intention of seeking formal accreditation.[44] In the fall of 1950, FCC abandoned its four-year curriculum and became a junior college with a four-year program in Bible and Religious Education. Cope and the board agreed that "it is a mistake for the school to attempt competition on a four-year academic level with other heavily endowed and luxuriously equipped colleges so early in its existence."[45] Florida Christian College did not wish to become a "big school," Cope insisted, rather, the board aimed to retain a small-school environment in which faculty members gave a "great amount of personal attention to each student." In 1951, Cope reported that "every college student [at FCC] this past year was a Christian," an extraordinary ambience even among colleges operated by members of the churches of Christ. Student conduct was rigidly controlled. Cope assured parents that "we make no apology for having regulations, some of which, no doubt, are considered by many as 'old fogy.'"[46]

During the early 1950s, Cope tried to steer Florida Christian College in a noninstitutional direction without completely alienating the school from mainstream churches. Nonetheless, the college came to be identified as a hotbed of noninstitutional radicalism. The board's decision to refuse church contributions placed the noninstitutional imprimatur on it, and by 1949, editor Fanning Yater Tant of the *Gospel Guardian* began touting FCC as "a place where any Christian parent could send a son or daughter with assurance and confidence."[47]

During the first half of the decade of the fifties, the FCC lectureship program generally drew speakers from both sides of the widening divide in churches of Christ, although the program tilted markedly toward noninstitutional preachers. *Gospel Advocate* editor B. C. Goodpasture was scheduled to speak at the college in 1950, but canceled his appearance because of illness. In 1951, G. H. P. Showalter, editor of the *Firm Foundation,* was a featured lecturer. In 1951, in response to a request from the Broadway Church in Lubbock, the college provided an open forum in which Otis Gatewood reported on his work in Europe and answered questions. The lecture programs through 1955 included preachers who supported church contributions to institutions, but each year the proportion weighed more and more in the direction of those who opposed institutionalism. By the middle of the 1950s, the FCC lectureship alone provided a platform for preachers adamantly opposed to sponsoring churches and other institutional practices.

The 1951 lectureship was a crucial juncture in defining the college. Jim Cope hoped that the program would provide a showcase for open discussion of institutional issues; he recruited James W. Adams to present the noninstitutional position and Gatewood to defend the sponsoring-church model. The audience was heavily tilted toward the noninstitutional cause, and hostile preachers in the audience vigorously grilled Gatewood after his presentation. James D. Bales, a respected and conservative professor at Harding College, requested an opportunity to defend institutionalism, and he received a post-presentation grilling similar to that which greeted Gatewood. Historian Earl Irvin West and Bales, both moderates who hoped the issues could be peaceably settled, wrote glowing summaries of the 1951 lectures, commending particularly the audience's "willingness to hear both sides."[48] Yater Tant's account in the *Gospel Guardian* was hopeful, even elated. He reported that there was no "sarcasm, ridicule, or any unworthy or unbecoming speech" in the freewheeling discussions. Rather, the open forums had provided "every opportunity for a full, free, unlimited and unrestricted discussion of the questions."[49]

Others disagreed with these rosy assessments of the exchanges at the lectures. Raymond C. Walker, a preacher from Jacksonville, Florida, wrote an open letter, published in the *Gospel Advocate,* outlining why "my description of those lectures cannot be given in terms that glow." Walker theorized that the "lectures were sponsored by the college and conducted by the Guardian." He believed that the "cards were stacked" against Gatewood and that the discussion that followed his presentation pitted "the college and the Guardian (in the main) versus Gatewood and a few of the rest of us."[50] The FCC board of directors circulated a formal statement denying Walker's charges. Goodpasture published the board's statement and wrote that he was "gratified that the board seeks to show that the college is not under the domination of any paper, particularly the Guardian." Clearly, however, Goodpasture remained unconvinced: "Many have thought that its [FCC's] head was lying on the lap of the Guardian; and that the lectureship was proof of it." He advised the FCC board to "exercise a little caution in their lectures and say things that are calculated to build up and expand the church rather than permit the college to be used as a sounding board for some individual to grind a personal ax."[51]

Cope and other leaders at FCC tried doggedly to maintain some sort of relationship with the growing institutional segment of the brotherhood. After the exchange over Walker's charges, Clinton D. Hamilton wrote an article in the *Gospel Advocate* urging people on both sides to "discuss issues on the basis of their scripturalness and not on the basis of what this brother or that group says about it."[52] Cope continued to report on the progress of the school in the *Advocate* and the *Firm Foundation* and to advertise the college in those papers, still featuring the Bible Department as the college's main asset. "Would you like your child to study Bible under these men?" asked a 1955 advertisement that featured pictures of James R. Cope, Homer Hailey, Clinton Hamilton, Pat Hardeman, Roland Lewis, Bob F. Owen, Harry Payne, Harry Pickup, Sr., and Franklin T. Puckett.[53]

By the end of the decade, the uneasy relationship between the college and the leadership of mainstream churches of Christ had become extremely precarious. In July 1958, Cope purchased a full-page advertisement in the *Gospel Advocate,* telling the history of the school and announcing future plans.[54] The advertisement had no doctrinal content, but its appearance in the *Advocate* raised a storm of protest.[55] Goodpasture reported that he had been "raked over the coals" for publishing it; he published nine scathing indictments of Cope and Florida Christian College. As editor of the *Advocate,* Goodpasture reported, his policy had been to allow advertising if he thought "there is reasonable hope of rescuing a college from its unsound teaching."[56] Perhaps he had been wrong in this case. By 1958, it was too late for an institution to straddle the fence in the internecine war dividing the churches of Christ.

The Bible Department: The FCC Brain Trust

Given his priorities, it was no surprise that Jim Cope regarded the recruitment of a high-profile Bible Department as the best strategy for building the college. He was remarkably successful. Three young men followed Cope to FCC from Freed-Hardeman: Clinton Hamilton, Cope's fellow faculty member, and two bright students, Bill Humble and Pat Hardeman. In 1950, Aaron W. Dicus and Harry Pickup, Sr., joined the Bible faculty; in 1951, Hailey came; and in 1952, G. K. Wallace, a widely know preacher and former director of Maude Carpenter Children's Home in Wichita, arrived. In 1952, Cope boasted that the college's Bible staff—Hailey, Wallace, Hamilton, Hardeman, Humble, Dicus, Pickup, and Cope—was an "unexcelled corps of Bible teachers." The Bible Department was the school's drawing card: "While seeking to give the very best in academic fields, we seek constantly to keep before the minds of our students the word of God by teachers well recognized for their knowledge, soundness, and ability to instruct young people."[57] Looking back years later, Bill Humble agreed that the "Bible department was the heart of the school" and that Cope used it effectively to gain "brotherhood support."[58]

At FCC, Homer Hailey was back in a Bible school environment. Hailey and Jim Cope saw eye to eye on virtually every question. They worked smoothly as a team, although the two of them never became close personal friends. Hailey and Dean Dicus had a respectful and cordial relationship, although they disagreed on several biblical questions, including their views of the eldership.

Among the older faculty members at FCC, Hailey's best friend was Harry Pickup, Sr. For three and a half decades, Pickup served in a variety of administrative capacities and sometimes taught Bible courses at the school. The two men loved one another from their first encounter. Hailey regarded Pickup as "one of the greatest men I have ever known," a "devout man," and an "excellent student of the Bible." Pickup stood in "awe" of Hailey, judging him to be a "great scholar." He believed that Hailey had the profoundest "concept of the word of God" that he had ever encountered; near the end of his life, Pickup could not recollect disagreeing with Hailey about any biblical question. Both men were down-to-earth, unaffected human beings, and they felt at ease with one another and confided in one another.[59]

Intellectually, Hailey was drawn to the young Bible teachers that Cope had recruited, and they adored him. The students dubbed a cadre including Clinton Hamilton, Pat Hardeman, Bill Humble, and Eugene W. Clevenger the "brain trust," and Hailey was soon convinced that they were "unusually brilliant young men."[60] The Bible Department staff was a volatile mix, and Hailey brought a degree of "stability" to their discussions.[61] Bill Humble recalled that Hailey "held us down, and we needed holding down."[62]

There was an extraordinary camaraderie in the Bible Department during Hailey's early years on campus. Each of the younger men established his own relationship with Hailey. Bill Humble, a devout man and a serious Bible student, lifted weights with Hailey and walked and talked with him in the evenings. Hailey was overwhelmed by the brilliance of Pat Hardeman, as were others who encountered his flashing intellect. Hailey believed that Hardeman "could see through a question better than any man I had ever seen." Hailey thought that Hardeman would become "a second Alexander Campbell"; the two of them bonded in a relationship of mutual respect.[63]

Clinton Hamilton was Hailey's closest intellectual companion during the twenty-two years they spent together at FCC. Hamilton was a meticulous and well-organized student of the Bible, a master of logic and precise expression, and Hailey immediately marked him as a "splendid thinker."[64] In 1993, Hamilton reflected on their friendship: "We often studied together, talked about subjects for sermons and issues under discussion among brethren. We walked together at night and conversed as we walked along the Temple Terrace Golf Club fairways. Those conversations tended to be very introspective, frank, open, and revealing. In whatever context, our conversations about issues and people were candid and cryptic because we had implicit confidence in the honorableness of the other."[65] Jim Cope judged that Hamilton, more than anyone else associated with FCC, came to know "Hailey the Bible student."[66]

Launching the Preceptor

In November 1951, shortly after Hailey's arrival at Florida Christian College, the members of the Bible faculty launched a new monthly periodical, the *Preceptor*. The initial issue of the paper was financed by one-hundred-dollar donations from Cope, Hailey, Humble, Hardeman, Hamilton, and Clevenger. In the *Gospel Advocate,* editor B. C. Goodpasture wished the new magazine "bon voyage," warning that the editors would discover many "troubled waters" on the sea of religious journalism.[67]

Jim Cope was the leader of the *Preceptor's* editorial corps, and he wrote the paper's opening editorial. Noting that there existed among the churches of Christ "an obvious unrest and disposition to do away with the existing order," Cope announced that the new magazine would be "a medium to provoke thinking and action in terms of inspired revelation." The "tenor of writings" in the new paper would provide a "balanced diet of positive and negative writings" and the editors would not allow the paper to be used by "saints or sinners to settle their personal feuds and fight their personal battles." Cope observed that none of the editors presumed to have a "haughty superior knowledge" nor did they have a "holier-than-thou attitude."[68] Clearly, the editors hoped to fight the institutional battle on a new level, free from the bitter personal feuding that had marked the *Gospel Guardian*.

For three and a half years the *Preceptor* was edited in Florida. During its early months the paper featured regular columns written by each of the original editors. Clinton Hamilton wrote a long series of articles on the history and doctrine of

Roman Catholicism under the title "Christianity and Catholicism"; Bill Humble wrote regularly under the heading "Restoration and Reaction." Hailey's column, entitled "Interpretation and Application," was generally filled with exegesis of biblical text, but he also wrote on traditional moral themes. The magazine offered a varied fare, including a regular column for parents and teachers written by Mrs. Oscar Foy, a widely respected teacher, and exchanges on such controversial topics as the marital qualifications of elders.

In 1955 the *Preceptor* was sold to a group of Texas Christians. Luther G. Roberts edited the paper briefly before being succeeded by Stanley J. Lovett, who continued to edit it for many years. Cope explained that the FCC editors had "become increasingly encumbered with other duties" that precluded their continued publication of the magazine.[69] However, it had also become clear that the paper might be a political liability to FCC. Clinton Hamilton and Bill Humble continued for a time to contribute regularly to the *Preceptor,* and some of the other original editors wrote for the magazine sporadically, but after leaving Florida it soon began to take on a different personality. In later years, most of the original editors of the *Preceptor* judged it to have been a unique and high-quality endeavor. Bill Humble considered it a "great paper,"[70] and Hailey believed that it was the "best paper this side of the restoration papers."[71]

The launching of the *Preceptor* thrust Florida Christian College and its Bible faculty headlong into the boiling institutional controversy in the churches of Christ. In his final editorial Cope declared that the editors had "sought to steer a middle-of-the-road course and avoid extremes." He insisted that the paper had "espoused no 'hobby'" and had "aligned itself with no 'brotherhood movement.'"[72] It was true that Cope had continued to call for "full and free discussion of the issues troubling Israel," and thus imagined that he had not taken sides in the fight, but the *Preceptor* never occupied the middle of the road.[73] By the end of 1951, Hamilton, Hardeman, Humble, Clevenger, and Cope were on the noninstitutional bandwagon. Among the original editors, only Hailey was not wholeheartedly committed to the cause.

The *Preceptor* bristled with articles challenging sponsoring churches and church support for institutions. Jim Cope wrote the most detailed articles, but the younger men were the fire-eaters. Pat Hardeman chastised the prevalence of "Dale Carnegie preaching" and urged the need for "more 'disputing' (Acts 19:8), contending, debating, preaching and living, of the kind that defeated Digressive tendencies a few years back."[74] Bill Humble warned that many wished to transform the church into a "complacent modernistic social club" and urged his brethren to "repudiate all doctrinal softness in the church and purge it!"[75]

The launching of the *Preceptor* had raised the institutional controversy to a new level. By 1951 the *Gospel Guardian*'s reputation for negativism and personal recrimination had seriously damaged its influence. The *Preceptor* scrupulously avoided personal attacks and offered a much broader array of articles, while at the same time discussing institutional issues in detail. In his yearly reviews, Cope repeatedly noted that the magazine "endeavored to deal with *principles,* not with *personalities,*" and to be "dignified" but not "stilted."[76] The paper's respected board of editors and its nonconfrontational tactics, Jim Cope believed, "made brethren conscious that they were violating their principles."[77]

In the long run, the *Preceptor* changed the institutional debate in a more important way. The *Gospel Guardian*'s assault on institutionalism had been very much in the Foy E. Wallace, Jr., mold—not only was it highly personal and abrasive, but it was also extremely technical and biblical. The editors of the *Preceptor* were not only less personal, but also they offered a much broader-based critique of the institutional developments in the church, appealing to the separatist consciousness in restoration thinking. For instance, in 1952 Jim Cope argued that the raging doctrinal debate reflected changed attitudes caused by teachers in church-related schools who had been trained by "modernistic teachers."[78] Eugene Clevenger expressed the separationist theme most clearly. In an article entitled "We Are a Different People," Clevenger theorized that "one of the greatest factors within the church today that is hindering the cause of Christ is a morbid fear . . . of being different." Things were out of order in the churches, Clevenger warned, because of the loss of "this consciousness of being different."[79]

Homer Hailey also captured the general sense of anxiety felt by conservatives in churches of Christ in the early 1950s. Still unpersuaded about some of the specific doctrinal questions involved in the institutional debate, Hailey wrote repeatedly in the *Preceptor* about the diverging attitudes that were separating brethren. In his strongest direct statement on the institutional issue, Hailey noted that it appeared to him "that the question of institutionalism is one of shifting responsibilities from the shoulders where God has put them to 'new carts' of man's own devising."[80] Nonetheless, Hailey's critiques remained vague. In his first editorial in the *Preceptor*, Hailey warned that "it is possible for a Christian to lose sight of the truly great things as God views them, and to substitute the things of no moment with God which appear great to him." Concerned about the "wave of enthusiasm in the church today to do all things in a 'big' way," Hailey warned that the "vital question is that of *motive* in striving for the small or great."[81] Hailey's writings in the early 1950s, like those of his fellow editors of the *Preceptor*, tried to move the institutional debate into the area of attitudes and motives.

The Painful Personal Choice to Separate

When Homer Hailey arrived at Florida Christian College in the fall of 1951 he was undecided about some of the issues being debated in the churches; however, much in his past pointed him toward noninstitutionalism. Most of the preachers whom Hailey had admired while a young preacher—Shepherd, Nichol, Arceneaux—were conservative by nature, though they played little role in the institutional controversy. Hailey drove Early Arceneaux to the airport after he had spoken at the FCC Lectures in 1952. Hailey recalled that the older preacher told him that he had "helped fight for years, but I am going to leave this to you younger men."[82] Hailey never understood the apparent switch of Foy E. Wallace, Jr., whom he greatly admired, but he attributed it to "prejudice against certain men that had angered or offended him."[83]

Looking back over Hailey's life, conservatism was a constant in his character. His move from the Central Church in Los Angeles to Honolulu had been triggered by fears of a growing "hookup between Central Church and Pepperdine College."[84] His departure from Abilene Christian College was an instinctive reaction against that school's reach for respectability. In his book *Attitudes and Consequences,* Hailey outlined a general scheme of digression in the nineteenth century that he would later identify with the churches of Christ division in the fifties and sixties. In a 1949 article in the *Gospel Guardian,* Hailey outlined his concerns about the general drift in the churches: "Shall the church of today follow the pattern [of digression], or shall it weather the present storm? . . . With rumblings of modernism coming out of the west; with the threat of discord and apathy, of softness and worldliness, of growing indifference to doctrine and the New Testament pattern arising in other sections, what shall be the result?"[85] Hailey's writings in the *Preceptor* highlighted the same kinds of general concerns.

Still, Hailey was slow to study the issues. He found it particularly difficult to abandon church-supported orphan homes. His article commending the Maude Carpenter Children's Home in Wichita was printed widely in the papers read by members of the churches of Christ in 1949 and was reprinted by Yater Tant in the *Gospel Guardian.*[86] Well into the 1950s, Hailey continued to preach in churches that supported institutions, and he shared many of the attitudes of his mainstream brethren. He was incensed by the treatment of American missionaries in Italy, and he wrote an editorial in the *Preceptor* asking readers to support them.[87] Like many other preachers who later changed their minds, in the early 1950s Hailey thought that the "Herald of Truth" was "a great thing." He later concluded, as did many others, that he had been "brain washed" to believe that any work under the oversight of a local eldership was scriptural.[88]

While preaching in Honolulu, Hailey wrote an article entitled "Keepers of Orthodoxy" that would later be an embarrassment to him. His motive, he later surmised, was the feeling experienced by most preachers in mission fields who come to think that "others are not properly concerned with world evangelism and that they are fussing over minor things."[89] In the article, Hailey bemoaned the paltry support given to missionaries and regretted that the "church of Christ has provided no hospitals." He complained, "But though the church may not do anything like support a man while he gives his life to work among American Indians; it may not send a shipload of food, clothing, and implements to the destitute and babies, nor send gospel teachers and preachers into suffering lands; it may build no hospitals, care for no foreign lands—it does have its 'keepers of orthodoxy.'" Struggling to build a church in Hawaii, he was offended by the bickering at home.[90] He was grieved by the constant displays of "personal feuds, characterized by vituperation, satire, sarcasm, and personal animosities" that filled the American papers.[91]

While Hailey's views on institutionalism were still "fuzzy" in the early fifties,[92] he was embarrassed when B. C. Goodpasture republished his "Keepers of Orthodoxy" article in the *Gospel Advocate* in June 1952. He sheepishly wrote an explanation entitled "Clubs Unwittingly Loosed": "Now and then a man writes or says something that unwittingly puts him in the wrong group, or which unwittingly puts into the hands of enemies of the truth a club with which to browbeat those who are standing for the truth. Such seems to have been the unfortunate consequences of an article entitled 'Keepers of Orthodoxy.'" He had not intended to "give comfort or encouragement to a rising element of digression within our ranks"; he only wanted to condemn the "pharisaical spirit that says and does not."[93] Even so, Hailey did not in 1952 repudiate any of the specific remarks included in the article.

Hailey's move to Florida Christian College no doubt influenced his subsequent actions. He was surrounded by young men who were running toward the battle. He and Clinton Hamilton spent many hours in their offices and walking on the golf course in the evenings, arguing and rearguing the question of church support for orphan homes. Hailey demurred, though he saw "seeds of digression" in many places, and he never contested the noninstitutional writings of his committed young friends.

The routine of teaching at FCC also delayed Hailey's decision. His daily schedule was hectic. Teaching a heavy load, preaching regularly in Tampa and in meetings during the summers, and caring for his children and a wife in declining health, Hailey simply had no time to study the issues in depth. He read a few of the vast number of articles being published on the subject, but he never attended a debate. Not until his former Abilene colleague J. D. Thomas wrote *We Be Brethren* did Hailey study the question. While in a meeting in Indiana, living in the home of an elder in the church who was a rural mail carrier, Hailey read Thomas's book and discussed it with his host. The book "opened my eyes," Hailey later recalled, convincing him that church support for orphan homes was a part of the whole nexus of institutional issues. More and more, he became convinced that "many of the brethren who went with the liberal camp did not have real convictions."[94]

Hailey's slowness did not sit well with some of the more militant preachers in the noninstitutional camp. Some refused to attend his meetings, and he was privately criticized.[95] At the same time, Hailey's stance was of incalculable importance to the noninstitutional movement. Stung by Foy E. Wallace, Jr.'s charge that the noninstitutional movement was led by a few "immature, novice, smart-alecks," Cecil Willis responded, "Quite frankly, we think men like Homer Hailey, Roy Cogdill, Hugh Clark, Frank Puckett, and James Adams . . . can compare favorably even with Wallace."[96] "Some men . . . felt that I was a little soft," Hailey recalled many years later, "but I did it my way."[97] Hailey's way was to delay until circumstances forced him to study and make up his mind. Then he took a stand. It was not so much that he was averse to a fight: "if you back me up to the wall, I'll come out fighting," he later insisted.[98] His deliberateness was caused by a stubborn independence; in his own time he would act on the "basis of what is right."[99] Colly Caldwell, who became president of Florida College in 1991, recalled Hailey's open-mindedness when he was in his classroom: "He would want to be very careful on anything. . . . He was always willing to keep an open mind on anything we studied. . . . He didn't mind saying he had changed on something. . . . He resented preachers who would get up in debate and say they had never changed. He admitted that he had changed on lots of things, important things."[100]

No one did more to push Hailey out of the middle of the road on the institutional question than B. C. Goodpasture. The republication of Hailey's "Keepers of Orthodoxy" article in 1952 was an effort to show that Hailey was drifting away from his former views and an unsubtle warning to Hailey that he could be injured by the *Gospel Advocate*. Goodpasture maintained a cordial relationship with Hailey through the mid-1950s; in 1954 Hailey contributed an innocuous article to the *Gospel Advocate* on the subject of building a good congregational library.[101]

In 1958, as lines hardened and as the parade of preachers writing confessions renouncing "antism" reached a torrent in the *Gospel Advocate*, Goodpasture targeted Hailey as a man with conservative convictions who still had a wide influence in the churches of Christ. He sought to diminish that influence. Thus, in 1958, he once again reprinted the "Keepers of Orthodoxy" article, this time on the front page of the *Gospel Advocate,* with the notation that it was "reprinted by request."[102] In a response that had every appearance of being orchestrated, the front page and the editorial page of the *Gospel Advocate* carried a series of comments on the article written by influential preachers. Writing on the editorial page, Gus Nichols announced that he was "made glad" when he saw the article by Hailey, but feigned surprise and disappointment upon discovering that the article was a reprint. Nichols held out an olive branch to Hailey: "I love Brother Hailey because he is a lovable man and has not lost the milk of human kindness from his soul. While he might not now endorse every word of his article and could see some tendencies needing to be curbed, even as the rest of us, still the general tenor of his article rings true to the tune of brotherly love, of which we hear and see so little in modern times."[103] A few weeks later, Goodpasture placed on the front page of the *Advocate* an article by James F. Kurfees, a physician, commending Hailey's ideas and urging that "we cannot allow bitterness, self-appointed saviors of the flock, and visionless, ignorant men to stop the forward progress of the Lord's church."[104]

This time, Hailey sent a more vigorous repudiation of the article, which Goodpasture printed under the title "Hailey Corrects Hailey." In this new article, he wrote, "Upon reading the article, I cannot imagine why I wrote some of the things in it, or why I should have allowed it to have been published." Obviously embarrassed, Hailey protested: "Some of the things contained in the article, together with the general tone and insinuations of it, I repudiate, as being out of harmony with my usual thinking." He specifically withdrew his suggestion that it was permissible for "the church to build and maintain hospitals" and warned that his assumption that the New Testament made no distinction between individual and church action was based on "loose thinking."[105] Goodpasture had no intention of letting Hailey off the hook easily. He published

Hailey's reply, noting that it was "written in good spirit," but he insisted that Hailey's new position was filled with inconsistencies.[106] Goodpasture's vendetta against Hailey, and the few other preachers who held conservative views but still preached widely throughout mainstream churches of Christ, increased after the exchange. Actually, Hailey had already begun to experience a crescendo of canceled meetings. In the mid-1950s, many Texas churches, influenced by the leaders of Abilene Christian College, began canceling the meetings of preachers accused of "antism," and Hailey did not escape this scrutiny.

However, it was Goodpasture who particularly irked Hailey. Hailey was angered by the strategy of repeatedly running an article that no longer expressed his views; shortly after the 1958 exchange, Goodpasture sealed Hailey's animosity by publishing a description, without mentioning Hailey's name, of an embarrassing incident that occurred in Lawrenceburg, Tennessee. While water-skiing with the local preacher, Hailey lost his false teeth. Goodpasture's description was lighthearted, but Hailey considered it an "insinuating insult."[107]

Hailey was convinced that Goodpasture aimed to "destroy my influence" and that he did it in an "underhanded way." Hailey later recalled, "He had control of a lot of people," and he used that power ruthlessly. If he had not had moral scruples, Hailey recalled, "I would have bought me a ticket and flown up to Nashville and beat the face off of him, gone to jail, paid my fine, and come home." He compromised by imagining Goodpasture's face on his punching bag when he did his daily workouts. "I would beat it to a pulp," he recalled. It took a while, but Hailey "prayed that God would remove the bitterness" and "God changed me."[108] Still, years later, Goodpasture's name brought a flash of irritation to Hailey's countenance.

Long after others had abandoned hope for unity in the churches of Christ, Hailey had assumed that he could continue to have fellowship with those who disagreed with him about institutionalism. By the end of the fifties, he knew he was wrong. He repeatedly encountered the attitude of "line up or be castigated." In 1960, he wrote in the *Gospel Guardian*, "One need not necessarily become militant in his opposition to these movements, it is sufficient merely to question their right to operate in order to bring the wrath of the mighty upon him."[109] Hailey discovered slowly that the middle of the road had vanished.

Even in the early 1960s, Hailey, like a few other individuals, had a reputation so broad, and a spirit so free from personal rancor, that he maintained the respect of people on both sides of the dividing church. Between 1959 and 1964 Batsell Barrett Baxter and M. Norvel Young collected information for three editions of a volume called *Preachers of Today*, coming about as close as possible to providing a clerical listing for churches of Christ. The editors sent out five thousand requests for information for the 1952 edition and received 1,360 replies. Even though debate on institutional issues was ravaging the churches in the 1950s, the book listed most of the leading "antis" in both 1952 and 1959, including Yater Tant, James R. Cope, Pat Hardeman, and Clinton Hamilton.[110] However, by 1964 almost all noninstitutional preachers had disappeared from the listing; most refused to supply the requested information. The only significant noninstitutional preachers whose names were listed were Benjamin Lee Fudge and Doyle Banta from Limestone County, Alabama, an area where the lines of fellowship remained blurred for many years; Harris Dark, a maverick member of the David Lipscomb College faculty; and Homer Hailey.[111]

Hailey recognized that in the institutional division he was never "as radical as some fellows."[112] He believed that extremists had allowed the supporters of institutions to select the battleground, and they "made us look like a bunch of nincompoop fools."[113] His friend Harry Pickup, Sr., guessed that Hailey moved slowly because he believed that many good people would finally see a fatal drift toward liberalism and cut loose from the institutional approach.[114] In the end, the thing that Hailey most regretted was that the division separated him from his old friends. He continued to love those "who went the other way," and, through the years, they could have his friendship "if they wanted it," but by 1960 insurmountable barriers were in place that made communication difficult.

At a personal level, division in the churches of Christ has to do mostly with one's interaction with local churches. For most people, that involves little more than selecting a congregation to attend. For nationally prominent preachers and widely traveled evangelists like Homer Hailey, division was defined when one could no longer preach in certain congregations or appear on certain lecture programs. Long before Goodpasture began paying particular attention to him, Hailey had begun to have meetings canceled in Texas and Oklahoma because of the influence of Abilene Christian College. Over and over in the late 1950s, he was contacted by the elders of local churches asking him for an assurance that he would not preach his views opposing institutions. He never did preach on the subject during those years without a specific invitation to do so, but he systematically refused to give such assurances.

The 1950s were tense and heavyhearted years, quite unlike the dynamic years of preaching in meetings in decades past. Hailey returned to old haunts and felt that the air was filled with tension; old friends refused to visit his meetings, even when he returned to Abilene. It was incomprehensible to Hailey. Twenty-seven churches that had invited him to hold meetings told him not to come. He did not want a division, and he did not cause it, but he was a part of it. After 1960, Homer Hailey, like everyone else in churches of Christ, was forced to decide where he would live his life.

Teaching, Preaching, and Writing

For all of the sound and fury in the religious periodicals of the 1950s and 1960s, Homer Hailey's life, like the lives of other preachers and members of churches of Christ, went on in familiar ways. The trauma of division touched Hailey, and occasionally got his attention, but he was never preoccupied with the controversy. His years in Temple Terrace were a blur of teaching, preaching, and writing. He worked tirelessly, almost recklessly, and he left behind a legacy that still hovers over the small campus of Florida College.

Hailey's duties as vice-president of Florida Christian College were perfunctory. He did serve as a member of a number of administrative committees at the college and he advised Jim Cope on various questions, but his main contribution was to bring credibility to the Bible Department and a conservative aura to the campus. On moral questions he brought impeccable credentials to his new job. The college encouraged social activities that brought "young men and women together in a wholesome spirit," Hailey wrote in the *Preceptor,* but it strictly prohibited "petting, fondling, holding hands and similar liberties."[115] Hailey was a conservative influence on the campus, opposing the formation of social clubs and the introduction of intercollegiate athletics. All such activities, Hailey believed, were "inconsistent with the kind of thing I wanted developed."[116]

For twenty-one years, Hailey served as a member of the dreaded Discipline Committee. Through the years, scores of young people paraded before the committee—sometimes for infractions seriously challenging the moral commitment of the school, but more often for relatively minor departures from the rigid rules in place in the 1950s. "As a whole they were the finest kids on earth," Hailey recalled, but a few were going to "kick out of the traces." The committee taught him a "good deal about human nature," including the fact that contrition besets offenders only after all alibis are exhausted. "Then he was sorry," Hailey said of the wrongdoer, "but he was sorry he got caught."

For all of his moral conservatism, Hailey was the soft touch on the Discipline Committee, along with his close friend

Harry Pickup, Sr. Some of the younger faculty members would send students home "at the drop of a hat," and Hailey judged that Clinton Hamilton was a better interrogator than Perry Mason. However, he and Pickup were older and both had lived full lives before making their decisions to be preachers. It was "hard to be strict" when you had done the same things in your youth, observed Pickup.[117] Hailey could accept moral weakness more easily than disrespect for authority. He understood, and accepted, a lapse into fornication better than someone setting off firecrackers in the dormitory. "We tried to be fair," he recalled in later years. "We didn't want the school destroyed."[118]

Hailey's focus at Florida College was on training young preachers, as it had been at ACC. He became the sponsor for the Sower's Club, attending the meetings of the aspiring preachers and helping them with their speeches. He taught a course on missions for many years but was disappointed that the class never got much response. Hailey believed that the students were not as idealistic as those he had taught at ACC immediately after the war.[119] While that was perhaps true, circumstances had also changed. Once Florida College became clearly identified with the noninstitutional position, opportunities for preaching overseas were virtually nonexistent because of a lack of funding. The mentality of the 1950s in noninstitutional churches was one of survival. All across the country, noninstitutional people were forced to build new congregations made up of people estranged from other churches.

Homer Hailey left an incalculable legacy in the students he taught at Florida College. Nearly every influential preacher in noninstitutional churches of Christ passed through his classes, as did nearly every current member of the Florida College Bible Department. Hailey insisted that the curriculum of the Bible Department be centered on a study of the biblical text; students who remained in the program for four years studied the entire Bible. "Anything the others didn't want to teach," Hailey recalled, "I taught." He taught a heavy load of classes, ranging from fifteen to twenty-one hours each week, and, at one time or another, he taught nearly every course in the college curriculum.[120]

Every day was a blur of activity—class preparation, teaching, committee meetings, and counseling students. Hailey rose early to prepare for his morning classes and studied late into the evening. "I was always sleepy," he later recalled, though the registrar always provided Hailey a schedule break to allow time for an after-lunch nap. There was little time for frivolity or small talk. Behind his office desk was a sign instructing all visitors to "Come to the Point." Like most teachers, Hailey learned that grading papers was the "hardest thing to find time to do." In later years, he surmised that his tardy grading provided the most frequent criticism from his students, but many of his students thought it was "more of a problem for him than for us."[121]

Florida Christian College changed its name in 1963 to Florida College, partly in response to a complaint that no secular institution should be called "Christian." The student body also changed in the 1960s, for the worse, Hailey thought. In the 1950s the college attracted many older preacher students and became something of a training ground for a cadre of noninstitutional leaders. In the long run, however, the marking of the school as an "anti" institution cut it off from a large number of churches of Christ, and it proved to be difficult to gain loyal supporters among people who held radical noninstitutional views. For a time in the 1960s, the college actively recruited students from outside the churches of Christ; that decision, in Hailey's opinion, nearly "ruined the school."[122] By the 1970s the student body was once again overwhelmingly recruited from the conservative churches of Christ, but it was a younger and more traditional group of students.

The faculty also changed in the 1960s. By the end of the 1960s the young "brain trust" of the early fifties had broken up. Eugene Clevenger and Bill Humble both completed graduate degrees in religion and ultimately joined the faculty of Abilene Christian University. Humble's departure was good spirited; he had recanted none of his anti-institutional views when he decided to accept a job preaching in Kansas City. Burdened by a huge teaching load, and struggling to survive on an annual salary of twenty-seven hundred dollars, Humble simply burned out. In the late 1950s he preached in Louisville, where he befriended two other local preachers, Harold Hazelip and Wesley Jones, and witnessed some of the bitterest congregational brawls in the institutional division. He was repulsed by the "divisive spirit" displayed by some of the conservatives in the Louisville divisions.[123] After completing a degree at Iowa University, Humble began a distinguished career as a teacher and administrator at ACC. He and Hailey remained friends; during a visit in the early sixties, they noted that the two of them had migrated past one another going in opposite directions. As might be expected, Humble was initially received with some reservations by many of his Abilene colleagues because "he had never made a statement withdrawing himself" from his early noninstitutional views.[124]

The departure of Pat Hardeman from Florida College was much stormier. The flashy, fiery young Hardeman had been a rising star on the Florida College campus from 1949 through 1952, when he decided to take a leave of absence to complete a doctoral degree in philosophy at the University of Illinois. During those years, he later recalled, "I talked so much, either in preaching, debating, or overload teaching tasks, that I had little time for more than routine studies."[125] Hardeman returned to the school in 1955 with a doctorate in hand and a part-time appointment at the University of Tampa. He was a changed man, less conservative in theology, and often abrasive and condescending in his dealings with Jim Cope and Clinton Hamilton.[126] After repeated clashes with the college administration over such issues as social drinking, swimming, and dancing, Hardeman left Florida College to teach at Tampa University.[127]

In Homer Hailey's mind, the college never regained the

mystique of the "great years" of the early 1950s. He admired many of his colleagues in later years, but the school never again had "the feel" that existed in those early embattled years when the college was girding to defend the truth. Hailey felt a sense of urgency in those early days, as well as a unity of purpose, that was difficult to sustain through the years. Perhaps, he thought, it was he who had changed. At any rate, as he neared retirement age, it seemed to him that "the whole world is tired."[128]

Of course, many of Hailey's old friends remained. He and Clinton Hamilton were neighbors, companions, and kindred spirits in the study of the Bible. When Hamilton left the college in 1968 to become dean of Broward Community College in South Florida, Hailey lost his closest intellectual comrade at the college. Harry Pickup, Sr., remained an adoring friend; whatever the subject, in his mind, "Homer was 99% of the time right about it."[129] In addition, Hailey and Bob Owen continued to enjoy a father-son relationship. Hailey's wife always knew that he had been talking with Owen when he came home with a new joke to tell her.

He also made new friends. Franklin Puckett and Hailey were loyal friends during the few years that Puckett was at the school. Louis W. Garrett, who came to the school in 1950 and served as dean from 1968 to 1975, had a "good mind," and he and Hailey frequently discussed the Bible together.[130] Garrett's wife, Margie, was one of Hailey's foremost supporters and the lifelong editor of his convoluted prose. During his last years of teaching at Florida College, many of his own students returned to become faculty members—Colly Caldwell, Melvin Curry, and Phil Roberts. Hailey befriended them, encouraged them, and became a model for them.[131]

During his years in Tampa, Hailey preached at several different congregations: Central, Temple Terrace, Cork, Clearwater, and Fortieth Street. Saturdays were reserved for sermon preparation, a duty Hailey never took lightly, and Wednesday evenings and Sundays were given to preaching, visiting, and counseling. Like many of the other professors at Florida College, Hailey was forced to preach to supplement his meager salary, but he would hardly have been idle on Sundays under any circumstances.[132]

As soon as the school term ended in the spring, Hailey set out on a round of gospel meetings, as he had for more than two decades. The summer meetings were another necessary financial crutch for the Hailey family. Frequently, Hailey had to borrow money to get to his first meeting, but by the end of the summer he had built up a nest egg to tide the family over through the coming year. Partly because he needed to save money, and partly because Florida was so far away from the West and Northwest where he held many of his meetings, Hailey was often away from home for weeks at a time; one summer he did not return home for four months. Often, he preached every evening for weeks on end. Homer felt "obligated" to preach, and he usually scheduled meetings four years in advance. The thought of taking a vacation never occurred to him, nor to most of the members of his family.[133]

The institutional controversy had an impact on Hailey's meeting schedule, but, despite cancellations, he never missed a full summer schedule. Providentially, he believed, each cancellation was followed by a request for a meeting from a newly formed noninstitutional congregation. As he had done for many years, he continued to schedule meetings as he received requests, never showing a "preference" based on the size or prestige of a congregation.[134]

The nature of Hailey's meetings changed during these years, as the character of meetings changed throughout churches of Christ. He reported his activities to both the *Gospel Advocate* and the *Preceptor* during the early 1950s when he continued to preach in many old familiar places and spent enjoyable times with men from whom he would soon be separated: Basil Doran, Cecil Wright, and Frank Shepherd.[135] After the institutional division, most of Hailey's meetings were in smaller congregations that were building anew after church splits, and more often than not his sermons were directed toward building up a local church. He made new friends and had many warm reunions with old friends who had taken the noninstitutional side. Hailey always enjoyed staying in the homes of members during his meetings, as opposed to hotels, relishing the hospitality and conviviality.[136]

After 1952, Hailey was never again invited to appear on a college lectureship except at Florida College. At the Florida College Lectures he became a fixture, the premier exhibit to advertise the Bible faculty to visitors. Sometimes he spoke on such eminently practical themes as "What Is a Christian," but more often he offered classes on the teachings of the Old Testament prophets, frequently with a modern twist, such as "Ancient Prophets and Modern Trends," or on the Book of Revelation.

Hailey wrote sporadically for periodicals during his years at Florida College. He was most active during the years that he helped to edit the *Preceptor,* but he also wrote occasionally for the *Gospel Guardian.* In the 1960s, when Yater Tant and the *Guardian* became less singularly focused on the institutional fight, Hailey wrote frequently for his old friend on such noncontroversial topics as "Thou Shalt Not Steal" and "God's Answer to Man's Need."[137] He also contributed occasional articles to *Truth Magazine* and other papers that were read by members of noninstitutional churches of Christ.

More significant in the long run was the publication of Hailey's third book in 1972, *Commentary on the Minor Prophets.* Hailey had taught a course on the minor prophets for many years and he had developed a syllabus that was nearly one hundred pages long. Through the years Hailey became acquainted with Herman Baker, one of the owners of Baker Book House, a widely known publisher of religious books. Because Florida College used a variety of the publisher's books as texts, Baker visited the campus from time to time and struck up a friendship with Hailey. The two went to lunch together when Baker was in town, and they occasionally corresponded. Hailey found Baker to be a "very conservative" man with a "deep faith" and the two became "good friends."[138] Homer told Baker about his work and the publisher encouraged him to write a book.

During the 1970 to 1971 academic year, Hailey was given a reduced teaching load to provide him with time to write. He borrowed an office at the Temple Terrace church where he could sequester himself to work. He wrote on a rigorous schedule, noting in the book's preface that he wanted to be certain that he would finish the work "before advancing age makes such a work impossible." He had no way of knowing that more than two decades later he would still be studying and writing. Hailey's book on the minor prophets established a pattern of work that he repeated in most of his later writing. He composed in longhand, then typed a manuscript that he sent to his friends Clinton Hamilton and Melvin Curry for corrections. Hailey's prose was rambling, conversational, and disjointed, and he depended heavily on Margie H. Garrett, his longtime friend who worked in the Development Office at Florida College, to "correct the sentence structure" and make his thoughts clear.[139]

Hailey's aim in writing about the minor prophets was to strike a "happy medium" between the extremely shallow commentaries on the subject and the scholarly and ponderous commentary of Carl Keil and Franz Delitzsch. After an introductory section entitled "General Observations," Hailey outlined each of the books and then provided verse-by-verse comments. Hailey emphasized that it was important to "understand the political, moral, social, and religious conditions at the time in which the prophet lived and preached," the relation of the Jewish nation to the "heathen nations" around them, and, particularly, "the prophet's teaching of a future kingdom and king to be fulfilled in one who was to come." Hailey's anti-premillennial ideas surfaced repeatedly in the book; for instance, he noted that the prophet Micah "did not envision a time when God would dominate and control the world by force, or an age when all men of all political kingdoms would live at peace on this earth. Only in God's spiritual kingdom established by Christ would this blessed experience be realized."[140] While the book provided a solid introduction to the minor prophets, Hailey made no pretense of offering new interpretative insights; it was rather a common-sense summary of the available scholarship.

Hailey's book on the minor prophets was a critical and marketing success. It was the "most popular and widely used" of any book he ever wrote. *Christianity Today* magazine chose Hailey's book as one of the twenty-five most significant religious books published in 1972. Twenty-five years later the book was still being sold, having been reprinted ten times by Baker Book House.

In 1973, just before retiring from Florida College, Hailey finished another book, *That You May Believe,* that was also published by Baker Book House. Based on the Gospel of John, the book "set forth the claims of Jesus and the evidence he gave to sustain it."[141] *That You May Believe* was also an expansion of class notes that Hailey had accumulated through the years. Although well received, the book was not reprinted by Baker and, in 1982, Hailey secured the rights to republish the work and a new edition was released by Nevada Publications, a printing business operated by one of Hailey's longtime friends, Stanley W. Paher.

Losing Lois

In many ways, the public life of Homer Hailey was Homer Hailey. But he was also a social person. He remained dedicated to health, carefully monitoring his diet and working out regularly with barbells in his backyard. A parade of friends joined him to lift weights and enjoy his company, and at one time he taught a class in weight lifting for young women.[142] At the same time, he was a loyal husband and father.

By the time the Hailey family moved to Florida in 1952, Lois

Hailey was a fitness enthusiast all his life. While Hailey was working out in a gym in Austin, Texas, the owner of the gym requested his picture, which was subsequently printed in *Strength* magazine in July 1957. It had the following caption: "Rev. Homer Hailey, is a Church of Christ minister, Vice-President of Florida Christian College, who believes in vigorous as well as victorious living. He was a victim of cancer, and began weight training after 40. Over six feet tall, he then weighed 120 lbs. He gained over 45 lbs. of solid muscle, and his agility and strength belies his 53 years. While in Texas he trained at Leo Murdock's Austin Health Club."

was a very sick woman. Her "terrible nervous spells" made her a virtual recluse in the Hailey home. She attended church services and occasionally attended a social function at the college, but mostly she stayed at home and cared for the children. Lois struggled valiantly to care for the five Hailey children, and her children adored her. Homer was busy; to some of his closest friends it appeared that he "had to neglect his family because it was demanded of him."[143] With regard to Lois, some felt that Homer did not "appreciate her sickness."[144] In later years, Hailey agreed that he had been "unobserving" in his relationship with Lois and that, like most busy men, "I could have used a lot of help."[145]

Harry Pickup, Sr., and his wife probably came to know Lois better than any of the other family friends in Florida. They dropped in to visit with her regularly, especially when Homer was away from home in meetings, and they usually found her in bed. "She was a very humble person," recalled Pickup. Struggling with her illness, Lois "tried to be as little trouble as possible, so that Homer could do the things demanded of him." Only after her death would the extent of her unselfish struggle become clear.[146]

In the spring of 1954, Lois's health deteriorated rapidly and she began to lapse into periods of unconsciousness. She continued to consult physicians, as she had through the years, and one doctor speculated that she was epileptic. While Homer was away in a meeting in Valdosta, Georgia, she suffered a serious seizure and friends hospitalized her. Because of her symptoms, she was placed in the psychiatric ward; when he returned home, Hailey had to go through a mountain of red tape to get her released. Thoroughly shaken by the experience, Lois made Homer promise to never put her in the hospital again.

At the end of April, while Homer was again away in a meeting, the young woman who helped in the Hailey home found Lois unconscious. The college nurse and the Pickups telephoned Homer. He requested that they not hospitalize her, but when he returned home he saw no other alternative and called an ambulance. Lois was dead when she arrived at the hospital. The funeral services for Lois were held in the Highland Church in Abilene, and Paul Southern delivered the funeral sermon.[147] G. K. Wallace, who, along with Southern, had been a classmate of Homer and Lois at ACC, wrote a eulogy that was published in several papers. Her suffering and death were a "puzzle," Wallace wrote: "We will never know why that good Christian people have to suffer so long and so seriously."[148]

An autopsy was performed on Lois and it was determined that she "died because of the presence of an extremely rare type of brain tumor." The report concluded that the "faulty development" had occurred "even before the birth of the individual" and that the slow-growing tumor was placed in the brain in a location "such as to have made its surgical removal impossible." "In retrospect," the report concluded, "there can be no doubt that her sudden losses of consciousness were all due" to the tumor.[149]

The autopsy report explained much about the long and lingering illness of Lois. Homer was saddened, and he was lonely, but he was relieved to gain an understanding of the difficulties borne by his wife. Only in hindsight could anyone, especially Homer, have known how courageous a life Lois had lived. Eighteen years after her death, the dedication in Hailey's book on the minor prophets carried an inscription expressing thoughts that he no doubt would have liked to have told her before she died: "To Lois, the mother of my children, whose faithful and sacrificing care for the home made possible my hours of study, teaching, and preaching through the early years of life."[150]

Homer held his round of meetings in the summer of 1954, for the first time understanding the full extent of service that Lois had rendered in keeping the family together. He considered asking his mother, Mamie, to come to live with the family, and she did visit. However, as Liz Pickup recalled, she stayed only twenty-four hours with the children before boarding the bus back to Texas.[151] Roma was married in the late spring, and Mary Lois held the family together for a year, but she also married a year after the death of her mother. Hailey employed students from the college to live in and care for the two boys and Carol Ann, but he ended up doing a good deal of the cooking himself.[152]

Love at First Sight

The late spring of 1955 began for the Hailey family in a familiar routine. After arranging for someone to care for the children, Hailey embarked on his cycle of summer meetings, beginning with a trip to Honolulu on which he was accompanied by his mother. In July, while preaching in West Texas, Hailey received a call from his friend Basil Overton, telling him that he needed to reschedule the dates for an August meeting in Paducah, Kentucky. Suddenly, Hailey was confronted with an open period of two weeks in early August, time that he could not afford to waste. Several people had told him to let them know if he had an opening during the summer, and, "after thinking it over for a few minutes, and maybe praying some about it," he decided to call Carl Spain who was preaching at the Graham Street Church in Abilene. The church quickly extended Hailey an invitation to hold a ten-day meeting beginning on August 1.[153]

The Graham Street meeting began on Monday; the building was full each evening with old friends, and Hailey enjoyed staying in the home of Lois's mother, Mrs. Manly. The following Sunday morning, August 7, Mildred Spain introduced Hailey to a strikingly beautiful woman, Widna Kirby, who attended for the first time on that day. "Preachers are also human," Hailey later noted as he reported saying to himself, "Wow, what an attractive woman." He noted that she was not accompanied by a husband, but he assumed that the two of them had been separated in leaving the services. That evening, as Widna was leaving the service, Hailey's instincts led him to ask, "Is your husband here tonight?" Widna explained that she was a widow who had moved to Abilene so that her two sons could attend ACC.

Hailey had not given a great deal of thought to getting remarried in the fifteen months since the death of Lois. On his way to the Abilene meeting he spent an evening with his cousin Gladys; he told her that getting married "was the thing farthest from my mind." In response to her questions, Hailey kidded, "When I find a woman the right age, and of course that means a lot younger than I am . . . pretty, the right size, who is a Christian who would be interested in my work and willing to keep my children and look after them when I am away, who owns a big ranch in West Texas all cluttered up with oil wells, then I'll really get interested."[154]

One week later he was as infatuated as a teenager. After his conversation with Widna on Sunday evening, Homer penned a note to her: "May I take the liberty of writing you a note tonight? This morning when I met you I thought, since you were a member of the Graham Street Church and hadn't been to the meeting till today, that you must be one of those Sunday morning Christians. Further, the thought flashed through my mind that you were the wife of an oil man who had moved to Abilene since last I was here. Imagine my surprise tonight to learn that you had been out of town with an injured son, and that you are a widow. May I say that I have been charmed by your grace, and may I be so bold as to say, your beauty as well. . . . I trust that, although there are only three more nights of the meeting, that we may become better acquainted during those three days. . . . I am grateful to our mutual friend, Mildred, for introducing us. Sincerely yours, Homer Hailey."[155] After that, things happened fast.

On Monday evening Homer talked with Widna at great length after services; after that, he and his old friend Olan Hicks stayed up late into the evening discussing the beautiful widow. "Olan told me six months later," Hailey recalled, "that he knew I was gone."[156] Time was running out, however. Homer and Widna talked again for a long time after services on Tuesday evening, and he called his friend Mildred Spain aside and asked, "How old is she, Mildred?" Told that Widna was thirty-eight, Homer retorted, "Too young, she wouldn't be interested in a fellow as old as I am. . . . Guess I'll forget it."

Mildred Spain assured Homer that Widna was interested; in fact, she had specifically returned home for the meeting because she wanted to meet him.

Late Tuesday night, Hailey's two sons, Rob and Dennis, arrived in Abilene to visit with their grandmother, and Homer arranged a visit the next afternoon to Widna's home where they met her mother and her son Richard. The meeting went well. "I thought I had never seen anybody as pretty in my life," Homer recalled. "I knew right then I was going to marry that woman or bust a hamstring trying. I was gone, plumb gone." On Wednesday evening Homer invited Widna and Mildred Spain out to the Manly home where he showed pictures of his trip to Honolulu. Then everyone left and Homer went back to town to catch a late bus to his next meeting. In the rush and excitement, he had forgotten to ask Widna's first name, knowing her only as Mrs. Kirby, and he did not know her address.[157]

Homer had arrived at the Graham Street meeting with no thoughts of matrimony; Widna came with a curiosity that soon blossomed into a full-scale entrapment campaign. Homer was a sitting duck. Born in Franklin Springs, Georgia, and reared in Alabama, Widna radiated the grace, charm, and beauty of a southern belle. In 1935, at age seventeen, Widna married Oliver Kirby, a policeman in Auburn. The Kirby family were members of the churches of Christ and Widna was baptized at age twenty-two; she was a faithful Christian, taking her sons to church, usually without their father. In October 1951, Oliver Kirby moved to Enterprise, Alabama, to become chief of police but died in June 1952 as a result of a longtime heart disease.[158]

The Kirbys had two sons, Richard and Gordon; both of the boys had attended church services regularly with their mother, and Richard decided that he wanted to be a preacher. When he graduated from high school in 1954, Widna sold the family home and she and the boys loaded their meager possessions into an old Plymouth and moved to Abilene so that Richard could enroll at ACC. Widna secured a job in a department store and the two boys entered school, Richard at ACC and Gordon at Abilene High School. Then tragedy struck. While practicing tumbling in the ACC gymnasium, Gordon broke his neck and lay for days in a coma. He finally regained consciousness, but remained paralyzed from the chest down. After many trying days, Gordon was accepted at the Warm Springs Foundation in Gonzales, Texas, for therapy. In July, Widna took him there and secured a job working in a local hospital. It was from there that she returned on the Sunday of August 7, 1955, to attend the Graham Street meeting.

Months earlier, a visitor to the store where Widna worked had told her, "Mrs. Kirby, you need a husband. You ought to meet Homer Hailey; he would make you a good one." Widna replied, "Some time I may have the opportunity to meet him, who knows." She wanted a husband; her only demands were that he had to be a Christian, he must be more than thirty-eight years old, and he must be taller than she.[159] Her son Richard sent her a bulletin from the Graham Street Church because it contained a note about Gordon, and Widna noticed as well an announcement about the beginning of the meeting with Homer Hailey in August. "Homer Hailey," she thought. "At least this is the chance to look him over, and meet him." She wanted to visit Richard and friends, so she hitched a ride with a friend, arrived in Abilene at five in the morning, slept a couple of hours, and quickly dressed for church. She reminded Mildred Spain that she had been promised an introduction; she liked what she had seen and heard. When Homer left Abilene on Wednesday evening, having never asked her name and address, she was disappointed. She returned to Gonzales assuming that time and distance would bring an end to a promising beginning.

Hailey tossed and turned restlessly on the bus in the early morning hours of August 11. He could not get his mind off the widow Kirby; indeed, he did not want to get his mind off the widow Kirby. Two nights later, Homer wrote Mildred Spain asking for Widna's name and address. Mildred called Widna to let her know that Homer had taken the bait and a few days later Widna received a letter from Paducah, Kentucky, where Homer was preaching. After the first exchange, letters came daily. Homer's first two letters were addressed "Dear Sister Kirby," but after that it was "Dear Widna." He discussed the romance with all of his children; they were less taken with the idea than he, but the boys became more agreeable as he talked with them about how it would be good to have a woman around the house again to help with the chores.

Hailey arrived home on September 3, and he called Georgia Deane Cope, his former student and the wife of the president of FCC, and confided in her. He knew that the whole affair sounded outrageous: "The idea of a man falling in love with a woman and making up his mind to marry her after having known her for only four days! And having been with her not more than two or three hours during that whole time!"[160] Georgia Deane Cope was sympathetic, so Homer wrote to Widna inviting her to come to Tampa for a visit. She accepted, and on the evening of September 10 she arrived, beautiful as he remembered, and he took her to stay with the Pickups.

The whirlwind courtship began in earnest the next day, a Saturday, with Homer fixing breakfast. Widna joined the family and toured the house that had been scrubbed clean for three days before her arrival. Homer's two boys were on their best behavior under threat of serious punishment. On Sunday, after church services, Homer and Widna ate lunch in the school cafeteria. "Homer was showing her off," recalled Bob Owen. "She was a very attractive woman."[161] After lunch the two of them went over to the Pickup's, where no one was home, and sat in the living room, and, at two o'clock on September 11, Homer blurted out: "Widna, we both know why you are here. You have had nearly two days to look the situation over. Would you consent to share the remainder of life and its work with me as a preacher's wife?" She knew it was coming, but she was surprised that it came on the second day of the visit. The deal was struck—they would marry around Thanksgiving—and Homer spent the remainder of her week's visit "floating in the clouds."[162]

"There is no fool like an old fool," Hailey told his friend Bob Owen.[163] "It could have been the biggest tragedy in the world," he later reflected.[164] Actually, they both knew a great deal about one another after their twenty hours together. Homer Hailey's persona was a matter of public record, and his private personality was exactly what it appeared to be. He had checked on Widna with Furman Cauthen, the preacher in Auburn who knew her best, and her character was flawless. Intuitively, they both knew that it was the right thing.

Hailey could hardly wait. Coincidentally, he, Harry Pickup, Sr., and Jim Cope were all scheduled to hold meetings in the Nashville area in early October, so Homer called and asked Widna to move the wedding date up to October 5. She agreed. After looking at his calendar carefully, he determined that he could arrive on October 4: another call, and Widna agreed to set the date up. Both of them made hectic preparations. Homer rode to Nashville with the Pickups, driving into the early morning hours of October 4. Widna arrived at five A.M., and Hailey's daughters flew in from Winston-Salem later in the morning.

On the afternoon of October 4, 1955, Harry Pickup, Sr., said the ceremony for his beloved friend in the home of one of their Nashville acquaintances. Jim Cope had just finished a week of meetings in Nashville and he and Georgia Deane Cope acted as best man and matron of honor. A few other old friends from the area attended, including Batsell Barrett Baxter, Hailey's student when he taught at Abilene Christian High School. Harry Pickup, Sr., asked Homer if he would be a "good wife to Widna," a line that followed him the rest of his days. It was not true, as Harry W. Pickup, Jr., frequently told in later years, that Hailey used a blackboard when he said "yes" at his wedding.[165] Hailey's daughters, still somewhat skep-

Homer Hailey and Widna Kirby Hailey at their wedding reception in Nashville, Tennessee, October 4, 1955.

tical about their father's decision, served the refreshments. "It was a gala occasion," Hailey recalled, and he and Widna were "supremely happy."

Clinton Hamilton had suggested that the Haileys spend their honeymoon in nearby Montgomery Bell Inn in a beautiful public park near Dickson, Tennessee. They borrowed the Pickup's car and spent "one of the happiest weeks that a couple could hope ever to live" in the park. On Sunday both

Pickup and Hailey began meetings in Nashville. The church where Hailey was preaching put the newlyweds in a suite in the James Robertson Hotel and the honeymoon continued. They all rode back to Tampa in the Pickup's station wagon.

All in all, it was a remarkable love story. He was fifty-two and she was thirty-eight. Both would consider remarriage only under the most restricted circumstances, and yet both of them longed for a companion. She was more than he could have ever dreamed of finding in a wife, and, quite clearly, Widna adored Homer Hailey from the first moment that she heard him preach.

My Kids and Your Kids

Widna returned to Gonzales on October 20, 1955, to make preparations for moving Gordon to Florida. That evening, after watching her plane depart, Homer wrote to her, as he would every night for twenty years when they were apart: "Widna, there hasn't been one disappointment to me in any way. You have measured up to every hope and yearning I had dared conceive. Surely, I could have found no more."[166] During Thanksgiving holidays at the college Homer drove to Texas, picked up Widna and Gordon, and returned to Temple Terrace to set up his new household. "It was no problem," he wrote years later. "It has been one continuous honeymoon since."[167]

It was an extraordinary marriage. Homer and Widna adored one another from the day they married, and the feeling never dimmed. Because Widna needed to stay close to Gordon to care for him, she rarely traveled with Homer. Homer often included poems in his daily letters to her. "We never had a fight," Widna later recalled. "He won't fight."[168]

Widna brought a new degree of financial stability to the household. She was a careful planner and tried to tuck back a bit of money for Homer to use as he began his summer meeting schedule. When he returned from his round of meetings, they would live through the year on the savings. "We kids never knew how poor we were," recalled Rob Hailey. The family survived, but frequently there was no meat on the table. They ate lots of cornbread, greens, and salad. Homer "never made a big issue of it," however, so neither did anyone else.[169]

Life was not an ongoing honeymoon for Widna. "She had a hard time," remembered her friend and neighbor Liz Pickup.[170] Widna soon found herself knee deep in a home filled with my kids and your kids, and she battled to win respect from the Hailey children. Homer captured the dilemma: "You're going to have problems if you have two sets of kids."[171] Both of Widna's sons, Gordon and Richard, lived in the Hailey home. Widna's children were housed in one end of the house and the Hailey kids, Rob, Dennis, and Carol Ann, were at the other end. Gordon demanded much of Widna's attention because of his disability, and the Hailey children soon felt that she showed favoritism toward her own children. Richard was studious and did not like to help with the yard work that fell to the lot of Rob and Dennis. Carol Ann deeply resented her new mother, her feelings being colored by the two married Hailey daughters, Roma and Mary Lois, neither of whom approved of the marriage.

In the years that followed the marriage, the family careened from one child crisis to the next—most of them trivial, but some semi-serious. The Hailey boys "were rounders," recalled Bob Owen, doing a little recreational drinking and smoking as they passed through adolescence.[172] "When you grow up preacher's kids," recalled Rob Hailey, "you always want to do something different."[173] Carol Ann's rebellion was more serious. Widna's presence cramped the style of the Hailey children because for many years their mother had been too ill to supervise them and Homer had been too busy. With increasing frequency, Widna became the prosecutor, reporting the children's misdeeds to Homer when he returned home. More often than not, "Homer would let the boys off at a lame excuse." In the eyes of some of the family friends, Widna never had "any support."[174]

In many ways, Homer was oblivious to the problems at home, deliriously happy with his new wife and companion and soon back into his old routine of studying, teaching, and preaching. As always in the past, at the beginning of the summer, Homer went away on his round of summer meetings, leaving Widna to manage an unruly house. Homer's son Dennis recalled that he "never saw him in the summer," but he knew what his father was doing and he never felt neglected. He rarely talked with his father when he was home, but he knew that he could approach him if a need arose. Additionally, the family carefully guarded the ritual of having dinner together each evening.

Hailey's loose approach to rearing his children was an inheritance from his own past. He was from the old school that believed that children raised themselves and that they needed relatively little attention. When dealing with his children, as with other things in life, Hailey sought to solve problems quickly and get back to his work, which was his life. When the turmoil at home reached insufferable dimensions, Hailey called his children together for a candid talk. He listened to their problems, and things were better for a time. Homer was never a "holy Joe"; he believed that all youngsters would have some problems growing up.

Rob Hailey was the most adventurous prankster in the family; he had the sparkling personality of his father. When he entered Florida College one could have predicted that he and the school's stringent code of behavior were on a collision course. Noted as the most skilled evader of the daily chapel services at Florida College, Rob ultimately found himself in deep trouble. A good student, in his chemistry class he learned how to make grapefruit wine. He set up a still in the dormitory and the smell soon attracted the attention of the dorm supervisors. Called before the Discipline Committee while his father was away in a meeting, Rob was suspended for three days. Disgusted because he would lose credits, he quit school. Even in later years Rob felt that the punishment "was a little more severe" than necessary. He felt he had been singled out as an example because he was Homer Hailey's son. After all, he noted, "They had a rule on drinking, but they didn't have one on making it."[175]

In time, the children began to leave home, Carol Ann first, then Rob and Dennis. All of them finished college, Dennis after a stint in the Navy Seabees. In later years, Carol Ann settled in Tampa and reconciled with Homer and Widna. Dennis lived in Phoenix where he became a highly successful CPA. Rob began a promising career with IBM before resigning and returning to the Manly ranch to become a West Texas rancher.

Through the years, Hailey's relationship with his children was sometimes shaky. Roma and Mary Lois, the two older daughters, became reconciled to his second marriage years later, but they always remembered Lois as the center of their home life. Even more, Roma resented the distant relationship that she had with her father, both before and after the death of her mother. In a sense, they were victims of Hailey's choice to be a public figure. Everyone regretted the distance between them at times, including Homer, but it was the result of a conscious choice on his part—and it was a type of family relationship not uncommon in his time.[176]

In later years, reflecting on his family life, Hailey regretted that he had not involved his children in his work to a greater degree. Had they known more about what he was doing, had they shared in his labors, perhaps they would have appreciated him more. Yet, he felt that he "did a lot of things right as a parent." He disciplined his children when necessary, he felt, and generally exercised "proper judgment." The family ate dinner together every evening, something that his children remembered vividly, and they read the Bible together.[177]

Time heals many of the real and imagined hurts between those who love one another, and in Hailey's declining years most of the old family tensions receded into the background. In the years after his retirement, the family members drew closer together. When he retired in 1973 from Florida College all of his children save Dennis surprised him by attending the celebrations. The children had all more or less made their peace with Homer and Widna. In 1989 he journeyed to Gloucester, Virginia, to perform the marriage ceremony for his grandson Scott, relishing the experience of being with the next generation of his family.

The Last Days of Mamie Collins Hailey

Beginning in 1960, Widna had to adjust to the presence of another Hailey. Mamie Collins Hailey moved into an apartment in Temple Terrace so she "could hear Homer preach the rest of her life." Homer had visited his mother occasionally through the years that she lived in Hallsville, Texas, but when she moved to Temple Terrace he called on her every day. "Homer was her pride and joy," and she also came to love Widna.[178]

Mamie Collins became something of a legend in Temple Terrace in the years before her death in 1970. She made her own clothes and always dressed neatly in a long dress and bonnet. Intellectually active to the very end of her life, she pored over *National Geographic, Arizona Highways, Reader's Digest,* and the local newspaper; she had no patience with anyone who was uninformed about current affairs. She listened faithfully to radio broadcasts of baseball games and was a passionate St. Louis Cardinals fan. She remained extremely outspoken, a "rugged individualist" who could be both "crusty" and "offensive."[179]

For all her cantankerousness, Mamie confided to her friend Liz Pickup that her Temple Terrace years were "the happiest time of her life and she had more friends."[180] Particularly, she loved Widna. "She gave me a hard time all the time," Widna recalled. "Nothing I ever bought her was pretty." Upon being

Mamie Collins Hailey receiving a plaque from Florida College president James R. Cope shortly before her death in 1970. An indomitable frontier woman, famous for her bonnets, she spent the last ten years of her life in Temple Terrace, Florida, near her beloved son, Homer.

given some material that Widna had picked out, Granny audibly whispered, "It's just as hard to make an ugly dress as it is a pretty one." However, when she inherited money from her Uncle Roger, she gave Widna a thousand dollars.[181] Mamie died quickly after a series of strokes in August 1970. She "wore out," Homer observed, "just as the Lord intended it."[182]

Farewell to Florida College

Hailey taught a reduced load at Florida College in the 1972 to 1973 academic year and made preparations to move to Arizona. The Copes and Owenses staged a retirement reception for him in April 1972 that was attended by four of Hailey's children. "It was time for me to leave," Hailey surmised. "I was getting worn out. I would teach school for eight months and head for meetings for three or four months. No vacation. No anything."[183]

Hailey left Florida College laden with honors. In 1972 the students dedicated the yearbook to him and the college gave him its annual "Friend of Youth" award. "His impact on others," noted the *Florida College News Bulletin,* "is perhaps best told through the life and work of literally hundreds of young men whom he has taught and influenced for good."[184] Hailey's old friend Jim Cope wrote an impressive epithet for his companion: "In the 38 years I have been involved as student, teacher or administrator in three different colleges of the nature of Florida College, I have never known any other man so immensely loved and respected by students and teachers alike."[185]

7

Arizona Retirement, Reluctant Notoriety

1973–1999

A Home in Tucson

ANTICIPATING LEAVING teaching in 1971, Homer Hailey made a trip to Arizona to look over potential retirement sites. "Everybody wants to go back where they were as a kid," Hailey later recalled. In 1971 his thoughts returned to the carefree days of his youth, to memories of the "real West."[1] Hailey considered Willcox, but he remembered the fierce winds that scoured the plains and looked elsewhere. He also thought of settling on a ranch, but that was not practical for Widna and Gordon. Widna was reluctant to leave Florida and her friends, and some of their Florida friends did not think that they would really move. However, they had no idea how deep Hailey's roots were embedded in frontier Arizona; he knew that Florida "wasn't me." James R. Cope dreaded the loss of Hailey, and he facetiously begged Widna to refuse to move.

Hailey visited with Charlie Mann in Phoenix and Harry Mann in Tucson. He had known the Mann brothers since the 1930s, when he began holding meetings in Arizona. Both of them tried to recruit Hailey as a neighbor, and he decided to move to Tucson. It was a beautiful town with a good airport that made it possible for him to fly to his busy schedule of meetings. The hospital facilities were adequate to care for Gordon's needs. He bought a lot next to the home of Harry

Mann and returned to Florida. Harry Mann contracted to build the home for him, and Homer spent the next fall in Tucson working as a laborer on a home that he designed with an eye toward easing Widna's burden of caring for Gordon. It was western to the core, blending imperceptibly into the desert landscape.

At the close of the spring term, the Haileys sold their home in Florida, and Homer, Widna, and Gordon embarked on a new life. Widna stopped on the way to visit friends in Alabama while Homer drove ahead to Tucson to ready the house for her arrival. Homer had the refrigerator stocked and stood bursting with pride when Widna arrived to inspect his handiwork on July 18, 1973. The day was "boiling hot," Widna recalled, and she saw little beauty in the desert yard surrounding the house. She didn't say much, but Widna thought to herself, "How can I ever spend the rest of my life here?"[2] Homer left almost immediately for a meeting, leaving Gordon and a downcast wife behind. Only with the passing of time did she come to love the desert as Homer did.[3]

Retiring had not been a difficult decision for Hailey. He believed that "God has used me richly," and that the time had come to turn another page. He thought he was "losing my zip" in the classroom and he longed for time to study and write. He soon established a new pattern of work that made his retirement years some of the most productive of his life.[4]

Much remained the same in the Hailey household. He continued to flourish on exercise and a strict health-food diet. All around the country those who hosted Hailey in their homes during meetings became familiar with his daily potion of brewer's yeast, water, wheat germ, bran flakes, safflower oil, and molasses. "It isn't so bad tasting," said Hailey in defense of the acrid-smelling mix. He believed that it accounted for his longevity and vitality. It seemed to work. When Homer was seventy-two his son Rob visited and the two of them hiked to the bottom of the Grand Canyon and back out.[5] Some people dread old age, but Homer welcomed it as the "best of life." The secret to a good old age, he believed, was to eat correctly, exercise, and "keep your mind on good things."[6]

Of course, he continued to preach. Writing in *Vanguard* in 1981, Hailey asked, "Shall I quit preaching?" Hailey wrote, "In the face of an indifferent world to spiritual things and an unconcerned church to spiritual growth," preachers were tempted to "quit preaching and try something else." However, "despondency" had little room in Hailey's mind. Nearing eighty, he urged others to leave "weakness and self-pity" behind and "turn to the work with a renewed zeal."[7] Still vigorous, Hailey scheduled more meetings than ever after returning to Arizona; in some years he preached twenty-four weeks. In addition, Hailey filled in for local congregations in the Tucson area, preaching while they were searching for regular preachers.

In October 1982, just past his seventy-ninth birthday, Hailey addressed a letter to the churches where he had meetings scheduled in the future requesting that they be canceled. "For fifty-two or three years I have spent all the time in meetings that I could spare from local church or class-room work," Hailey wrote. It was now time, he believed, "to stay home and pursue a different line of work in the Lord's vineyard." In the future, he intended to speak only on "special occasions."[8]

Hailey did not elaborate about his reasons in his form letter, but several factors prompted him to become less active. First, he felt that Widna and Gordon needed more of his attention. Second, he was tired of traveling; he wanted to stay home, visit Willcox occasionally, and savor his beloved desert. He continued to conduct a heavy correspondence with old friends and strangers who wrote asking questions. In addition, he entertained a steady stream of visitors at his home in Tucson—old friends, family, and former students.

Hailey also began preaching at a little congregation in Oracle. The church in the tiny mining village high in the mountains thirty miles north of Tucson was near death, having only about fifteen members. It met only once each Sunday.

Even though the church had supported institutions in the past, and they knew that Hailey was an "anti," the few remaining members implored him to preach for them. He accepted, and preached regularly for the congregation for fifteen years, persevering even though it was "a very discouraging place." He baptized a few people in the little town, and the church grew to a membership of twenty-six before being depleted by deaths and members moving away.[9]

Hailey also spoke in five or six meetings or lectureships each year. He was a fixture on the lectureship program at Florida College during the 1980s, returning time after time as the featured speaker. Like many others in the 1980s, Hailey also opened communications with old friends in institutional churches of Christ. In the mid-1980s he preached several Sundays for the "liberal" church in Willcox. "They know where I stand," Hailey observed, "and they thought I was great." In fact, Hailey surmised, the little church was not very "liberal," and he hoped to be able to open lines of communication with them.[10]

By 1988, Hailey had begun once again to increase his meeting schedule. His annual commitments rose to sixteen before slowly dwindling to a few each year in the 1990s. He also continued his yearly pilgrimages to the Florida College Lectures until 1990, when that relationship was abruptly interrupted and he was embroiled, for the first time in his life, in the center of a controversy in the noninstitutional churches of Christ.

Studying and Writing

In his later life, Homer Hailey's reputation was inextricably linked with a steady flow of books. Escaping the grinding round of teaching and grading papers had been the chief attraction that lured him into retirement. In Arizona, his routine allowed more time for leisurely study. He secluded himself in his book-lined study each morning to work from eight until one o'clock. After lunch and a nap he worked sporadically un-

Homer Hailey in his study in his Tucson home in 1986. Here he wrote a steady stream of books well into his nineties.

til time for his thirty-minute workout. He still set aside Saturdays to study for his Sunday lessons.

Throughout the 1980s, Hailey continued to write for several periodicals circulated among members of churches of Christ. In 1975, he agreed to be a member of the board of editors for *Vanguard,* a new magazine launched by Fanning Yater Tant. Hailey headed a group that included Franklin T. Puckett, Clinton D. Hamilton, Robert H. Farish, Hoyt H. Houchen,

Peter J. Wilson, L. A. Mott, Jr., Harry W. Pickup, Jr., Jack Holt, and Ed Harrell. Hailey was the superstar upon whom Tant pinned much of his hope for the magazine's future. Tant wrote, "Homer Hailey, dean of Bible teachers, is one of the most distinguished preachers and Bible scholars of modern times. Beloved by thousands of former students, and constantly sought as both preacher and teacher, Brother Hailey speaks with a voice of authority in Biblical matters that spans the world."[11] Hailey loved Yater Tant and he wrote regularly for *Vanguard* throughout the paper's life, mostly on familiar Old Testament themes. He also supported Tant's appeals for financial assistance.[12] As the circulation of the magazine dwindled in the late 1980s, and its editor came under attack from some of his former friends, Hailey repeatedly came to Tant's aid. He wrote extensively for *Vanguard* in its final years. Hailey also contributed occasionally to other journals; he wrote two articles published in the *Guardian of Truth* in 1987, one of them a featured editorial entitled "The Prophets Speak of Calvary."[13] In 1985, Stanley W. Paher published a compilation of Hailey articles in two volumes entitled *Hailey's Comments*.[14]

Primarily, however, Hailey wrote books. Spurred by the success of his commentary on the minor prophets, Hailey explored several new book projects. Soon he began to work on a commentary on the book of Revelation. He had long avoided a serious study of the book because Foy E. Wallace, Jr., whom Hailey still greatly admired, had published a commentary on the book in 1966.[15] However, Hailey concluded that Wallace's book was the "sorriest thing he ever did," and he soon was hard at work on the subject.[16]

Writing was hard work for Hailey. He developed a contraction in his hands that prohibited him from typing for fifteen years before he finally had an operation to relieve the condition. Nothing came easy. "I am not a good writer," he later complained. "I am not a good thinker at the typewriter."[17] He continued to lean heavily on his closest friends, Clinton Hamilton and Melvin Curry, to read his texts and he was especially dependent on Margie H. Garrett "for her invaluable help in correcting sentences and for her suggestions toward their proper structure."[18]

If Hailey had no illusions about his stylistic limitations, neither was he vain about the depth of his scholarship. "I am not a scholar," he conceded, "I am just a student."[19] Hailey's method of writing was fairly well set by the time he reached Arizona. Above all, he wanted to give readers his common-sense interpretation of the text. He made a "deliberate choice" not to immerse himself in the thoughts of others.[20] "My idea of writing a book," Hailey reflected, "is not to fill it up with a lot of quotations of what men have said, but analyze what they said, digest what they said, and then make it your own." So, he assembled a dozen commentaries, read them, and "picked what is good." His favorites were the works of R. C. H. Lenski and Carl Keil and Franz Delitzsch, mostly because they helped him with linguistic problems that he did not have the expertise to explore.[21] He also depended heavily on word studies to compensate for his inability to read ancient languages well.

Hailey made slow progress on his Revelation commentary, burdened by a heavy schedule of meetings and with regular classes at the Country Club and Northside churches in Tucson. Dissatisfied with Wallace's conclusion that Revelation was written in Nero's time (A.D. 64–68), Hailey based his commentary on the assumption that the book was written much later, about A.D. 91–96. Hailey reviewed a variety of interpretative schemes commonly used by commentators—"futurist," "continuous historical," "philosophy of history," "preterits," and "historical background"—and called his interpretative framework "eclectic." His book used "a combination of some aspects of all five views." His general conclusion was that the "grand theme of Revelation is that of war and conflict between good and evil resulting in victory for the righteous and defeat for the wicked."[22] Published by Baker Book House in 1979, the commentary was well received, though it did not have the lasting popularity of his book on the minor prophets.[23]

After finishing his commentary on Revelation, Hailey toyed with several ideas. He began a book on the wisdom literature of the Old Testament, but "it didn't work."[24] One day he began reading a manuscript he had written years earlier while living in Honolulu, and he liked it. He sent it to Clinton Hamilton to read and Hamilton urged him to turn it into a book. In later years, Hailey surmised that such seasoning was good for any manuscript. "If you want to write," he advised, "you should start early and lay stuff back."[25]

The book that resulted was entitled *From Creation to the Day of Eternity.*[26] Hailey submitted the manuscript to Baker Book House, as he had his other manuscripts, and they declined to publish it. Hailey suspected that Baker would not publish the manuscript because it was a book that was written "strictly for our brethren."[27] The work was a brief survey of the entire Bible; Hailey's purpose was to trace the story of "God's grace." He wrote, "It has been my purpose in writing this book to set forth the divine plan in simple language, beginning with God and the creation, tracing the plan to its consummation in the 'day of eternity.'"[28] The book opened a publishing relationship between Hailey and independent Nevada publisher Stanley Paher, who subsequently republished several of Hailey's books that had gone out of print. While the book was never as widely circulated as Hailey's commentaries, it was well known among members of churches of Christ.

In 1982, after canceling his meeting schedule to allow himself more time to stay home and write, Hailey began working on what he considered the most difficult of his book projects, a commentary on Isaiah. Initially, he intended to write only about the messianic passages in the book, but he concluded that those passages could not stand alone. He struggled with the often obscure passages in the book, getting help with difficult Hebrew linguistic questions wherever he could find it. The book was published by Baker Book House in 1985.

Hailey was drained by the experience of writing the Isaiah commentary. However, projects kept popping into his fertile mind. He considered writing a commentary on the books of Ephesians and Colossians, a study that would "cut the tap root of every ism." Instead, he turned to another theme he had repeatedly written about in articles: prayer and providence. Hailey believed that God "still rules in the kingdoms of men" and that he used those "given over to idolatry" to punish the heathen nations that were "ripe for destruction." Hailey was convinced that "this nation was the logical place for the restoration movement to start" because of the morality and wholesomeness of early America, but that the United States had become "worse than lots of nations."[29] Prophetic principles served as a warning to modern nations.

Hailey once again submitted his manuscript to Baker Book House and it was rejected. "I don't believe a Calvinist can accept the providence of God," he later surmised.[30] He was again drained as he neared completion of the project. He wrote to his old friend John Kilgore, "Am still trying to get work done on the book, but very slow. Have it ready to begin my final typing of it—then to Margie—and then to my typist—then (probably) retire from writing."[31]

In the 1990s Hailey was seriously distracted from his writing when he became the center of a controversy because of his views on divorce and remarriage. Under fire, he spent hours restudying his controversial position on the subject. Persuaded that he was correct, he wrote a pamphlet explaining his view. Urged by many of his friends not to publish the booklet, the wounded Hailey insisted that he wanted his view in print for the sake of posterity.

We Love Homer Hailey, but . . .

Homer Hailey was an unlikely candidate to become the center of a controversy within noninstitutional churches of Christ. Although he had garnered a degree of fame and a very large following of admirers through his preaching, teaching, and writing, he had never aspired to being a "brotherhood leader."

He made his mind up slowly during the institutional controversy, almost reluctantly, and, aside from his exchanges with B. C. Goodpasture about his article on orphan homes, he had never been involved in a direct exchange on any controversial subject. In 1988, while retired, holding a limited schedule of meetings, and preaching regularly to about two dozen people in Oracle, Arizona, Hailey unexpectedly became the center of a national dispute.

Homer Hailey, like every other member of the churches of Christ, held some views not shared by a majority. He raised eyebrows with a series of articles on the eldership in the *Preceptor* in the 1950s. Hailey believed that a pastor system had evolved in churches of Christ that placed evangelists in charge of the spiritual welfare of churches and reduced elders to the role of financial overseers. In attacking that abuse, Hailey was on safe ground, but he went further. He insisted that the word *authority* was never used in connection with elders, and that the leaders of local churches assumed too much authority. "It makes them mad to say that," Hailey conjectured, insisting that he did not oppose properly constituted elderships.[32]

Even more controversially, Hailey urged less stress be placed on the biological qualification requiring elders to have children and more on the spiritual merits of candidates. In a distinctly minority opinion, Hailey insisted that "the number of children" in one's family was indifferent in the appointment of elders. Indeed, he believed that a childless man could serve as a bishop.[33] Preaching in Hawaii in 1991, Hailey said with typical gusto, "You can count his kids and see whether or not they've been baptized . . . just like counting the attendance and dollars. . . . I get so indignant when I preach regarding elders. We get hung up on the physical, when Paul is stressing the spiritual. We are over-burdening this thing by putting interpretations that emphasize the minor rather than the major."[34] Finally, Hailey believed that in the New Testament, evangelists had the authority to designate elders, another view that was by no means universally accepted.

Through the years, Hailey's views on the eldership "struck a lot of fire." He was accused of not believing in elders in local churches, a charge that he vehemently denied. Most of those who disagreed with him overlooked his teaching on this subject and others, because, in Harry Pickup, Jr.'s words, Hailey had "paid the price for standing for the truth when it has cost him." Furthermore, Pickup noted, Hailey's life was without "blemish" and he had always preached his views candidly but with discretion.[35]

Hailey held several other views that placed him in a minority in the churches of Christ. All through his life, he believed that "God set the Holy Spirit in my heart to relate me to Him," an idea that many considered a dangerous concession to subjectivism and Calvinistic concepts of grace.[36] He also remained a conscientious objector, insisting that "you have to hate to be a soldier."[37] However, after the close of World War II pacifism was little discussed in churches of Christ, and few people were troubled by Hailey's lingering opposition to war.

Of much more concern to many people was Hailey's view on divorce and remarriage. On this issue he was in a distinct minority on a subject that many felt symbolized the moral decline of America. Hailey's biblical exegesis on divorce and remarriage matured through the years, but he first formed his belief while preaching at the Fifth and Highland Church in Abilene in the 1930s. An ardent proponent of personal evangelism, Hailey recalled being instructed by the church's elders not to baptize a certain prospect he had been teaching unless the man would separate from his wife. Hailey was shocked by the seeming harshness of the directive. He began a serious study of the subject, and reached the conclusion that "God did not say a thing" about breaking up marriages when people became Christians. For many years, Hailey's analysis of the subject did not progress far beyond that conclusion. He continued to believe that "divorce and remarriage is contrary to God's law," but he was not convinced that "God dealt with the question with regard to the heathen." Consequently, he concluded, "These people who are telling individuals . . . you have got to separate . . . are acting where God never did legislate and they are setting themselves up as judges in this matter."[38]

In later years, Hailey elaborated on his views on divorce and remarriage. He read little of what others had written in crafting his own positions, studying the Bible text as he did in other matters. He resented the charge made by those who attacked him that he endorsed the "Fuqua position," because he had never read any of the controversial writings of E. C. Fuqua.[39] Hailey concluded that the restrictions placed by Jesus on divorce and remarriage in Matthew chapters 5 and 19 "deal with those who are in covenant relationship with God" and that Jesus never "dealt with the condition of the Gentiles in this matter."[40] Alien sinners who divorced were guilty of "covenant breaking," Hailey believed, and they should repent of that evil when they became Christians, but they were not bound by the restraints on divorce and remarriage that Jesus had placed on Christians.[41]

Hailey knew that his conclusions were controversial and he "never made it an issue." "I only recall preaching it twice," Hailey stated in 1988, "in California and in Alabama by request."[42] James W. Adams remembered an occasion when Hailey preached on the subject in Anaheim, California, at the request of the church's elders: "While it provoked discussion elsewhere in Southern California, it did not materially disturb the West Anaheim congregation, create trouble, divide the church, or result in a proliferation of divorces and remarriages."[43] Most of the teachers and students at Florida College knew about Hailey's views and they occasionally discussed the subject with him. "Anybody ask me about it, I would tell them," Hailey insisted, but "I didn't try to promote it."[44] "They all differed from me," Hailey recalled. But it was not a problem. "When it came up in class, I would tell them briefly" and then proceed to other subjects.[45]

Hailey was challenged from time to time because of his views on divorce and remarriage. His most consistent critic was preacher and editor J. T. Smith. After Hailey stated his position publicly in the sermon in Anaheim, California, in 1976, Smith challenged his former teacher. Smith confessed that he had "known for some time brother Hailey's position," but he had never before heard him "express it before an audience of people." He offered Hailey an opportunity to reply to his rebuttal in the pages of his church bulletin and concluded, "Nothing suffers from honest investigation—but error."[46] Six years later, in 1982, in an article discussing "false doctrine and false teachers," Smith named Hailey, along with others, as a proponent of false doctrine. "I understand from the standpoint of the overall knowledge of the Bible I do not even come to the top of his boots," Smith wrote, but "I feel compelled to . . . answer . . . because I believe it is false doctrine."[47]

Despite sporadic attacks from Smith and others, by and large Hailey's view on divorce and remarriage detracted little from his prestige and influence among the people in noninstitutional churches of Christ. Partly, he escaped attack because of the historical realities in the noninstitutional churches of Christ in the 1960s and 1970s. Those ostracized from the mainstream felt so besieged during those bitterly divisive years that they bonded together in spite of a broad array of doctrinal differences. Partly, Hailey's extraordinary reputation protected him from attack. "His vast storehouse of knowledge on other subjects" made people overlook his controversial position on divorce, observed Jim Cope. Cope was well aware of Hailey's views on divorce and remarriage when he hired him to head the Bible Department at Florida Christian College, but he also knew that Hailey would never be schismatic: "I've always felt that he would say what he believed and then he would turn it loose as soon as he could."[48] One could hardly "write him off as an incompetent," reasoned Cope's successor as president of Florida College, Bob F. Owen. Additionally, above all, he had been a "peacemaker," content to express his conviction and "let the other fellow make the application."[49]

The issue that engulfed Homer Hailey in controversy in 1988 was quite old. Never in the history of the restoration movement had a settled opinion existed on the subject of divorce and remarriage, though discussions on the subject were often derailed by more pressing concerns. Furthermore, at the local level, there was considerable diversity in the practices followed by congregations.

In 1979, institutional churches of Christ were rocked by a controversy on the subject when James D. Bales, a highly respected and conservative professor of Christian Doctrine at Harding University, published a booklet entitled *Not Under Bondage*.[50] Bales interpreted 1 Corinthians 7:10–15 in a way that established three separate marriage laws: one for Christians, another for couples in which one partner was a Christian, and a third governing the marriages of those who were not Christians. It would be presumptuous, he insisted, to bind laws on alien sinners that did not apply to them.

The Bales booklet sparked a quick and hostile counterattack from the *Spiritual Sword* and other conservatives within the institutional churches of Christ. In 1975, the *Spiritual Sword* devoted an entire issue to the subject of divorce and remarriage. Editor Thomas B. Warren cataloged the various "false doctrines" on the subject, including the idea that "those who divorced and remarried before entering the church do not sin in so doing even when such action is in violation of the conditions set forth in Matthew 19:9 if the civil law to which they are amenable is obeyed."[51] Bales wrote an article in the issue that vaguely stated his position and called for a willingness to "re-study our position and consider the arguments brought against it."[52]

As attacks on him multiplied, Bales fought back. In a pamphlet published in 1980 entitled *Shall We Splinter?* Bales warned that "there are a handful of brethren who are trying to push these matters to the point of disfellowshipping." He pointed out that his attackers did not agree with one another on some of the difficult questions posed by the biblical teaching about divorce and remarriage, and that consistency demanded that they cease to fellowship one another, thus causing a splintering rather than a split. Mostly, however, Bales assembled an array of material demonstrating the historical diversity within the restoration movement on the subject of divorce and remarriage. He cataloged the preachers in the past who had disagreed in some respect with the majority view on divorce and remarriage, all of whom insisted that churches had a right to tolerate a degree of diversity on the subject. Bales reached back into restoration history to note the unconventional views of Alexander Campbell, Walter Scott, David Lipscomb, and F. B. Srygley, and then documented an astonishing diversity among such early twentieth-century preachers as R. L. Whiteside, N. B. Hardeman, H. Leo Boles, C. R. Nichol, and G. C. Brewer.[53] Perhaps most telling was his appeal to some of the most conservative pioneers of the past century. For instance, in 1945, the leader of early noninstitutional attacks, W. W. Otey, urged that "people . . . divorced for 'any cause,'" could hardly expect to become leaders in local churches but that they should be granted "fellowship in the worship, and all the spiritual help that can be given them."[54] According to Bales, John T. Lewis, the patriarch of the noninstitutional churches in North Alabama, refused to urge separation on couples who had been divorced and remarried before becoming Christians and he "performed a wedding ceremony involving a young Christian woman to a man who had been divorced."[55] Perhaps most embarrassing to his *Spiritual Sword* attackers, Bales published a letter from Foy E. Wallace, Jr., chiding editor Thomas Warren for "binding procedures which the Lord did not prescribe." Concurring with Bales's interpretation of 1 Corinthians 7, Wallace pointed out that he had made a similar interpretation of the text in his book on the Sermon on the Mount.[56] In that book he wrote, "The course of some preachers in demanding separations and the breaking up of family relations, and the refusal to even baptize certain ones whose marriage status does not measure up to his standard of approval, is a presumptuous procedure. It reveals the tendency to displace God as the Judge of us all, and a preacher ascends to the bench."[57]

After the flurry over Bales's book, the divorce and remarriage issue continued to be widely debated among conservatives in the institutional wing of the movement. In 1975, Reuel Lemmons, editor of the *Firm Foundation*, reported that "we receive letters containing variations of this divorce and remarriage question more often than any other."[58] The *Spiritual Sword* continued to try to impose a church-wide orthodoxy on the subject, and in 1992, in a move that appeared related to the Hailey controversy in the noninstitutional churches of Christ, the Spiritual Sword lectureship, an annual event sponsored by the Getwell church in Memphis, featured the subject of "Marriage, Divorce, and Remarriage."[59]

The Divorce Debate in Noninstitutional Churches of Christ

To some extent, the debate triggered by the Bales discussion spilled over into noninstitutional churches of Christ. While the first broad airing of the subject in the papers read by noninstitutional Christians did not occur until the late 1970s, several earlier spats made it clear that those who opposed institutionalism were by no means united in their views on divorce and remarriage. As early as 1962, Charles A. Holt, a leading debater, questioned the assumption that every church must conduct "a survey of the members, examine their marriages and certainly their divorces, and FORCE all those judged to be 'living in adultery' to accept and act upon . . . our deduction and conclusion or else withdraw from them." Wary of the consequences of open debate on divorce and remarriage, Holt warned that there were "too many 'trigger-happy' brethren among us" and that the movement was in danger of becoming "factious."[60]

In 1963, editor Yater Tant opened the pages of the *Gospel Guardian* to a discussion on "the marriage question" between Lloyd Moyer and Gene Frost. Tant, whose own private views on the subject of divorce and remarriage were similar to those of Bales, noted that he had "been reluctant to open the pages of the *Guardian* to a full scale discussion of this subject, knowing how tense and emotion-packed discussions of this theme often become." However, he believed that the time had come when the subject could profitably be discussed and that the two disputants would remain in "full fellowship with one another in the Lord," even if they remained "far apart" in their beliefs on divorce and remarriage.[61] For the remainder of the decade of the sixties, most preachers were willing to leave the issue alone.

In the late 1970s, the Bales controversy triggered discussions on the subject in noninstitutional circles, leading to the most extended and heated clash up to that point between editors of noninstitutional papers. That exchange began when James W. Adams, the respected and arch-conservative editor of the *Gospel Guardian,* defended himself against rumors that he supported a "permissive point of view toward divorce and remarriage." Adams urged restraint in debating the issue: "The divorce and remarriage question is highly complex. . . . Over-simplification of the issue coupled with arbitrary dictums have obscured rather than exposed truth on the question. Too many hesitate not to play god with the lives of other people." Disgusted by ideologists on both sides of the issue, Adams wrote, "I do not know as much as some brethren. Where I am uncertain, I move with great caution."[62]

Adams insisted that "the practice of a single individual in these areas does not of necessity involve the conscience or practice of another individual." Because one's marital status was not a "congregational" problem, a person's individual conscience should be respected: "The theory of 'unity in diversity' can be practiced within prescribed limits in these areas where it cannot be practiced in the area of congregational activity." Adams implored those pressing for an exclusive orthodoxy on the issue to lower their voices: "I am attempting only to appeal to the good sense of serious, reflecting, dedicated brethren of good will *not to press their views* in these areas to the inevitable destruction of fellowship and peace."[63]

Adams was soon locked in an acrimonious exchange with those he styled "the infallible-judges-of-the-validity-of-every-case-of-divorce-and-remarriage group." He labeled those who wished to establish a binding orthodoxy throughout the churches of Christ "Johnny-come-lately-Sommerites" and appealed to "brethren of influence and ability" to "stop our progress toward oblivion on the road of 'partyism.'"[64] Adams believed that it was counterproductive to debate the controversial topic publicly and he was stung when some marked him as a compromiser: "Each tells me unabashedly how sad it is that I 'once stood so nobly against error in the fight over institutionalism' and now have succumbed to false doctrine and compromise. They get out their crying towels and weep over my defection while, at the same time, they are berating me for either 'fellowshipping whoremongers and adulterers' (from one side's point of view) or for aiding, abetting, and joining forces with 'reputation assassins and human creed makers' from the other side's point of view." Adams hoped that "the innocent and unsuspecting" would not become "embroiled in this unnecessarily divisive struggle over these old, controverted matters that, like the poor, 'are ever with us.'"[65]

Adams believed that no good would come from public debates on the subject of marriage and divorce. "For some time now," he wrote, "persons on both sides of the controversy have been literally itching ('burning') to project these problems and diverse points of view into a 'brotherhood issue' with resultant severance of fellowship."[66] While not opposed to religious debating, Adams remained convinced that such encounters often resulted in the formation of "distinct 'parties' among the churches," and he continued to believe that a subject such as divorce and remarriage could best be studied "in the forum provided by the papers circulating among the brethren and the churches."[67] In all honesty, he despaired that the question would be settled: "These matters have been discussed to and fro and over and over and still are being discussed. There are about as many points of view as there are men who discuss them. . . . Yet, the divergent points of view continue. We are simply going to have to live with our differences, or we are going to fragment the churches into a motley mess of divided cliques all loudly proclaiming to the world: '*We are the one true church; you see it as we do because that's what Jesus said; it's simply a matter of faith!*'"[68]

Adams was directly challenged by H. E. Phillips, one of the founding editors of *Searching the Scriptures* and a consistent defender of the majority view on divorce and remarriage, and by Connie W. Adams, the editor of the magazine. H. E. Phillips was particularly offended by the James Adams articles because he had been scheduled to participate in a debate on the subject before becoming ill. He bristled at Adams's charge that some brethren were "over-zealous" in pressing the "so-called 'Marriage issue.'" The issue was real, Phillips protested, and one could not be "over-zealous" in "defending the truth." Furthermore, Phillips believed that biblical truth concerning divorce and remarriage was simple; what was under discussion was not a matter of "opinion," but "truth and error." Recognizing that his uncompromising stand would "bring the wrath of the gods upon me," Phillips laid down his challenge: "I cannot, in good conscience, remain silent any longer with reference to a number of articles that have appeared in bulletins and in some papers that suggest a compromise on the divorce and adulterous remarriage issue to avoid division. When error is introduced among the people of God, scriptural division is inevitable as long as the error is believed and practiced." Phillips had no desire to promote "partyism," but he intended to "oppose false teachers and their works without compromise."[69]

Searching the Scriptures editor Connie W. Adams, whose opposition to deviant views on marriage and divorce was consistent and frank, defended Phillips and other debaters—J. T. Smith, Gene Frost, and Maurice Barnett—but at the same time acknowledged "the right of each congregation to handle such problems as they arise, without outside meddling." Connie Adams was indignant because "able, faithful and godly men have been abused and branded as radical partisans for defending God's standard of purity in such matters."[70] Deeply concerned about the "purity" of the church in the midst of the nation's decaying morality, Connie Adams insisted that the question needed to be debated lest "churches through the land . . . be filled with moral corruption."[71] A conspiracy of silence for the sake of peace was both dangerous and wrong.

After this 1978 confrontation, divorce and remarriage was discussed at a more subdued level in noninstitutional circles. J. T. Smith wrote on the subject from time to time in *Searching the Scriptures*,[72] and in the *Guardian of Truth*, editor Mike Willis wrote an extensive series defending his somewhat unconventional view, which discounted as a "smoke screen" the arguments of those who believed that "the innocent party in an unscriptural divorce is obligated to live a celibate life or be reconciled to her husband," but methodically refuted a variety of more liberal views.[73]

Hailey in the Center of the Storm

Hailey inadvertently moved to the center of a bitter debate in March 1988 when he accepted an invitation from a small church in Belen, New Mexico, to present his views about divorce and remarriage to the church, which had been grappling with a local problem. The church subsequently invited Ron Halbrook from Baytown, Texas, to present a rebuttal. The Belen church insisted that they had never intended to cause a controversy. In a statement issued after a controversy erupted, the members said that they wished to hear "both sides of the issue"; neither Hailey nor Halbrook "*forced* upon us their teaching," and both men "came here as gentlemen, with sincerity and a calm spirit." The congregation then made "a decision that we believed to be correct in God's sight."[74]

Hailey understood that his class in Belen was a "private meeting," though he did agree that the session could be taped.[75] Soon a videotape of Hailey's presentation was in circulation, along with a critique by Halbrook, and in November the *Guardian of Truth* carried an account of the proceedings from Halbrook's point of view. While the reporter stood "in awe of his command of the Scripture and ability to expound upon it," and did not question that Hailey "meant well" in his visit to Belen, he believed the result was that "there was greater confusion" after Hailey left than before he arrived. The article in the *Guardian* expressed hope that "an open and thorough investigation of the subject will result as we lovingly discuss the oracles of God."[76]

Even before the *Guardian of Truth* account of the Belen proceedings, there were inklings that Hailey was about to be attacked. In *Torch,* a small journal edited by J. T. Smith, an editorial note in May 1988 named Hailey: "Sometimes it is difficult to understand how brethren think. Let me give you an example of what I mean. If a brother who is not very well known in the brotherhood has the truth and stands strong on a controversial issue (like the marriage and divorce question) while another brother who is a 'prominent brotherhood figure' teaches error on the same subject, it seems strange to me that brethren will shun using the man with the truth while continually using the 'prominent figure' who teaches error that will cause people to lose their souls in Hell. Case in point, J. T. Smith and Homer Hailey."[77] After receiving "a number of inquiries" about his note, Smith published several articles restating his long-held objections to Hailey's view and labeling him a "false teacher." Smith acknowledged that some felt "compelled by . . . conscience to make brethren aware of one issue, and those who espouse it," and he had long sought to bring uniformity to the beliefs of his brethren on the question of divorce and remarriage.[78]

Several of the papers circulated among noninstitutional churches of Christ picked up on the Belen controversy, declaring themselves orthodox on the subject of divorce and remarriage and specifically warning against Homer Hailey. In a departure from the magazine's stated policies of not engaging in controversy and debate, Ed Harrell wrote an article in *Christianity Magazine,* the most widely circulated journal in noninstitutional circles, entitled "Homer Hailey: False Teacher?" Harrell did not endorse Hailey's views on divorce and remarriage, but his article pointed to the historical tolerance that had long existed within the restoration movement on subjects involving private conscience and noted that Hailey was a man who had "won wide esteem among Christians in spite of his views on the subject of divorce and remarriage." In an abrasive statement that angered many of those who had criticized Hailey's presentation in Belen, Harrell called "the recent personal attacks" on Hailey an "unheroic assault on an 85-year-old warrior."[79]

In the same issue of *Christianity Magazine,* a brief statement written by Hailey appeared in response to the attacks on him. He stated that he had held his views for forty-five years and that, while he had never "felt impelled to crusade" for his view, "I have never hesitated to express it when asked." Hailey was grieved that "all at once I find myself under attack by some, being charged as a false teacher, unfit for the fellowship of certain ones who differ from me." Hailey explained his understanding of the Belen incident and expressed some chagrin that the video "had been given wide circulation so that what was to have been a private study has become a brotherhood issue, which is regrettable." He concluded, "I do not intend to contribute to any division in the church over this issue," though he reserved the right to write in the future a "full presentation of the scriptural grounds for my position."[80] In a private letter to Ron Halbrook, Hailey repeated his understanding that he had "presented my views in a private meeting . . . a privilege we all cherish."[81] Hailey's rebuttal was subsequently published in the *Guardian of Truth* with comments by editor Mike Willis. Willis urged Hailey to "express his views that they may be tested to see whether or not they are from God." "I wish that I could see a way for a tolerance about this matter," Willis wrote, but he insisted that "false doctrine which leads to sin cannot be acceptable before God."[82]

The most immediate practical consequence of the controversy was Hailey's withdrawal from the lectureship program at Florida College in January 1989. In an official statement read at the opening of the lectures, President Bob F. Owen explained Hailey's absence: "During this past summer brother Hailey heard that some were not going to attend the lectures because he would be a speaker and one preacher intended to circulate an article urging others not to attend for this cause. Hearing this, brother Hailey called me and said he would not be on the program this year because he did not want to hurt the college or the lectureship."[83] It was a stunning and highly visible absence because the lecture theme for the year was the Old Testament prophets and the intent had been to highlight Hailey's scholarship; nearly every speaker quoted his writings profusely. Owen expressed a widely held sentiment: "I regret his not being here and I regret the problems that have arisen."[84]

Hailey was angered and hurt by the personal attacks on him. "It stung me deep," he said in 1989. He had been treated like "an old fellow in his dotage," Hailey believed, and he had been "sold down the river" by some who had posed as his friends.[85] He was disgusted by the tactics of his assailants, seeing them as men who had no purpose in life except to "get after guys." Of J. T. Smith, Hailey remarked, "I had him in classes, but I didn't teach him anything."[86] He was discouraged and disappointed: "I didn't want to spend my last years wrangling about something that would never be settled."[87]

Hailey wanted to strike back, even though he was eighty-five years old. He was a "mild-mannered boy," he confessed, but if his attackers thought he would not answer, "they are crazy."[88] As the discussion continued into the 1990s, it was hardly surprising that Hailey decided to write a defense of his views on divorce and remarriage. Many of his friends regretted his decision to answer because they felt that it would raise the debate to a new level. "If the right people had approached him and sat down and reasoned with him," mused his old friend Harry Pickup, Jr., "he probably would not have said as much as he has."[89] Many agreed with Clinton Hamilton's assessment, expressed in an open forum at the Florida College Lectures in February 1991, that Hailey had been goaded into making statements by "young men" with their own agendas.[90] Nonetheless, Hamilton, Ed Harrell, and others among Hailey's friends acknowledged that his public advocacy of his controversial views on divorce and remarriage made him a more schismatic figure.

In 1991 Hailey published a pamphlet entitled *The Divorced and Remarried Who Would Come to God* in which he fully developed his ideas. Hailey advised that he had "no intention of entering into or carrying on a discussion of the subject," and he urged readers to "read the material, accept it, reject it, or continue to study the question."[91] The publication of Hailey's pamphlet was surrounded by a spate of other short books on the question. Jerry Bassett published *Rethinking Marriage, Divorce and Remarriage,* defending many of the same views supported by Hailey,[92] and Mike Willis noted that Hailey's "false doctrines were immediately answered by several competent brethren."[93] Tracts critiquing the Hailey pamphlet were written by Maurice Barnett, Donnie Rader, and Gary Fisher and Dennis Allan, and most of the papers circulated among noninstitutional churches published extensive reviews of his position.[94] Probably the ablest of the critiques was Weldon Warnock's series of articles published first in the *Guardian of Truth* and subsequently in a tract. Warnock argued that Hailey's views on divorce and remarriage showed no respect for the Bible doctrine of repentance that required every penitent to "stop doing whatever is offensive to God."[95]

Hailey persevered through the attacks, but he considered the year after Belen a "wasted year."[96] Like James Bales and James Adams before him, Hailey was stunned that he had been singled out as a target. He was aware that two of his chief critics, Ron Halbrook and Mike Willis, held different views on the subject of divorce and remarriage, and he insisted that all positions on the subject were to some degree "controversial," including those that demanded that couples break up their marriages when they became Christians.[97] He was disappointed that so many had closed minds on the subject and were unwilling to "go to the Bible to see what I believed." It seemed to Hailey that the commitment to open-mindedness had vanished in a movement more and more tyrannized by "sectarian arguments."[98] "I've had some meetings canceled because some brethren said I hold strange views on marriage and divorce," Hailey told a group in Hawaii. "I suspect a lot of things are strange to some brethren, because all they've heard is tradition. Truth scares some people. Putting your mind in neutral is a lot more comfortable."[99]

Confronting the Fellowship Issue in Noninstitutional Churches

The dispute on divorce and remarriage that occurred at the end of the 1980s in noninstitutional churches of Christ, which in turn triggered yet another discussion of fellowship, served notice that those churches had entered a new cycle in their history. By the 1980s much had changed in noninstitutional churches of Christ that rendered the group ripe for internal bickering and controversy. Those who had opposed institutionalism had lived with an illusion of unity for two decades, even though they disagreed with one another about many significant doctrinal issues. So long as they kept all of their guns trained on the dangers of institutionalism, other differences rarely became targets. Once the institutional division had become a relic of history, as it had by the 1980s, and a new post-division generation filled the churches, the fighting tradition reappeared, intent on purifying the ranks of the noninstitutional churches of Christ.

Actually, a number of skirmishes erupted in noninstitutional circles in the decades of the 1970s and 1980s, generally initiated by *Truth Magazine* and other militant papers. One such controversy centered on a discussion of grace and the meaning of "unity in diversity" and led to the departure of Edward Fudge, who for a time edited the *Gospel Guardian,* and several other young men. The so-called "Neo-Calvinist" controversy also damaged the reputations of William E. Wallace and baseball celebrity and preacher Lindy McDaniel.[100] While Fudge and several other younger men clearly came to hold views that were incompatible with those of their brethren, the so-called "grace-fellowship" debate took on a life of its own and ultimately resulted in irresponsible attacks on the orthodoxy of such stalwarts as Leslie Diestelkamp, Eugene Britnell, Robert F. Turner, Robert C. Welch, Yater Tant, and Doyle Banta.[101] Turner was shocked and miffed when he was named by *Truth Magazine* editor Mike Willis in 1981. In his autobiography he wrote, "Also, in '81 an irresponsible editor of a paper charged me with six gross errors, offering out-of-context excepts from *Plain Talk* for proof. When I learned of it and wrote denying all six positions, he replied, 'you have not said in print . . . letter . . . [or] articles what you have said in private.' I had never seen the editor, nor had any other such conversations taken place. Then he wrote, 'It was with the hope that you would clarify your position that you have been mentioned' and 'we are giving you opportunity to reply.' Isn't that nice? Charges, with no proof, and the victim is guilty until he proves himself innocent. Ten years later he says he had misjudged my 'intentions' (hmmm!) and is 'sorry for any grief or difficulty . . . caused.' Just a sample of pressures created by inflated editors in their haste to police the brethren."[102]

The highly charged debate on divorce and remarriage that began in 1988, like the discussion of grace a decade earlier, led inexorably to discussions of fellowship. Predictably, much of the argument on both sides repeated the rhetoric of past generations who had grappled with the thorny dilemma of balancing a commitment to truth with a unity that tolerated contradictory biblical interpretations.

People were uncomfortable when disagreements arose, but notions about "brotherhood fellowship" were particularly hard to market in the "wild democracy" of noninstitutional churches of Christ. While all parties in the divorce and remarriage controversy agreed that each local church determined its own boundaries of fellowship, Hailey's critics nonetheless longed for some mechanism that would mark those whose teaching countenanced the acceptance of "adulterers" into local churches. Some went further, demanding the condemnation of anyone who associated with those who were "false teachers" on the question of divorce and remarriage and, indeed, with anyone who associated with those who continued to countenance the marked "false teachers."

When Yater Tant published articles by Lloyd Moyer and Gene Frost on the subject in 1964, he prefaced the discussion with an article about fellowship: "Let us all realize that 'the marriage question' does NOT affect the organization, work, or worship of the congregation at all. And there is no action by any congregation that forces a man to violate his conscience. If brethren can understand that this is a 'personal question' (like the matter of carnal warfare, the head covering for a Christian woman, whether or not a Christian has the right to vote, etc.) the discussion can be truly profitable and helpful." On the other hand, Tant warned, if "any one seeks to *force* his views on the congregation . . . then we have indeed opened up Pandora's box of troubles."[103] Tant believed that each divorced "couple . . . must decide for themselves . . . what God would have them do."[104]

In his 1978 exchange on the subject, James W. Adams zeroed in on the schismatic implications of using the term *false teacher* to describe conscientious brethren with whom one disagreed. He wrote, "Phillips and Connie Adams seem agitated over my insistence that the marriage question not become a test of fellowship among conservative churches. If they are serious in wanting it to become such, let them be consistent. . . . Do you just apply [this test] to some preacher here or there who may disagree with your concepts?" Adams pointed out that Phillips opposed Christians in "combat service in carnal warfare," judging all such to be "potential manslayers." "Is 'manslaying' less bad than 'adultery'?" Adams asked. He concluded, "Brethren, we cannot make everything about which we disagree a test of fellowship. Some things individuals practice about which we differ are just going to have to be tolerated. We are just going to have to let the Lord decide about some things. I confess that I do not have all the answers to all problems in these realms. We can live together concerning these matters if we are satisfied not to *press* our divergent views. Let those with permissive views hold them, not press them. Let those with conservative views in these matters not arrogate to themselves prerogatives of judgment that belong only to 'Him who judgeth wisely.' . . . My plea is for sanity, forbearance, and tolerance in these areas of disagreement in which the matter is individual and not collective in character."[105] H. E. Phillips replied that he was "far less concerned about brotherhood fellowship, where adultery and fornication in unscriptural marriages are winked at in order to secure and maintain fellowship, than I am in publicly debating . . . the truth and error of divorce and remarriage."[106]

The debate on the subject of fellowship that began in 1988 elicited a new batch of studies on the subject, including a booklet by Samuel G. Dawson, *Fellowship: With God and with His People,*[107] a sixteen-month series of articles written in *Christian-*

ity Magazine by Ed Harrell,[108] and several extensive reviews of Harrell's series in the *Guardian of Truth*.[109] In January 1992 the *Guardian of Truth* devoted an entire issue to the subject of "fellowship and the divorce and remarriage issue."[110] The "fellowship issue" came to supersede the "divorce and remarriage issue" as the center of controversy in the nineties.

Generally speaking, as in the case of most squabbles in the restoration movement, the fellowship debate in noninstitutional churches of Christ in the late eighties and nineties tended to divide the group into cliques surrounding opposing editorial positions. As the sole educational institution that received its support from members of noninstitutional churches, Florida College was placed in an awkward political position by the fellowship debate. The demands that Hailey be excluded from the 1989 lecture program at the college threatened to impose a brotherhood orthodoxy that placed Florida College in considerable jeopardy. President Owen expressed the college's view on the subject: "Those of us associated with Florida College do not envision our role as determining fellowship for our brethren in the Lord. We do not knowingly endorse or support those who are immoral or those who are factious but this does not preclude use of honorable men with whom some doctrinal differences exist. To do so would preclude using practically any person."[111] Indeed, the Florida College faculty included people who held a wide variety of views on divorce and remarriage and other disputed subjects.

To some people in noninstitutional churches, the fellowship controversy in the 1990s was symbolic of a new softness that pointed toward a new digression. Indeed, they saw Hailey and those who defended him as harbingers of a nascent liberalism in noninstitutional churches of Christ. In a sermon entitled "Trends Pointing toward a New Apostasy," preached widely throughout the country and subsequently published in a booklet, Ron Halbrook compared the trends in noninstitutional churches to the tensions that preceded the institutional division in the decades of the 1930s and 1940s.[112] The long list of symptoms of laxity Halbrook identified, in addition to winking at heretical teachings on divorce and remarriage, included reading "too heavily & with too little discernment the literature of evangelical writers," the emergence of "false concepts on grace & unity," the development of a "positive mental attitude philosophy," which he connected with such magazines as *Vanguard* and *Christianity Magazine,* and a tendency to be pliable on such "worldliness" as social drinking and dancing. "At the heart of all these trends," Halbrook concluded, "is a common softness—a tendency to drift, to relax, & to compromise [the] standard of truth—*therefore* potential for some or all of these trends to contribute to a larger movement of apostasy."[113] Halbrook ranged widely in his criticisms, but he particularly focused on the dangers posed by *Christianity Magazine,* which he saw as a reincarnation of the *Christian Leader,* a "source and a center for compromise."[114]

Halbrook's jeremiad sounded much like the pre–World War II warnings of the likes of J. D. Tant. Many of the older leaders in noninstitutional churches of Christ shared some of his misgivings. In a 1981 lecture at Florida College, Ed Harrell warned, "As long as brethren honor those who have no credentials but a knowledge of the word of God . . . who are unafraid to speak their mind, who care preeminently that the truth prevail, who have no fear of open confrontation—that long, and just that long, can they feel secure about themselves. When the time comes that the churches honor respectable managers (and surely it will come again, though, I think, not in my lifetime) it will then be time for every Christian to look in the mirror."[115]

Like the debates in the 1920s and 1930s in the churches of Christ, the arguments in noninstitutional churches of Christ in the 1980s and 1990s pitted like-minded people against one another. For all of the fussing and fighting at the end of the century, people in noninstitutional churches uniformly looked backwards for examples and authority. Everyone who wrote on the controversial themes of the nineties was a biblical conservative, intent on grounding his arguments in Scripture and willing to engage in honorable exchange. They had rediscovered the restoration truism that biblical literalists often become cranky and factious.

In such a setting it was impossible to define conservative and liberal boundaries using a single-issue litmus test. As Ed Harrell said in a public discussion with Mike Willis at Florida College in 1991, "I am reasonably certain that I stand to the right of Mike Willis on most of the unsettled questions that trouble our common conscience. . . . I regard Mike Willis as a brother not because I think he is right about every question, nor because we disagree only about unimportant matters, but because I believe that we are united by the singular intent to do God's will, and to defend our actions with a 'thus saith the Lord.'"[116] Still led by a generation of veterans of the institutional division, noninstitutional churches of Christ in the nineties were hardly fertile ground for "liberalism."

On the other hand, the profile of noninstitutional churches of Christ was changing, and, as in the years before World War II, those changes did signal the appearance of sociological and ideological differences within the movement. Contrary to the opinion of Leroy Garrett that the noninstitutional movement was headed down a "steady path toward extinction" because of its proclivity for strife and dissension,[117] in the eighties and nineties the group appeared to be growing rapidly. Many members of the Christian church defected to the churches of Christ in the 1930s, and Douglas A. Foster pointed to a similar pattern in the 1990s: "Not surprisingly, leaders in the anti-institutional churches are increasingly calling conservatives in 'liberal' mainstream churches of Christ to come over to them, and with some success."[118] As church growth accelerated and larger congregations multiplied, warnings about changing attitudes and doctrinal laxity could hardly be dismissed as figments of Ron Halbrook's imagination.

Nonetheless, alignments in the noninstitutional movement in the 1990s remained untidy and filled with ironies. In December 1987, just before joining in the attacks on Hailey, the *Guardian of Truth* published a glowing tribute to James W. Adams, the man who in 1978 repudiated the "opinions and pompous pronouncements of hot-headed zealots" whose zeal on the divorce and remarriage issue threatened to create parties in the churches of Christ.[119] "May God bless brother Adams," wrote Ron Halbrook in 1987, "for the good he has done and raise up other men who will be like him."[120] Hailey's harshest critics continued to advertise his books and recommend them, and they reprinted articles that he had written.[121] In 1980, the *Guardian of Truth* placed one of Mike Willis's articles on marriage, divorce, and remarriage on the page facing an advertisement of Hailey's first book, *Let's Go Fishing for Men.*[122] Such ironies, of course, were the stuff of restoration history.

It was transparently clear in the 1990s that the camps in the noninstitutional movement were neither clear nor stable. Marshall E. Patton, a widely respected preacher from Huntsville, Alabama, who wrote for *Searching the Scriptures* for many years, supported a somewhat deviant view on divorce and remarriage and in 1991 wrote a long series of articles that argued that Romans chapter 14 provided a basis for disagreements in matters of faith.[123] Melvin Curry, Hailey's successor as head of the Bible Department at Florida College, defended the same position in the *Guardian of Truth* in January 1979. "It must be recognized," Curry wrote, "that matters of difference between strong and weak brothers are not necessarily to be considered indifferent matters. At least one party in a dispute usually believes that participation in such activities would constitute sin." Curry insisted that "brethren have been able to disagree on hundreds of issues without withholding fellowship from one another" when such questions did not involve common activities. He appealed for freedom of expression: "Paul does not intimate that Christians are to cease from arguing their differences. Brethren must be free to preach and teach what they believe to be the truth, always being careful to listen to opposite views, and, above all else, studying what God has to say on the issue at hand."[124]

Conflicting cliques waxed and waned in noninstitutional churches of Christ in the 1990s. The *Guardian of Truth* remained in the vanguard of the attack on Hailey and *Christianity Magazine,* but its writers were in turn under siege from the witty and iconoclastic editor of *Sentry Magazine,* Floyd Chappelear. In 1996, Chappelear roasted the *Guardian of Truth* in an entire issue of his magazine.[125] At the same time, a fierce Christological debate had erupted that pitted a number of *Guardian of Truth* writers, and particularly Gene Frost, editor of the *Gospel Anchor,* against the associate editor of *Faith and Facts,* John A. Welch.[126] Welch protested that Mike Willis, Tom Roberts, Harry Osborne, Maurice Barnett, Dudley Ross Spears, and J. T. Smith were ready at all times to attack "positive preaching," but they were unwilling to "defend their cause when the real enemy is before them."[127]

For all the sound and fury, no broad-based platform for division existed among noninstitutional churches of Christ in the 1990s. No nexus of issues had emerged that clearly pointed to a divided mind in the movement. It seemed more likely, as in the case of the rebaptism controversy of the 1920s, that the debate over divorce and remarriage would rage for decades before either waning or, less likely, ending with the general acceptance of one position or the other.

Strains in a Common Mind

The kinds of tensions in noninstitutional churches of Christ at the close of the twentieth century were typical of those of periods of growth and expansion in the restoration movement when disagreement and debate provided doctrinal focus in the loose and unorganized movement. Frustrating and debilitating as the bickering was to those involved, and despite the broader signs of change that were visible on the horizon, in the 1990s, the noninstitutional churches of Christ had not reached one of those broad sociological and intellectual divides such as those that created permanent schisms in the 1890s and 1950s.

On the other hand, the clashes on divorce and remarriage and fellowship illustrated the continued dissonance between the underlying themes in restoration thought. Some of the early critics of institutionalism had been driven largely by a propositional understanding of the concept of restoration that, rooted firmly in a Baconian, common-sense hermeneutic, tended toward a sectarian view of the church. Others were motivated by a more general commitment to the principle of restoration, remaining open to change and acknowledging the ongoing nature of the search for the ancient order. The divorce and remarriage debate highlighted once again a tension between these fundamental motifs in restoration thought. Every person in noninstitutional churches of Christ was a distinctive personal mix of both concepts, but some defined their religious identity more narrowly and propositionally, while others had a higher tolerance for dissent and uncertainty.

These two diverging mind sets were illustrated by the writings of Mike Willis in the *Guardian of Truth* and Ed Harrell in *Christianity Magazine*. For Willis, fellowship involved a simple principle: "In matters of sin, fellowship must *not be extended* . . . in matters of authorized liberties, we must *receive one another*." Willis insisted that matters such as pacifism fell in the category of "authorized liberty," and he offered an extensive argument to prove that military service was not prohibited by the New Testament.[128] Frustrated by what he deemed a lack of clarity on the part of those who defended Hailey, Mike Willis demanded a concrete definition of the boundaries of fellowship: "Those who do not believe that we can understand the Bible alike need to come up with a list of those things that all men are expected to believe alike and those which men are unable to understand alike. Are we expected to understand these following items alike? Divorce and remarriage? Fellowship? The humanity/deity of Christ? Church support of human institutions (missionary societies, colleges, orphan homes)? Church worship? The action, purpose, and subject of baptism? The inspiration of the Scriptures? The deity of Christ? Belief in God? . . . We are moving away from the basic tenets of Scripture when we justify divisions among us on the grounds that we do not believe that men can understand the Bible alike."[129]

Sensitive to criticisms that writers for the *Guardian of Truth* did not themselves agree about the subject of divorce and remarriage, in 1996, Ron Halbrook sought to define precisely the limits of disagreement that could be tolerated. He listed twenty-one positions on which "brethren advocating the same fundamental truths on marriage, divorce, and remarriage have differed without dividing in my 30 years of preaching experience." The twenty-one variations he deemed acceptable because, he asserted, they existed among brethren who "share a common playing field of truth and differ only as to whether a given situation constitutes an infraction of the rules shared by all."[130] Still, in the minds of Willis and Halbrook, Homer Hailey's view was clear-cut heresy.

Ed Harrell's view of the restoration movement was more historical and less tidy. He argued that members of churches of Christ had been united historically by a commitment to a common-sense hermeneutic in finding New Testament patterns, but, at the same time, acknowledged that the movement had always tolerated a degree of diversity among those who judged one another honorable seekers of truth. Harrell accepted the truism that unity-in-diversity did indeed exist within the restoration movement, as James W. Adams had ten years earlier, but sought rational limits to that diversity, arguing that the "bounds" of fellowship were limited by a number of factors, including "factiousness," "clear and open immorality," "a good conscience," and "judgments about the *clarity* of New Testament instruction." Fellowship decisions, Harrell wrote, were sometimes "informed by my estimation of the honesty and sincerity of a brother."[131] It was these sorts of judgments, he argued, that had compelled him to separate from institutional brethren who seemed to no longer share his basic hermeneutical assumptions, while at the same time continuing to fellowship Homer Hailey and others with whom he had serious differences of faith.

Harrell's ideas drew on a separatist tradition that still remained quite strong in noninstitutional churches of Christ.[132] In the 1990s, such thinking was manifest in the highly spiritual writing of Paul Earnhart on the Sermon on the Mount[133] and in the writings of many younger preachers. Through the years, no one more intelligibly captured that separatist outlook, with its central commitment to New Testament primitivism, than Robert F. Turner. In a 1982 lecture at Florida College, Turner insisted that "there are some things in which we can and must be the same," but, at the same time, he acknowledged that the single principle that united restorers was an "earnest desire and honest effort" to follow truth. Turner elaborated on the difference between principled commitment and creedal correctness: "There can be no genuine fellowship between one man who earnestly desires to know God's will and do it and another who travels the path of human wisdom and majority rule. In reality, the bond of 'Christian' fellowship among saints is not so much the uniformity of practice, or even of doctrinal conclusions per se (these being the *fruits*), but it is rather the spirit and attitude that produces such fruits. For example, two men who do the same thing religiously—one because he sincerely believes God wants it that way, and the other because he likes it that way and has no intention of changing, regardless of God's word—may be less unified than two men whose practice is different, but who are both sincerely searching for truth and are willing to conform to all truth found. The first two will drift further apart; the second two will be drawn together in the paths of God. . . . Biblical unity, as a practical reality among men, is the common ground and sharing relationship experienced by those who make seeking after God their life's work. Biblical unity is not a goal achieved and placed on our trophy shelf, but is an open-ended way of life. . . . It cannot be bottled and capped by any human level of understanding but must remain a challenging mountain upon which all truth-seekers climb. We *have* the Biblical unity available to fallible creatures, *in the process of seeking it.*"[134]

Turner used a 1994 exchange with Ron Halbrook as an occasion to reassert his generalist view on the division of the fifties: "For several years in the fifties I left home, family and guaranteed support, to try to meet the special need of that day. But I also know that balance is necessary. It was wrong then to conclude a church was 'sound in faith' merely because it did not support sponsoring elders or orphan homes. If any made such claim, liberal brethren were right in saying those 'issues' had become their creed. A church, and a preacher, must be measured by much more than what they believe about some special problem, important though it may be."[135]

These conflicting attitudes were placed in clear focus in 1994 when the elders of the church in West Columbia, Texas, drafted a list of twenty-eight questions to be answered by preachers with whom the church had a relationship because they wanted to be certain they were using "the Lord's money wisely in supporting men who are proclaiming the gospel in its entirety and 'with all boldness.'" When they were criticized for creating a creed, Ron Halbrook sprang to their defense. Halbrook insisted that the elders did not intend "to create a creed," but he and the church were soon engulfed by a tidal wave of charges that they had done precisely that.[136] Halbrook found himself answering to some of the most vocal attackers of Homer Hailey, including *Gospel Truths* editor J. T. Smith, who urged that it was time to "cease and desist . . . sending out the catechism."[137] Among other things, Smith pointed out that Halbrook's "creed" omitted "Marshall Patton's position and the mental divorce position on divorce and remarriage," two of Halbrook's twenty-one acceptable deviations that were offensive to Smith.[138]

Robert F. Turner challenged the questionnaire in an exchange with Halbrook in the *Guardian of Truth*. Granting the "good intentions" of the elders of the West Columbia church, he insisted that "the elements of a creed are present in what was done."[139] Halbrook replied that "the real danger is not elders asking questions but brethren winking at unmistakable signs of a new apostasy."[140] However, with no "personal animosity" and "fully believing in the writer's good intentions," Turner insisted that the questionnaire did show "creedal tendencies." He repeated in the *Guardian of Truth* his long-held and often-articulated understanding of the general Christian commitment: "In seeking to teach others we explain the N. T. as we believe it to be. . . . What else can we do? But here we face a critical point. We must not build their faith on our beliefs, but strive to 'sanctify the Lord God' in their hearts, so that they build their faith from his teaching. We are asked, 'What does the church of Christ teach on divorce?' I reply, 'The church is not the source of any teaching. God's word says . . . ' I have no right to set forth my beliefs as the standard for others. What the Holy Spirit wrote is completely adequate for that. My own beliefs must be constantly subject to testing by that rule."[141]

At the end of the exchange, Ron Halbrook insisted that he and Turner were not far apart. In practice, he was correct. On the other hand, Halbrook and Turner did represent opposite ends of the spectrum of restoration thinking. Halbrook, who was fond of quoting Roy E. Cogdill, was a classic propositional thinker; his attacks on Hailey and others led inexorably to the drawing of well-defined and rigid doctrinal boundaries. Such thinking was fundamentally flawed in the eyes of Robert Turner, whose grasp of a people committed to the general principle of following truth had made him the most important conceptualizer of the noninstitutional vision in the 1960s.

The Hailey/divorce and remarriage/fellowship controversy highlighted again both the cohesive and divisive tendencies in churches of Christ. The controversy caused much heat, and probably damaged the reputations of Hailey and those who defended and attacked him. On the other hand, noninstitutional churches of Christ in the 1990s continued to survive as a community of faith in the midst of acrimonious debate.

Digging for Roots

By the 1990s, noninstitutional churches of Christ had become something of a microcosm of the larger movement. Some in noninstitutional churches were drawn to the conservatives in the institutional churches of Christ who themselves waged war on divorce and remarriage heretics and who, beset by progressive critics, also sought a propositional definition of the "brotherhood" that would eliminate the perils of an open and free environment of nonsectarian debate. Hopeful of finding some common ground, hundreds of preachers assembled in three meetings to discuss their differences, the first in 1968 in Arlington, Texas, and the second two in the 1970s in Dallas and Nashville. Old friends who had been separated for years by institutional disagreements explored unsuccessfully the possibility of bridging the old chasm.[142] By the 1970s they belonged to distinct religious groups with very different agendas.

More surprising was a rapport that developed between the progressive left wing within the institutional churches of Christ and those in noninstitutional churches who held quite traditional doctrinal views. To some degree, however, they shared a respect for restoration primitivism and separationist sentiments. The writings of such progressives as Richard T. Hughes, Douglas Foster, Michael W. Casey, and C. Leonard Allen owed a good deal to Ed Harrell's sociological critiques of the restoration movement, and these men frequently shared platforms with him to bemoan the loss of the separationist ("apocalyptic," to use Hughes's term) vision in mainstream churches of Christ. Nonetheless, while their critiques of mainstream churches of Christ were strikingly similar, the progressives looked forward to evangelical thought and modern scholarship for new insights and directions, while those with a separatist vision in noninstitutional churches continued to look back to the New Testament, using traditional hermeneutical tools.

People throughout the restoration movement continued to feel ties of kinship because they still held many ideas in common. Homer Hailey illustrated the combination of loyalties that often made people seem inconsistent and unpredictable. His love for Foy E. Wallace, Jr., made him overlook Wallace's personality flaws. Hailey knew that Wallace was "self-assured and self-confident," and he knew that he himself was "not of that disposition" and did not like controversy, but his love for Wallace never waned. He regarded him as the "greatest pulpit man I ever saw."[143] Others, including Roy Cogdill, had tried to fill his shoes, Hailey observed, but they "couldn't do it."[144]

On the other hand, Hailey never cared much for those who emulated Wallace's heresy-hunting tactics. He was never close to Cogdill: "I have never been an admirer of Roy Cogdill. I could tolerate him but I was never close to him. . . . He was a lawyer and he had a legalistic spirit. . . . Everyone else admired him so I never said much."[145] He decried the tendency of many of the papers to promote controversy: "I'm pretty well of the opinion that the church would have been better off if no one had ever written for one."[146] "One of the things that discourages people is that they see this lack of love and enthusiasm among us," Hailey said in a sermon. "They ought to see something in us that they want."[147] He was equally disgusted that many seemed totally unconcerned about teaching the gospel to the lost. He wrote to his old friend Yater Tant, "Yater, I don't know what is wrong with our people; I have tried to figure it out—maybe they are like I am, just so busy doing this and that. . . . Most of our brethren are not doing anything in most places. . . . Well, let's keep on trying to get the old fire going again."[148]

Hailey was intrigued by the honors he received late in his life from such places as Pepperdine University and Abilene Christian University. His name still resonated in such places. He was remembered as one of the best of the generation that rejected pomp and denominational pride, called people back to the Bible, and built the churches of Christ. William S. Banowsky, in his controversial speech "The Christ-Centered Church" delivered at the Abilene Christian University Lectures in 1996, began with a personal recollection that momentarily reconnected the disjointed movement: "Mother and Dad met on this campus and were married by their Bible teacher, Homer Hailey, in the parlor of Zellner Hall."[149] In his book on fellowship that was aimed primarily at understanding the growing schism in the institutional churches of Christ, F. LaGard Smith came to the defense of Homer Hailey, "a godly man greatly wronged—a spiritual giant whose last years are being wasted in ignominy." From his office on the plush Malibu campus of Pepperdine University, Smith lamented the persecution of "one of God's finest."[150] Such attention surprised Hailey, and made him wonder: "Do they think I am weak or liberal? Maybe because I'm not aggressive. . . . I don't know why."[151]

In some ways, these distant relatives in restoration still shared a common vision. Hailey had long grasped the sociological dynamics at work in the restoration movement; indeed, his book *Attitudes and Consequences in the Restoration Movement* had sketched out the patterns of division in churches of Christ.[152] In 1988, when C. Leonard Allen, Richard T. Hughes, and Michael R. Weed wrote *The Worldly Church,* Hailey believed they had "nailed down" the problems confronting the churches of Christ and he endorsed their "call for biblical renewal."[153] "Radicalism alienated some of those fellows," Hailey judged late in his life, and he wondered whether a better spirit might have saved these good-spirited progressives.[154]

Hailey shared much with the progressives in the institutional churches of Christ, but they were also worlds apart. He rejected the narrow propositional, creedal approach to restoration thinking that could be found in both institutional and noninstitutional churches of Christ, and he responded enthusiastically to the progressive exposés of a denominational and worldly church of Christ, but Hailey would never have been comfortable in the left wing of the churches of Christ. During a visit to Abilene in the 1980s, he sat through a service in an institutional congregation and felt extremely uncomfortable.[155] For all of the affronts he suffered from his noninstitutional brethren in his declining years, he had ended up where he belonged.

8

Homer Hailey

Persona and Legacy

Westerner

FROM HIS EARLIEST MEMORIES of train rides and wagon trips into the unorganized territory of Arizona, Homer Hailey imbibed the spirit of the American West. "There is something about the bigness of Arizona," Hailey reminisced. "When you hit the Davis Mountains, your soul begins to expand." Whatever one's state of mind, after a ride through the desert, viewing the upraised arms of saguaro, one's "problems evaporate." Had he not been a preacher, Hailey would have liked to have been a forest ranger, roaming across the primal landscapes of Arizona.[1]

Hailey's character was honed in the simplicity of frontier life. He learned not to worry: "There is something about this country that is not conducive to worry. . . . [with the] simpler life and the bigness of this country, you just don't worry." One learned to live life really, without fluff and clutter. Many modern young people were reared in the midst of "confusion," Hailey bemoaned, a luxury that frontier youngsters were spared: "I never knew what confusion was. I've never been confused. I always knew I was going to have to work. . . . I knew where I was going."[2] Always a "happy fellow," he never mistook happiness for "exuberance," and he never engaged in self-pity and maudlin nostalgia.[3]

The pragmatic realism of the American frontiersman was branded deep into Hailey's character. He loved Western music; he did not appreciate the music of the "long hairs"—either the classics or rock.[4] Hailey was always "gentlemanly around women" and never "vulgar," yet Harry W. Pickup, Jr., remembered that Hailey's "humor was earthy," rooted in the manly banter of cowboys and frontiersmen.[5] Never a joke teller, Hailey had a "marvelous sense of humor" that sparkled in barbed repartee.[6] Hailey's passion for physical fitness, his early fondness of boxing, and his love of guns were all a part of his Western persona. He had a sense of frontier justice that was restrained only by his Christian convictions. "God gave a man a temper," Hailey maintained, and he saw nothing wrong with "righteous indignation." He struggled to "learn to control it."[7] Nonetheless, when told by Harry Pickup, Jr., that someone had misrepresented him, Hailey replied, "Picky, I should have beaten the devil out of him a long time ago."[8] "He was such a human kind of a guy," recalled James R. Cope, but no one ever doubted that "he was a fair fighter."[9]

Hailey believed in "hero admiration"; he was convinced that modern youth lacked heroes with character. He frequently ticked off the predictable role models that he had cherished from the time he was a youth—George Washington, Robert E. Lee, and "Stonewall" Jackson. There were other heroes who fit neatly into his background—"Jack Dempsey, and possibly an old western outlaw or two and a few Indian fighters of earlier days."[10] Hailey admired Will Rogers: "I don't know what we would have done in that Depression without Will Rogers." Hailey respected Cochise, who had "a streak of honor about him," and, begrudgingly, Geronimo, because "those fellows were willing to fight for their homeland," although he regarded Geronimo as a "skunk." He had a similar admiration for modern Americans who showed true grit—Douglas MacArthur, Dwight D. Eisenhower, and Harry Truman.[11]

Like most westerners, Hailey was an arch-conservative patriot. His prejudices ran deep against the "punks in the 1960s" who tried to destroy "patriotism."[12] Hailey never imagined that the United States was a "Christian nation," but when he was young, he recalled, "at least it was decent."[13] He bemoaned the rampant materialism he saw in modern society and the breakdown of families.[14] The United States had become "so corrupt and so wicked that I don't see how we can last."[15] "We are asking for judgment," Hailey told an audience in Honolulu in 1980, "and God's going to give it to us—it will curl the hair of all of us and put the beauty parlors out of business."[16] Hailey believed that God still ruled in the destiny of nations. He wrote in his commentary on the minor prophets, "National sin demands national repentance. As this applied to Nineveh, so it applies to the nations of today."[17]

Much about politics in modern America disturbed Hailey. A committed conservative who believed that "Hoover would have worked it out" during the Depression had he been given a chance, Hailey was convinced that Franklin D. Roosevelt moved the country toward "socialism" and "communism," pandering to "people who want something for nothing." Hailey's hall of political heroes was predictable—Barry Goldwater, Ronald Reagan, George Wallace, and Richard Nixon. And his villains were just as predictable—the American Civil Liberties Union ("an atheistic, communist gang"), Lyndon Johnson (who "out-Roosevelted Roosevelt"), and John F. Kennedy.[18]

Hailey was incensed most by what he saw as an increasing unwillingness on the part of the government to take "vengeance on evil doers." Disgusted by the plague of drugs, Hailey insisted that "you can stop . . . this stuff if you want to." He recommended shooting down the airplanes and sinking the boats that smuggled drugs into the country. Firmly opposed to Christians participating in war because wars were generally little more than a conspiracy by a "bunch of politicians," Hailey believed that capital punishment was "the Lord putting offenders to death through the government." Hailey sometimes spoke graphically and with gusto about the need to execute "arch-criminals." He suggested, "Make them comfortable in the electric chair." For the worst of them, he would be happy to "pull the switch" and "send them to hell where they belong."[19]

Hailey always admitted that he was a deeply prejudiced man. He was "violently prejudiced against the gay movement": "God Almighty made it a capital offense and destroyed cities because of it."[20] In addition, he confessed, "Racially, I'd be a little prejudiced." Looking back, Hailey came to see that much of his prejudice came from his "environment and background," and he "tried to overcome it."

Hailey's prejudices were always general, never personal. He loved black Christians as sincerely as white. Having once been rebuked by a colleague because of a prejudicial racial remark he made in a chapel service at Florida College, Hailey asked permission to speak to the assembly the next day. He apologized to the entire chapel assembly and tried to explain to them the personal background that had caused such prejudices in his life.[21] Colly Caldwell vividly remembered sitting in Hailey's classroom when the news came that John F. Kennedy had been shot: "He sincerely prayed for Kennedy. . . . We were all moved."[22] Even his deepest political prejudices were overwhelmed by his Christian anticipation of "victory." He told his friend John Kilgore, "I may vote again, but I may not," because, in the end, the world could only be changed by "changing the hearts of people."[23]

Christian

The image of Homer Hailey that would endure in the memories of "countless [people] who have been imprinted" by the acquaintance with him, wrote his friend Clinton D. Hamilton, was that of a man of "godly character, devout faith, and great knowledge of holy writ."[24] Throughout his life, Hailey carefully preserved his moral integrity. He always enjoyed the company of women, but he never allowed "sexual temptation" to occupy his mind, "because it was wrong." Hailey believed that modern preachers were peculiarly tempted by sexual sins because the nation was a "sex-oriented society" and because modern counseling techniques "contribute to the problem." His answer to temptation was "just not to think of it."[25] "A man's escape from temptation," he advised, "is through the power of God."[26]

Never unctuous or sanctimonious, Hailey was a profoundly spiritual man. "Prayer has had a very important place in my life," he revealed to John Kilgore. He regarded the lack of spiritual commitment to prayer to be the weakest link in the restoration heritage: "Very few of God's people ever learn to pray."[27]

The central motif in Homer Hailey's life was an unwavering, common-sense faith in God. He could never remember a time in his life when he had "a doubt about the existence of God." He found nothing in the Bible "difficult to accept." He told John Kilgore, "I have no problem with anything that the Bible says that I understand. My problem is in understanding fully what it is saying. Once I understand what it is saying, I have no problem." Acknowledging that the Bible might sometimes "challenge my imagination," Hailey noted that nonetheless "when I accept God, anything he says is easy to accept." Most of the practical problems that people encountered in life could be traced to a "lack of faith in God."[28]

Hailey's religious faith was always practical and nonspeculative. He thought deeply about the mysteries of Christianity, but he was uncomfortable in opaque theological waters. He believed profoundly that man was a creature with a free will and that from the beginning God "did not know what man would do," having a "plan for man had he not sinned" and "also a plan revealed in the gospel should he sin." However, he confessed that such ideas ventured into a "realm that is too deep for me." After preaching a sermon on the nature of God, he concluded that the subject was "too big for me." He also had speculated about whether human beings were dual or triune in nature, but he concluded, "Matters of this kind have always been difficult for me, because by nature I am not a fellow disposed to get into things like that. A thing that I can't prove one way or the other and know absolutely, I don't give it too much mind."[29]

Hailey's study, writing, and preaching all reflected his practical turn of mind. "Higher education is more theory than it is practical things," he concluded early in life; too often, a doctoral degree was simply an "ego trip." The same practical bent limited his reading: "I want to read something that is true. . . . I never did read Calvin. . . . I figured he was wrong."[30]

There was not an ounce of pretense in Hailey. He recognized his limitations as a scholar; he knew he had not read widely, and, at the end of his life, he confessed, "I'm very ignorant." He never imagined that he was a "leader type" and he systematically refused to be pushed into positions of prominence that demanded administrative skills.[31]

Those closest to him found Hailey to be unswervingly honest and honorable in discussion. Clinton Hamilton wrote, "As we have had discussions on topics on which we have had some disagreement, he has never been arrogant, haughty, or irritable. His arguments have been buttressed by what he believes the Bible teaches. . . . Arguments and repartee are not his long suits. Stating truth with grand sweeps, eloquence, and simple elegance, he does as well as, or better than, any of his fellows."[32] "If he believed a certain thing was right," recalled his friend Harry W. Pickup, Sr., "he'd show you he was right and he'd let you know that [was] what he was going to do."[33] In the classroom, recalled Colly Caldwell, Hailey entertained questions and readily discussed them, but he would not "sit around and argue about it." He was soon back on his lesson because "he had so much to tell his students about what the Scripture said."[34]

Hailey was "very careful about what he would say publicly, particularly about personalities," recalled Jim Cope.[35] For many years his views on divorce and remarriage were little known. "I have always been hesitant to go out on a limb," Hailey stated in later years.[36] Partly, Hailey simply wanted to go on about his work without being interrupted by squabbling; partly, he was impatient discussing subjects that seemed beyond settlement at the time; partly, he saw the complexity of many issues that others reduced to simple solutions; and partly, as stated by Bill Humble in 1988, he "stands for what he believes and is going to preach it, but he is non-judgmental."[37]

If Hailey had a major character flaw it was his naivete. Widna was a realist who bristled at the slightest criticism of Homer; her husband playfully called her "Suspicia." "My wife has a memory problem," Hailey joked, "She can't forget anything."[38] Her judgment of Homer's "weakest point" was telling: "He is too good for his own good. He will let people do things to him. . . . He judges other people by himself."[39] Hailey's problem, said his friend Harry Pickup, Jr., was that he was "naive in terms of issues." He lacked the political instincts of B. C. Goodpasture, Roy E. Cogdill, or Fanning Yater Tant and was incapable of reacting to political pressures to gain popularity. Because he was totally devoid of "the denominational spirit that characterizes many of our preachers," observed Bob Owen, "he [was] not much of a line-drawer." Never an "issue-seeker or a flag waver, his ticket [was] 'I'll tell you what the Bible says.'"[40]

Hailey's personality showed through in his preaching. "I never set out to be a big preacher," he said late in his life. "All I ever wanted to do was to do the Lord's work. . . . To make people see the truth."[41] Year after year as he departed to conduct summer meetings, he was all business. The routine that he preferred, and for many years almost insisted upon, was two services a day, interrupted by one meal, a nap, and an afternoon of study. "I don't want to do any sightseeing or playing golf," Hailey insisted: he went to a church in order to communicate the vital truths of the Scriptures.[42] His "greatest joy" was to stand in the pulpit; he could hardly wait to get to the meeting house so he could begin to preach.[43]

At the end of his life, Homer Hailey remained mystified by his success. "After fifty-five years, I don't know how to preach," he told John Kilgore. Always bothered by a "poor speaking voice," Hailey thought his preaching was mediocre: "I don't like to listen to myself. . . . I'm not what I would call a good speaker. . . . I was not a great preacher." In his own estimation, his sermons were never entertaining and seldom sensational; they were usually just "plain vanilla."[44] In some ways, even his strongest supporters agreed. "There was nothing novel about his preaching," Harry Pickup, Jr., recalled; indeed, people liked him because his sermons were devoid of "novel interpretations."[45]

Hailey's immense popularity in churches of Christ was easily explained. First, people stood in awe of his startling command of Scriptures. Not only did Hailey flawlessly quote scores of biblical passages in every sermon, a practice he began early in his life, but he also had the "ability to put Scriptures together in a logical arrangement." His audiences were astounded by his ability to quote hundreds of verses in a lesson without referring to the biblical text, but they were even more amazed by the extraordinary sweep of his biblical knowledge that took him blithely through the obscure recesses of prophetic passages and other remote texts where few preachers ventured. Added to the display of learning that was a part of every Hailey presentation was a transparently fervent and sincere spirit. "I was zealous for what I was doing," Hailey recalled. "There is nothing sham about me."[46] Homer Hailey was a man filled to the brim with the Scriptures; he had little interest in other matters.

Hailey counseled young preachers beginning in the days when he was a part-time faculty member at Abilene Christian College. The first quality necessary to preach, he believed, was "dedication to the Lord." He knew "a few preachers" who had "ego problems," and he overlooked the faults of his friends, but most of the preachers he knew were "good old boys who came out of the woods." It was those good-spirited men, men with deep "desires to see souls saved," who had built the churches of Christ in Hailey's lifetime.[47]

The second quality demanded for good preaching was study. He advised young men to establish a routine of serious study: "Learn what God said. And then try to pray for the wisdom to make the right application of it . . . so that Jesus Christ will be exalted and not you." Hailey never liked to deliver a sermon without at least an hour of preparation, going over already familiar texts, re-memorizing passages. When his preaching "flopped," it was generally because he was tired, or he had not had sufficient time to study, or he was speaking on a theme that was "beyond my grasp at the time."[48]

Most of Hailey's friends believed that his greatest talent was as a teacher. Some of Hailey's students might take the material they had learned from him and "do better with it in the pulpit than he did," surmised Jim Cope, but Hailey had few peers in the classroom because he had a "unique ability to draw things together."[49] One can "go deeper" in the classroom, Hailey noted, because the teacher was not bound by severe time restraints. "We don't meet often enough" in church services, Hailey complained, and too often people simply accepted the teaching without question. In the classroom, young people had "inquiring minds" and they "want to know the why."[50]

The secret to Hailey's success as a teacher and as a preacher was preparation. After many years of teaching a heavy load, Hailey systematically tried to spend two hours of "specific preparation" before teaching each class.[51] Colly Caldwell recalled, "He never was falling back on what he knew before. He always restudied everything. . . . He always had something fresh."[52] He entered every class in hopes that he could "challenge my students." Hailey's formula was simple: "Know your material, love your work, have control of your class."[53] In the words of Melvin Curry, he was "a teacher who walked humbly with God."[54]

People Remembered

In ninety-five years of living, much of it in the public eye, one's life intertwines with those of many others. Homer Hailey recalled a long stream of people who had influenced his life for good. There was his mother, Mamie, a "very unique woman," "a pioneer type," who bequeathed to him an "interest in life" and a will to live in the midst of adversity.[55] Additionally, there were Mrs. Huffman and Mrs. Browning, the two women who encouraged Hailey as a young Christian and who turned him toward preaching.[56] Several of his teachers influenced him, including the venerable R. C. Bell at Abilene.[57] In his early years as a preacher, Hailey was molded and impressed by the hearty pioneers of the older generation—Frank B. Shepherd, Early Arceneaux, C. R. Nichol, and, above all, Foy E. Wallace, Jr.

Hailey believed that he became a "composite" of the personalities of the older men of the generation that preceded him. He ticked them off at the end of his life: C. R. Nichol was a "master debater," "a shrewd operator, a sharp blade"; Early Arceneaux was the "greatest logician among us" whose "cold blooded" commitment to truth Hailey sought to emulate; the preaching of C. M. Pullias, who prolifically quoted Scripture, became a model for Hailey's famous pulpit manner; R. L. Whiteside was a fine student of the Scriptures, though Hailey found him "so dry" as a preacher that he was ineffective. The list of old-time acquaintances went on and on—H. Leo Boles, J. D. Tant, N. B. Hardeman, and, of course, his hero of heroes, Foy E. Wallace, Jr.[58]

The institutional division in the churches of Christ ruptured many friendships that Hailey had cherished. In the 1950s Hailey stopped to visit his old friend Gus Nichols in Alabama and found him "cordial but not warm."[59] It was a story repeated often by those who lived through those trying years. However, those older associations were replaced by new ones.

Hailey came to know and love most of the leaders of the non-institutional movement. Hailey had a "great admiration for brother John T. Lewis," the patriarch of churches in the Birmingham area. Contrary to the views of many who considered Lewis cantankerous, Hailey found him to be moderate and reasonable in defending his views on women wearing a covering, kneeling in prayer, and other doctrinal questions. Lewis had a similar respect for Hailey.[60] Hailey was a "great admirer" of Bryan Vinson, Sr., of Texas, regarding him as "very sound in all of his thinking."[61] He and Yater Tant were fast friends who remained loyal to one another through various adversities.

Hailey's strongest personal ties in the last half of his life were with his colleagues at Florida College and friends he made in the Florida churches where he preached. Perhaps his closest friends in the Tampa area were Ed Britt, who preached in the small community of Cork, and his wife, Ginny. Well into his nineties Hailey continued to visit Cork to preach in meetings and visit with the Britts. He relished his early association with Pat Hardeman, Bill Humble, Eugene Clevenger, and Louis W. Garrett. Garrett's wife, Margie, was his loyal friend and indispensable editor. He shared deep personal friendships with Harry Pickup, Sr., Franklin Puckett, Melvin Curry, and Bob Owen. He had a profound personal respect for his other colleagues, James R. Cope, James P. Miller, and many others.

Hailey was not essentially a social person. "Homer never spent his time gregariously," recalled Bob Owen. "Hanging back of his desk was a little sign that said, 'Come to the Point.' " Owen continued, "It is hard to get into a conversation with Homer, and not get into a Bible conversation."[62] That was the basis for Hailey's profound and deep personal friendship with Clinton Hamilton.[63] They were kindred spirits. Hamilton reminisced, "Our walks together, our talks about subjects of mutual interest, and our prayers together in various places, including stops on the golf course during walks in the night, all linger as wonderful memories."[64]

People Who Remember

The list of lives touched by Homer Hailey is long indeed. Leading the roster would be the students. Many of them—Bob Owen, Melvin Curry, Colly Caldwell—left their own imprints on Florida College. "You come as close as anyone I know to having the mind of Paul," scribbled Melvin Curry in a note to Hailey after hearing him lecture. "I love you like a father." After thirty-three years of teaching at Abilene Christian College and Florida College, he was a father figure to thousands. How could one measure the influence that he had exerted on so many young lives? Most of his students carried away memories of the breadth and sweep of Hailey's lectures. A few wrote letters to tell him. "Your classes this year have been so very enriching for me," wrote a young woman in 1975. "I hope that there will be a day that I can in turn influence some life as you have mine." Another young woman wrote in 1970, "I want to thank you for all that you have done for me this year. You have helped to make my life richer and fuller by the example that you set for all around you and your dedication to God. . . . *Thank you* so much for all the wonderful lessons. I feel now that I have come closer to God and I feel I will come to know Him better as I further my studies in His Word."[65]

None of Hailey's students were more loyal to him than the group of "preacher boys" he taught at Abilene in the years immediately after World War II—a group that included Bob Owen, Bill Fling, Robert Bolton, Dudley Stout, Paul Faulkner, Johnny Ramsey, and LeRoy McDonald. Even the institutional division never totally separated Hailey from the men who had shared his enthusiasm during those years. They loved him profoundly. One of them wrote to him in 1970, "You will probably never know the extent of the great influence you have been on so many people in your life, but I . . . express my sincere appreciation to you for the Godly life you have lived and the great help you have been to me personally."[66]

Hailey had a profound influence on a generation of preachers. "As I sit here studying John and reading your book," a young man wrote to Hailey in 1975, "I am reminded of the great debt I owe you for introducing me to a true love of the Scriptures. . . . I am now a preacher myself . . . with children of my own and the responsibilities of teaching God's word. Because of your gift to me, I have made it my goal to give the same gift to as many others as are disposed to accept it. I have already seen eyes light up with new love for the Scriptures. . . . I believe [their understanding] is [because of] you as well[,] hence this note from me." Another young man wrote in 1982, "Ten years have passed since I left Florida College, but you would be surprised to know how often you have been remembered for your sermons, lectures and other discussions. . . . I'm sure that you have taught some who have become gospel preachers who preach to large crowds and have well known reputations among God's people. But, there are many others who have been greatly influenced by you and you will probably not know, without such a letter as this. I'm sure that there are many, like myself, who will never be widely known among the church." As a final example, one of his Arizona friends wrote to him in 1987, "Homer, I know the time will come when you won't be among us anymore, but I want you to know that you have been the strongest influence in my preaching efforts. . . . We dearly love you for this and will never forget the example you have set for us to follow."[67]

Sometimes Hailey's dual influences as teacher and preacher were virtually indistinguishable. In 1987, he received a note from a former student, signed "A fellow Christian." The man wrote, "When I first came to FC in 1964, I wasn't a Christian, but I was able to recognize your scholarship." In 1987 the writer was a deacon in a local church, and he had taken his sons to a meeting to hear Hailey preach: "Take heart, we are listening. . . . Thank you for your influence, and being the stable rock in righteousness. . . . My children share my enthusiastic thirst to share your knowledge." Such letters accumulated through the years, from individuals, from elders, from entire congregations: "Thanks for coming our way. . . . Generations yet unborn will be blessed as the result of your lifetime of study and teaching. We thank you for what you shared with us, and honor you for your life."[68]

Hailey's unique standing in the American restoration movement was recognized by Pepperdine University. In April 1987, during the annual lectureship program, Pepperdine University President David Davenport presented Hailey with a Christian Service Award. When the award was conferred at a "preachers-elders" dinner, Hailey received a standing ovation from the hundreds in the audience after delivering a short acceptance speech. The generous recognition had been arranged by Jerry Rushford, the lectureship director and head of the Religion Department at Pepperdine, and the proceedings included tributes from several of Hailey's old acquaintances. Hailey's friend and colleague during his early years at Florida College, Bill Humble, spoke movingly of Hailey's "remarkable influence on the young preachers in his classes." Humble recalled an incident at Abilene Christian University when Hailey returned for a class reunion: "Dr. Paul Faulkner introduced him in chapel. As Paul tried to tell the ACU student body what bro. Hailey had meant to him, his voice was choked with emotion. That is typical, I think, of the impact bro. Hailey had on so many young preachers."[69]

The Pepperdine honor was laden with meaning, both for Homer Hailey and for the restoration movement. It showed, as Humble put it, that amidst the differences that had estranged former brethren, all "can still honor a great servant of the Lord." Hailey was careful that his brief acceptance speech implied no "compromise of his convictions." He spoke on a theme he had preached for fifty years, calling "young preachers to be faithful to the old ways." Bill Humble believed the occasion illustrated that "we are still one brotherhood and one body, even though we may not see eye-to-eye on every single disputed issue."[70] It probably proved less than that. It was rather the nostalgic death rattle of a generation who remembered a united church. The occasion was, no doubt, as Humble remembered, "a beautiful occasion," reminding separated brethren why they had loved one another, but it was little more.

Still, both at a personal and at a public level, Hailey's life reached across the walls that compartmentalized churches of Christ in the years after World War II. He maintained cordial, and sometimes close, relationships with former students who by the 1990s were scattered across the spectrum of churches of Christ. In 1997, Hailey was honored by Abilene Christian University for his life of service. Asked to speak for two minutes, the ninety-four-year-old warrior launched into a twenty-minute lecture on the legacy of the past. "He really raked us over," recalled Abilene historian Douglas A. Foster. In a fitting closing of the circle, in 1998 Hailey returned to Temple Terrace to be honored by Florida College along with other pioneer faculty members.

Nonagenarian

Widna's health declined rapidly in the 1990s. She remained committed to serving Gordon even as her own health failed. In 1996, Gordon spent much of September, October, and November in the hospital and Widna slept little as she cared for him. On the morning of January 8, 1997, she died, worn out by the exertions of a life of service to those whom she loved. Gordon's health continued to deteriorate and on February 6, four weeks and a day after the passing of his mother, he also died in Tucson. The two were buried in Roanoake, Alabama, beside the grave of Widna's first husband. In a final personal tragedy in 1997, Hailey's oldest daughter, Roma, died on December 26.

Hailey considered a number of alternatives after the death of Widna. He wanted to return to Abilene to live on the Manly ranch with his son Rob and his family, but after a long visit, he decided it would not be wise. He had difficulty walking on the rough ground at the ranch. He returned to Tucson, sold his house, and moved into an apartment constructed with him in mind by Ruby Stroup, a loyal friend to Widna and to him. Ruby had been devoted to Homer ever since his return to Tucson, typing all of his manuscripts and acting as his secretary, and she was Widna's closest friend and confidant. She admired Homer and had drunk deeply of his teaching. At age ninety-four, he called her the "Shumanite woman" who was prepared to rescue him in his last years. She and Homer had the same ideas about nutrition; he still drank his protein health drink each day and ate one healthful meal.[71]

Never one to look back, always an activist, Homer Hailey still bristled with new ideas and exciting discoveries in his nineties. He jotted off papers on troublesome texts and continued to write books. He had always had a one-track mind, he reasoned: "When I am writing a book my whole life is in it. When I am in a meeting, my whole life is in it."[72] Year after year—reaching into his ninety-fifth year—the study routine continued. He wrote a commentary on the book of Job, and another study of God's eternal plan and the covenants, both of which were published by the Religious Supply Company in Louisville.[73] At age ninety-five, he looked ahead.[74] "I have a little hankering to write a book on the Edomites," he said in a 1997 conversation, and then his mind wandered on: "I think I could write a pretty good book on Ezekiel. . . . But it is too late now. . . . I would like to write a book on Daniel. . . . Daniel for the twenty-first century. I believe I could do a good job of that."[75]

All one can do with life is "fill it up," Hailey said with no signs of regret. All in all, life had been "wonderful."[76] "I don't know anything I would change," Hailey told John Kilgore. He lost on nearly "every investment I ever made," but he never really cared about money. He was saddened by the untimely death of Lois, but her suffering prepared him for the loss.

Overall, he could not recall "having a real sorrow." He had an unfailing ability to put both his failures and his successes behind him. He told Kilgore, "It is not my disposition, if I ever accomplish anything, to brag on it. . . . I haven't done anything great. Just wrote those books and taught those kids and preached my head off all during those years."[77] That was pretty much it.

Like all parents, Hailey worried most about his children. They had sometimes disappointed him spiritually. However, he exhorted them to faithfulness, and he prayed for them. "Let them know you are concerned and pray," that was all a parent could do, Hailey reasoned. In the end, things turned out well. He was thankful that in his nineties he had the respect and love of his children and grandchildren. The Hailey clan gathered in Nashville in 1993 to celebrate his ninetieth birthday and again on the Manly ranch in 1997 in his ninety-fourth year. Homer bristled with pride as the wholesome group of children and grandchildren gathered around him, no one smoking, drinking, or cursing; almost all of them active church members.[78] His eldest daughter, Roma, died in December 1997, but all of his other children stayed in touch with him regularly.

Homer Hailey possessed a profound confidence in the providence of God. He believed that "God was directing my life to the end that he had in mind." If one prays that God's will be done in his life, it will be so. "I've seen the providence of God in my life all the way through," Hailey insisted. Thus, he could live at peace with every decision he had made; he could see the hand of God in his encounter with the Huffmans in Willcox, in his journey to Abilene, in his decision to move to Florida, and in the magical moment he met Widna. God had blessed him richly for his service: "I have been respected and honored by people." He had never asked for so much, and he would have followed the path of God's providential leading without it, but he received the happiness and joy with satisfaction and thankfulness.

Oracle

Homer Hailey maintained an active schedule into 1999. He continued to write, he still preached and taught classes in congregations all over the country, though he usually declined to travel far from home, and he entertained a constant stream of friends and former students who visited him in Tucson. On Sundays, he went to Oracle. The drive from Tucson to Oracle was a steady upward grade for twenty-nine miles, the crisp desert air exaggerating the brightness of the desert horizon. An old mining town, Oracle remained at the end of the twentieth century a village mired in its frontier past—still secluded from the floods of tourists who clogged Tucson.

Since 1980, on most Sundays Homer Hailey had driven up the highway from Tucson to Oracle to preach and teach. In 1996, he turned the preaching over to George Peck, a seventy-year-old whom Hailey had trained for years, though Hailey continued to teach a morning class. Widna and Gordon accompanied him until they were no longer able to make the trip, and Ruby Stroup drove him to Oracle after that. The neat little building usually held about ten people on Sundays. Anyone who visited Oracle would hear Homer Hailey sweep through the pages of the Bible with a nimbleness and erudition rarely encountered at the end of the twentieth century. He had lost little of his legendary recall of Scripture, and he ranged gracefully from Exodus to Revelation, visiting remote passages here and there in Isaiah and Ezekiel, speaking passionately on "the man of sin" in 2 Thessalonians, chapter 2. Each week there was a refreshing enthusiasm as he presented "new views that I have developed in my studies."

The scene in Oracle on Sunday mornings was almost surreal. In front of ten students stood a gnarled master craftsman, a man who had been many places and influenced countless lives. Was it possible and was it fitting that this story should end in Oracle? It was all right. Homer Hailey had lived his life full cycle and had come back home. He first preached to a little group of women in Willcox. He traveled far and learned much, he received honors and won the respect and love of thousands, but all he had ever intended to do was preach the gospel. So, in the midst of his tenth decade, he studied his lesson on Saturday, engrossed in the grand themes that had filled his mind for years on end, and on Sunday he crafted a fresh message filled with truths newly grasped. Everything else had always been peripheral.

Notes

1. Homer Hailey and the Churches of Christ: An Institutional History and a Personal Saga

1. See Richard T. Hughes, ed., *The American Quest for the Primitive Church* (Chicago: University of Illinois Press, 1988); Richard T. Hughes and C. Leonard Allen, *Illusions of Innocence: Protestant Primitivism in America, 1630–1875* (Chicago: University of Chicago Press, 1988).
2. See Nathan Hatch, *The Democratization of American Christianity* (New Haven: Yale University Press, 1989).
3. For an overview of the restoration movement, including bibliographical citations, see David Edwin Harrell, Jr., "Restorationism and the Stone-Campbell Movement," in Charles H. Lippy and Peter W. Williams, eds., *Encyclopedia of the American Religious Experience* (3 vols.; New York: Charles Scribner's Sons, 1988), vol. 2, pp. 845–58.
4. David Lipscomb, "Strange Developments," *Gospel Advocate,* January 23, 1884, p. 49.
5. *Missouri Christian Lectures* (Kansas City: J. W. Smart, 1886), pp. 101–2.
6. George Smith, "No Man Wishes Women to Keep Silence in the Churches," *Christian Standard,* October 7, 1893, p. 798.
7. See Bureau of the Census, *Religious Bodies: 1926* (2 vols.; Washington: Government Printing Office, 1929), vol. 2, pp. 394–400, 466–78.
8. Ibid., p. 400.
9. Winfred Ernest Garrison and Alfred T. DeGroot, *The Disci-*

ples of Christ: A History (St. Louis: Christian Board of Publication, 1948), p. 405.

10. *List of the Preachers of the Churches of Christ* (Nashville: McQuiddy Printing, 1906).
11. Ibid., pp. 30–31.
12. On this point, see the section entitled "A Cleavage Becomes a Division," in Garrison and DeGroot, *Disciples of Christ,* pp. 404–6.
13. Richard T. Hughes, *Reviving the Ancient Faith* (Grand Rapids: William B. Eerdmans, 1996).
14. For information on the growth of Harrison County, see Randolph B. Campbell, *A Southern Community in Crisis: Harrison County, Texas, 1850–1880* (Austin: Texas State Historical Association, n.d.).
15. Ibid., pp. 367–95.
16. Nancy Blakeley Ruff, *Harrison County, Texas* (Baltimore: Gateway Press, 1987), p. 165.
17. Vernon B. Schultz, *Southwestern Town: The Story of Willcox, Arizona* (n.p.: Board of Regents of the Universities and State College of Arizona, 1964), pp. 89–96.
18. Ibid., p. 160.
19. See Stephen Daniel Eckstein, Jr., *History of the Churches of Christ in Texas, 1824–1950* (Austin: Firm Foundation Publishing, 1963), pp. 239–62.
20. "Showalter and Otey," *Firm Foundation,* October 9, 1951, p. 7. See Ed Harrell, "The Bounds of Christian Unity (11)," *Christianity Magazine,* December 1989, p. 358.
21. Leroy Garrett, *The Stone-Campbell Movement: An Anecdotal History of Three Churches* (Joplin: College Press Publishing, 1981), pp. 400–401, 582.
22. *Firm Foundation,* September 1884, p. 1.
23. See Earl Irvin West, *The Search for the Ancient Order* (4 vols.; Indianapolis: Religious Book Service, 1950), vol. 2, pp. 397–404.
24. Rob Hailey, interview with the author, August 11, 1988, Abilene, Texas.
25. For a good description of the physical setting of the Sulphur Springs Valley, see Schultz, *Southwestern Town,* pp. 1–15.
26. Homer Hailey, taped conversations with John Kilgore, Tucson, Arizona, tape no. 3.

27. Kilgore tape no. 2; Homer Hailey, interview with the author, March 19, 1993, Tucson, Arizona.
28. Kilgore tape no. 2.
29. Garrison and DeGroot, *Disciples of Christ,* p. 394.
30. Bureau of the Census, *Religious Bodies: 1926,* vol. 2, p. 473.
31. Kilgore tape no. 3.
32. Bureau of the Census, *Religious Bodies: 1926,* vol. 2, p. 477.
33. Thomas R. Burnett, "Burnett's Budget," *Gospel Advocate,* July 4, 1895, p. 419.
34. Kilgore tape no. 3.

2. *The Churches of Christ, 1920–1950: A Heritage of Controversy*

1. Homer Hailey, taped conversations with John Kilgore, Tucson, Arizona, tapes no. 5 and 8.
2. Foy E. Wallace, Jr., "The Gospel Guardian," *Gospel Guardian,* October 1935, p. 2.
3. *Firm Foundation,* February 18, 1941, p. 4. Richard Hughes stated that "the loss of cultural respectability Churches of Christ experienced in the aftermath of their separation from the Disciples in 1906" combined with the trauma of World War I to retard any serious growth in the early years of the twentieth century. *Reviving the Ancient Faith* (Grand Rapids: William B. Eerdmans, 1996), p. 145.
4. Bureau of the Census, *Religious Bodies: 1936* (3 vols.; Washington: United States Government Printing Office, 1941), vol. 2, pp. 462–70.
5. See Robert E. Hooper, *A Distinct People* (West Monroe, Louisiana: Howard Publishing, 1993), p. 80.
6. Ibid.
7. Cled E. Wallace, "Strict in His Demands," *Gospel Advocate,* September 7, 1933, p. 844.
8. G. H. P. Showalter, "History of the Church during the Last Fifty Years," *Firm Foundation,* February 25, 1941, p. 4.
9. *Firm Foundation,* March 1, 1939, p. 4.
10. *List of the Preachers of the Churches of Christ* (Nashville: McQuiddy Printing, 1906), pp. 30–31.
11. Quoted in Robert E. Hooper, *Crying in the Wilderness: A Biography of David Lipscomb* (Nashville: David Lipscomb College, 1977), p. 313.

12. See Hughes, *Reviving the Ancient Faith,* p. 194; Leroy Garrett, *The Stone-Campbell Movement: The Story of the American Restoration Movement* (rev. ed.; n.p.: College Press Publishing, 1997), p. 395.
13. Wallace, "The Gospel Guardian," p. 2.
14. Frank B. Shepherd, "Rethinking Our Religion," *Gospel Guardian,* October 1935, p. 21.
15. Foy E. Wallace, Jr., "Broken Cisterns," *Firm Foundation,* September 1, 1936, p. 1.
16. L. L. Brigance, "Common Sense," *Bible Banner,* September 1939, p. 24.
17. Wallace, "Broken Cisterns," p. 1.
18. Will J. Cullum, "The Division, and Sin of Hobby Riding," *Firm Foundation,* February 4, 1938, p. 6.
19. Ibid.
20. See Hughes, *Reviving the Ancient Faith,* p. 219; Garrett, *The Stone-Campbell Movement,* pp. 435–38.
21. Mac Lynn, *Churches of Christ in the United States* (Nashville: Gospel Advocate Co., 1991), pp. ix–x. Two debates on the Bible class issue are Joe S. Warlick and George W. Phillips, *A Debate on the Sunday School Question* (Dallas: n.p., 1925), and Roy Deaver and Lester Hathaway, *Debate on the Bible Class Question* (Abilene: Chronicle Publishing, 1952).
22. Guy N. Woods, "The Menace of the Y. P. M. Society," *Firm Foundation,* March 17, 1936, p. 1.
23. Otis Gatewood, "Reply to Guy N. Woods, Y. P. M.," *Firm Foundation,* August 9, 1938, p. 3.
24. G. H. P. Showalter, [Editorial], *Firm Foundation,* October 21, 1930, p. 2.
25. W. T. Kidwell, "Answers to Queries," *Firm Foundation,* October 13, 1931, p. 2.
26. G. H. P. Showalter, "Marriage, Divorce, Salvation," *Firm Foundation,* October 10, 1939, p. 4.
27. Quoted in Hughes, *Reviving the Ancient Faith,* p. 193.
28. Garrett, *The Stone-Campbell Movement,* p. 84.
29. Foy E. Wallace, Jr., "Concerning Factions," *Gospel Advocate,* August 3, 1933, p. 732.
30. B. C. Goodpasture, "Religious Papers and Divided Churches," *Gospel Advocate,* July 20, 1933, p. 684.
31. See David Edwin Harrell, Jr., *Quest for a Christian America*

(Nashville: Disciples of Christ Historical Society, 1966), pp. 139–74.

32. J. D. Tant, "War: Its Effect upon the Church," *Gospel Advocate*, July 14, 1898, p. 443. See also Fanning Yater Tant, *J. D. Tant: Texas Preacher* (Lufkin, Texas: Gospel Guardian Co., 1958), p. 201.
33. David Lipscomb, *Civil Government: Its Origin, Mission and Destiny, and the Christian's Relation to It* (Reprint; Nashville: Gospel Advocate Co., 1957).
34. See Hooper, *Crying in the Wilderness*, pp. 110–22.
35. David Lipscomb, "Christians and Politics," *Gospel Advocate*, July 15, 1880, p. 446. See David Edwin Harrell, Jr., *The Social Sources of Division in the Disciples of Christ, 1865–1900* (Athens: Publishing Systems, 1973), pp. 26–30.
36. See Michael W. Casey, "From Pacifism to Patriotism: The Emergence of Civil Religion in the Churches of Christ during World War I," *Mennonite Quarterly Review*, July 1992, pp. 376–90. Casey has done excellent research on pacifism in the twentieth-century churches of Christ. See also Michael W. Casey, "Cordell Christian College," *Chronicles of Oklahoma* 76 (Spring 1998): 20–37.
37. Hooper, *Crying in the Wilderness*, p. xiii.
38. Quoted in Casey, "From Pacifism to Patriotism," p. 381.
39. Ibid.
40. Ibid., p. 386.
41. Foy E. Wallace, Jr., "The Mind of the Brethren on the War Subject," *Firm Foundation*, May 1, 1934, p. 4; see Earl Irvin West, *The Search for the Ancient Order* (4 vols.; Germantown, Tennessee: Religious Book Service, 1987), vol. 4, p. 348.
42. W. W. Otey, "Attitude of Church toward War," *Firm Foundation*, October 22, 1935, p. 1.
43. See Michael W. Casey, "Warriors against War: The Pacifists of the Churches of Christ in World War Two," unpublished manuscript in the possession of the author, p. 4.
44. G. H. P. Showalter, "The Relation of Christians to War," *Firm Foundation*, April 14, 1942, p. 4.
45. Cled E. Wallace, "The Gospel Advocate and the Goose-Step," *Bible Banner*, June 1945, p. 9. See also Cled E. Wallace, "An Editor Tiptoes around a Vexing Problem," *Bible Banner*, February 1943, pp. 6–7.

46. West, *Search for the Ancient Order,* vol. 4, p. 348.
47. John T. Lewis, *The Christian and Government* (Birmingham: John T. Lewis, 1945). In his booklet, Lewis reviewed the attacks on pacifism made by Foy E. Wallace, Jr. See Hughes, *Reviving the Ancient Faith,* p. 261.
48. See Terry J. Gardner's account of Wallace's reversal, "Foy E. Wallace, Jr.: The Bible Banner Years, Part One," *Faith and Facts,* January 1997, pp. 62–68.
49. N. B. Hardeman, "The Banner Boys Become Enraged," *Firm Foundation,* October 28, 1947, pp. 1–3.
50. Quoted in Casey, "Warriors against War," p. 11.
51. Cled E. Wallace, "More for the Record," *Bible Banner,* September 1944, p. 2.
52. Cled E. Wallace, "The Gospel Advocate and the Goose-Step," p. 9.
53. Casey, "Warriors against War," p. 12.
54. Don Carlos Janes, "Conscientious Objectors," *Firm Foundation,* February 17, 1942, p. 7; see West, *Search for the Ancient Order,* vol. 4, pp. 346–52.
55. G. H. P. Showalter, "Church of Christ Men in Civilian Public Service Camps," *Firm Foundation,* April 27, 1943, p. 12.
56. Chester Estes, "Concerning Conscientious Objectors to Combatant Service," *Firm Foundation,* November 10, 1942, pp. 4–5.
57. Murrey W. Wilson, "Concerning Conscientious Objectors to Combatant Service," *Firm Foundation,* October 27, 1942, p. 4.
58. "Service Committee for Conscientious Objectors," *Firm Foundation,* November 23, 1943, p. 9; "Conscientious Objectors' Fund Grows Rapidly," *Christian Chronicle,* July 21, 1943, pp. 3, 8.
59. W. W. Otey, "Keep the Record Straight," *Firm Foundation,* August 12, 1947, p. 7.
60. W. W. Otey, "Who Are the Martyrs?" *Firm Foundation,* December 14, 1943, p. 3.
61. G. H. P. Showalter, "Still Confused," *Firm Foundation,* October 28, 1947, p. 3.
62. Richard T. Hughes has argued in a number of papers that this is the defining theme in the restoration movement. Hughes stresses premillennialism as the primary theological carrier of the movement's sense of cultural alienation. Richard T. Hughes, "People without Memory: Churches of

Christ and the Triumph of American Progress," unpublished paper in the possession of the author.

63. Casey, "Warriors against War," p. 27.
64. West, *Search for the Ancient Order,* p. 185. See pp. 179–211.
65. For an introduction to the rise of dispensational premillennialism in America see George M. Marsden, *Fundamentalism and American Culture: The Shaping of Twentieth-Century Evangelicalism* (New York: Oxford University Press, 1980).
66. See Hughes's chapter "A Shifting Worldview: The Premillennial Controversy," in *Reviving the Ancient Faith,* pp. 137–67.
67. See Harrell, *Quest for a Christian America,* pp. 39–53; Harrell, *The Social Sources of Division,* pp. 24–25.
68. See Hughes, "People without Memory."
69. Ibid., p. 39.
70. See West, *Search for the Ancient Order,* vol. 4, pp. 179–82; William E. Wallace, "Profile of a Movement," typescript manuscript in the possession of the author, n.d., n.p.
71. See Hooper, *Crying in the Wilderness,* pp. 317–18.
72. See H. Leo Boles and R. H. Boll, *Unfilled Prophecy: A Discussion on Prophetic Themes* (Nashville: Gospel Advocate Co., 1928), pp. 5, 181.
73. H. Leo Boles, "Boles-Boll Debate," *Gospel Advocate,* November 3, 1927, p. 1051.
74. West, *Search for the Ancient Order,* vol. 4, p. 185.
75. *Neal-Wallace Discussion* (Nashville: Gospel Advocate Co., 1933), pp. 194, 217. Quoted in William E. Wallace, "Profile."
76. Quoted in Wallace, "Profile."
77. Foy E. Wallace, Jr., *Modern Millennial Theories Exposed* (Houston: Roy E. Cogdill, 1945) and *God's Prophetic Word* (Houston: Roy E. Cogdill, 1946).
78. West, *Search for the Ancient Order,* vol. 4, p. 204.
79. William E. Wallace, "Profile."
80. J. N. Armstrong, "A College President Goes on Record: Again," *Bible Banner,* February 1939, pp. 5–9.
81. Foy E. Wallace, Jr., "The Common Ground of Fellowship," *Gospel Guardian,* October 1935, p. 3.
82. See West, *Search for the Ancient Order,* vol. 4, p. 186.
83. John T. Lewis, "The Cause, Curse and Cure of Whispering Campaigns," *Bible Banner,* September 1939, pp. 6–7.

84. Wallace, "Broken Cisterns," p. 1.
85. See West, *Search for the Ancient Order,* vol. 4, pp. 182–210.
86. G. H. P. Showalter, "Twisting and Turning," *Firm Foundation,* October 31, 1939, p. 4.
87. Foy E. Wallace, Jr., "The Gospel Advocate's Restated Policy," *Bible Banner,* December 1940, pp. 2–3.
88. See Foy E. Wallace, Jr., "The Advocate's Adamant Attitude," *Bible Banner,* June 1943, pp. 14–16.
89. Fanning Yater Tant, interview with the author, August 20, 1988, Birmingham, Alabama.
90. See West, *Search for the Ancient Order,* vol. 4, pp. 204–7; William E. Wallace, "Profile."
91. See Wallace, "Profile."
92. Hughes, *Reviving the Ancient Faith,* p. 160.
93. L. C. Sears, *For Freedom: The Biography of John Nelson Armstrong* (Austin: Sweet Publishing, 1969), p. 287.
94. Hughes, *Reviving the Ancient Faith,* p. 228.
95. Ibid., p. 166.
96. Hughes, "People without Memory," p. 3.
97. Ibid., p. 36.
98. Hughes, *Reviving the Ancient Faith,* p. 145.
99. Roy E. Cogdill, "Claude F. Witty and the Dallas Meeting," *Firm Foundation,* October 1, 1935, p. 2; Tant interview.
100. Hughes, *Reviving the Ancient Faith,* p. 149.
101. See Hooper, *A Distinct People,* pp. 238–40.
102. David E. Harrell, "The Sectional Origins of the Churches of Christ," *Journal of Southern History,* vol. 30 (August 1964), p. 277.
103. Hughes, *Reviving the Ancient Faith,* p. 224.
104. Ibid., p. 150.
105. For discussions of the rise of institutionalism in the churches of Christ, see Michael W. Casey, *Saddlebags, City Streets, and Cyberspace: A History of Preaching in the Churches of Christ* (Abilene: ACU Press, 1995), pp. 37–46; Hughes, *Reviving the Ancient Faith,* pp. 217–53.
106. See G. C. Brewer, "About Organizations," *Gospel Advocate,* September 28, 1933, pp. 914–15, 925.
107. Wallace, "Broken Cisterns," p. 1.
108. Bureau of the Census, *Religious Bodies: 1936,* vol. 2, p. 470.
109. See William E. Wallace, "Profile."

110. Terry J. Gardner, "Foy E. Wallace, Jr.," *Faith and Facts,* July 1996, p. 39.
111. C. A. Norred, "A Homily on Benevolences," *Gospel Guardian,* March-April 1936, p. 39.
112. Foy E. Wallace, Jr., "The Morrow Foundation," *Gospel Advocate,* May 25, 1933, pp. 492–93. See William E. Wallace, "Profile."
113. See Hughes, *Reviving the Ancient Faith,* pp. 228–30; Steve Wolfgang, "A Life of Humble Fear: The Biography of Daniel Sommer, 1850–1940" (M.A. thesis, Butler University, 1975); William E. Wallace, "Profile."
114. F. B. Srygley, "Brother Daniel Sommer's Visit to Nashville," *Gospel Advocate,* March 9, 1933, pp. 228–29; "Brother Sommer's Visit to Nashville," *Gospel Advocate,* April 13, 1933, pp. 348–49.
115. G. H. P. Showalter, "Bethany College," *Firm Foundation,* August 5, 1947, p. 9.
116. Wallace, "The Gospel Guardian," p. 2.
117. Foy E. Wallace, Jr., "Jehovah-Nissi: The Lord My Banner," *Bible Banner,* July 1938, p. 5.
118. Hugh M. Tiner, "Dancing in 'A Play,' " *Firm Foundation,* April 23, 1946, p. 4.
119. G. H. P. Showalter, "Should Our Christian College Be Standard?" *Firm Foundation,* October 27, 1936, p. 6; " 'Christian Education'—What Others Say," *Firm Foundation,* December 22, 1936, p. 4.
120. Isaac E. Tackett, "Abilene Christian College Is Not Guilty," *Firm Foundation,* January 5, 1937, pp. 4–5.
121. William E. Wallace, "Profile."
122. Ibid.; Hughes, *Reviving the Ancient Faith,* pp. 228–35.
123. G. C. Brewer, "About Organizations," *Gospel Advocate,* October 12, 1932, pp. 962–63.
124. R. L. Whiteside, "Some Questions," *Firm Foundation,* November 11, 1930, p. 5; J. W. Chism, "An Open Letter to the Regents of Abilene Christian College," *Firm Foundation,* December 2, 1930, p. 3.
125. C. R. Nichol, "Religious Digest," *Firm Foundation,* August 11, 1931, p. 1.
126. Don Morris, "Abilene Christian College," *Firm Foundation,* May 6, 1947, p. 3.

127. See Hughes, *Reviving the Ancient Faith,* pp. 231–33.
128. See G. C. Brewer, "Foy Versus Foy," *Firm Foundation,* September 9, 1947, p. 6.
129. See William E. Wallace, "Profile."
130. Foy E. Wallace, Jr., "The Blight of Hobbyism," *Gospel Advocate,* June 15, 1933, p. 566.
131. William E. Wallace, "Profile."
132. Foy E. Wallace, Jr., "Concerning Christian Colleges," *Firm Foundation,* January 19, 1937, pp. 1, 3.
133. Hooper, *A Distinct People,* pp. 285–86.
134. Frank S. Mead, *Handbook of Denominations* (5th ed.; Nashville: Abingdon, 1970), p. 85.
135. West, *Search for the Ancient Order,* vol. 4, p. 354.
136. Ibid., pp. 353–98.
137. G. C. Brewer, "Evangelizing the World in the Post War Period," *Firm Foundation,* February 16, 1943, pp. 7–8.
138. G. C. Brewer, "Broadway Church . . . ," *Christian Chronicle,* July 14, 1943, pp. 3, 8.
139. G. C. Brewer, "More about the After-the-War Missionary Program and Other Post-War Problems," *Firm Foundation,* July 13, 1943, pp. 5–6.
140. George S. Benson, "Evangelizing the World in the Post-War Period," *Firm Foundation,* March 23, 1943, p. 9. For biographical information on George S. Benson, see Edward L. Hicks, *Sometimes Wrong but Never in Doubt: George S. Benson and the Education of the New Religious Right* (Knoxville: University of Tennessee Press, 1994), and John C. Stevens, *Before Any Were Willing: The Story of George S. Benson* ([Searcy: Harding University], 1991).
141. Ulrich R. Beeson, "After-the-War Missionary Program," *Firm Foundation,* September 14, 1943, p. 3. See Atheleton Crawson, "The World as a Field: After the War," *Firm Foundation,* April 6, 1943, pp. 6–7.
142. Jimmie Lovell, "It Can Be Done," *Firm Foundation,* August 15, 1944, p. 7.
143. See "A Request for Information," *Firm Foundation,* March 7, 1944, p. 11; P. D. Wilmeth, "Getting Acquainted with Our Preaching Brethren," *Firm Foundation,* March 3, 1942, p. 3; "The Utah Campaigns," *Firm Foundation,* June 15, 1943, pp. 8–9; "Utah Campaigns for 1944 and Accomplishments in

Utah Campaigns of 1943," *Firm Foundation,* April 18, 1944, pp. 8–9.

144. *Firm Foundation,* February 16, 1943, pp. 1–2. See West, *Search for the Ancient Order,* vol. 4, pp. 352–55; Harvie M. Pruitt, "Germany," *Gospel Advocate,* October 1997, pp. 22–24.
145. M. Norvel Young, "Otis Gatewood to Make Survey," *Firm Foundation,* July 31, 1945, p. 13.
146. "Sherrod and Gatewood Leave for Europe," *Firm Foundation,* July 9, 1946, p. 11.
147. M. Norvel Young, "General Clay Admits Two Missionaries to Germany," *Firm Foundation,* June 24, 1947, p. 10; "Three Families of Workers Arrive in Europe," *Christian Chronicle,* May 28, 1947, p. 1.
148. M. Norvel Young, "Gatewood Requests Food for Starving and Undernourished," *Firm Foundation,* September 2, 1947, p. 4.
149. "German Mission Work," *Firm Foundation,* November 7, 1950, p. 3.
150. *The Lubbock Lectures on Mission Work* (Lubbock: Broadway Church of Christ, 1946), pp. 5, 40–41. Quoted in William E. Wallace, "Profile."
151. "Opportunities in Japan and China," *Firm Foundation,* September 2, 1947, pp. 2–3.
152. "Memphis Church to Send McMillan on Survey Trip in Japan," *Christian Chronicle,* August 27, 1947, p. 1.
153. "Churches Laying Plans for Hailey to Make Religious Survey in Japan This Fall," *Christian Chronicle,* October 1, 1947, p. 1.
154. Homer Hailey, interview with the author, March 19, 1993, Tucson, Arizona.
155. See *Christian Chronicle,* November 24, 1948, p. 8.
156. "$70,000 Program for Italy Undertaken by Brownfield, Texas Church," *Christian Chronicle,* March 31, 1948, p. 5.
157. "Abilene Christian College Lectureship," *Firm Foundation,* March 18, 1947, p. 7.
158. Ibid., p. 8.
159. William E. Wallace, "Profile."
160. "Some Preachers Meetings," *Firm Foundation,* February 15, 1938, p. 4.

161. See Earl Irvin West, *The Life and Time of David Lipscomb* (Henderson, Tennessee: Religious Book Service, 1954), p. 271
162. O. C. Lambert, *Gospel Guardian,* March-April 1936, p. 4. Quoted in William E. Wallace, "Profile."
163. *Torch,* August 1950, p. 25. Quoted in Wallace, "Profile."
164. For information on the growth of colleges, see West, *Search for the Ancient Order,* vol. 4, pp. 69–108; for information on orphan homes, see pp. 109–26.
165. Mead, *Handbook of Denominations,* p. 85.
166. See William E. Wallace, "Profile."
167. R. N. Alexander, "Why Abilene Christian College Is Asking for $43,000,000," *Firm Foundation,* July 16, 1946, p. 5.
168. "Worldwide Evangelism Planned," *Christian Chronicle,* July 7, 1943, pp. 1, 3.
169. "Gatewood to Teach Missionary Training Courses at Pepperdine," *Christian Chronicle,* August 2, 1944, pp. 1, 7.
170. *Abilene Christian College Bulletin,* March 1947.
171. G. H. P. Showalter, "The Power and Danger of the Christian College," *Firm Foundation,* April 8, 1947, p. 8.
172. W. W. Otey, "Please Suffer a Few Words," *Firm Foundation,* April 22, 1947, p. 3.
173. G. H. P. Showalter, "Some Observations of the Colleges," *Firm Foundation,* April 1, 1947, pp. 8–10.
174. J. D. Tant, "Who Are the Cowards," *Firm Foundation,* October 14, 1947, pp. 8–9.
175. For a good discussion of the early years of the postwar institutional crisis, see William E. Wallace, "Profile."
176. Roy E. Cogdill, "A Challenge to Wilburn Whittington," *Gospel Guardian,* March 22, 1956, p. 708. See Wallace, "Profile."
177. See, particularly, G. C. Brewer, "Brother Otey Misses the Mark and Wounds the Bystanders," *Firm Foundation,* June 10, 1947, pp. 1–3; W. W. Otey, "Keep the Issue Clear," *Firm Foundation,* November 11, 1947, pp. 6–7; W. W. Otey, "Hardeman and Otey," *Firm Foundation,* October 14, 1947, pp. 6–7.
178. Quoted in Wallace, "Profile."
179. G. H. P. Showalter, "The College," *Firm Foundation,* May 27, 1947, p. 8.

180. Glenn L. Wallace, "Support Abilene Christian College," *Firm Foundation,* August 19, 1947, p. 3.
181. G. H. P. Showalter, "Reflections," *Firm Foundation,* July 1, 1947, p. 8.
182. L. R. Wilson, "More about the Bible College Question," *Firm Foundation,* June 24, 1947, p. 3; "New College Organized," *Firm Foundation,* June 17, 1947, p. 9.
183. "New President of Florida Christian College Outlines Plans," *Christian Chronicle,* June 22, 1948, p. 7.
184. G. C. Brewer, "Sound and Unsound Men in Our Present Crisis," *Firm Foundation,* January 28, 1940, p. 2.
185. See William E. Wallace, "Profile."
186. G. C. Brewer, "About Organizations," *Gospel Advocate,* August 17, 1933, p. 780.
187. Wallace, "The Blight of Hobbyism," pp. 564–65.
188. Hardeman, "The Banner Boys Become Enraged," pp. 1–3; "The Principle and the Law Requested," *Firm Foundation,* July 15, 1947, p. 7.
189. Quoted in William E. Wallace, "Profile."
190. G. H. P. Showalter, "Old Folks' Homes, Children's Homes," *Firm Foundation,* June 24, 1947, pp. 9–10.
191. William E. Wallace, "Profile."
192. West, *Search for the Ancient Order,* vol. 4, p. 139.
193. G. H. P. Showalter, "The Spirit of Rivalry," *Firm Foundation,* September 21, 1948, p. 8.
194. James R. Cope, "Sectarianized Sinners or Sanctified Saints: Which?" *Firm Foundation,* December 16, 1947, pp. 1–2.
195. West, *Search for the Ancient Order,* vol. 4, p. 164; for a discussion of Wallace's influence, see pp. 164–78. Also see Hughes, *Reviving the Ancient Faith,* pp. 160–66; William E. Wallace, "Profile."
196. "The Fort Worth Debate," *Firm Foundation,* November 20, 1934, p. 1.
197. See William E. Wallace, "Hostile Profile," *Vanguard,* January 1984, pp. 11–12.
198. Terry J. Gardner wrote a fine series of articles on the life of Foy E. Wallace, Jr., in the quarterly *Faith and Facts.* The series began with "Young Foy: The Early Years, 1896–1938," April 1996, pp. 16–45.
199. Tant interview.

200. See Gardner, "Young Foy," pp. 24–26.
201. Ibid., p. 27.
202. G. C. Brewer, "Are You Afraid to Read This?" *Gospel Advocate*, October 26, 1933, p. 1020.
203. William E. Wallace, "Profile."
204. Gardner, "Young Foy," p. 33.
205. "The 'Gospel Guardian' Starts," *Firm Foundation,* November 5, 1935, p. 4.
206. "Another Forward Movement," *Firm Foundation,* September 1, 1936, p. 4.
207. See Gardner, "Young Foy," pp. 39–40.
208. Ibid., p. 40.
209. See Gardner, "Foy E. Wallace, Jr.: The Bible Banner Years, Part One," pp. 57–58.
210. Editorial, *Torch,* July 1950, p. 1.
211. "Developments on All Fronts," *Bible Banner,* January 1941, p. 2.
212. Hardeman, "The Banner Boys Become Enraged," p. 3.
213. Brewer, "Foy Versus Foy," p. 7.
214. Foy E. Wallace, Jr., "Cullings and Comments," *Bible Banner,* March 1945, pp. 32–45.
215. James W. Adams, "Foy E. Wallace, Jr.: Militant Warrior," in Melvin D. Curry, ed., *They Being Dead Yet Speak* (Temple Terrace, Florida: Florida College Bookstore, 1981), pp. 183–84.
216. Foy E. Wallace, Jr., "Concerning My Return to Nashville," *Firm Foundation,* May 25, 1937, p. 1.
217. N. B. Hardeman, "Then and Now," *Firm Foundation,* November 18, 1947, p. 3.
218. Taped recollections of Clinton D. Hamilton, October 10, 1998, Plantation, Florida.
219. James R. Cope, "N. B. Hardeman, Orator, Evangelist, Educator, and Debater," in Curry, *They Being Dead Yet Speak,* pp. 148–50.
220. Quoted in Cope, "N. B. Hardeman," p. 150.
221. William E. Wallace, "Profile."
222. Letter from N. B. Hardeman to B. C. Goodpasture, October 3, 1951, copy in the possession of the author. Tant interview; Wallace, "Profile."
223. See James Marvin Powell and Mary Nelle Hardeman Powers, *N. B. H.: A Biography of Nicholas Brodie Hardeman* (Nashville: Gospel Advocate Co., 1964).

224. See West, *Search for the Ancient Order,* vol. 4, pp. 152–64.
225. Casey, *Saddlebags,* p. 76.
226. For information on Brewer, see Grover Cleveland Brewer, *Forty Years on the Firing Line* (Kansas City: Old Paths Book Club, 1948); Grover Cleveland Brewer, *A Story of Toil and Tears and Love and Laughter* (Murfreesboro, Tennessee: Dehoff Publications, 1957); West, *Search for the Ancient Order,* vol. 4, pp. 140–52; Hughes, *Reviving the Ancient Faith,* pp. 185–88.
227. See J. E. Choate, *The Anchor That Holds: A Biography of Benton Cordell Goodpasture* (Nashville: Gospel Advocate Co., 1971), pp. 124–25; Leo Lipscomb Boles and J. E. Choate, *I'll Stand on the Rock: A Biography of H. Leo Boles* (Nashville: Gospel Advocate Co., 1965).
228. Lewis S. Maiden, Preface to Choate, *The Anchor That Holds,* pp. xiii–xvii.
229. See William E. Wallace, "Profile."
230. "The Gospel Advocate's Restated Policy," pp. 2–3.
231. West, *Search for the Ancient Order,* vol. 4, pp. 347–48.
232. See David Edwin Harrell, Jr., "B. C. Goodpasture: Leader of Institutional Thought," in Curry, *They Being Dead Yet Speak,* pp. 241–53.
233. Wallace, "Broken Cisterns," p. 1.
234. For a discussion of the colleges after World War II, see West, *Search for the Ancient Order,* vol. 4, pp. 126–32.
235. Ibid.
236. Roy H. Lanier, Sr., "Fighting Preachers and Debaters," *Gospel Advocate,* September 21, 1933, p. 899.
237. W. D. Bills, "Congregational Expansion," August 21, 1934, p. 2.
238. G. H. P. Showalter, "Matters Controversial," *Firm Foundation,* November 5, 1935, p. 4.
239. National Unity Meeting program, 1939, copy in the possession of the author.
240. See West, *Search for the Ancient Order,* vol. 4, pp. 231–34; William E. Wallace, "Profile."
241. Richard Hughes has an excellent section describing the origins of the new *Christian Leader.* See *Reviving the Ancient Faith,* pp. 194–210.
242. Quoted in Sears, *For Freedom,* p. 298.
243. Hughes, *Reviving the Ancient Faith,* p. 198.

244. See Choate, *The Anchor That Holds,* pp. 152–53; Sears, *For Freedom,* pp. 298–300.
245. Sears, *For Freedom,* p. 299.
246. Hughes, *Reviving the Ancient Faith,* p. 198.
247. See Hicks, *Sometimes Wrong but Never in Doubt;* Stevens, *Before Any Were Willing: The Story of George S. Benson,* pp. 128–37.
248. Letter from C. B. F. Young to Foy E. Wallace, Jr., January 27, 1941, copy in the possession of the author.
249. Letter from Clinton Davidson to H. Leo Boles, August 1, 1938, in the possession of the author.
250. Letter from H. Leo Boles to Clinton Davidson, August 18, 1938, in the possession of the author.
251. Hughes, *Reviving the Ancient Faith,* pp. 194–210.
252. *Gospel Proclaimer,* January 1939, p. 8.
253. On the founding of the *Twentieth Century Christian,* see Hughes, *Reviving the Ancient Faith,* pp. 210–14.
254. Circular letter written by Clinton Davidson, July 30, 1938, copy in the possession of the author.
255. See William E. Wallace, "Profile," appendix.
256. *Bible Banner,* November 1938, p. 13.
257. G. H. P. Showalter, "Two Methods of Teaching," *Firm Foundation,* September 1, 1942, p. 4.
258. W. W. Otey, "Debates," *Firm Foundation,* February 17, 1931, p. 5.
259. See Sears, *For Freedom,* p. 300.
260. See Hughes, *Reviving the Ancient Faith,* p. 203.
261. Choate, *The Anchor That Holds,* p. 153.
262. Quoted in Hughes, *Reviving the Ancient Faith,* p. 203.
263. Hughes, *Reviving the Ancient Faith,* p. 203.
264. Ibid., p. 178; Casey, *Saddlebags,* pp. 71–72.
265. Casey, *Saddlebags,* p. 54.
266. See Casey, *Saddlebags,* pp. 55–73; Hughes, *Reviving the Ancient Faith,* pp. 168–89.
267. Hughes, *Reviving the Ancient Faith,* p. 212.
268. See Hughes, *Reviving the Ancient Faith,* p. 187.
269. W. W. Otey, "Our Leadership," *Firm Foundation,* November 19, 1946, pp. 4–5. For a treatment of Otey's life, see Homer Cecil Willis, *W. W. Otey: Contender for the Faith* (Akron: Cecil Willis, 1964).
270. W. W. Otey, "Statement Challenged," *Firm Foundation,* April 25, 1950, p. 3.

271. W. W. Otey, "Controversy," *Firm Foundation,* February 24, 1948, p. 3.
272. W. W. Otey, "Which Road?" *Firm Foundation,* November 8, 1949, p. 6.
273. Ulrich R. Beeson, "The Boys Are Coming Home," *Firm Foundation,* February 20, 1945, p. 3.

3. Consummating the Institutional Division

1. See Terry J. Gardner, "Foy E. Wallace, Jr.: The Critical Decade, 1949–1959," *Faith and Facts,* April 1997, pp. 111–14. Gardner notes that Roy E. Cogdill had already assumed much of the editing work on the magazine.
2. Letter from Fanning Yater Tant to the author, January 6, 1996.
3. Ibid.
4. William E. Wallace, "Profile of a Movement," typescript manuscript in the possession of the author, n.d., n.p.
5. For William Wallace's version of the Wallace-Tant disagreement, see Wallace, "Profile." Tant's recollection is contained in a letter dated January 6, 1996, in the possession of the author.
6. Wallace, "Profile." William Wallace, Foy's son, summarized his father's charges against Tant in a letter: William E. Wallace to Fanning Yater Tant, October 30, 1952, copy in the possession of the author. Tant and William E. Wallace corresponded regularly for forty years, beginning in the 1950s, and Tant's view of this dispute is amply discussed in that correspondence. See, for instance, Fanning Yater Tant to Wm. E. Wallace, November 8, 1952, copy in the possession of the author.
7. James W. Adams, who was present at the organizational meeting, believed that Tant had acted "unwisely," but, at the same time, he thought that Wallace's objections were "childish and trivial" and that the controversy occurred because "Foy was in a bad state of mind." Letter from James W. Adams to the author, August 12, 1998.
8. See Fanning Yater Tant to William E. Wallace, April 17, 1953, copy in the possession of the author.
9. See Gardner, "Foy E. Wallace, Jr.: The Critical Decade," pp. 26–27.

10. For an overview of the Italian mission, see Gerald Paden, "Italy," *Gospel Advocate,* October 1997, pp. 14–17.
11. "Italian Gov't Orders Closing of School," *Christian Chronicle,* December 14, 1949, p. 1.
12. See "Officials, Flooded with Requests," *Christian Chronicle,* January 4, 1950, pp. 1, 4; "Italian Situation Develops into International Crisis," *Christian Chronicle,* January 11, 1950, pp. 1, 5.
13. Ibid.
14. Cled E. Wallace, "That Rock Fight in Italy," *Gospel Guardian,* January 19, 1950, pp. 1, 5. See William E. Wallace, "Rock Fight in Italy," *Vanguard,* July 1983, pp. 179–80.
15. Cled E. Wallace, "In the Middle of the Rock Fight," *Gospel Guardian,* February 2, 1950, p. 6.
16. Cled E. Wallace, "Getting Me Straightened Out," *Gospel Guardian,* March 2, 1950, p. 6.
17. Cled E. Wallace, "That Disgusted Brotherhood," *Gospel Guardian,* April 6, 1950, p. 2. See also Fanning Yater Tant, "Let Us Study the Question," *Gospel Guardian,* April 6, 1950, p. 4.
18. William Wallace, "Unwarranted Editorial Liberty," *Vanguard,* August 1983, p. 206.
19. Letter from James W. Adams to the author, August 12, 1998.
20. Yater Tant, "Not Alone—We Hope," *Gospel Guardian,* April 20, 1950, p. 2.
21. Yater Tant, "Surveying the Scene," *Gospel Guardian,* February 23, 1950, p. 2.
22. "Union Avenue Church Supports Man to Devote Full Time to Promoting," *Christian Chronicle,* July 14, 1948, p. 3.
23. G. K. Wallace, "Orphan Homes," *Gospel Guardian,* November 17, 1949, pp. 1, 3. Similarly, Glenn L. Wallace published an article in favor of churches "pooling their resources" in volume 5 of the *Preceptor.*
24. "The 'Special,'" *Gospel Guardian,* May 3 and 10, 1956, pp. 1, 3.
25. Ibid.
26. Homer Hailey, "The Church and Human Organizations," *Gospel Guardian,* 1956–57, pp. 22, 23, 26.
27. For a discussion of the new noninstitutional papers, see William E. Wallace, "Profile."

28. Bryan Vinson, Jr., "Is There a Need for 'Truth'?" *Truth Magazine,* November 1956, p. 2.
29. Bryan Vinson, Jr., "Extreme Left . . . Or the Middle of the Road," *Truth Magazine,* July 1957, p. 2.
30. See Robert F. Turner, "Attitudes toward Current Issues," *Truth Magazine,* June 1957, pp. 2, 17, 18, 21.
31. William E. Wallace, "Profile."
32. Charles A. Holt, "Controversy and Preaching," *Gospel Guardian,* August 29, 1957, p. 257.
33. See Wallace, "Profile."
34. Letter from Fanning Yater Tant to William E. Wallace, May 14, 1954, copy in the possession of the author.
35. Letter from James W. Adams to the author, August 18, 1998.
36. Yater Tant, "The Lesser of Two Evils," *Gospel Guardian,* 1956–57, p. 188.
37. See John T. Lewis, "John T. Lewis and Childhaven," *Gospel Advocate,* May 17, 1951, p. 309; John T. Lewis, "Childhaven," *Gospel Advocate,* April 26, 1951, p. 264; John T. Lewis, "Shall It Be a Review of My Tract?" *Gospel Advocate,* September 13, 1951, p. 579; G. C. Brewer, "Shall We Review Brother Lewis' Tract on Childhaven?" *Gospel Advocate,* June 7, 1951, pp. 356–57; W. W. Otey, "Keep the Question Clear," *Firm Foundation,* November 21, 1950, pp. 6, 7; W. W. Otey, "Can We? Will We? Should We?" *Firm Foundation,* May 2, 1950, pp. 1–3; G. H. P Showalter, "Concerning the Way Things Are Done by the Churches," *Firm Foundation,* December 12, 1951, p. 8; G. H. P. Showalter, "The 'Cooperations,'" *Firm Foundation,* July 17, 1951, pp. 8, 9; G. H. P. Showalter, "Concerning the Co-Operation Meetings," *Firm Foundation,* October 9, 1951, pp. 8, 9.
38. James W. Adams, "The Present Controversy Reviewed," *Firm Foundation,* June 20, 1950, pp. 3, 4.
39. E. W. McMillan, "Letting Facts Speak for Themselves," *Firm Foundation,* July 31, 1951, p. 5.
40. W. W. Otey, "Brother Otey's Shameful Misrepresentations," *Gospel Guardian,* May 15, 1952, p. 3.
41. Showalter, "The 'Cooperations,'" p. 9.
42. Quoted in William E. Wallace, "Personalities," *Vanguard,* October 1983, pp. 274–75.
43. J. E. Choate, *The Anchor That Holds: A Biography of Benton*

Cordell Goodpasture (Nashville: Gospel Advocate Co., 1971), p. xix.

44. Letter from N. B. Hardeman to B. C. Goodpasture, December 21, 1957, copy in the possession of the author.
45. A discussion of this fight may be found in Gardner, "Foy E. Wallace, Jr.: The Critical Decade," pp. 120–21.
46. William E. Wallace, "Profile."
47. B. C. Goodpasture, "The Voice of the Turtle," *Gospel Advocate,* July 12, 1951, p. 434. See Fanning Yater Tant, "Voice of the Turtle," *Gospel Guardian,* April 19, 1951, pp. 4–5.
48. Letter from Fanning Yater Tant to William E. Wallace, December 20, 1952, copy in the possession of the author.
49. See William E. Wallace, "The Voice of the Turtle," *Vanguard,* February 1984, p. 39.
50. B. C. Goodpasture, "What Is That to Thee," *Gospel Advocate,* August 23, 1951, p. 530. See William E. Wallace, "A Tributary of Bitterness," *Vanguard,* November 1983, pp. 290–91; William E. Wallace, "Trouble in Lufkin," *Vanguard,* December 1983, pp. 318–19.
51. Roy E. Cogdill, "The Advocate Editor Can't Take It," *Gospel Guardian,* November 29, 1951, pp. 8–10.
52. B. C. Goodpasture, "It Is Time to Name the Man," *Gospel Advocate,* November 1, 1951, p. 690.
53. Letter from N. B. Hardeman to B. C. Goodpasture, October 3, 1951, copy in the possession of the author.
54. William E. Wallace, "The Voice of the Turtle," p. 40.
55. See James D. Bales, "The Diocesan Decree," *Firm Foundation,* June 6, 1950, pp. 1–2; "The Gospel Guardian Plan," *Firm Foundation,* January 23, 1951, pp. 1–5; "There Is a Better Way," *Firm Foundation,* April 10, 1951, pp. 6–8; "Brother Bales Does and He Doesn't," *Firm Foundation,* April 17, 1951, pp. 6–8.
56. Cecil N. Wright, "Cooperation on a Scriptural Basis," *Firm Foundation,* July 25, 1950, p. 3; August 8, 1950, pp. 1–3
57. Cecil N. Wright, "The Cooperation Controversy (No. 8)," *Gospel Advocate,* August 16, 1951, p. 519.
58. See series of four articles in *Gospel Guardian,* beginning with "'The Cooperation Controversy' Reviewed—No. 1," October 18, 1951, pp. 4, 9.
59. Goodpasture, "What Is That to Thee," p. 530.

60. William E. Wallace, "The Voice of the Turtle," p. 40.
61. See "Urgent Appeal for Immediate Aid in Nationwide Broadcast Plans," *Christian Chronicle,* November 14, 1951, pp. 1, 8.
62. See William E. Wallace, "Herald of Truth—30 Years 1952–1982," *Vanguard,* August 1982, pp. 216–17; Cecil N. Wright, "The Herald of Truth Discussion," *Gospel Advocate,* April 1, 1954, pp. 251–53.
63. See William E. Wallace, "A Great Gulf Forms," *Vanguard,* May 1984, pp. 131–32.
64. E. R. Harper, "That Conversion," *Gospel Advocate,* March 25, 1954, pp. 231–33.
65. For a description of the debates of the 1950s, see Wallace, "Profile." A few of the more prominent were published as follows: *Harper-Tant Debate* (Abilene: Christian Chronicle Publishing, 1956); *The Cogdill-Woods Debate* (Lufkin, Texas: Gospel Guardian Co., 1958); William L. Totty, ed., *The Indianapolis Debate* (Lufkin, Texas: Gospel Guardian Co., 1955); *The Woods-Porter Debate on Orphan Homes and Homes for the Aged* (Nashville: Gospel Advocate Co., 1956); *Wallace-Holt Debate* (Nashville: Gospel Advocate Co., 1960).
66. Reuel Lemmons, "The Harper-Tant Debate," *Firm Foundation,* April 5, 1955, p. 214.
67. *Harper-Tant Debate,* p. 8.
68. Yater Tant, "The Deed That Will Live in Infamy," *Gospel Guardian,* August 16, 1956, p. 236.
69. *The Cogdill-Woods Debate.*
70. See Guy N. Woods, "The Birmingham Debate—'Gospel Guardian' Style!" *Gospel Advocate,* September 25, 1958, pp. 610–12.
71. Guy N. Woods, "Orphanages and Homes for the Aged," *Gospel Advocate,* December 16, 1954, p. 994.
72. Thomas B. Warren, "Cooperation between New Testament Churches," *Gospel Advocate,* December 15, 1955, pp. 1136–40.
73. J. D. Thomas, *We Be Brethren* (Abilene: Biblical Research Press, 1958), p. vii.
74. Ibid., p. 9.
75. Yater Tant, "Brother Thomas' New Book," *Gospel Guardian,* 1958, pp. 340 41.

76. Roy E. Cogdill, "'We Be Brethren'—A Review," *Gospel Guardian,* August 20, 1959, pp. 225, 236–38.
77. Reuel Lemmons, "Can a Church Engage in a Work Larger Than Its Local Capacity?" *Firm Foundation,* November 15, 1955, p. 742.
78. Reuel Lemmons, "The Inconsistency of Anti-ism," *Firm Foundation,* November 29, 1955, pp. 774–75.
79. See "Editorial," *Firm Foundation,* February 1, 1955, pp. 66–67; Reuel Lemmons, "Outside Interference with Local Autonomy," October 4, 1955, p. 646.
80. Roy H. Lanier, Sr., "The Middle of the Road, No. 3," *Firm Foundation,* February 26, 1957, pp. 133, 136.
81. See Guy N. Woods, "A Shocking Editorial (No. 1)," *Gospel Advocate,* March 27, 1958, pp. 194–97.
82. Ibid.; "Lanier—In the Middle of the *Wrong* Road!" *Gospel Advocate,* April 11, 1957, 226–29.
83. Woods, "A Shocking Editorial (No. 1)," p. 194.
84. Yater Tant, "Both Right—Both Wrong," *Gospel Guardian,* 1957–58, p. 52.
85. Guy N. Woods, "A Meeting of the Minds," *Gospel Advocate,* May 8, 1958, pp. 289, 298.
86. Letter from Colly Caldwell to the author, undated.
87. Fanning Yater Tant, "Present Issues—and a Suggested Solution (I)," *Gospel Guardian,* May 29, 1958, pp. 65, 76–77; Reuel Lemmons, "Concerning Brother Yater Tant's Proposition," *Gospel Guardian,* May 29, 1958, pp. 66–67.
88. Robert F. Turner, "Ruminating with the Editor," *Firm Foundation,* October 4, 1960, p. 629.
89. Reuel Lemmons, "Brother Turner Wishes to be Heard Again," *Firm Foundation,* October 4, 1960, p. 626.
90. Turner, "Ruminating with the Editor," pp. 629, 635. See also Robert F. Turner, "Units of the 'Church Universal,'" *Firm Foundation,* August 2, 1960, pp. 483, 489.
91. Harry Pickup, Jr., "Institutionalism: A Virulent Cancer," *Firm Foundation,* May 11, 1965, pp. 295, 299.
92. Reuel Lemmons, "Institutionalism," *Firm Foundation,* May 11, 1965, p. 290.
93. Reuel Lemmons, "We Like It in the Middle of the Road," *Firm Foundation,* July 5, 1960, p. 418.
94. Reuel Lemmons, "There Is Still a Need to Go Back," *Firm Foundation,* September 6, 1960, p. 562.

95. Reuel Lemmons, "The Further They Go the Worse They Get," *Firm Foundation,* October 26, 1965, p. 674.
96. Reuel Lemmons, "Keep the Door Open," *Firm Foundation,* September 14, 1965, p. 578; "The Right to Disagree," *Firm Foundation,* July 19, 1960, p. 450.
97. Reuel Lemmons, "We Like It in the Middle of the Road," p. 418.
98. See J. W. Roberts, "Brother Porter's Review (No. 2)," *Gospel Advocate,* December 1, 1955, pp. 1077, 1091; E. R. Harper, "Adams Answered on the Society," *Gospel Advocate,* June 24, 1954, pp. 492–95.
99. B. C. Goodpasture, "Colleges and Orphan Homes—Who Has Changed?" *Gospel Advocate,* August 20, 1953, pp. 522–23. The article was reprinted in 1957 and 1959. See *Gospel Advocate,* June 29, 1957, pp. 386–88, and August 20, 1959, pp. 530–32.
100. See B. C. Goodpasture, "Church Cooperation," *Gospel Advocate,* November 25, 1954, pp. 922–23; H. Leo Boles, "Colleges and Church Autonomy," *Gospel Advocate,* April 9, 1953, p. 210.
101. See B. C. Goodpasture, "Another False Statement Exposed," *Gospel Advocate,* December 19, 1957, pp. 802–4.
102. B. C. Goodpasture, "Both Sides!" *Gospel Advocate,* March 19, 1953, p. 162.
103. Bill L. Rogers, "Quibbling Over Quarantines and Prating Against Principles," *Gospel Advocate,* September 22, 1955, pp. 845–46; see William E. Wallace, "Profile."
104. Earl West and B. C. Goodpasture, "A Statement and an Explanation," *Gospel Advocate,* September 19, 1957, p. 594.
105. See B. C. Goodpasture, "Brother Crouch's Statement," *Gospel Advocate,* July 24, 1958, p. 466.
106. See B. C. Goodpasture, "Brother Hardeman's Forthright Statement," and Pat Hardeman, "A Statement of Conviction," *Gospel Advocate,* March 13, 1958, p. 162.
107. Pat Hardeman, "Who Says Who Is a 'Modernist'?" *Gospel Advocate,* September 4, 1958, pp. 566–69.
108. Letter from N. B. Hardeman to B. C. Goodpasture, September 9, 1958, copy in the possession of the author.
109. Pat Hardeman, "The Gospel Versus Dogmatism," *Gospel Advocate,* August 21, 1958, pp. 529, 539.
110. See James P. Miller, "Let the Record Speak for Itself," *Gospel*

Guardian, November 26, 1959, p. 452; Clinton D. Hamilton and Louis W. Garrett, "An Interview with Pat Hardeman," *Gospel Guardian,* December 10, 1959, pp. 481, 492.

111. B. C. Goodpasture, "Concerning Pat Hardeman," *Gospel Advocate,* October 29, 1959, pp. 690, 691.
112. B. C. Goodpasture, "Keeping the Record Straight," *Gospel Advocate,* July 23, 1959, pp. 466–67.
113. Cecil B. Douthitt, "Keeping the Record Straight," *Gospel Guardian,* July 30, 1959, p. 177.
114. Roy E. Cogdill, "Slander—Gospel Advocate Style," *Gospel Guardian,* January 1, 1959, pp. 532–38.
115. Hugo McCord, "By This Shall All Men Know," *Gospel Advocate,* November 21, 1957, p. 738.
116. G. K. Wallace, "The Underground Movement," *Gospel Advocate,* February 5, 1959, p. 81.
117. "The Restrictive Clause for the Deed," *Gospel Advocate,* October 2, 1958, p. 626.
118. "A New Paper—A Statement of Aim and Policy," *Spiritual Sword,* January 1958, p. 4.
119. B. C. Goodpasture, "The Spiritual Sword," *Gospel Advocate,* February 6, 1958, pp. 82–83.
120. Yater Tant, "Foolish Talk About a 'Major Division,'" *Gospel Guardian,* 1957–58, p. 723.
121. Johnny Ramsey, "Politics and Pressure," *Firm Foundation,* February 23, 1960, p. 120.
122. Yater Tant, "A Listing of Preachers," *Gospel Guardian,* August 27, 1959, p. 244.
123. Choate, *The Anchor That Holds,* p. 179.
124. Robert F. Turner, "They Ask, 'Are You "Anti,"'" *Truth Magazine,* September 1959, pp. 268–69.
125. Ira Y. Rice, Jr., "While Brethren Squabble," *Gospel Advocate,* January 10, 1957, p. 19.
126. Robert C. Welch, "Dean Gardner Picking the Winner," *Gospel Guardian,* April 17, 1958, p. 769.
127. Reuel Lemmons, "Our Foolish Contentions," *Firm Foundation,* August 25, 1961, p. 530.
128. Reuel Lemmons, "The Determination to Form a Sect," *Firm Foundation,* January 30, 1962, p. 66.
129. Yater Tant, "A Sifting," *Gospel Guardian,* 1961–62, p. 404.
130. Lemmons, "Our Foolish Contentions," p. 530.
131. Tant, "Foolish Talk About a 'Major Division,'" pp. 723–25.

132. Earl Irvin West, *The Search for the Ancient Order* (4 vols.; Germantown, Tennessee: Religious Book Service, 1987), vol. 4, p. v.
133. Ibid.
134. J. D. Tant, "What I Think," *Firm Foundation,* April 22, 1930, p. 3.
135. "From Brother Tant," *Firm Foundation,* June 18, 1940, p. 4.
136. Cled Wallace, "Brother Tant's Picture," *Gospel Advocate,* September 7, 1933, p. 844.
137. *Firm Foundation,* September 1, 1941, p. 4.
138. Foy E. Wallace, Jr., "The Gospel Guardian," *Gospel Guardian,* October 1935, p. 2.
139. Foy E. Wallace, "The Bible Banner—Past, Present and Future," *Bible Banner,* June 1945, p. 4.
140. G. H. P. Showalter, "Threatened Dangers Ahead," *Firm Foundation,* February 15, 1938, p. 4.
141. H. Leo Boles, "The Education of Preachers," *Gospel Advocate,* February 23, 1933, p. 184.
142. Glenn L. Wallace, "The Modernism Among Us," *Firm Foundation,* August 29, 1950, pp. 1–2.
143. Robert M. Alexander, "College Trained Preachers," *Christian Chronicle,* March 19, 1947, p. 2.
144. Robert E. Hooper, *A Distinct People* (West Monroe, Louisiana: Howard Publishing, 1993), pp. 181–206.
145. Ibid., p. 181.
146. Michael W. Casey, *Saddlebags, City Streets, and Cyberspace: A History of Preaching in the Churches of Christ* (Abilene: ACU Press, 1995), p. 123; see also pp. 111–24.
147. Ibid., p. 111.
148. Ibid., pp. 117–18; Batsell Barrett Baxter, *Speaking for the Master: A Study of Public Speaking for Christian Men* (New York: Macmillan, 1954).
149. Hooper, *A Distinct People,* p. 205.
150. Quoted in Hooper, *A Distinct People,* p. 206.
151. George F. Ketcham, ed., *Yearbook of American Churches* (n.p.: National Council of Churches of Christ in America, 1951), pp. 42, 235.
152. Frank S. Mead, *Handbook of Denominations* (5th ed., Nashville: Abingdon Press, 1970), pp. 85–86.
153. See Hooper, *A Distinct People,* pp. 183–85.
154. See Hooper, *A Distinct People,* p. 285.

155. See Richard T. Hughes, *Reviving the Ancient Faith* (Grand Rapids: William B. Eerdmans, 1996), p. 235.
156. See Hooper, *A Distinct People,* p. 285.
157. See Hooper, *A Distinct People,* pp. 284–86.
158. Henry P. Van Dusen, "Third Force in Christendom," *Life,* June 9, 1958, p. 113.
159. Dean M. Kelley, *Why Conservative Churches Are Growing* (New York: Harper & Row, 1972).
160. For a description of North's work at Madison, see Hooper, *A Distinct People,* pp. 194–99.
161. See *Gospel Advocate,* March 19, 1959, p. 179.
162. Quoted in Hooper, *A Distinct People,* p. 198.
163. Bailey McBride, "Church Growth," *Christian Chronicle,* February 1982, p. 16.
164. Cleon Lyles, "Little Men Obscure the Greatness of the Church," *Firm Foundation,* October 27, 1953, p. 9.
165. Reuel Lemmons, "The Cause of Christ in Manhattan," *Firm Foundation,* May 10, 1955, p. 302.
166. G. C. Brewer, "Is It Nothing to You," *Firm Foundation,* May 10, 1955, p. 316.
167. Hooper, *A Distinct People,* p. 178.
168. See Hughes, *Reviving the Ancient Faith,* pp. 248–49.
169. M. Norvel Young, "Britannica Yearbook Article Concerning Church," *Firm Foundation,* November 30, 1965, p. 760.
170. See Hooper, *A Distinct People,* pp. 198–205.
171. Hooper, *A Distinct People,* p. 190; see also pp. 187–90.
172. Hughes, *Reviving the Ancient Faith,* pp. 239–44.
173. Quoted in Hooper, *A Distinct People,* p. 284.
174. Paul Hunton, "We Can Preach the Gospel to Every Creature in Our Generation," *Gospel Advocate,* December 17, 1959, p. 801.
175. Hughes, *Reviving the Ancient Faith,* p. 224.
176. Hunton, "We Can Preach the Gospel to Every Creature in Our Generation," p. 801.
177. Joe K. Alley, "The Mustard Tree Is Growing Again," *Gospel Advocate,* September 8, 1955, p. 804.
178. "The Changed Emphasis," *Christian Chronicle,* November 13, 1946, p. 2.
179. G. H. P. Showalter, "Instructions From the Director of the Census in Washington," *Firm Foundation,* January 28, 1947,

pp. 8–9; [M. Norvel Young], "Census Bureau Disappointed at Our Response So Far," *Firm Foundation,* May 6, 1947, p. 11; "Broadway Church in Lubbock, Texas, Named by Government to Take 1946 Census," *Christian Chronicle,* November 13, 1946, p. 6.

180. "Complete Census Will Enlarge Concessions of Radio Time to Congregations," *Christian Chronicle,* February 19, 1947, p. 6.
181. "Post-War Church Problems Must Be Met," *Christian Chronicle,* August 22, 1945, p. 2.
182. Ulrich R. Beeson, "The Boys Are Coming Home," *Firm Foundation,* February 20, 1945, pp. 2–3.
183. G. C. Brewer, "Evangelizing the World in the Post War Period," *Firm Foundation,* February 16, 1943, p. 1.
184. Ibid.
185. Cecil B. Douthitt, "Ten Billion Years and the Great Commission," *Firm Foundation,* October 21, 1947, pp. 1–2.
186. Cled E. Wallace, "That Rock Fight in Italy," pp. 1, 5.
187. "Hardeman-Doran Meeting Big Success Dallas Elders Say," *Christian Chronicle,* December 1, 1943, p. 1.
188. Hughes, *Reviving the Ancient Faith,* p. 224.
189. Ibid., p. 210.
190. Casey, *Saddlebags,* p. 92; see also pp. 91–101.
191. James Bales, interview with the author, November 25, 1981, Searcy, Arkansas.
192. "A Brother Is Arraigned in Court and Tried for Preaching the Gospel in Italy," *Voice of Freedom,* January 1953, p. 10.
193. L. R. Wilson, "Editorial Comments," *Voice of Freedom,* October 1959, p. 146.
194. Hughes, *Reviving the Ancient Faith,* p. 155; see also pp. 151–60.
195. Ibid., p. 155.
196. Bales interview.
197. Hughes, *Reviving the Ancient Faith,* p. 160; see also pp. 156–60.
198. Hooper, *A Distinct People,* p. 252; see also pp. 238–54.
199. Ibid., p. 253.
200. Ibid., p. 254.
201. For a sample of works by David Edwin Harrell, Jr., see *Quest for a Christian America* (Nashville: Disciples of Christ Histori-

cal Society, 1966); *The Social Sources of Division in the Disciples of Christ* (Athens: Publishing Systems, 1973); "The Sectional Origins of the Churches of Christ," *Journal of Southern History*, vol. 30 (August 1964), pp. 261–77; "The Disciples of Christ and Social Force in Tennessee, 1865–1900," East Tennessee Historical Society, Publication No. 38 (1966), pp. 30–47.

202. Harrell, "Sectional Origins," p. 277, n. 58.
203. Hughes, *Reviving the Ancient Faith*, pp. 224–25.
204. Casey, *Saddlebags*, p. 54.
205. Foy E. Wallace, Jr., "Broken Cisterns," *Firm Foundation*, September 1, 1936, p. 1.
206. W. W. Otey, "Controversy," *Firm Foundation*, February 24, 1948, p. 3.
207. W. W. Otey, "A Scrap of History," *Firm Foundation*, August 26, 1947, p. 4.
208. Robert F. Turner, "History of Current 'Sponsoring Church,'" *Gospel Guardian*, 1965–66, p. 57.
209. Harold Dowdy, "Three Pound Chicken Lays a Five Pound Egg," *Gospel Guardian*, 1962–63, p. 646.
210. Yater Tant, "A Dash of Ice Water," *Gospel Guardian*, April 30, 1959, p. 804.
211. C. D. Crouch, "Churches of Christ—Statistics," *Gospel Guardian*, January 22, 1959, p. 587.
212. Tant, "A Dash of Ice Water," p. 804.
213. Bryan Vinson, Sr., "The Birth of a Denomination," *Truth Magazine*, June 1961, pp. 206–8.
214. George T. Jones, "The Largest Church of Christ Gathering . . . in the History of the Denomination," *Gospel Guardian*, July 31, 1958, p. 194.
215. Hoyt H. Houchen, "Doing Things in a Big Way," *Gospel Guardian*, 1962–63, p. 246.
216. Ed Harrell, "Thoughts on Dishonesty," *Gospel Guardian*, September 24, 1959, pp. 312–14.
217. J. D. Thomas, "'Liberalism' and 'Social Gospel,'" *Gospel Advocate*, May 21, 1959, pp. 324–26.
218. Hughes, *Reviving the Ancient Faith*, p. 252.
219. Ibid., p. 244.
220. See C. Leonard Allen, Richard T. Hughes, and Michael R. Weed, *The Worldly Church* (Abilene: ACU Press, 1988); C. Leonard Allen and Richard T. Hughes, *Discovering Our*

Roots (Abilene: ACU Press, 1988); C. Leonard Allen, *The Cruciform Church* (Abilene: ACU Press, 1990).

221. David Edwin Harrel [*sic*], Jr., "The Emergence of the 'Church of Christ' Denomination" (Lufkin, Texas: Gospel Guardian Company, n.d.).
222. Ibid., p. 28.
223. Leroy Garrett chastises those who yield "to the claims of social determinism." See Leroy Garrett, *The Stone-Campbell Movement: The Story of the American Restoration Movement* (rev. ed.; n.p.: College Press Publishing, 1997), pp. 351, 352. Garrett caricatures the writings of David Edwin Harrell, Jr., and Richard Hughes, suggesting, particularly in the case of Harrell, that they ignore theological and doctrinal matters in favor of sociological theories that undermine "moral responsibility." In fact, neither author shows any sympathy for "social determinism."
224. Douglas A. Foster, *Will the Cycle Be Unbroken?* (Abilene: ACU Press, 1994), p. 1.
225. Hughes, *Reviving the Ancient Faith,* pp. 217–53.
226. Ibid., p. 352.
227. Ibid., p. 228.
228. Ibid., p. 228.
229. Ibid., p. 218.

4. The Mainstream Becomes a Divided Stream

1. Richard T. Hughes, *Reviving the Ancient Faith* (Grand Rapids: William B. Eerdmans, 1996), p. 244.
2. For a good summary of Wallace's last years, see Terry J. Gardner, "Into the Sunset: Foy E. Wallace, Jr., 1960–1969," *Faith and Facts,* October 1998, pp. 313–33.
3. Reuel Lemmons, "For General Information," *Firm Foundation,* November 29, 1955, p. 775.
4. Reuel Lemmons, "Paper Yokes and Party Labels," *Firm Foundation,* May 26, 1959, p. 325.
5. Quoted in William E. Wallace, "Profile of a Movement," typescript manuscript in the possession of the author, n.d., n.p.
6. Letter from William E. Wallace to Fanning Yater Tant, October 22, 1994, copy in the possession of the author.
7. See Wallace, "Profile."

8. See Gardner, "Into the Sunset," p. 317; letter from Fanning Yater Tant to William E. Wallace, December 19, 1955, copy in the possession of the author.
9. Gardner, "Into the Sunset," pp. 321–24.
10. Ibid., p. 151.
11. Letter from Fanning Yater Tant to William E. Wallace, March 25, 1980, copy in the possession of the author.
12. For a good summary on Leroy Garrett and Carl Ketcherside, see Hughes, *Reviving the Ancient Faith,* pp. 313–17.
13. Leroy Garrett, *The Stone-Campbell Movement: The Story of the American Restoration Movement* (rev. ed.; n.p.: College Press Publishing, 1997), p. 535.
14. Roy H. Lanier, Jr., "Controversies in the Church," *Spiritual Sword,* January 1995, p. 21.
15. Hughes, *Reviving the Ancient Faith,* p. 313.
16. Quoted in H. A. (Buster) Dobbs, "Fatal Error," *Firm Foundation,* July 1996, p. 4.
17. See David Edwin Harrell, Jr., *The Social Sources of Division in the Disciples of Christ, 1865–1900* (Athens: Publishing Systems, 1973), pp. 15–16.
18. Hughes, *Reviving the Ancient Faith,* pp. 313–16.
19. A good overview of the discipling movement in the churches of Christ may be found in Flavil R. Yeakley, Jr., ed., *The Discipling Dilemma: A Study of the Discipling Movement among Churches of Christ* (Nashville: Gospel Advocate Co., 1988). For a thorough doctrinal summary of the movement in the churches of Christ, see Maurice Barnett, *The Discipling Movement* (2d ed., rev. and enl.; Phoenix: Maurice Barnett, 1989).
20. See Hughes, *Reviving the Ancient Faith,* pp. 357–63.
21. Lanier, "Controversies in the Church," p. 21.
22. Quoted in Garrett, *The Stone-Campbell Movement,* p. 441.
23. Robert E. Hooper, *A Distinct People* (West Monroe, Louisiana: Howard Publishing, 1993), p. 302.
24. For a comparison with the Christadelphia movement, see David Edwin Harrell, Jr., "Restorationism and the Stone-Campbell Tradition," in Charles H. Lippy and Peter W. Williams, eds., *Encyclopedia of the American Religious Experience* (3 vols.; New York: Charles Scribner's Sons, 1988), vol. 2, pp. 851–52.

25. Hughes, *Reviving the Ancient Faith,* p. 352.
26. Robert Meyers, *Voices of Concern* (St. Louis: Mission Messenger, 1966), p. 32.
27. Richard Hughes, himself a part of the "progressive" generation of the sixties, writes with feeling about the pioneer educators of the period. See Hughes, *Reviving the Ancient Faith,* pp. 317–25.
28. See Hughes, *Reviving the Ancient Faith,* p. 310.
29. Quoted in Michael W. Casey, *Saddlebags, City Streets, and Cyberspace: A History of Preaching in the Churches of Christ* (Abilene: ACU Press, 1995), p. 132.
30. Hughes, *Reviving the Ancient Faith,* pp. 317–23.
31. Ibid., p. 317.
32. Ibid., p. 320.
33. Ibid., p. 323.
34. Ibid., p. 307.
35. Douglas A. Foster, *Will the Cycle Be Unbroken?* (Abilene: ACU Press, 1994), p. 54. See Hooper, *A Distinct People,* p. 289.
36. Hughes, *Reviving the Ancient Faith,* p. 341.
37. See Hughes, *Reviving the Ancient Faith,* pp. 341–43; Casey, *Saddlebags,* pp. 157–75.
38. For a discussion of the clashes on the Holy Spirit in the late 1960s, see Hughes, *Reviving the Ancient Faith,* pp. 333–41.
39. See Hughes, *Reviving the Ancient Faith,* p. 341.
40. Ibid., p. 348.
41. Ibid., p. 325.
42. Ibid., p. 327.
43. Ibid., p. 349.
44. Denny Boultinghouse, "Dear Brother," *Image,* January/February 1996, pp. 5–6.
45. Hughes, *Reviving the Ancient Faith,* p. 308; see also pp. 307–51.
46. Ibid., p. 326; see also pp. 325–33.
47. See Thomas Warren, "Our Aim," *Spiritual Sword,* October 1969, pp. 1–3.
48. See Hughes, *Reviving the Ancient Faith,* p. 330.
49. See Ira Y. Rice, Jr., *Axe at the Root* (Dallas: privately published, 1966).
50. Quoted in Hooper, *A Distinct People,* p. 297.
51. Hughes, *Reviving the Ancient Faith,* p. 330.

52. "Bible Colleges," *Christian Chronicle,* January 1996, p. 31.
53. Hughes, *Reviving the Ancient Faith,* p. 330.
54. Hooper, *A Distinct People,* p. 301.
55. Hugo McCord, "Are We Drifting," *Spiritual Sword,* October 1993, p. 10.
56. Lanier, "Controversies in the Church," p. 21.
57. Foster, *Will the Cycle Be Unbroken,* pp. 55–56.
58. David Edwin Harrel [*sic*], Jr., "The Emergence of the 'Church of Christ' Denomination" (Lufkin, Texas: Gospel Guardian Co., n.d.).
59. "Thoughts on Overcoming Church's Identity Crisis," *Christian Chronicle,* September 1996, p. 20.
60. Mel Hailey, Douglas A. Foster, and Thomas L. Winter, "Ministers' Beliefs," *Christian Chronicle,* July 1996, pp. 15–17.
61. Hughes, *Reviving the Ancient Faith,* p. 351.
62. "Editorial: On the Fragmentation and Healing of the Church," *Christian Chronicle,* August 1996, p. 20.
63. See Hooper, *A Distinct People,* pp. 286–89.
64. Charlie Coil, "2001: A Faith Odyssey," *Image,* January/February 1995, p. 31.
65. See Lynn Anderson, "Big, Sick, Denomination: Revisited," *Wineskins* [January/February 1996], pp. 34–38.
66. Mike Cope, "Is It an Identity Crisis?" *Wineskins,* March/April 1996, p. 4.
67. Hughes, *Reviving the Ancient Faith,* p. 308. Hughes, who was himself a part of the progressive movement of the sixties and an editor of *Mission,* believed that "many progressives of the 1960s stood in the apocalyptic and ethical heritage of Barton W. Stone"; *Reviving the Ancient Faith,* p. 325.
68. C. Leonard Allen, *Distant Voices: Discovering a Forgotten Past for a Changing Church* (Abilene: ACU Press, 1993).
69. See Hughes, *Reviving the Ancient Faith,* pp. 364–72.
70. "Wineskins: A Purpose Statement," *Wineskins,* May 1992, pp. 5–6.
71. Hughes, *Reviving the Ancient Faith,* p. 325.
72. Ibid., p. 372.
73. Hooper, *A Distinct People,* p. 304.
74. Andre Resner, "Christmas at Matthew's House," *Wineskins,* November 1992, pp. 5–7.
75. William Woodson, "An Article Deserving Rebuke," *Spiritual Sword,* October 1993, p. 22.

76. H. A. (Buster) Dobbs, "What Lies Ahead," *Firm Foundation,* January 1996, p. 2.
77. Jerry Moffitt, "Liberalism," *Firm Foundation,* January 1996, p. 16.
78. Alan E. Highers, "The Winds of Change," *Spiritual Sword,* October 1993, p. 4.
79. Alan E. Highers, "Precious Memories," *Spiritual Sword,* January 1995, p. 2.
80. Harvey Porter, "Love the Brotherhood," *Gospel Advocate,* December 1993, p. 13.
81. Wayne Jackson, "The Current Crisis," *Spiritual Sword,* October 1993, p. 15.
82. Leroy Brownlow, "And They Wanted Change," *Gospel Advocate,* December 1993, pp. 20–22. See Leroy Brownlow, "Is the Church Fluid and Open to Change?" *Gospel Advocate,* October 1993, pp. 6–7; Willard Collins, "Change, Change and More Change," *Gospel Advocate,* December 1993, p. 64.
83. See Bill Lockwood, "The Christian Chronicle and Evolution," *Firm Foundation,* March 1995, pp. 1, 6; J. E. Choate, "Golden Calf Syndrome," *Firm Foundation,* November 1996, pp. 18–20; "The ACU Lectureship Speech," *Spiritual Sword,* October 1993, p. 46–47.
84. Royce Money, *People with a Purpose* (Abilene: Abilene Christian University, 1992), n.p.
85. See Money, *People with a Purpose,* and "The ACU Lectureship Speech," *Spiritual Sword,* October 1993, p. 47.
86. Money, *People with a Purpose.*
87. "Abilene Christian University Facilities Requested for 1995 Seminar on 'The New Testament Church,'" *Firm Foundation,* January 1995, p. 18.
88. Gregory Alan Tidwell, "The Eternal Restoration," *Gospel Advocate,* October 1993, p. 11.
89. Roy J. Hearn, "Ancient Landmarks," *Gospel Advocate,* May 1997, p. 17.
90. James D. Bales, "From Within," *Gospel Advocate,* February 1993, p. 9.
91. F. Furman Kearley, "Unity—Desired but not Essential," *Gospel Advocate,* February 1993, p. 5.
92. See Hooper, *A Distinct People,* pp. 287–306.
93. Hooper acknowledges that the halt in declining member-

ship owed much to the success of the International Church of Christ. See *A Distinct People,* p. 308.

94. Two articles pointing out the complexity of the transitions taking place in the churches of Christ are Joe Beam, "What Is Happening to Us?" *Wineskins,* May 1996, p. 23, and Michael R. Weed and Gary Holloway, "The Gospel in Urban Vessels," *Discipliana,* September 1995, p. 109.
95. Hughes, *Reviving the Ancient Faith,* p. 350. See the Hughes section entitled "Rethinking the Restoration Vision," pp. 363–73.
96. Hughes, *Reviving the Ancient Faith,* p. 366.
97. Randy Harris, "Come Holy Spirit?" *Wineskins,* March/April 1996, pp. 16–19.
98. Lynn Anderson, "Right-Brain Christians in a Left-Brain Church," *Wineskins,* July 1992, pp. 27–30.
99. "Editorial: Pendulum Swings Between Dogma and Devotion," *Christian Chronicle,* November 1996, p. 20.
100. Quoted in Hughes, *Reviving the Ancient Faith,* p. 368. On the new hermeneutic, see pp. 363–73.
101. Thomas H. Olbricht, *Hearing God's Voice: My Life with Scripture in the Churches of Christ* (Abilene: ACU Press, 1996).
102. Gary D. Collier, *The Forgotten Treasures* (Austin: Howard Publishing, 1995), p. 98.
103. C. Leonard Allen, *The Cruciform Church: Becoming a Cross-Shaped People in a Secular World* (Abilene: ACU Press, 1990).
104. Bill Love, *The Core Gospel: On Restoring the Crux of the Matter* (Abilene: ACU Press, 1992).
105. Rubel Shelly and Randy Harris, *The Second Incarnation: A Theology for the Twenty-First Century Church* (West Monroe, Louisiana: Howard Publishing, 1992).
106. Darryl Tippens, "Reading the Bible in an Age of Crisis," *Wineskins,* January/February 1994, pp. 9–14.
107. Rubel Shelly, *I Just Want to Be a Christian* (Nashville: Twentieth Century Christian, 1984). For a thorough discussion of Shelly's role in the progressive movement, see Hughes, *Reviving the Ancient Faith,* pp. 363–73, including footnotes 37, 41, 47, and 52.
108. Rubel Shelly, "A Christ-Centered Hermeneutic," *Wineskins,* January/February 1994, p. 5. See this entire issue for a series of articles urging a rethinking of the hermeneutical basis of the restoration movement.

109. *The Restoration Movement and Unity* (Henderson, Tennessee: Freed-Hardeman College, 1986), p. 140.
110. See "The Eighteenth Annual Spiritual Sword Lectureship," *Spiritual Sword,* October 1993, p. 49; J. E. Choate, "The Best Kept Secret of Our Liberal Brethren: The 'Hermeneutic of Suspicion,'" *Firm Foundation,* May 1995, pp. 1, 5–6.
111. Lanier, "Controversies in the Church," p. 22.
112. H. A. (Buster) Dobbs, "New Hermeneutic Again," *Firm Foundation,* November 1995, p. 3.
113. H. A. (Buster) Dobbs, "Fellowship and Revelation," *Firm Foundation,* August 1996, p. 5.
114. C. Leonard Allen, Richard T. Hughes, and Michael R. Weed, *The Worldly Church* (Abilene: ACU Press, 1988), p. 47.
115. "Editorial: On the Fragmentation and the Healing of the Church," p. 20.
116. Allen, *Distant Voices,* p. 4.
117. Hughes, *Reviving the Ancient Faith,* p. 306.
118. See Hughes, *Reviving the Ancient Faith,* pp. 375–84.
119. J. E. Choate, "Reviving the Ancient Faith: The Story of the Churches of Christ in America," *Firm Foundation,* September 1996, p. 14.
120. Ibid., p. 14.
121. Alan E. Highers, "Trojan Horse in the Church," *Spiritual Sword,* April 1994, p. 7.
122. F. LaGard Smith, *The Cultural Church* (Nashville: Twentieth Century Christian, 1992).
123. Alan E. Highers, "From the Woodland," *Spiritual Sword,* April 1994, p. 45.
124. Mike Cope, "Christians Only—Not the Only Christians," *Wineskins,* April/May 1997, pp. 6–10. See Denny Boultinghouse, "Christians Only, but not the Only Christians," *Image,* May/June 1995, p. 5; Mike Cope, "Is It an Identity Crisis," pp. 4–5.
125. Foster, *Will the Cycle Be Unbroken,* pp. 22–23.
126. Max Lucado, "Life at Sea on the Good Ship Fellowship," *Wineskins,* March/April 1996, p. 21.
127. Dobbs, "Fellowship and Revelation," p. 2.
128. Wayne Jackson, "Who Are These Other Sheep?" *Firm Foundation,* November 1996, p. 9.
129. Jim Laws, "The Biblical View of Fellowship," *Spiritual Sword,* October 1993, pp. 17–21.

130. James S. Woodruff, *The Church in Transition* (Searcy, Arkansas: Bible House, 1990).
131. Ibid., p. 174.
132. Cecil May, Jr., "Levels of Fellowship," *Gospel Advocate,* August 1993, p. 22.
133. F. LaGard Smith, *Who Is My Brother?* (Malibu, California: Cotswold Publishing, 1997).
134. Ibid., pp. 77–79.
135. Ibid., p. 78.
136. Ibid., pp. 253–354. For an example of the emphasis placed on baptism as the mark of fellowship with Christ, see Jimmy Jividen, "Fellowship Challenges Today," *Gospel Advocate,* August 1993, p. 13.
137. E. Claude Gardner, "Save Our Children," *Spiritual Sword,* October 1993, pp. 40–43; *Gospel Advocate,* December 1993, pp. 17–19.
138. J. E. Choate, "Christian Jubilee Has Developed a 'Jacob's Limp,'" *Firm Foundation,* April 1995, p. 20.
139. William S. Banowsky, "The Christ-Centered Church," *Wineskins,* April/May 1997, pp. 32–38.
140. Alan Highers, "The Banowsky Speech at ACU," *Firm Foundation,* November 1996, pp. 1, 6–8.
141. Richard T. Hughes, "Strengths of Our Heritage," *Wineskins,* April/May 1997, pp. 12–16.
142. Rubel Shelly, "A Call to Biblical Action," *Image,* January/February 1995, p. 16.
143. Rubel Shelly, "A Passion for Nonsectarian Faith," *Wineskins,* January/February 1993, pp. 4–6.
144. Noble Patterson, "Foy E. Wallace, Jr.: A Remembrance!" *Firm Foundation,* January 1996, pp. 11–12; *Christian Chronicle,* March 1996, p. 18.
145. H. A. (Buster) Dobbs, "Foy E. Wallace, Jr.: A Remembrance!" *Firm Foundation,* January 1996, p. 12.
146. William S. Banowsky, "The Christ-Centered Church," *Image,* March/April 1996, p. 26.
147. Thomas H. Olbricht, "Reuel Lemmons," *Image,* July/August 1995, pp. 6a–9a.
148. "Abilene Christian University Facilities Requested," p. 18.
149. H. A. (Buster) Dobbs, "Fatal Error," *Firm Foundation,* July 1996, p. 6.
150. Hailey, Foster, and Winter, "Ministers' Beliefs," pp. 15–17.

1. G. H. P Showalter, "History of the Church During the Last Fifty Years," *Firm Foundation,* March 11, 1941, p. 4.
2. *Prickly Pear: 1930* (Abilene Christian College yearbook), p. 24. See Don Morris, "Abilene Christian College," *Firm Foundation,* August 22, 1939, p. 7.
3. Homer Hailey, taped conversations with John Kilgore, Tucson, Arizona, tape no. 3.
4. Paul Southern, interview with the author, August 10, 1988, Abilene, Texas.
5. See "Abilene Elects New President," *Firm Foundation,* January 12, 1932, p. 4.
6. *Prickly Pear: 1930,* p. 25.
7. Walter Adams, interview with the author, August 11, 1988, Abilene, Texas.
8. See O. E. Payne, *Instrumental Music Is Scriptural* (Cincinnati: Standard Publishing, 1920); Marshall Clement Kurfees, *Instrumental Music in Worship* (Nashville: McQuiddy Publishing, 1911); Ira Matthews Boswell and N. B. Hardeman, *Discussion on Instrumental Music in Worship* (Nashville: Gospel Advocate Co., 1924).
9. Kilgore tape no. 3.
10. Ibid.
11. *Prickly Pear: 1930,* p. 24.
12. Adams interview.
13. Kilgore tape no. 3.
14. *Prickly Pear: 1927,* p. 79.
15. *Prickly Pear: 1929,* p. 117.
16. "Mission Work among Negroes Is Started by College Students," *Optimist,* October 24, 1929, p. 2.
17. "Hailey Reports Good Attendance at Negro Mission Last Monday," *Optimist,* March 6, 1930, p. 3.
18. Kilgore tape no. 1.
19. "Many Interesting Incidents Fill Life of Preacher Boys," *Optimist,* February 14, 1929, p. 2.
20. See "Preaching the Word," *Optimist,* November 1, 1928, p. 2.
21. Ibid., p. 2.
22. "Hailey Wins First Place in Cox Speaking Contest," *Optimist,* April 10, 1930, p. 1.

23. "Homer Hailey Speaks Last Sunday Morning," *Optimist,* April 3, 1930, p. 2.
24. "Seniors Name Speakers for Commencement," *Optimist,* April 24, 1930, p. 1.
25. *Prickly Pear: 1929,* p. 149.
26. Ibid.
27. Homer Hailey, "Chronology," unpublished manuscript in the possession of the author.
28. F. B. Shepherd, "Into All the World," *Gospel Advocate,* August 28, 1930, p. 833.
29. For an account of much of the activity of this summer, see Homer L. Hailey, "Needy Fields," *Gospel Advocate,* August 28, 1930, pp. 832–33.
30. "Workers' Activities," *Firm Foundation,* August 26, 1930, p. 5.
31. "Workers' Activities," *Firm Foundation,* September 16, 1930, p. 5.
32. "Workers' Activities," *Firm Foundation,* October 28, 1930, p. 5.
33. See Hailey, "Needy Fields," pp. 832–33.
34. Kilgore tape no. 3.
35. *Prickly Pear: 1930,* pp. 116, 122, 146.
36. See *Prickly Pear: 1928,* p. 154; "Players to Appear in Comedy Tonight," *Optimist,* October 10, 1929, pp. 1, 4.
37. "W Club Will Present Old Maids' Convention Next Monday Evening," *Optimist,* April 10, 1930, pp. 1, 2.
38. "Ko-Jo-Kai Girls Are Honored with Outing," *Optimist,* May 23, 1939, p. 3.
39. "Lois Manly Honors Friends Saturday," *Optimist,* April 10, 1930, p. 4.
40. "Hailey Will Be Principal of Academy," *Optimist,* May 15, 1930, p. 1; Kilgore tape no. 3.
41. See Hailey, "Chronology."
42. Kilgore tape no. 1.
43. "Workers' Activities," *Firm Foundation,* July 7, 1931, p. 7.
44. *Firm Foundation,* August 25, 1931, p. 5.
45. *Firm Foundation,* October 13, 1931, p. 5. See also Hailey, "Chronology."
46. *Firm Foundation,* November 10, 1931, p. 7.
47. Hailey, "Chronology."
48. *Firm Foundation,* February 16, 1932, p. 5.

49. See *Firm Foundation,* September 6, 1932, p. 6; Kilgore tape no. 4; Hailey, "Chronology."
50. *Firm Foundation,* May 31, 1932, p. 5.
51. *Firm Foundation,* October 4, 1932, p. 4.
52. "Highland Church to Award Contract for Two Story Building," *Optimist,* January 30, 1930, p. 1.
53. Kilgore tapes, nos. 1 and 4.
54. Kilgore tape no. 4.
55. "Highland Church Dedicated Sunday," *Optimist,* September 29, 1938, p. 1.
56. Kilgore tape no. 4; Hailey, "Chronology."
57. "Homer Hailey Resigns Highland Work After 11 Years of Fruitful Preaching, Teaching," *Christian Chronicle,* June 9, 1943, p. 3.
58. Adams interview.
59. Kilgore tape no. 4.
60. "Homer Hailey Resigns Highland Work," p. 3. See Homer Hailey, "Are We Kidding Ourselves," *Christian Chronicle,* June 30, 1943, p. 2.
61. Homer Hailey, *Let's Go Fishing for Men* (Abilene: Christian Chronicle Publishing, 1951); Kilgore tapes, nos. 4 and 9.
62. Harry W. Pickup, Jr., interview with the author, April 28, 1988, Tampa, Florida.
63. See *Firm Foundation,* July 11, 1933, p. 7; July 25, 1933, p. 6; August 22, 1933, p. 6; September 12, 1933, p. 5; September 26, 1933, p. 3.
64. *Firm Foundation,* May 8, 1934, p. 6.
65. *Firm Foundation,* September 14, 1937, p. 3.
66. See *Firm Foundation,* July 18, 1939, p. 6; August 15, 1939, p. 5.
67. *Firm Foundation,* May 24, 1938, p. 6. See *Firm Foundation,* May 3, 1938, p. 4; "Hailey to Hold Denver Meeting," *Optimist,* April 14, 1938, p. 1.
68. *Firm Foundation,* November 4, 1941, p. 6.
69. *Firm Foundation,* May 27, 1941, p. 5; October 1, 1940, p. 6; September 6, 1938, p. 7; November 18, 1941, p. 8.
70. Homer Hailey, interview with the author, August 2, 1988, Tucson, Arizona.
71. See *Firm Foundation,* August 7, 1934, p. 5; October 1, 1940, p. 6; September 22, 1942, p. 6.

72. See *Firm Foundation,* August 21, 1934, p. 5; September 1, 1942, p. 6; August 20, 1935, p. 5.
73. *Firm Foundation,* July 10, 1934, p. 6. See also *Firm Foundation,* June 26, 1934, p. 5.
74. *Firm Foundation,* September 1, 1936, p. 5.
75. *Firm Foundation,* November 18, 1941, p. 8; July 18, 1939, p. 6.
76. *Firm Foundation,* August 30, 1938, p. 5; October 27, 1942, p. 7; August 15, 1939, p. 5.
77. *Firm Foundation,* September 6, 1938, p. 7; May 3, 1938, p. 4; June 4, 1940, p. 5.
78. *Firm Foundation,* August 21, 1934, p. 5; August 26, 1941, p. 7; November 18, 1941, p. 8.
79. *Firm Foundation,* November 18, 1941, p. 8; February 17, 1942, p. 5.
80. *Firm Foundation,* August 6, 1940, p. 6.
81. Kilgore tape no. 4.
82. Ibid.; Georgia Deane Cope, interview with the author, April 27, 1988, Tampa, Florida.
83. Letter from James W. Adams to the author, August 12, 1998.
84. *Abilene Christian College Bible Lectures, 1934* (Austin, Texas: Firm Foundation Publishing House, n.d.), pp. 30, 31. See also pp. 17–31.
85. *Abilene Christian College Bible Lectures, 1937* (Abilene: Abilene Christian College, 1937), pp. 9–13.
86. *Abilene Christian College Bible Lectures, 1939* (Austin, Texas: Firm Foundation Publishing House, n.d.), p. 40. See also pp. 32–41.
87. In 1937, Hailey joined old-timers Curtis Porter, Early Arceneaux, and L. R. Wilson on a lecture program in Waco, Texas. None of them would probably have approved the sponsoring format a few years later. *Firm Foundation,* October 17, 1937, p. 6. See also "Southern, Hailey, Scott on Lecture," *Optimist,* October 20, 1938, p. 1; "College Speakers in Anson Lectures," *Optimist,* December 12, 1935, p. 1.
88. *Firm Foundation,* April 6, 1943, p. 13.
89. *Firm Foundation,* September 28, 1943, p. 14; Hailey, "Chronology."
90. Kilgore tape no. 9.
91. *Firm Foundation,* July 6, 1937, p. 5.
92. "Homer Hailey Resigns Highland Work," p. 3.

93. Homer Hailey, "Work of James E. White," *Bible Banner,* March 1941, p. 6. See Homer Hailey, "The Indian Work," *Bible Banner,* December 1942, p. 13.
94. James F. Cox, "Abilene Christian College," *Firm Foundation,* August 21, 1934, p. 8.
95. *Bulletin Abilene Christian College . . . 1934–35,* June 1934, pp. 5–21.
96. Ibid., p. 1.
97. Ibid., p. 3.
98. See "Hailey Resignation Takes Effect Soon," *Optimist,* January 13, 1938, p. 1.
99. Garvin Beauchamp, interview with the author, August 10, 1988, Abilene, Texas.
100. Georgia Deane Cope interview.
101. "Hailey Counsels Forum Attendants," *Optimist,* October 14, 1937, p. 3. See also "Hailey Addresses Forum on Reasoning," *Optimist,* October 24, 1935, p. 1.
102. "Hailey Gives Farewell to Mission Class," *Optimist,* February 3, 1938, p. 3.
103. Beauchamp interview.
104. "Homer Hailey Chosen Speaker by Seniors," *Optimist,* March 24, 1938, p. 1.
105. See "Hailey Will Preach Here April 3–10," *Optimist,* March 17, 1938, p. 1; "Homer Hailey in Midst of College Church's Annual Spring Meeting," *Optimist,* April 7, 1938, p. 1.
106. Beauchamp interview; Kilgore tape no. 4; Hailey, "Chronology."
107. See "Hailey Entertains Senior Students," *Optimist,* February 3, 1938, p. 3; "Hailey Ranch Scene of GATA Frolic," *Optimist,* March 10, 1938, p. 3; Kilgore tape no. 4; Beauchamp interview.
108. Kilgore tape no. 4; Hailey, "Chronology."
109. Kilgore tape no. 4.
110. See "Helena, Montana," *Firm Foundation,* May 11, 1943, p. 9; Hailey, "Chronology."
111. See *Firm Foundation,* May 4, 1943, p. 11; July 6, 1943, p. 10; August 10, 1943, p. 10; August 24, 1943, p. 12; September 14, 1943, p. 15.
112. "Many Preachers Plan Moves for September," *Christian Chronicle,* August 4, 1943, p. 1.
113. Kilgore tape no. 1; Georgia Deane Cope interview.

114. Kilgore tape no. 4.
115. "Fifteen Preachers to Take Part in Fourth Annual Lectures in Dallas," *Christian Chronicle,* January 19, 1944, p. 1.
116. Kilgore tape no. 4.
117. Kilgore tape no. 4; Southern interview; Adams interview.
118. Adams interview.
119. *Firm Foundation,* November 18, 1930, p. 6. See "Roberson's Life Marked by Scholarship, Service," *Optimist,* May 22, 1951, p. 4.
120. Southern interview.
121. Southern interview; Kilgore tape no. 4.
122. J. L. Hines, "The 'Free-For-All' at Abilene Christian College," *Bible Banner,* December 1940, pp. 14–15.
123. Don H. Morris, "A Clear-Cut Statement by the President of Abilene Christian College," *Bible Banner,* January 1941, pp. 8–9.
124. Foy E. Wallace, Jr., "Brother Roberson's 'A-Millennium,'" *Bible Banner,* May 1941, pp. 4–5.
125. Ibid.
126. Foy E. Wallace, Jr., "The 'Millennium' in 'What Jesus Taught,'" *Bible Banner,* March 1941, pp. 4–5; "Concerning the Colleges," *Bible Banner,* February 1941, p. 10.
127. Letter from Homer Hailey to the author, February 23, 1998. Content used by permission.
128. See *Firm Foundation,* July 11, 1944, p. 12; August 15, 1944, p. 12; Hailey, "Chronology."
129. "Hailey Will Go to Central Church in Los Angeles, Calif.," *Christian Chronicle,* September 6, 1944, p. 1.
130. See *Firm Foundation,* September 26, 1944, p. 12; October 10, 1944, p. 15; November 14, 1944, p. 11; December 5, 1944, p. 12; December 19, 1944, p. 10.
131. Kilgore tapes, nos. 1 and 4.
132. Kilgore tape no. 4.
133. "From Brother Homer Hailey," *Firm Foundation,* May 8, 1945, p. 11; "Hailey Begins Work in Los Angeles," *Christian Chronicle,* May 2, 1945, p. 1.
134. Kilgore tapes, nos. 1 and 4.
135. "From Brother Homer Hailey," p. 11.
136. "Homer Hailey in Meeting with Tucson, Ariz. Church," *Christian Chronicle,* October 10, 1945, p. 1.
137. Hailey, "Chronology."

138. Kilgore tapes, nos. 1 and 4.

139. Homer Hailey, *Attitudes and Consequences in the Restoration Movement* (Kansas City: Old Paths Book Club, 1945); See "Old Path Book Club to Issue Hailey's Book," *Christian Chronicle,* October 31, 1945, p. 4.

140. "Hawaiian Mission to be Sponsored from Los Angeles," *Christian Chronicle,* February 27, 1946, pp. 1, 4.

141. "Hailey to Open Bible School," *Christian Chronicle,* January 23, 1946, p. 1; "Hailey Family Sails March 18 for Hawaii Work," *Christian Chronicle,* March 20, 1946, p. 1.

142. Kilgore tape no. 4.

143. Hailey, "Chronology."

144. "From California," *Firm Foundation,* May 7, 1946, p. 4.

145. "Honolulu Bible School Opens," *Christian Chronicle,* December 11, 1946, p. 2.

146. Kilgore tape no. 4; Homer Hailey, "The Honolulu Work," *Firm Foundation,* October 14, 1947, p. 9.

147. "Homer Hailey in Honolulu," *Firm Foundation,* June 10, 1947, p. 9.

148. Hailey, "The Honolulu Work," p. 9. Also see *Firm Foundation,* March 2, 1948, p. 12.

149. Kilgore tape no. 4.

150. Ibid.

151. "ACC Lectures to Draw Record Crowds," *Christian Chronicle,* February 19, 1947, pp. 1, 7.

152. "Lectures on World Evangelism Arouse High Enthusiasm among Record Audiences Attending," *Christian Chronicle,* March 5, 1947, pp. 1, 7.

153. "Hailey to Return to States in Apr.," *Christian Chronicle,* March 10, 1948, p. 1.

154. Kilgore tape no. 1.

155. Hailey, "Chronology."

156. Kilgore tape no. 1.

157. "Homer Hailey Now Holding Meeting on Campus," *Optimist,* October 27, 1948, p. 1.

158. "Abilene Christian College Lectureship," *Firm Foundation,* March 18, 1947, p. 7.

159. Southern interview. See "Abilene Christian College," *Firm Foundation,* July 2, 1946, pp. 5, 6.

160. "Abilene Christian College," *Firm Foundation,* August 1, 1950, p. 6.

161. "Abilene Christian College," *Firm Foundation,* December 2, 1947, p. 2.
162. *Firm Foundation,* July 27, 1948, p. 15; *Christian Chronicle,* July 14, 1948, p. 5.
163. *Firm Foundation,* August 9, 1949, p. 9.
164. *Firm Foundation,* September 20, 1949, p. 10.
165. See *Firm Foundation,* August 9, 1949, p. 11.
166. "Special Lectures in Fort Worth," *Firm Foundation,* March 14, 1950, pp. 8, 9.
167. "God Can Use You, Hailey Declares," *Optimist,* December 15, 1948, p. 1.
168. Kilgore tape no. 5.
169. Hailey, *Let's Go Fishing for Men;* see *Christian Chronicle,* January 10, 1951, p. 1; February 7, 1951, p. 3.
170. "Central Christian College Announces First Lectures of Annual Series Planned," *Christian Chronicle,* March 14, 1951, p. 1.
171. Southern interview.
172. "Paul Southern Named Bible Department Head," *Optimist,* May 22, 1951, p. 6; see also "Southern Named New Head of ACC Bible Dept.," *Christian Chronicle,* May 30, 1951, p. 1.
173. Kilgore tape no. 5; Southern interview.
174. R. M. Alexander, "Why Abilene Christian College Is Asking for $3,000,000," *Firm Foundation,* July 16, 1946, pp. 5–6.
175. Adams interview.
176. *Abilene Christian College Bulletin: 1951–52,* vol. 35 (May 1951), pp. 6–13.
177. There was a touch of irony in Southern's experience as head of the Bible Department at ACC. During his long tenure, which lasted until 1970, his own academic credentials and values became a point of controversy. A younger group of publishing scholars who joined the Bible faculty increasingly criticized colleagues who were less rigorous in their scholarship and were trained at less prestigious universities. "People who didn't go to Harvard or Yale or Princeton," Southern complained, "were . . . not real scholars." As the university reached a new level of academic aspirations in the 1970s, Southern's educational status and his approach became a liability rather than an asset. Southern and his generation were replaced by a group of religion scholars much more attuned to the broader community of academic

professionals engaged in the scientific study of religion. In short, Southern became enmeshed in the progressive-traditional division in institutional churches discussed in Chapter 4 of this book. Southern interview.

178. "An Announcement Full of Hope for the Future," *Firm Foundation,* March 16, 1943, p. 16.
179. "Abilene Christian College Campaign," *Firm Foundation,* August 13, 1946, p. 15; Don H. Morris, "Abilene Christian College," *Firm Foundation,* May 6, 1947, pp. 1–3.
180. Bob F. Owen, interview with the author, April 30, 1988, Tampa, Florida. The growing importance of donors is clearly reflected in the *Optimist* during the late 1940s and early 1950s.
181. Southern interview.
182. Beauchamp interview.
183. Kilgore tape no. 1.
184. Ibid.
185. Owen interview; Kilgore tape no. 5.
186. Hailey, "Chronology."
187. See "Hailey Named Vice Pres. of Florida Christian College," *Christian Chronicle,* June 6, 1951, p. 1.
188. Hailey, "Chronology."

6. Hailey in the Eye of the Storm: The Florida Years

1. See Cecil Willis, *W. W. Otey: Contender for the Faith* (Akron: Cecil Willis, 1964), pp. 250–61.
2. Quoted in L. C. Sears, *For Freedom: The Biography of John Nelson Armstrong* (Austin: Sweet Publishing, 1969), p. 291.
3. "Preacher Stresses Work Done by Chronicle," *Christian Chronicle,* May 3, 1944, p. 1.
4. Homer Hailey, *What Will This Babbler Say?* (Abilene: Otis Gatewood, Ben W. Newhouse, John Fairs Nichols, [1932]), pp. 70–74.
5. See Homer Hailey, "Shall History Repeat Itself?" *Bible Banner,* May 1941, p. 6; Homer Hailey, "The Man on the Other Side," *Bible Banner,* January 1941, p. 6.
6. Homer Hailey, taped conversations with John Kilgore, Tucson, Arizona, tapes no. 5, 8, and 9.
7. Kilgore tapes, nos. 11 and 12.

8. Homer Hailey, interview with the author, August 2, 1988, Tucson, Arizona.
9. Kilgore tape no. 9; *Bible Banner,* October 1940, p. 42.
10. *Torch,* September 1950, back cover.
11. Homer Hailey, "The Curse of Negligence," *Bible Banner,* March 1940, p. 13.
12. Homer Hailey, "The Inner Threat of Softness," *Bible Banner,* January 1941, p. 5; Homer Hailey, "America's Religious Heritage," *Bible Banner,* November 1940, p. 5.
13. Homer Hailey, "The Man on the Other Side"; Homer Hailey, "Standing Up," *Bible Banner,* April 1940, p. 7.
14. Homer Hailey, "Clinton Davidson in Abilene," *Bible Banner,* July 1940, p. 2.
15. Homer Hailey, "The Digression of the Digressives," *Bible Banner,* July 1941, pp. 8–9.
16. See Don H. Morris, "A Clear-Cut Statement by the President of Abilene Christian College," *Bible Banner,* January 1941, pp. 8–9.
17. Homer Hailey, "Christians: By Conviction or Convenience," *Bible Banner,* October 1942, p. 8.
18. Homer Hailey, "God's Call to Expansion," *Bible Banner,* January 1942, pp. 13–14.
19. Homer Hailey, "Some Modern New Carts," *Bible Banner,* September 1942, p. 15.
20. "Hailey and Baley Address Assembly on Armistice," *Optimist,* November 12, 1936, p. 1.
21. Kilgore tape no. 5.
22. "Homer Hailey Speaks to GTC, Men's Forum," *Optimist,* January 19, 1951, p. 1.
23. See Homer Hailey, "The Christian and Ball Games," *Gospel Broadcast,* March 27, 1941, p. 12.
24. Kilgore tape no. 12.
25. James R. Cope, interview with the author, April 29, 1988, Tampa, Florida.
26. Homer Hailey, "Dependent Children," *Firm Foundation,* October 25, 1949, pp. 3–4. See also "Hailey on Annual Tipton Home Program," *Optimist,* November 17, 1938, p. 1.
27. Kilgore tape no. 9.
28. Kilgore tapes, nos. 1 and 5.
29. Letter from Homer Hailey to the author, December 29, 1998.

30. Cope interview.
31. Cope interview; Bob F. Owen, interview with the author, April 29, 1988, Tampa, Florida; Kilgore tape no. 5.
32. James R. Cope, "Homer Hailey Goes to Florida Christian College," *Gospel Advocate,* July 5, 1951, p. 429.
33. Harry W. Pickup, Jr., interview with the author, April 28, 1988, Tampa, Florida.
34. Owen interview.
35. Bill Humble, interview with the author, August 10, 1988, Abilene, Texas.
36. An excellent popular history of Florida College was published in 1996: Margie H. Garrett, ed., *Making a Difference* ([Temple Terrace]: Florida College, 1996).
37. L. R. Wilson, "Leaving Florida Christian College," *Firm Foundation,* January 18, 1949, pp. 1–2.
38. C. Ed Owings, "Florida Christian College Names New President," *Firm Foundation,* April 12, 1949, pp. 2, 3.
39. L. R. Wilson, "Our Program for Florida Christian College," *Firm Foundation,* December 18, 1945, pp. 6, 7; January 8, 1949, pp. 8, 9.
40. Harry Pickup, "Florida Christian College," *Firm Foundation,* February 15, 1949, pp. 8, 9.
41. Owings, "Florida Christian College Names New President," pp. 2, 3. For an extensive treatment of Cope's presidency, written by Clinton D. Hamilton, see Garrett, ed., *Making a Difference,* pp. 46–87.
42. E. H. Ijams, "Former Lipscomb President Speaks," *Firm Foundation,* April 12, 1949, p. 3.
43. Yater Tant, "Florida Christian College Looks Ahead," *Gospel Guardian,* May 31, 1949, p. 5.
44. James R. Cope, "A Brief Look at Florida Christian College," *Firm Foundation,* June 13, 1950, p. 4.
45. James R. Cope, "Rumors and the Record," *Firm Foundation,* April 18, 1950, p. 7.
46. James R. Cope, "Florida Christian College Closes Another Session," *Gospel Advocate,* June 15, 1951, p. 375.
47. Yater Tant, "Jim Cope and Florida Christian College, *Gospel Guardian,* June 2, 1949, p. 2; ". . . And We Need It Now," *Gospel Guardian,* March 30, 1950, p. 2.
48. James D. Bales, "Florida Christian College Lectureship," *Firm Foundation,* April 3, 1951, p. 15; Earl West, "Florida

Christian College Lectures," *Firm Foundation,* March 20, 1951, p. 14.

49. Yater Tant, "Those Florida Lectures," *Gospel Guardian,* March 15, 1951, p. 4.
50. Raymond C. Walker, "An Open Letter to My Brethren," *Gospel Advocate,* August 16, 1951, pp. 516–17.
51. "A Letter from the Board of Directors of Florida Christian College Concerning R. C. Walker's 'Open Letter,'" *Gospel Advocate,* September 27, 1951, pp. 610–11.
52. Clinton D. Hamilton, "Issues and Personalities," *Gospel Advocate,* August 23, 1951, p. 534.
53. *Gospel Advocate,* August 11, 1955, p. 715. See James R. Cope, "Florida Christian College—Changes and Prospects," *Gospel Advocate,* May 27, 1954, pp. 410–11; James R. Cope, "A Brief Look at Florida Christian College," *Gospel Advocate,* June 14, 1955, p. 604.
54. James R. Cope, "Florida Christian College: Retrospect and Prospect," *Gospel Advocate,* July 17, 1958, p. 463.
55. Letter from Eddie G. Couch to B. C. Goodpasture, August 28, 1958, copy in the possession of the author.
56. B. C. Goodpasture, "The Florida Christian College Advertisement," *Gospel Advocate,* August 21, 1958, pp. 530–31.
57. James R. Cope, "Florida Christian College," *Gospel Advocate,* June 26, 1952, p. 421.
58. Humble interview.
59. Kilgore tapes, nos. 6 and 13.
60. See Walker, "An Open Letter to My Brethren," p. 517.
61. Kilgore tape no. 5.
62. Humble interview.
63. Kilgore tape no. 12.
64. Hailey interview.
65. Letter from Clinton D. Hamilton to the author, March 5, 1993.
66. Cope interview.
67. B. C. Goodpasture, "The Preceptor," *Gospel Advocate,* November 22, 1951, p. 738.
68. James R. Cope, "The Preceptor," *Preceptor,* November 1951, pp. 2, 3.
69. James R. Cope, "The Preceptor Changes Hands," *Preceptor,* October 1955, p. 434.

70. Humble interview.
71. Kilgore tape no. 9.
72. Cope, "The Preceptor Changes Hands," p. 434.
73. James R. Cope, "I Am Concerned," *Preceptor,* September 1955, p. 410.
74. Pat Hardeman, "What Foes Tomorrow?" *Preceptor,* January 1952, p. 2.
75. Bill Humble, "The Doctrinal Purity of the Church," *Preceptor,* February 1952, p. 2.
76. James R. Cope, "Our Second Year Closes," *Preceptor,* October 1953, p. 1.
77. Cope interview. Also Hailey interview; Humble interview; Kilgore tape no. 9.
78. James R. Cope, "'Traditional' and 'Creed-Bound' Preaching," *Preceptor,* November 1952, p. 2.
79. Eugene Clevenger, "We Are a Different People," *Preceptor,* April 1952, p. 2.
80. Homer Hailey, "New Carts," *Preceptor,* April 1952, pp. 14–15. See also Homer Hailey, "Thinking Straight," *Preceptor,* November 1951, pp. 6–7.
81. Homer Hailey, "The 'Big' and the 'Little,'" *Preceptor,* March 1952, p. 2.
82. Kilgore tape no. 8.
83. Ibid.
84. Hailey interview.
85. Homer Hailey, "Organization—the Successor to Unity," *Gospel Guardian,* November 17, 1949, p. 4.
86. Homer Hailey, "Dependent Children," *Gospel Guardian,* November 24, 1949, p. 5.
87. Homer Hailey, "Italy and Incense," *Preceptor,* October 1952, p. 2.
88. Kilgore tape no. 11.
89. Ibid.
90. Kilgore tape no. 13.
91. Homer Hailey, "Keepers of Orthodoxy," *Gospel Advocate,* June 19, 1952, p. 399.
92. Pickup interview.
93. Homer Hailey, "Clubs Unwittingly Loosed," *Gospel Advocate,* July 10, 1952, pp. 442, 447.
94. Kilgore tape no. 11.

95. Kilgore tape no. 1.
96. Cecil Willis, "Foy E. Wallace, Jr. Then and Now or 'How the Mighty Have Fallen,'" *Truth Magazine,* August 1964, p. 246.
97. Kilgore tapes, nos. 9 and 11.
98. Hailey interview.
99. Kilgore tape no. 11.
100. Kilgore tape no. 14.
101. Homer Hailey, "Building up the Church through a Good Church Library," *Gospel Advocate,* August 19, 1954, pp. 646–47.
102. Homer Hailey, "Keepers of Orthodoxy," *Gospel Advocate,* November 20, 1958, pp. 740, 746.
103. "Homer Hailey's Article," *Gospel Advocate,* December 4, 1958, p. 770.
104. James F. Kurfees, "More about the 'Keepers of Orthodoxy,'" *Gospel Advocate,* January 1, 1959, pp. 1, 8.
105. Homer Hailey, "Hailey Corrects Hailey," *Gospel Advocate,* January 22, 1959, p. 50.
106. B. C. Goodpasture, "Brother Hailey's Article," *Gospel Advocate,* January 22, 1959, p. 50.
107. Kilgore tapes, nos. 9 and 12; Hailey interview.
108. Kilgore tape no. 9; Hailey interview.
109. Homer Hailey, "Centralized Control," *Gospel Guardian,* February 22, 1960, pp. 130, 140.
110. Batsell Barrett Baxter and M. Norvel Young, eds., *Preachers of Today* (Nashville: Christian Press, [1952]); Batsell Barrett Baxter and M. Norvel Young, eds., *Preachers of Today* (Nashville: Gospel Advocate Co., 1959).
111. Batsell Barrett Baxter and M. Norvel Young, eds., *Preachers of Today* (Nashville: Gospel Advocate Co., 1964).
112. Homer Hailey, interview with the author, August 3, 1988.
113. Kilgore tape no. 11.
114. Kilgore tape no. 13.
115. Homer Hailey, "Meeting a Need," *Preceptor,* July 1953, pp. 4, 5.
116. Kilgore tape no. 5.
117. Kilgore tape no. 13.
118. Kilgore tape no. 5.
119. Ibid.
120. Kilgore tapes, nos. 5 and 6.
121. Kilgore tapes, nos. 6 and 13.

122. Kilgore tape no. 6.
123. Humble interview.
124. Paul Southern, interview with the author, August 10, 1988, Abilene, Texas.
125. Pat Hardeman, "Why?" in Robert Meyers, *Voices of Concern* (St. Louis: Mission Messenger, 1966), p. 91.
126. Hardeman, "Why?" p. 93.
127. Cope interview.
128. Kilgore tape no. 5.
129. Kilgore tape no. 13.
130. Kilgore tape no. 6.
131. Kilgore tape no. 14.
132. Kilgore tapes, nos. 5 and 6.
133. Kilgore tape no. 6.
134. Hailey interview, August 2, 1988.
135. See "Notes and News," *Gospel Advocate,* March 13, 1952, p. 169; July 10, 1952, p. 448; August 21, 1952, p. 546; September 18, 1952, p. 608; Homer Hailey, "Attention, Former Members of the Church in Honolulu," *Gospel Advocate,* January 13, 1955, pp. 32–33; "Hither, Thither, and Yon," *Preceptor,* August 1953, p. 22.
136. Hailey interview, August 2, 1988.
137. See *Gospel Guardian,* September 22, 1949, pp. 1, 7; July 11, 1963, pp. 1, 12.
138. Kilgore tape no. 9.
139. Ibid.
140. Homer Hailey, *A Commentary on the Minor Prophets* (10th ed., Grand Rapids: Baker Book House, 1987), pp. 21–24, 206; see also pp. 204–21.
141. Kilgore tape no. 9; Homer Hailey, "Chronology," unpublished manuscript in the possession of the author.
142. Kilgore tapes, nos. 5 and 6.
143. Kilgore tape no. 13. Harry W. Pickup, Sr., interview with the author, April 28, 1988, Tampa, Florida.
144. Owen interview.
145. Kilgore tape no. 10.
146. Kilgore tape no. 13.
147. Kilgore tapes, nos. 5, 6, and 13.
148. G. K. Wallace, "Mrs. Homer Hailey," *Gospel Advocate,* June 3, 1954, pp. 430–31.
149. Ibid.

150. Hailey, *Minor Prophets,* dedication.
151. Kilgore tape no. 13.
152. Kilgore tape no. 5; Hailey, "Chronology."
153. [Homer Hailey], "Courtin' by Correspondence," unpublished mimeographed manuscript, copy in the possession of the author; Kilgore tape no. 5; Homer Hailey, interview with the author, August 25, 1989, Tucson, Arizona.
154. "Courtin' by Correspondence."
155. Letter from Homer Hailey to Widna Kirby, August 8, 1955, mimeographed copy in the possession of the author.
156. "Courtin' by Correspondence."
157. "Courtin' by Correspondence"; Kilgore tape no. 5.
158. Hailey interview, August 25, 1989.
159. Widna Hailey, interview with the author, August 25, 1989, Tucson, Arizona.
160. "Courtin' by Correspondence."
161. Owen interview.
162. "Courtin' by Correspondence."
163. Owen interview.
164. Homer Hailey interview, August 25, 1989.
165. Harry Pickup, Jr., interview.
166. Letter from Homer Hailey to Widna Hailey, October 20, 1955, mimeographed copy in the possession of the author.
167. "Courtin' by Correspondence."
168. Widna Hailey interview.
169. Rob Hailey, interview with the author, August 2, 1988, Abilene, Texas.
170. Kilgore tape no. 13.
171. Kilgore tape no. 6.
172. Owen interview.
173. Rob Hailey interview.
174. Owen interview; Kilgore tape no. 6.
175. Rob Hailey interview; Kilgore tape no. 6.
176. Kilgore tapes, nos. 6, 13, and 14.
177. Kilgore tape no. 10; Dennis Hailey, interview with the author, August 5, 1988, Phoenix, Arizona.
178. Widna Hailey interview.
179. Harry Pickup, Jr., interview.
180. Kilgore tape no. 13.
181. Widna Hailey interview.
182. Kilgore tape no. 10.

183. Kilgore tape no. 1.
184. "Homer Hailey," *Florida College News Bulletin,* May 1972, pp. 2–3.
185. James R. Cope, "Honor to Whom Honor," *Florida College News Bulletin,* May 1972, p. 4.

7. Arizona Retirement, Reluctant Notoriety: 1973–1999

1. Homer Hailey, interview with the author, August 2, 1988, Tucson, Arizona; Rob Hailey, interview with the author, August 11, 1988, Abilene, Texas; Homer Hailey, taped conversations with John Kilgore, Tucson, Arizona, tape no. 1.
2. Homer Hailey, interview with the author, August 25, 1989, Tucson, Arizona.
3. Kilgore tapes, nos. 1 and 6.
4. Kilgore tape no. 6.
5. Kilgore tape no. 12; Rob Hailey interview.
6. Kilgore tape no. 7.
7. Homer Hailey, "Shall I Quit Preaching?" *Vanguard,* January 1981, pp. 1, 14.
8. Letter from Homer Hailey, dated October 18, 1992.
9. Kilgore tape no. 1; Hailey interview, August 2, 1988; Homer Hailey, "Chronology," unpublished manuscript in the possession of the author.
10. Kilgore tape no. 3.
11. Yater Tant, "Your Board of Editors," *Vanguard,* January 9, 1975, pp. 4–5.
12. Fanning Yater Tant, "'Fellow-Workers' in the Gospel," *Vanguard,* October 14, 1976, p. 2.
13. Homer Hailey, "The Prophets Speak of Calvary," *Guardian of Truth,* October 1, 1987, pp. 610, 643; Homer Hailey, "The Problem of Suffering," *Guardian of Truth,* May 21, 1987, pp. 304–7.
14. Homer Hailey, *Hailey's Comments* (Las Vegas: Nevada Publications, 1985).
15. Foy E. Wallace, Jr., *The Book of Revelation* (Nashville: Foy E. Wallace, Jr., Publications, 1966).
16. Kilgore tape no. 6.
17. Kilgore tape no. 9.

18. Homer Hailey, *A Commentary on the Minor Prophets* (Grand Rapids: Baker Book House, 1972), p. 8.
19. Hailey interview, August 2, 1988.
20. Harry W. Pickup, Jr., interview with the author, April 28, 1988, Tampa, Florida.
21. Kilgore tape no. 9.
22. Homer Hailey, *Revelation: An Introduction and Commentary* (Grand Rapids: Baker Book House, 1979), pp. 15–53.
23. Kilgore tape no. 9.
24. Kilgore tape no. 6.
25. Kilgore tapes, nos. 6 and 9.
26. Homer Hailey, *From Creation to the Day of Eternity* (2d ed., Las Vegas: Nevada Publications, 1982).
27. Kilgore tape no. 9.
28. Hailey, *From Creation,* p. vii.
29. Hailey interview, August 2, 1988.
30. Hailey interview, August 25, 1989.
31. Letter from Homer Hailey to John Kilgore, July 1, 1986, copy of handwritten letter in the possession of the author.
32. Homer Hailey, interview with the author, July 16, 1997, Tucson, Arizona.
33. Kilgore tape no. 11; Hailey interview, July 16, 1997.
34. "Homer Haileyisms," mimeographed manuscript assembled by Don Givens, copy in the possession of the author.
35. Pickup interview.
36. Hailey interview, July 16, 1997.
37. Hailey interview, August 2, 1988.
38. Kilgore tape no. 11; Hailey interview, August 25, 1989.
39. Letter from Homer Hailey to the author, December 29, 1998.
40. Kilgore tape no. 11.
41. Hailey interview, August 25, 1989.
42. Homer Hailey, interview with the author, August 3, 1988, Tucson, Arizona.
43. Letter from James W. Adams to the author, August 12, 1998.
44. Hailey interview, August 25, 1989.
45. Hailey interview, August 3, 1988; Kilgore tape no. 11.
46. J. T. Smith, "Homer Hailey's Position on Divorce and Remarriage," *The Bible Says,* August 15, 1976.
47. J. T. Smith, "A Difficult Task #2," *North Miami Avenue Bulletin,* June 27, 1982.

48. James R. Cope, interview with the author, April 29, 1988, Tampa, Florida.
49. Bob F. Owen, interview with the author, April 29, 1988, Tampa, Florida.
50. James D. Bales, *Not Under Bondage* (Searcy, Arkansas: J. D. Bales, 1979).
51. Thomas B. Warren, "A General Look at Divorce & Remarriage," *Spiritual Sword,* January 1975, pp. 1–9.
52. James D. Bales, "We Must Neither Bind Nor Loose Where God Has Not Done So," *Spiritual Sword,* January 1975, pp. 9–11.
53. James D. Bales, *Shall We Splinter* (Searcy, Arkansas: James D. Bales, n.d.).
54. W. W. Otey, "Teaching—Practice," *Gospel Advocate,* August 16, 1945, p. 1.
55. Bales, *Shall We Splinter,* p. 35.
56. Bales, *Shall We Splinter,* pp. 60–70.
57. Foy E. Wallace, Jr., *The Sermon on the Mount and the Civil State* (Nashville: Foy E. Wallace, Jr., Publications, n.d.), p. 40.
58. Reuel Lemmons, "Divorce and Remarriage," *Firm Foundation,* March 25, 1975, p. 178.
59. See *Firm Foundation,* October 1992, p. 9.
60. Charles A. Holt, "News and Views," *Gospel Guardian,* February 1, 1962, pp. 598, 607. An early debate on the subject of divorce was published as *Dabney-Frost Debate on Marriage, Divorce and Remarriage* (Fort Worth: Massey, 1959).
61. Yater Tant, "Articles on 'The Marriage Question,'" *Gospel Guardian,* August 22, 1963, pp. 244, 249.
62. James W. Adams, "Speak for Yourself, John," *Gospel Guardian,* January 15, 1978, pp. 28–29.
63. James W. Adams, "False Conclusions from Just Principles," *Gospel Guardian,* June 1, 1976, pp. 244–45.
64. James W. Adams, "Johnny Come-Lately-Sommerites," *Gospel Guardian,* February 1, 1978, pp. 52–53.
65. James W. Adams, "Every Way of Man Is Right in His Own Eyes," *Gospel Guardian,* May 15, 1978, pp. 220–21.
66. James W. Adams, "While I Was Musing the Fire Burned," *Gospel Guardian,* July 1978, pp. 268–69.
67. James W. Adams, "Attempting to Fight the Lord's Battles with 'Carnal Weapons,'" *Gospel Guardian*, September 1978, pp. 332–33.

68. James W. Adams, "Identical Abominations," *Gospel Guardian,* August 1978, p. 304.
69. H. E. Phillips, "Judgment or Conviction?" *Searching the Scriptures,* July 1978, pp. 101–3. See H. E. Phillips, "Medley of Matters," *Searching the Scriptures,* October 1978, pp. 205–6.
70. Connie W. Adams, "First Pure, Then Peaceable," *Searching the Scriptures,* July 1978, p. 127. A published debate dating from this period was *The Smith-Lovelady Debate* (Brooks, Kentucky: Searching the Scriptures, 1976).
71. Connie W. Adams, "Some Extreme Position," *Searching the Scriptures,* June 1978, pp. 104–5.
72. See J. T. Smith, "A Second 'Putting Away,'" *Searching the Scriptures,* January 1981, pp. 313–15.
73. See Mike Willis, "Marriage, Divorce, and Remarriage," *Guardian of Truth,* March 27, 1980, pp. 211–13; April 3, 1980, pp. 228–30; April 10, 1980, pp. 244–46.
74. "Open Letter to Samuel G. Dawson," mimeographed letter signed by Tim P. Stevens for the church in Belen, New Mexico.
75. Hailey interview, August 25, 1989.
76. Ron Halbrook et al., "Recent Studies with Homer Hailey on Divorce and Remarriage," *Guardian of Truth,* November 17, 1988, pp. 689–91.
77. J. T. Smith, "Brethren Do Strange Things," *Torch,* May 1988, p. 103.
78. See J. T. Smith, "Homer Hailey's Teaching on Divorce and Remarriage," *Torch,* June 1988, pp. 141–42; J. T. Smith, "Did I Misrepresent Homer Hailey?" *Torch,* August 1988, pp. 170–76.
79. Ed Harrell, "Homer Hailey: False Teacher?" *Christianity Magazine,* November 1988, pp. 326, 328, 329.
80. Homer Hailey, "Homer Hailey Speaks," *Christianity Magazine,* November 1988, p. 327.
81. Letter from Homer Hailey to Ron Halbrook, October 17, 1988. Quoted by permission.
82. Mike Willis, "Editor's Note," *Guardian of Truth,* February 2, 1989, pp. 70–71.
83. Bob F. Owen, "Policy Statement Made at Florida College Lectures, Monday, January 30, 1989," mimeographed copy in the possession of the author.
84. Ibid.

85. Hailey interview, August 25, 1989.
86. Ibid.; Homer Hailey interview, August 2, 1988.
87. Homer Hailey, interview with the author, March 20, 1993, Tucson, Arizona.
88. Hailey interview, August 25, 1989.
89. Pickup interview.
90. "Open Forum," Florida College Lectures, February 5, 1991.
91. Homer Hailey, *The Divorced and Remarried Who Would Come to God* (Las Vegas: Nevada Publications, 1991), p. 7.
92. Jerry Bassett, *Rethinking Marriage, Divorce and Remarriage* (Eugene, Oregon: Western Printers, 1991).
93. Mike Willis, "Fellowship and the Divorce and Remarriage Issue," *Guardian of Truth,* January 2, 1992, p. 1.
94. See Maurice Barnett, *Alien Sinner and the Law of Christ* (Phoenix: Westside Church of Christ, 1991); Gary Fisher and Dennis G. Allan, *Is It Lawful? A Comprehensive Study of Divorce and Remarriage* (n.p.: Allan and Fisher, 1989); Donnie Rader, *Divorce and Remarriage: What Does the Text Say?* (Louisville: Donnie Rader, 1989). A good treatment in a periodical is Royce P. Bell, "Concerning Those Who Would Come to God: A Review of Homer Hailey," *Gospel Anchor,* June 1994, pp. 194–98.
95. Weldon E. Warnock, "A Review of *The Divorced and Remarried Who Would Come to God* by Homer Hailey," *Guardian of Truth,* May 2, 1991, pp. 273–76; Weldon Warnock, *A Review of Homer Hailey's The Divorced and Remarried Who Would Come to God* (Bowling Green: Guardian of Truth Foundation, 1991).
96. Hailey interview, August 25, 1989.
97. Hailey interviews, August 2 and August 3, 1988.
98. Hailey interview, August 3, 1988.
99. "Homer Haileyisms."
100. For an introduction to the "Neo-Calvinism" clash, see Tom Roberts, ed., *Neo Calvinism in the Church of Christ* (Fairmont, Indiana: Cogdill Foundation, 1980); Edward Fudge, "A Final Word about 'Truth,'" *Gospel Guardian,* November 8, 1973, p. 420.
101. An example of the clash on "continuous cleansing," may be found in *Patton-Diestelkamp on Continuous Cleansing* (Indianapolis: Faith and Facts, n.d.).
102. Robert F. Turner, *What It Is, Is Preaching* (Lakeland, Florida: Harwell/Lewis Publishing, 1998), p. 134.

103. Tant, "Articles on 'The Marriage Question,'" pp. 244, 249.
104. Yater Tant, "More on the Marriage Question," *Gospel Guardian,* August 29, 1963, p. 267.
105. Adams, "Identical Abominations," pp. 303–4.
106. H. E. Phillips, "Judge Righteous Judgment," *Searching the Scriptures,* December 1978, p. 254.
107. Samuel G. Dawson, *Fellowship: With God and with His People* (Santa Maria, California: Gospel Themes Press, 1988).
108. See Ed Harrell, "The Bounds of Christian Unity," *Christianity Magazine,* February 1989–May 1990.
109. Mike Willis, "When Apostasy Occurs," *Guardian of Truth,* April 19, 1990, pp. 226ff; "What Saith the Scriptures?" *Guardian of Truth,* August 2, 1990, pp. 457ff. For a good summary of the literature spawned by the debate, see Mike Willis, "Divorce and Remarriage and Fellowship," *Guardian of Truth,* February 7, 1991, pp. 80–88.
110. See *Guardian of Truth,* January 2, 1992.
111. Bob F. Owen, "Policy Statement," mimeographed manuscript, copy in the possession of the author.
112. Ron Halbrook, *Trends Pointing toward a New Apostasy* (Bowling Green, Kentucky: Guardian of Truth Foundation, 1992).
113. Ron Halbrook, "Trends Pointing toward a New Apostasy," mimeographed notes in the possession of the author, pp. 1–7.
114. Ron Halbrook, *Trends Pointing toward a New Apostasy* (6th ed., Bowling Green, Kentucky: Guardian of Truth Foundation, 1997), p. 42–44.
115. Melvin D. Curry, ed., *They Being Dead Yet Speak* (Temple Terrace: Florida College Bookstore, 1981), pp. 252–53.
116. Ed Harrell, "Divorce and Fellowship," manuscript of speech delivered at Florida College Lectures, 1991, in the possession of the author.
117. Leroy Garrett, *The Stone-Campbell Movement* (rev. ed.; n.p.: College Press Publishing, 1997), p. 435.
118. Douglas A. Foster, *Will the Cycle Be Unbroken?* (Abilene: ACU Press, 1994), p. 56.
119. See *Guardian of Truth,* December 3, 1987. See particularly Mike Willis, "A Tribute to James W. Adams," p. 711.
120. Ron Halbrook, "James W. Adams vs. a New Unity Movement," *Guardian of Truth,* December 3, 1987, p. 719.

121. See *Searching the Scriptures*, December 1978, p. 258. Hailey's commentary on Revelation was advertised just three pages removed from H. E. Phillips's response to James W. Adams.
122. See *Truth Magazine,* April 10, 1980, pp. 242–43.
123. See Marshall E. Patton, "Divorce and Remarriage," *Searching the Scriptures,* January 1977, pp. 249–51. See *Faith and Facts,* January 1991, pp. 5–59.
124. Melvin Curry, "Follow after Things Which Make Peace," *Truth Magazine,* January 4, 1979, pp. 28–30.
125. See Floyd Chappelear, "A Call for Concern," *Sentry Magazine,* September 30, 1996, pp. 1–5.
126. See "Debate on Corruption," *Gospel Anchor,* November 1993, pp. 42–43. The "deity issue" was debated in a variety of forms in the 1990s. See *The O'Neal-Welch Debate* (Bessemer, Alabama: Thomas G. O'Neal, 1996).
127. See John A. Welch, "Letters and Such," *Faith and Facts,* October 1998, p. 352.
128. Mike Willis, "Just Like the War Question," *Guardian of Truth,* January 2, 1992, pp. 18–20. See also Mike Willis, *Can We Understand the Bible Alike?* (Bowling Green: Guardian of Truth Publications, n.d.).
129. Mike Willis, "Can We Understand the Bible Alike?" *Guardian of Truth,* July 3, 1997, pp. 407–8.
130. Ron Halbrook, "Are We Doomed to Divide over Every Difference on Divorce and Remarriage? (2)," *Guardian of Truth,* September 5, 1996, pp. 548–50.
131. Ed Harrell, "The Bounds of Christian Unity (16)," *Christianity Magazine,* May 1990, p. 134.
132. See Melvin D. Curry, Jr., "Being a Sojourner and Pilgrim in This World," *Christianity Magazine,* May 1998, p. 12.
133. See Paul Earnhart, *Invitation to a Spiritual Revolution* (Floyd's Knob, Kentucky: Gary Fisher, 1998).
134. Robert F. Turner, "Unity," *Focus Magazine,* January 1998, pp. 21–22. See also Robert F. Turner, *The People of God: A Study of the Church* (Lakeland, Florida: Harwell/Lewis Publishing, 1999).
135. Robert F. Turner, "Does 'The 28' Have the Elements of a Creed?" June 2, 1994, p. 341.
136. See "The Questionnaire," *Gospel Truths,* April 1994, pp. 75–78. The entire issue of *Gospel Truths* in April 1994 is a critique of the questionnaire.

137. J. T. Smith, "The Editor's Views on 'The Questionnaire,'" *Gospel Truths,* June 1994, pp. 122–24.
138. Ibid., p. 123.
139. Robert F. Turner, "A List of Questions Can Be a Human Creed," *Guardian of Truth,* June 2, 1994, pp. 336–37.
140. Ron Halbrook, "Not All Questions Make Human Creeds," *Guardian of Truth,* June 2, 1994, p. 339.
141. Turner, "Does 'The 28' Have the Elements of a Creed?" p. 341.
142. See *The Arlington Meeting* (Orlando: Cogdill Foundation, 1971); *The Nashville Meeting* (video, Arlington: Private Publication, 1988); James Steve Wolfgang, *History and Background of the Institutional Controversy* (Bowling Green: Guardian of Truth Foundation, 1989), a volume of historical analysis delivered at those meetings.
143. Homer Hailey, interview with the author, July 16, 1998, Tucson, Arizona.
144. Ibid.
145. Ibid.
146. Kilgore tape no. 9.
147. "Homer Haileyisms."
148. "A Letter from Homer Hailey," *Vanguard,* September 1983, p. 232.
149. William S. Banowsky, "The Christ-Centered Church," *Wineskins,* April/May 1997, p. 32.
150. F. LaGard Smith, *Who Is My Brother?* (Malibu: Cotswold Publishing, 1997), pp. 206–9.
151. Hailey interview, July 16, 1998.
152. Homer Hailey, *Attitudes and Consequences in the Restoration Movement* (Kansas City, Old Paths Book Club, 1945); Kilgore tape no. 11.
153. Hailey interview, August 2, 1988; C. Leonard Allen, Richard T. Hughes, and Michael R. Weed, *The Worldly Church* (Abilene: ACU Press, 1988).
154. Hailey interview, July 16, 1998.
155. Ibid.

8. Homer Hailey: Persona and Legacy

1. Homer Hailey, taped conversations with John Kilgore, Tucson, Arizona, tape no. 2.

2. Kilgore tape no. 2.
3. Kilgore tape no. 10.
4. Kilgore tape no. 12.
5. Harry W. Pickup, Jr., interview with the author, April 28, 1988, Tampa, Florida.
6. Bob F. Owen, interview with the author, April 29, 1988, Tampa, Florida.
7. Kilgore tape no. 10.
8. Pickup interview; Kilgore tapes, nos. 7, 11, and 12.
9. James R. Cope, interview with the author, April 29, 1988, Tampa, Florida.
10. Homer Hailey, "Feet of Clay," *Vanguard,* June 1981, p. 121.
11. Kilgore tape no. 12.
12. Ibid.
13. Kilgore tape no. 7.
14. Kilgore tape no. 6.
15. Kilgore tape no. 7.
16. "Homer Haileyisms," mimeographed manuscript assembled by Don Givens, copy in the possession of the author.
17. Homer Hailey, *A Commentary on the Minor Prophets* (10th ed., Grand Rapids: Baker Book House, 1987), p. 65.
18. Kilgore tapes, nos. 6, 7, and 14.
19. Kilgore tapes, nos. 6, 7, and 11.
20. Kilgore tape no. 6.
21. Pickup interview.
22. Kilgore tape no. 14.
23. Kilgore tape no. 7.
24. Homer Hailey, *Prayer and Providence* (Louisville: Religious Supply, 1993), p. iii.
25. Kilgore tapes, nos. 7 and 9.
26. Kilgore tape no. 10.
27. Ibid.
28. Kilgore tapes, nos. 9 and 10.
29. Kilgore tapes, nos. 9 and 10; letter from Homer Hailey to the author, February 23, 1998.
30. Kilgore tapes, nos. 8 and 9.
31. Kilgore tape no. 2; Pickup interview.
32. Foreword, *Prayer and Providence.*
33. Kilgore tape no. 13.
34. Kilgore tape no. 14.
35. Cope interview.

36. Kilgore tape no. 10.
37. Bill Humble, interview with the author, August 10, 1988, Tampa, Florida; Pickup interview.
38. Homer Hailey, interview with the author, March 20, 1993, Tucson, Arizona.
39. Widna Hailey, interview with the author, August 25, 1989, Tucson, Arizona.
40. Owen interview.
41. Kilgore tape no. 8.
42. Ibid.
43. Kilgore tape no. 7.
44. Kilgore tape no. 8.
45. Pickup interview.
46. Kilgore tape no. 8.
47. Kilgore tape no. 7.
48. Kilgore tapes, nos. 7 and 8.
49. Cope interview; Owen interview.
50. Homer Hailey, interview with the author, July 16, 1997, Tampa, Florida.
51. Owen interview.
52. Kilgore tape no. 14.
53. Kilgore tape no. 9.
54. Margie H. Garrett, ed., *Making a Difference* ([Temple Terrace]: Florida College, 1996), p. 60.
55. Kilgore tape no. 1.
56. Kilgore tape no. 3.
57. Kilgore tape no. 8.
58. Kilgore tapes, nos. 8 and 12.
59. Kilgore tape no. 13.
60. Kilgore tape no. 12.
61. Ibid.
62. Owen interview.
63. Kilgore tape no. 12.
64. Foreword, *Prayer and Providence*.
65. Letters to Homer Hailey, copies in the possession of the author.
66. Ibid.
67. Ibid.
68. Ibid.
69. Bill J. Humble, "A Tribute to Homer Hailey," mimeographed paper; Humble interview.

70. Humble interview.
71. Hailey interview, July 16, 1997.
72. Kilgore tape no. 10.
73. Hailey interview, July 16, 1997.
74. Kilgore tapes, nos. 1, 7, and 12.
75. Hailey interview, July 16, 1997.
76. Kilgore tapes, nos. 1 and 7.
77. Kilgore tape no. 1.
78. Hailey interviews, March 20, 1993, and July 16, 1997.

Bibliographical Essay on the Churches of Christ

The most important primary sources in writing a history of churches of Christ in the twentieth century are probably the scores of periodicals that were founded to mold opinion on various issues. Beyond that, I conducted many interviews and used a number of manuscript collections. In addition, members of churches of Christ are prolific book writers. The original sources that I found to be most useful are cited in the notes.

In a book so extensively documented, a general bibliography would be superfluous. However, it seems appropriate to make a few comments about the array of recent books that have appeared interpreting the history of the churches of Christ in the twentieth century. The most important and influential of these studies is Richard T. Hughes, *Reviving the Ancient Faith: The Story of the Churches of Christ in America* (Grand Rapids: William B. Eerdmans, 1996). In my book, I have discussed at length Hughes's arguments about the "apocalyptic world view" that he believes is the central ideological focus of the restoration movement, but his book is filled with new and challenging interpretations. Whereas Hughes quite strongly, though not exclusively, connects the distinctive sense of alienation in churches of Christ with premillennial ideas, Michael W. Casey has written a series of important articles about the centrality of a pacifist tradition in churches of Christ. Among his articles are "From Pacifism to Patriotism: The Emergence of Civil Religion in the Churches of Christ during World War I" (*Mennonite Quarterly Review,* July 1992, pp. 376–90); "Cordell Christian College" (*Chronicles of Oklahoma,* Spring 1988, pp. 20–37); and "Free Speech in Time of War: Government Surveillance of the Churches of Christ in World War I," with Michael A. Jordan in John J. McKay, editor, *Free Speech Yearbook* (Carbondale:

Southern Illinois University Press, 1997). Casey also has written an astute and resourceful interpretation of the history of the churches of Christ in a book about preaching styles: *Saddlebags, City Streets, and Cyberspace: A History of Preaching in the Churches of Christ* (Abilene: ACU Press, 1995). A third author who has written a notable interpretation of the movement, using sociological categories to compare the events of the twentieth century to the division between the Disciples of Christ/Christian Church and churches of Christ in the nineteenth century, is Douglas A. Foster, in his *Will the Cycle Be Unbroken?* (Abilene: ACU Press, 1994).

In addition to these fresh theoretical studies of the history of the churches of Christ, other, more conventional, books have added to the richness of the historical record. Earl Irvin West has written four volumes in a series begun in 1949 entitled *The Search for the Ancient Order*. Volume 3 (Indianapolis: Religious Book Service, 1979) and volume 4 (Germantown, Tennessee: Religious Book Service, 1987) provide a careful and detailed chronicling of the history of churches of Christ from 1900 to 1950. Written in the same narrative style is Robert E. Hooper's *A Distinct People: A History of the Churches of Christ in the Twentieth Century* (West Monroe, Louisiana: Howard Publishing, 1993). However, Hooper's book is conceptually sophisticated; he argues that the churches of Christ are best understood by a straightforward analysis of the words and actions of the broad mainstream that remained loyal to the idea of restoring New Testament Christianity. Two theologically conservative historians, J. E. Choate and William Woodson, who have independently written defensive treatments of the theology of churches of Christ, jointly authored a book in 1990: *Sounding Brass and Clanging Cymbals: The History and Significance of Instrumental Music in the Restoration Movement (1827–1968)* (Henderson, Tennessee: Freed-Hardeman University, 1990). Woodson earlier wrote *Standing for Their Faith: A History of Churches of Christ in Tennessee, 1900–1950* (Henderson, Tennessee: J & W Publications, 1979), and Choate has written a number of biographies, including *The Anchor That Holds: A Biography of Benton Cordell Goodpasture* (Nashville: Gospel Advocate Company, 1971).

A sometimes insightful, but always highly polemical, study of the restoration movement was written by Leroy Garrett: *The Stone-Campbell Movement: The Story of the American Restoration Movement* (rev. ed., n.p.: College Press Publishing, 1997). Two major scholars of American religion who are not members of the churches of Christ have written books interpreting the movement: Samuel S. Hill, *One*

Name but Several Faces: Variety in Popular Christian Denominations in Southern History (Athens: University of Georgia Press, 1996), and Paul Conkin, *American Originals: Homemade Varieties of Christianity* (Chapel Hill: University of North Carolina Press, 1997). I find both books unsatisfying, flawed by sweeping generalizations based on a limited understanding of the highly nuanced belief system within the churches of Christ.

A number of unpublished works have informed my writing about the churches of Christ. Extremely helpful is an unpublished manuscript written by William E. Wallace entitled "Profile of a Movement." Some of this material was published in *Vanguard* magazine in the 1970s. Other unpublished sources include Joseph Everett Bungard, "Becoming a Denomination: The Church-Sect Typology and the Stone-Campbell Movement" (Ph.D. dissertation, University of Kansas, 1985); James Stephen Wolfgang, "Fundamentalism and the Churches of Christ, 1910–1930" (M.A. thesis, Vanderbilt University, 1990) and "Science and Religious Issues in the American Restoration Movement" (Ph.D. dissertation, University of Kentucky, 1997); Jesse Curtis Pope, "The Restoration Ideal in American Religious Thought" (Ph.D. dissertation, Florida State University, 1990); and David M. Owen, "The Premillennial Movement in the Church of Christ" (M.A. thesis, Murray State University, 1989).

Before embarking on this book, I had written about the nineteenth-century history of the restoration movement in two volumes: *Quest for a Christian America: A Social History of the Disciples of Christ* (Nashville: Disciples of Christ Historical Society, 1966) and *The Social Sources of Division in the Disciples of Christ* (Athens, Georgia: Publishing Systems, 1973). I outlined many of the interpretations put forward here in earlier articles, including "The Sectional Origins of the Churches of Christ" (*Journal of Southern History*, August 1964, pp. 261–77); "Restoration and the Stone-Campbell Movement," in Charles Lippy and Peter W. Williams, editors, *Encyclopedia of the American Religious Experience* (3 vols., New York: Charles Scribner's Sons, 1988), volume 2, pp. 845–58; and "Epilogue," in Richard T. Hughes, editor, *The American Quest for the Primitive Church* (Urbana and Chicago: University of Illinois Press, 1988), pp. 239–45. My earliest speculations about the nature of a three-way division in the churches of Christ in the twentieth century were embedded in a polemical tract published in 1961: *The Emergence of the "Church of Christ" Denomination* (Lufkin, Texas: Gospel Guardian Company, n.d.).

Index

C

H

I

J

K

L

M

N

R

S

T

U

V

W

Y

About the Author

DAVID EDWIN HARRELL, JR., is the Daniel F. Breeden Eminent Scholar in the Humanities, Department of History, Auburn University. He received his B.A. from David Lipscomb College and his M.A. and Ph.D. from Vanderbilt University. He has written six other books on American religious history.